novum pro

AF086713

Susan Battersby

Around the World in Fifty Sites!
My story, our journey, your itinerary

novum pro

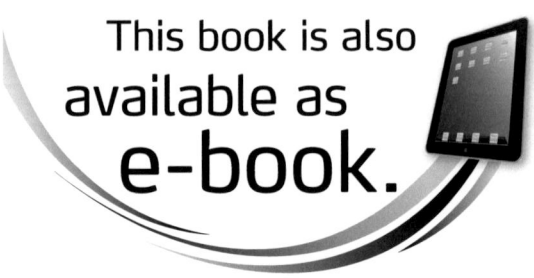

www.novum-publishing.co.uk

All rights of distribution, including via film, radio, and television, photomechanical reproduction, audio storage media, electronic data storage media, and the reprinting of portions of text, are reserved. Printed in the European Union on environmentally friendly, chlorine- and acid-free paper.	© 2019 novum publishing ISBN 978-3-99064-442-3 Editing: Hugo Chandler, BA Cover photo: Susan Battersby Cover design, layout & typesetting: novum publishing Internal illustrations: Susan Battersby **www.novum-publishing.co.uk**

Index

Dedication 9

Introduction 11

Chapter 1: Angel Falls, Venezuela (47) –
   August 2000 13
Chapter 2: Rome, Italy (35) – November 2000 21
Chapter 3: Luxor (34); Abu Simbel (48) and
   the Pyramids (17), Egypt – August 2001 29
Chapter 4: Las Vegas, USA (7) – November 2001 43
Chapter 5: Rio de Janeiro, Brazil (31) –
   March 2002, Our Honeymoon 51
Chapter 6: Paris, France (27) – June 2002 57
Chapter 7: Machu Picchu, Peru (14) – January 2003 68
Chapter 8: San Francisco (36) and Hawaii (24),
   USA – September 2003 76
Chapter 9: Taj Mahal, India (10) and Mount Everest,
   Nepal/Tibet (30) – October 2003 86
Chapter 10: Petra, Jordan (16) – March 2005 99
Chapter 11: Bangkok, Thailand (42), Sydney (8),
   Uluru (12), The Great Barrier Reef (2), Australia
   and Singapore (39) – November 2005 106
Chapter 12: Disney World, USA (3) – April 2006 134
Chapter 13: Lake Louise, Canada (11) and Alaska,
   USA (28) – August 2006 140
Chapter 14: Reykjavik, Iceland (44) – May 2007 161
Chapter 15: Seychelles (40) and Masai Mara,
   Kenya (32) – October 2007 166

Chapter 16: New York, USA (9) –
New Year 2007/08 183
Chapter 17: Barcelona, Spain (37) – March 2008 195
Chapter 18: Yosemite National Park (23),
The Grand Canyon (1), USA – May 2008 201
Chapter 19: Dubai, United Arab Emirates (38) –
November 2008 219
Chapter 20: Iguazu Falls, Argentina/Brazil (26) –
April 2009 227
Chapter 21: Venice, Italy (18) – June 2009 239
Chapter 22: Cape Town, South Africa (5) –
January 2010 252
Chapter 23: Angkor Wat, Cambodia (29) –
February 2010 258
Chapter 24: Golden Temple of Amritsar,
India (6) – May 2010 266
Chapter 25: Barbados (43) – November 2010 277
Chapter 26: Victoria Falls, Zimbabwe and
Zambia border (21) – January 2011 286
Chapter 27: Galapagos Islands, Ecuador (33) –
February 2011 301
Chapter 28: Chichen Itza, Mexico (13) – March 2011 315
Chapter 29: Hong Kong, China (22) and Bali,
Indonesia (49) – January 2012 325
Chapter 30: Bora Bora, French Polynesia (50) and
return to Hawaii (24) – February 2012 344
Chapter 31: Matterhorn, Switzerland (46) –
July 2012 360
Chapter 32: Terracotta Warriors (45) and
the Great Wall of China (20) – October 2012 372
Chapter 33: South Island (4) and North Island (25),
New Zealand – February 2013 389
Chapter 34: Niagara Falls (15), USA and Canada –
September 2013 416
Chapter 35: Sri Lanka (41) and The Maldives (19) –
December 2014 433

Epilogue 456

Appendix 1: Fifty Places to see Before You Die –
   in order of preference 462
Appendix 2: A list of countries that we have visited
   (and stepped foot on!) 465
Appendix 3: Territories, Islands and Dependencies
   that we have visited 468
Appendix 4: Glossary, references and useful e-mail
   and website addresses 469
Appendix 5: Some personal travel tips; money,
   airline benefits, security and cruising 470

Dedication

This book is dedicated to the two most important people in my life. Firstly, to Richard, as I could not have completed this journey without him. Since meeting him my life has been complete. Our love of travel has made this objective of seeing the fifty places to see before you die all the more meaningful and possible. He is my best friend, my travel companion and my soulmate. Thank you.

My second dedication is to my mother, who sadly was not here to see me complete this journey as she had died in June 2010 at the age of seventy-nine. When I first got the travel bug in 1994, I was single, but this did not stop me from travelling to exotic countries like China, India and Venezuela. Mum encouraged me to follow my heart and do my own thing, and I bless her for that support and backing. She told me once that a neighbour had asked her why she let me travel on my own and was she not worried about me? My Mum replied, "Yes," she did worry, "but you try stopping Sue!"

My two brothers and I always bought a plate for Mum to hang on the wall from every place that we visited. It became a friendly competition to try and find a new country where none of us had visited before. When she died, we still bought them for Dad, and, despite having Alzheimer's disease, he could always remember whether he had a plaque from any country we visited.

When I used to arrive home from any holiday, Mum was always the first person I phoned to tell her all about the trip; the things that I had seen and the people who I had met. Mum and Dad were so pleased when I met, and eventually married Richard, as they knew that there was now someone to care and to look after me after they had passed on. I miss her every day but I am sure that she is looking down and she is proud that I have achieved everything I had set out to do; in life as well as my travel objectives.

Dad passed away in January 2017 at the age of ninety-one. He had suffered from dementia for a number of years, and the family felt that we had lost him many years earlier, as he had lost interest in what we were doing, and he was not aware of what was happening around him. He still recognised us whenever we went to visit him, which was a blessing. Richard and I took Dad away a few times, firstly on a river cruise in Russia in 2011, and then to Lake Como, Northern Italy and Switzerland in 2012, which is featured as a chapter in this book, as that was when we saw the Matterhorn. We also took him to Jersey to attend my cousin's wedding. Except for his immediate family, we were the only ones who attended and Alastair was really pleased that his Uncle Vernon was there to represent his father's family.

I am sorry that I did not complete this book before he had passed away, as I am sure that there would have been a flicker of pride and recognition if he saw my name in print. Mum, Dad – rest in peace; you are gone but will never be forgotten.

Introduction

In 2002, the BBC aired a programme entitled "Fifty places to see before you die." The fifty places were voted for by the British public, and were shown in the order of number of votes for each place. These consisted of countries, natural sites, and buildings, and were located all over the world although, rather surprisingly, none of them were in the UK. I watched the programme with intrigue, to see which location would come first and also to see how many of the fifty sites we had already visited. Quite a few were already under our belt — bought the T-shirt, read the book, and had the photos to prove that we had been there. I was bewildered at how some of the locations had made it into the top fifty, but most of them were either already on my wish list or, after seeing this programme, were being jotted down as we watched! At that moment I decided to set this as our target for travel over the next few years, and from then on, most of the holidays that I booked were aimed at trying to tick off another location from the list.

Not every holiday covered the fifty places, as we still travelled to many other countries that included natural sites and buildings that were not included on the list, like Inle Lake in Myanmar, the Northern Lights in Norway and Kyoto in Japan. We also saw a lot more of a country than just the single site mentioned in the programme. As a result of this, not only have we seen all of the fifty places, some of them several times over; but we have also visited over a hundred countries in the process.

The list is still available on the internet, but there have been some small changes. For example, instead of Disney World, it shows Florida and instead of Lake Louise, it is now listed as the Rockies. My journey has been true to the original list that was shown in the programme, aired by the BBC, which has been burnt into my memory over the years and I can now recite the fifty, not in the right order, but I know every place by heart.

But my story does not actually start in 2002. It starts three years earlier in Venezuela when we ticked off the first of the fifty that we saw together. One of the key facts about achieving this list is that, not only have we seen all fifty places, but, we have seen all of them together. This is our story, not just a travel journal. I hope that this will be a tale of commitment and perseverance, showing that whatever it is that you set your mind to, if you are determined enough to achieve your dreams and goals, then there is nothing stopping you!

This book shows each of the places in the order that we saw them in since we had met. Some holidays enabled us to tick off several sites from the list at the same time. Each chapter details the place, the year that we saw it and the position it appears on the list of the fifty. I have included details of other sites in the area that may be of interest to anyone wanting to follow the same journey, as it is an interesting one!

This is not meant to be a guidebook: it is a personal travel journal. Since before Richard and I met, I have kept travel diaries and I have referred back to these for the inspiration I needed to write this book. I have included quite a lot of information about the places that we have visited, which has not all come from memory or from my diaries, but also from some additional research. Most of the information is personal and expressed from the heart. Where I have used Internet facts I have shown the source from which they were gathered.

Just a little explanation for the subtitle – My story, our journey, your itinerary! The first part is self-explanatory – I am telling my story from the diaries that I have written during my travels over the years. Our journey is referring to the fact that Richard and I have seen all the fifty places together since we met in August 2000. And finally, as the fifty places were chosen for the BBC by votes from the British public, then it is you who had decided on the places that we would visit, so it is actually your itinerary.

CHAPTER 1

Angel Falls, Venezuela (47) –
August 2000

I have to start my story here, as it is where Richard and I had met, and it is the first on the list that we both saw together. It was the first time in South America for both of us and the trip was an amazing one. It was run by Sovereign Small World and was aimed at both single travellers and groups. The actual tour was entitled "The Lost World of Conan Doyle", as we would go to see the tepuis that inspired Arthur Conan Doyle to write this book of dinosaurs and cavemen lost in the midst of time on top of these huge monoliths. Both Richard and I were amongst the four single travellers; there were two couples and a group of four ladies who made up our tour group of twelve.

Our journey started with a flight from Gatwick to Margarita Island where we stayed for one night before we flew to Puerto Ordaz on the mainland of Venezuela. The flight to the mainland was an adventure in itself—there were thirteen of us including our guide, Morton, and we were all squeezed into a small Cessna-type plane to make the crossing, which took a couple of hours. During our flight, it started to rain very heavily and you could see it pelting down onto the Orinoco River, which we could see way below us. There was lightning too, which made it a rather frightening experience. Richard was sitting behind the pilot and he told me later that the pilot was battling with the controls to try and keep the plane stable and in a straight line, as we headed for the runway. To say it was a relief when we landed in one piece was an understatement!

The hotel at Puerto Ordaz was very basic but clean and the food served that evening was pleasant. One thing that we did notice with all our hotels during the trip to Venezuela was the high walls and gates that surrounded the compounds. This stopped us from going out, but also kept us safe, by not letting anyone else in when the gates closed each night after we had returned from our tour. It was only when we were on holiday that we found out just how dangerous Venezuela was at that time; due to gang warfare as a result of the ruling President imprisoning the previous gang-leaders/drug barons, and now the other minor gang members were trying to get control of the illegal underworld. However, we never felt at threat or scared during the whole holiday, none of these problems affected us at all.

On our first full day in Venezuela our little group went to the banks of the Orinoco where we visited two forts built in the 1600s. These were both attacked by that famous pirate – Sir Walter Raleigh! These were the words of our guide, a Venezuelan. In England, Sir Walter Raleigh is a hero, not a pirate—it just goes to show how history is written as in the eyes of the victor and not that of the vanquished.

We then headed out onto the Orinoco Delta on a boat, where we went piranha fishing. Nobody caught one except for the guide, and we suspected that he was dragging a dead fish behind him during the whole trip, to be able to produce it if no-one was lucky enough with their endeavours! We were then informed that we were going to have a picnic on the Orinoco. The boat we were in was quite small and only big enough for the twelve people in our group, Morton and the boatman. It certainly did not offer a lot of room for us to eat in comfort. To our surprise, we stopped at a huge rock in the middle of the river and we all climbed ashore onto the rock, where we proceeded to have an excellent picnic with wine and beers. It was quite an experience and one of those events that will stay with you forever. We watched as other boats sped past us and waved to the bewildered passengers.

When the boat trip was over, we boarded our coach for the drive back to our hotel and this was the first time that we were given the local drink as a sundowner—Cuba Libre! It is a mix of dark rum, Coca-Cola and a slice of lime. I didn't like it very much as it was strong and, at that time, my preferred choice was vodka. But it was complimentary and after a long, hot day on the river, it was refreshing.

The next day we were taken to Cachamay Park for our breakfast. We were seated in a small restaurant facing the most amazing waterfall on the Caroni River, which was truly spectacular—breakfast was good too!

We walked through the Loefling Park which included a small zoo, where we got to see a jaguar as well as the Orinoco crocodile, giant sea otter and a caiman. We continued our journey into the Gran Sabana, a long drive, but we stopped for our sundowners on a bridge, built by Gustave Eiffel, located in the middle of the rain forest, miles from anywhere. This time I gave my drink away and it was Richard who accepted the extra tipple. That night we stayed at a camp where we were all allocated small "Wendy" houses for the night and had a lovely communal meal at the main building, located down winding paths away from our rooms.

The next day we headed for Santa Elena de Uriens, stopping at three waterfalls. The first had a seventy metre drop and was quite spectacular; the second was a series of shallow falls where we were able to take a swim if we wanted to. I just had a paddle as I am not a strong swimmer and the current was very strong in places. I slipped at one point and almost fell in! This was where we had our lunch which was a barbecue. The spot was very busy with locals as it was obviously a popular spot for them to enjoy their Sundays. The final waterfall was probably the most beautiful. We had to walk through the jungle to get to it but it was worth every step. We were rewarded with the sight of water falling over a wall of jasper. The red rock shone and glistened through the thin layer of water that slid down the sheer face into the clear, shallow river below. We were able to walk right up to the waterfall and taste the cool, refreshing water as it cascaded down the rock face. During our journey, we were able to see the table-top mountains in the distance, shrouded in mist and you could understand how these mysterious peaks gave Conan Doyle the idea of a lost world high on their eerie plateaus, inaccessible to man (well, not now that we can fly over them!). That evening we had a surprise as we went over the border into Brazil, where we drove onto a small hill to view the surrounding area, while we had our sundowners. By now I was getting used to this drink; now that I had reduced the amount of rum that Morton was pouring!

Our evening meal was served in a hall that looked more like a garage! There was a large central table laid for the whole group, plus Morton and our driver and we enjoyed our very first Brazilian barbeque. All manner of meats were served from skewers and carved directly onto our plate, accompanied by salads and vegetables. It was truly delicious. The next day, before we headed into Canaima, we went to visit a diamond merchant. The prices and quality of the stones he had to offer were quite amazing, but I was on a tight budget and could not go mad, so I bought a third of a carat diamond for one hundred and fifty dollars – this becomes a lot more significant later in my story, which is the reason I have mentioned it here.

On our sixth day in Venezuela we took our flight to Canaima where we would fly past Auyán-Tepui, the mountain where Angel Falls is located. We were all very disappointed as it was cloudy and wet and the chance of us seeing anything was pretty remote. As we took off I remember how low the clouds were, and that visibility was really poor and I thought that we had no chance of even a peek at these famous falls. But, as we approached, the clouds lifted and we had the most wonderful view of the world's tallest, single drop, waterfall.

The plane circled inside the Devil's Canyon, going very close to the cliff edge, which created thermals that rocked the plane. Two of our tour group were very ill, but for once, I did not suffer from the motion. The falls are named after Jimmie Angel who landed his plane on top of Auyán-Tepui in October 1937. He had flown over the tepui and had seen the falls four years earlier, but it was in 1937, after getting his planes wheels stuck in the mud, that Jimmie, his wife and two other passengers had to make their way down from the top of the highest tepui in Venezuela. It took them eleven days! But as a result of this, the waterfall was later named after him in his honour. His plane remained on top of the Auyán-Tepui for thirty-two years until it was airlifted off by a helicopter, and, in July 1960, Jimmie Angel's ashes were scattered here. The falls are a true natural wonder; falling for almost one mile in a sheer vertical, uninterrupted drop. It is difficult to get to the falls on foot as the tepui is isolated and surrounded by jungle, so to visit the falls means a strenuous hike, involving rafting upriver in the heat of Venezuela or rains depending on the season. It's much easier, and probably more spectacular, to see them from the air as you circle around the Devil's Canyon.

We were each allowed to go into the cockpit to be able to get a pilot's view of the falls, which cascaded from the tepui top to the river below in a single unbroken jet of water. I thought that

I would try and get a dramatic video showing the falls in reverse and I started to film the river, ready to lift the camera up the fall of water from the floor to the mountaintop. I then got a tap on my shoulder from the pilot who pointed out the opposite window from the one where I was filming and there was Angel Falls almost crashing onto the plane – I was looking the wrong way! My video sped round to film the more important feature of the falls rather than the river way below us! When I viewed the video later, you could see the whirl of the filming of the cockpit as I refocused my video on the right subject.

We arrived at our camp in Canaima exhilarated and delighted at our sighting of Angel Falls. The camp was beautiful, set right on the lagoon with the wall of Canaima Falls crashing down almost outside our door. This was by far the best accommodation we had had in Venezuela and the most beautiful location. We went to visit Sapo Falls which we travelled to by boat, firstly travelling very close to the powerful waters of Canaima Falls. We went on foot to the Sapo Falls and we were able to walk behind the rushing waters.

At first it wasn't too bad, the water was not too strong, just a little cold, but as we walked further along the slippery path that lay behind the falls, the water became a torrent and the force of it took your breath away. The path was not completely dry either as parts of it were hit by the water falling all around us. I closed my eyes in fear of losing my contact lenses and I took Morton's hand as he led us along the walkway to the other side. As we looked back, I could not believe the ferocity of the water that was cascading over the rock edge—but there was no chickening out now, as there was only one way back and that was under the falls again!

Venezuela is an amazing place and has to be one of the best holidays that I have ever had as every day there was something different. The sights were amazing, the views were spectacular and the adrenalin rush was exhilarating. After our week in Venezuela, we had a week of relaxation on Margarita Island staying at a hotel in Playa El Agua. It was perfect—our rooms were facing onto the pool, so you practically walked straight out of the door and into the blue waters if you wanted to. The town was ideal as there were lots of restaurants, bars and shops and a beautiful golden sandy beach with clear aqua blue waves crashing onto the shore.

The four single travellers, Richard, Mike, Isabel and I were staying at this hotel. The others were staying elsewhere on the island. As we had become close friends during the tour, we continued to enjoy one another's company for the remaining week of our holiday. This included our ritual sun-downers of rum and coke, which, by now, I really enjoyed and I had ditched the vodka completely. Richard had been a whisky drinker prior to this holiday, but he too was relishing this local drink. Between the four of us, we bought quite a few litres of the local rum to see us through the remaining part of the holiday and after one boozy night, Richard and I were left alone and, as you might say, the rest is history! That was the 10th of September 2000, and we have been together ever since, continuing to keep in contact on our return home to England and commuting between Sheffield and Leeswood, North Wales, to see one another every weekend until February 2001 when I moved to Sheffield to live with Richard. But we have another of our fifty places before that date!

Margarita is a beautiful Caribbean island which does not feature heavily on the tourist route. It has so much to offer with many excellent five-star hotels, beautiful beaches with soft, golden sand lapped by the clear, aqua blue waves from the ocean, and a lot of sites to keep you amused if you are not lounging by the pool.

Each year on the 8th of September, there is a fiesta in Espiritu del Valle to celebrate the discovery of the statue of the Virgin Mary found by locals, which now resides in the main church in this village. She is the patroness of the island, fishermen and the navy, keeping them safe whilst at sea. We were lucky enough to be on the island on this date and took a taxi to the village to be met by thousands of locals—it seemed like every living resident of the island was in the town square that morning.

There was a religious ceremony attended by many priests, nuns and local dignitaries that took place on the streets outside of the church. The statue of the Virgin, dressed in her finery, was paraded through the throngs of people for this special occasion. To our surprise, at the end of a hymn, the priests, choir and the crowds started to sing "Happy Birthday" to the statue! Now, coincidentally, this day was also Isabel's birthday, and as all these people were singing in Spanish we changed the words to celebrate Isabel's big day quietly, of course, so as not to offend anyone!

This village also had an interesting museum where the clothes of the statue, worn on other religious occasions, were on display and also all the donations and gifts bestowed on the patroness for keeping people safe. We also discovered that there was a tradition to "ask" the Virgin for requests and in return, you would bequeath a gift in exchange for your request being granted. These requests could be a good harvest, safe passage on a trip, good results in examinations and other things in this line. I thought I'd have a go and, silently, I asked the Virgin if she could arrange for me to be married within a year, and if this happened, that I would return the diamond that I had purchased on the main land. As it happened, although I was living with Richard within five months of this "wish", we did not get married until March 2002, which was eighteen months later, so when I didn't return the diamond, I did not feel that I had reneged on the deal! But I did have the diamond set into a gold tie stud as a wedding gift for Richard so that he had my memories of our holiday to keep forever.

Other places to visit on the island are Porlamar, La Asuncion, the Mangrove Lagoon, Juan Griego for the sunset, the artisan village and lots of other lovely nature spots for views of the island from mountaintops to off-roading in 4 x 4's over rugged landscapes. There are lots of tour operators who organise day trips to see many of these sights and who will also do catamaran cruises around the island.

CHAPTER 2

Rome, Italy (35) – November 2000

Two months and two days after meeting Richard, we had our first holiday together in the Eternal City, Rome. We stayed at the Eliseo, a lovely hotel located just off the Via Veneto that serves a great breakfast with views over Borghese Park towards Saint Peter's Basilica and the Vatican.

Where do you start with Rome? It is a beautiful city with so much to see and to do; with the most wonderful restaurants and bars; shops to die for; galleries, museums and architecture that is among the best in the world and, of course, a romantic atmosphere that is perfect for lovers, whatever their age!

I had been to Rome once before, just for a day trip but this was Richard's first time, so we wanted to try and fit as much into our short holiday as possible. Our location was ideal for walking to all the main sights in Rome and our first stop was at the Spanish Steps, before heading for the Piazza Popolo, which is a lovely square, free of traffic. Rome is built on seven hills and, if you gain some height and find walkways that are a little elevated, you are rewarded with fabulous views over the city.

Not only does the Via Veneto have many wonderful restaurants and shops, it also leads to the Trevi Fountain, a must when visiting Rome. The tradition is that you must throw a coin over your shoulder into the water and make a wish—this will mean that you will return to Rome someday. It was thirteen years before we returned, but the wish came true! All around the fountain are lots of little streets with many wonderful restaurants and bars. It is a very busy and popular tourist location and it is almost impossible to get a decent photograph in front of the fountain with no other people cluttering up your image. The Trevi Fountain is

actually a façade on the side of a building, but with the twisting statues of deities, horses and spouting water that crashes into the sparkling blue stone trough, it is a spectacular sight, one I would go back to time and time again.

There are so many sides to Rome – the Roman remains are still very prominent with the Forum and the Coliseum taking centre stage and the Pantheon, a former Roman temple dating back to 126 AD and completed by the emperor Hadrian. Of course, it is also the centre for the Roman Catholic Church and besides Saint Peter's Basilica and the Vatican, there are many beautiful churches all around Rome including Saint Paul's, which lies just outside the city walls. There are so many beautiful statues, squares and buildings including the Emmanuel Monument, the Piazza Navona and the Castle of Saint Angelo.

When in Rome, a must is a visit to the Vatican apartments and the Sistine Chapel. We thought that this small chamber was breath-taking and neck breaking as you strain to get the best view possible of this masterpiece. I cannot imagine how difficult it must have been to create such a wonderful piece of art as this – it certainly does Michelangelo justice! The queues for the Vatican can be huge but you can pre-book and I think that you can pay to visit at a specific time and then queue jump, legitimately!

Saint Peter's and the whole complex of the cathedral, square, columns and other buildings is a magnificent sight. The cathedral is huge and the statues and art inside are fabulous. You need either a tour guide or a good guidebook to understand everything that you are witnessing and to make sure that you don't miss anything. Another bonus of visiting Saint Peter's and the Vatican is that you are actually entering another country. The Vatican

City State is recognised by the United Nations as an independent country, and is listed as one of the one hundred and ninety-eight countries of the world. Correct number as of May 2014.

There are many websites that you can choose from, to find tours of Rome, including walking tours; night tours and very specific tours like the Angels and Demons tour; taking you to all the key sites mentioned in the Dan Brown book of the same name. We did this tour when we returned to Rome in 2015, which I detail later in this chapter. Try looking for some of the secret tours where they take you behind the scenes or to places that the normal tourist would not think about visiting. They can certainly make a trip more interesting.

Most evenings we would walk down the Via Veneto to find a restaurant for our evening meal and we were never disappointed. On one occasion, we decided to eat at one of the restaurants located on the street, protected from the elements by a glass shelter. There are many of these, but this particular one had a liveried gentleman outside to take you inside to be seated in the small but beautifully appointed restaurant. We had not looked at the menu outside, which we normally do, but we thought that it was sure to offer us something that we would both liked. When we were given the menu, I was surprised to find that there were no prices, but by the look on Richard's face, he certainly had the full details. I had a ladies' menu! This was the first time that this had happened. I have experienced the same thing since then in very high-class eateries, but the first time is always the best. We decided to go for the chateaubriand, which we would share, as it was Argentinian meat and Richard knew from experience that he enjoyed the country's beef. We both had starters and they were served under domed covers, both withdrawn at the same time by two waiters either side of us. The chateaubriand was flamed at our table and it was truly delicious, so tender – as a result of this we have eaten this dish on many occasions since, but the meal we had on the Via Veneto was by far the best. We had the selection of mini-desserts and with a bottle of wine, the bill came in at around one hundred pounds, which was a very expensive meal in 2000! We have had much more expensive meals since then, and, with inflation, the drop in the pound and time, our budget for food costs on holiday has increased immensely, but I really enjoy the opportunity to have a great meal in fine surroundings – it is something that can make, or break, a holiday, in my opinion.

There are many museums and galleries all over Rome, but we are not really interested in museums. However, there is one gallery that I must recommend. It is the Galleria Borghese, which is located in the park at the top of the Via Veneto. You have to book a timed visit for the gallery as this keeps the numbers down, and allows you to view the masterpieces on show in relative peace and quiet. We took the option of using a headphone guide so we could recognise and understand the pieces that we were looking at.

The two statues that blew us away were Apollo and Daphne and the Rape of Proserpina, both by Bernini. They looked like they were made from pliable wax rather than rock solid marble, they were so intricate and lifelike. Daphne is changing into a tree in the sculpture; the leaves and her skin where it is turning to bark are so delicate and detailed. On the other statue, Zeus's fingers are embedded into Proserpina's thigh as though it was living flesh and the tear on her cheek was just sheer brilliance. We walked around and around these two statues as we could not take it all in – pure genius!

We returned to Rome in July 2013 where we spent just two nights at the Hotel Cavalieri, a stupendous five-star hotel located on one of the seven hills, with amazing views over Rome. We were here for one reason – to see Roger Waters perform The Wall, live, at the Olympic Stadium. Needless to say, the concert was brilliant and it allowed us to have a little free time in this fabulous city. This time, we booked on a Segway Tour of the Roman remains. This is a great method of travelling and sightseeing at the same time—it is fun, certainly less tiring than walking everywhere, and with headphones, your guide can give you details and information while you are on the move. We have done Segway

Tours all over – in cities, including Rome, Florence, Barcelona, Budapest, Catania in Sicily and San Juan in Puerto Rico; along the beach in Saint Martin and through conservation areas in Saint Lucia and New Caledonia. Every time you are given a helmet and instructions on how to use the Segway, or a refresher lesson if you are repeat user. I have fallen off, once, in Saint Lucia because of going over uneven ground which was covered by a puddle. I'm glad I had the helmet as I fell backwards and cracked my head, but other than a bit of a scar on my elbow, I was fine. However we did see a serious accident once because of a woman messing around and getting too close to her husband's Segway – they collided and he fell off, breaking his ankle and he had to be taken to hospital, so it is important to follow the rules and the instructions. Don't let this put you off though – it really is great fun and we have enjoyed every excursion we've done.

We returned to Rome in May 2015 when we had an extended holiday in Italy. In fact we were there for a month. We had planned everything ourselves and we booked it all through the internet. On this occasion it went like clockwork! We flew into Catania in Sicily where we hired a car for the full holiday; starting off with seven days touring Sicily (Taormina is particularly lovely) and then crossing to the mainland on the ferry and, if you imagine Italy as a boot, we continued to drive up the toe, stayed in the instep at Palazzo Margherita in Bernalda, Francis Ford Coppola's hotel, continued to the heel, a rarely visited area of Italy called Puglia and then continued up the east coast and into the stirrup. We then crossed over to the west side staying at the Relais Chalons d'Orange, Alvito – a wonderful rural location offering fabulous food in an area where we did not come across any other tourists at all. Our next stop was for seven nights in Umbria, where we hired a villa and were joined by Richard's family – thirteen of us in all. We enjoyed visiting the local area, including a day in Assisi, but we also managed a few days of relaxation as we had been on the go for two weeks before this point.

After seven days, the others flew back home but we continued our holiday with three nights in Rome, four nights in Sorrento, where we visited Pompeii and the Amalfi Coast and finally spent two nights in the magnificent Villa Cimbrone in Ravello, where we celebrated Richard's birthday. It was a fabulous holiday – we saw so much of a part of Italy that is off the main tourist route and we had beautiful weather for most of our trip.

On this occasion, we stayed at Aldrovandi Villa Borghese in Rome – a beautiful, five-star hotel and a member of the Leading Hotels of the World. Our room was small; as this is a very expensive hotel, but it overlooked the Borghese Gardens and it had everything that we required. The outdoor area of the hotel was very pretty with lovely gardens and a pool and we certainly made the most of this charming place over a bottle or two of wine!

With two days to enjoy in the capital city, we did the aforementioned tour, Dan Brown's Angels and Demons, through Viator.com, which started from the Piazza del Popolo Square. We had a large group, as there were supposed to be two tour guides, but one had called in sick that morning. This was a bit of an inconvenience, but Roberto was so enthusiastic and knowledgeable that he made up for this, and we had no problems getting close enough to hear him and to see where he pointed as he retold the story. Some people on the tour had not read the book or seen the film and kept asking us what he was talking about! Not a good idea, as you really need to have an inkling of what happened, as you see the churches and the key sites that are named in the book. Don't rely on the film as this was changed by Hollywood and the book is so descriptive, keeping you on the edge of your seat as you read it, which I have done twice!

The first site is Santa Maria del Popolo which is the site of the first murder in Rome. I don't think that I'm giving anything away by saying this! We then had a coach take us to Piazza San Pietro (Saint Peter's Square) and then to Santa Maria della Vittoria – following the trail from the book. Our next stop, again by coach, was Piazza Navona for the Fountain of the Four Rivers. We had a short break here for a drink and a rest stop, before continuing to our final location, Castel Sant'Angelo. The view from the top overlooking the Vatican was worth every exhausting step we climbed, and it was here that Roberto wrapped up the story and we left him after having had a coach and a walking tour that lasted four hours and, we both agreed, was probably the best tour we have done – anywhere! To visit some of the smaller, less known churches was great as they are so ornate and full of sculptures and art that you would miss if you weren't doing a tour like this one. It wasn't just about the book either. We did learn a lot about the Roman Catholic Church, the history of Rome and the artists involved in creating the wondrous architecture and works of art.

We enjoyed a break back in Piazza Navona, where we had something to eat accompanied with a couple of bottles of wine, and we just watched the people of Roma pass us by on a glorious, sunny day. This is a lovely, large square with lots of restaurants and bars where you can sit out and enjoy the beautiful architecture surrounding the square and the fountain, designed by Bernini. I do love Rome as there is so much to do, places to see, wonderful shopping, plenty of great restaurants and excellent hotels. A great weekend break from the UK, as the flights are not too pricy or lengthy, and I would certainly not frown at returning as there are always new experiences for us to try.

CHAPTER 3

Luxor (34); Abu Simbel (48) and the Pyramids (17), Egypt – August 2001

In recent years, Egypt has seen a lot of turmoil and I would imagine that many people might be wary of visiting the country now. This is a shame as there is so much to see and the antiquities along the Nile are totally amazing when you realise how many years they have stood the test of time and the ravages of the Egyptian sun and desert.

In 2001, the first time we went to Egypt together, it was a relatively calm period, even though a few years' earlier tourists had been shot when visiting Queen Hatshepsut's temple near Luxor. We did witness the precautions that the government were taking to ensure that another incident of this nature did not reoccur, but we never felt threatened during our two-week holiday.

We booked our holiday through Kuoni, who offer a great variety of cruises on the Nile, tours of different locations in Egypt and the Middle East and have a great variety of hotels to choose from. This trip started with one night in a hotel in Luxor before we were transferred to our home for the next seven nights, the Nile Beauty. Most of the ships on the Nile are very similar—long, narrow and not very high. They are of different classes though and the Nile Beauty was a five-star ship. It was nicely appointed but the cabins on the lower decks were quite small. The public areas were large with a lounge area including the bar and restaurant, and upstairs on the open sun deck there were loungers, chairs and tables.

On our first full day in Egypt we went to see the Karnak and Luxor Temples. Karnak is by far the largest and in the best condition. It is located just outside the city.

Karnak is so much more than a temple, it is a whole complex of sanctuaries, kiosks, pylons, and obelisks dedicated to the Theban gods and the pharaohs. The site is huge, measuring one and a half kilometres by eight hundred metres. It was started by Ramses III but was built, added to, dismantled, rebuilt, enlarged and decorated over the next one thousand five hundred years.

From the entrance you pass down the processional avenue of ram-headed sphinxes that originally flanked a canal connecting the temple to the Nile. You cross a wooden bridge to enter the complex, passing a huge unfinished pylon as you enter the Amun Temple Enclosure. This is the first of a total of ten pylons in the complex.

As you walk into the temple, you enter the Great Court, the largest area of the temple. Here you will find the temple of Seti II and Ramesses III and two-colossal pink granite statues of

Ramses II, which he erected himself. They appear to guard the entrance to the temple gates.

Continuing your walk, and you come to the Great Hypostyle Hall with its one hundred and thirty-four towering papyrus-shaped stone pillars that look like a forest of stone, before you come to the Inner Temple and the obelisks of Hatshepsut, (the one still erect), which is the tallest obelisk in Egypt, standing 29.2 metres high. In the Inner Temple you will also find the Wall of Records, built by Tuthmosis III. Located on the northern side of the central court, this wall has some wonderful hieroglyphs and reliefs that are so clear and prominent that the guide could easily tell us the stories behind the pictures. She relayed all the fantastical tales of the Egyptian Gods, their lives, loves, deaths and reincarnations. It was very hot, but she held us spellbound as the temple walls came to life in front of us. Because the site is so big, it takes a few hours to walk around, seeing all the key monuments, obelisks, pillars and statues.

Continuing our journey around the complex we saw the Great Festival Hall of Tuthmosis III, where there is a small chapel for all the people who were not allowed to enter the temple's sacred enclosure; the Amun Temple Enclosure which has the sacred lake and the top half of Hatshepsut's fallen obelisk, as well as a stone statue of a scarab beetle; temples to Mut and Munthu and the open-air museum.[3]

In the evening we went to the sound and light show at Karnak. It starts at the only statue depicting the face of King Tutankhamun, a small sphinx near the entrance to the temple. As the lights shine on the different parts of the temple, voices depicting the Gods boom out and tell us the story of the building of the temple and the life of the Gods. As we walked through the complex, seeing the buildings at our leisure and lit up against the black sky, it really allowed the imagination to picture how imposing this place was when it was built. Unfortunately, the last part of the show where you sit in the amphitheatre over the lake, went on a bit too long, and we both got quite bored! It was still a great experience though.

Luxor temple lies within the heart of the city itself and is much smaller than Karnak. You start by walking along the avenue of the sphinxes, which is the path that used to run for three kilometres and connected the temples at Luxor and Karnak. At the entrance there are two imposing statues of Ramses II and a pink granite obelisk. There used to be six statues and two obelisks, but only the two statues remain and the other obelisk stands in the Place de la Concorde in Paris. All of the carvings on the walls inside the temple are in relief, quite mind-blowing that they could accomplish such fine detail three thousand years ago. The great court is surrounded by a double row of columns with lotus-bud capitals, more reliefs and several huge statues.

The hypostyle hall is the first inner room of the temple and features four rows of eight columns. The central chamber of the Temple of Amun was once stuccoed over by the Romans in the third century AD and was used as a cult sanctuary. This temple was visited by Alexander the Great who rebuilt the barque shrine and had his own image added to the reliefs, dressed in Egyptian regalia in his role as pharaoh, immortalising himself amongst the other Egyptian deities.

We returned to the Nile in July 2008 when we took a cruise with Voyages Jules Verne on the SS Misr, which used to be King Farouk's paddle steamer. This beautiful vessel is quite different from the normal Nile cruisers as most of the cabins have small balconies and the ship is made of wood and powered by a genuine steam paddle. It is quite luxurious inside and the cabins are very decadent. We had one of the suites that had a slightly larger balcony to the front of the boat – it is only just big enough to get a couple of chairs on it, but it was still a very pleasant location to watch the Nile embankment pass you by.

On this second cruise, which was a return journey to Luxor going as far as Aswan, we had the special treat of attending an evening concert at Luxor temple. We were told it was just for Voyages Jules Verne cruise passengers. There were several other boats under their patronage on the Nile, so it was quite exclusive. We entered the complex with the orchestra playing the

March from the opera Aida, which was truly fabulous and so atmospheric. There were strong lights aimed at the main buildings and statues, illuminating them to their full glory. We were escorted in small groups around the temple and each of the little cornerstones and alleyways was lit with torches so as to make the evening very special, and totally different from the view that we had during the day.

Once we returned to the entrance, we were treated to drinks and canapés while the orchestra played on with classical music befitting the whole evening. It was wonderful and probably the highlight of our second visit to Luxor.

Back to 2001, whilst we were still at our moorings in Luxor, we went to the Valley of the Kings. We crossed over the Nile and journeyed into the desert away from the fertile river and into the mountains. The Egyptians chose the left bank to bury their dead, as this is where the sun sets and the mountains have peaks that look a little like a pyramid, which was their preferred burial place when the dynasty was located in Cairo. There are a number of burial sites in addition to the Valley of the Kings, as you also have the Valley of the Queens and the Valley of the Noblemen.

When you visit the Valley of the Kings, your guide will give you some history and an explanation of the layout of the site and will probably take you into one of the tombs. We went into the tomb of Ramses III with our guide. Normally you are then given tickets to go and view two other tombs on your own. Some of them are very imposing – they go deep into the earth and decrease in size or twist around bends before entering the actual burial chamber itself. There are hieroglyphs on the walls dedicated to Anubis, the God of the underworld, death and otherworldly creatures and tales. All of these carvings and paintings were to help the body of the pharaoh enter the afterlife.

We went into King Tutankhamun's tomb, for which you have to pay extra; it is not included on the complementary tickets that you receive. In comparison with the other tombs we went into, this is very small and quite bare, only consisting of a pathway down, a single ante-chamber and then the burial chamber. But this is by far the most well-known of any of the tombs as it was discovered intact and full of the fine funerary treasure that now lie in the museum in Cairo. The sarcophagus has been put back into the burial chamber but not all of it as many of the inner compartments are on display in the museum in Cairo, along with the funeral mask and casket. I understand that the remains of the young pharaoh have been returned to lie in rest in his tomb.

Many people will say it is not worth going into this tomb, as it is so small and undecorated, but if you have grown up on the stories of Lord Carnarvon, Howard Carter and the curse of the mummy, then I would say pay the money and go in – you may never get the chance to do it again!

Away from the Valley of the Kings, you will find Queen Hatshepsut's Funerary Temple. This is carved into the mountain and there is quite a long walk from the car park to the entrance and in full heat, so be prepared! She ruled as a Pharaoh, not as a queen escort and she actually wore a false beard to prove her position in the hierarchy. Many of the statues were defaced after she died, but one still shows her image. The temple is very impressive and also very different from the tombs in the Valley.

One of the excursions that you can book in Luxor is a morning balloon flight. You are at the mercy of the winds as to where the balloon flies, but there is so much to see, you won't be disappointed! We started with magnificent views of Queen Hatshepsut's Temple and then we came over the Nile and we flew over Karnak Temple before finally coming to land quite gently in a field close by. There have been some horror stories about these balloon flights and recently one crashed and those on board were killed, so you are at the mercy of the pilot, the equipment and the winds, but we enjoyed our ride very much and have some wonderful photos to show for it.

We sailed down the Nile to Aswan, which took us three further nights, calling at other temples on the way including Edfu and Kom Ombo where there is a mummified crocodile. We went through locks, we bought Galabiyya's for the Egyptian night on board the Nile Beauty and we had time for some shopping and browsing at shops and stalls in both ports. In Aswan there is a lot to see including Philae Temple, the Aswan High Dam, the unfinished obelisk and the market.

We had a felucca ride around Kitchener's Island, but this was with the tour group and quite crowded. Later, when we checked into our hotel in Aswan, the Oberoi, we were treated to a private one, free of charge, with just one other couple. Even more special was our excursion in our own felucca to go to a Nubian restaurant located on an island near the old cataracts. We were the only ones in the restaurant and we were treated like royalty whilst dining on some fabulous local cuisine. We were then taken back by the felucca to our hotel – no catch, no money making scheme, just a genuine gesture and a wonderful evening costing us just forty pounds for the transfer, meal and a couple of beers but this was in 2001!

When you visit Philae Temple, you travel there by boat as the temple is built on an island. There are some wonderful buildings that are still intact, with carved columns, set against the blue of the Nile tributary, they are great subjects for a photograph. The main avenue, which has a number of different types of columns, is impressive but a lot of the reliefs on the walls were defaced as settlers who came from other countries thought that this would remove any power the Gods may have had at the site, when the main temple was turned into a Christian Church.

The market in Aswan is quite an experience. Prepare to be hassled and harassed. It did not matter how many times you said, "No thank you" to whatever it was they were offering you, they still kept badgering in the hope that you might change your mind. We always tried to be polite but at times it was difficult, as the tradesmen and hawkers are a continuous problem in Egypt. But we took it in our stride, and said, "No thank you" for the zillionth time and browsed the stalls at our leisure. The spices are remarkable and it was good to have them explained to us, as most of them I had never heard of. One stall owner offered a camel to Richard for me in exchange, but he was holding out for more! In one bag store, I got "trapped" behind the counter where I had been coaxed by the owner. He wouldn't "release" me until I purchased a bag! It was done in good spirit and I never felt threatened or at risk, so we just had a laugh, bought a bag, and moved on. We had gone in with the intention of buying a cloth beach bag, so again we did not feel as though we had been coerced into buying one.

Aswan is the point where you will depart on your excursion to Abu Simbel. There are options now to take a cruise on Lake

Nassau and you would then approach the temple from the water. I would imagine that this would be a fantastic way of getting your first glimpse of this glorious temple, but that was not on our itinerary on this occasion – maybe in the future when troubles are over in Egypt as it will be a different experience then.

Normally you go either by coach, which involves a long drive there and back in air-conditioned coaches, but you are looking at a round journey of eight hours—a long day in the heat of Egypt. Richard did this trip the previous time he had been on the Nile, so we were glad that the option for our tour through Kuoni was by plane. The flight from Aswan to Abu Simbel takes just twenty-five minutes plus all the hassle at the airport of course, but once we arrived, as there was no luggage, we all got straight onto a coach and off for our day trip at Abu Simbel.

Abu Simbel is an amazing site and we totally agreed that it should be on the fifty places to see list, but at forty-eighth, it is very low. There are two temples in the complex, the first, the Great Temple of Ramses II, was carved out of the mountain between 1274 and 1244 BC, being dedicated to several deities and to the pharaoh himself. Being built facing the river, the four colossal statues of Ramses II were designed to show the strength of the pharaoh to anyone visiting his lands from the south. Over the years, the temple was completely covered by sand and was lost to man until it was rediscovered, by chance, in 1813.

This temple was excavated to reveal a massive rock-cut façade standing thirty metres high and thirty-five metres wide with four colossal seated statues of Ramses II guarding the entrance although only three were found intact. As you enter the temple, which is small inside, there are a number of reliefs showing the battles and victories of Ramses II. These lead to the holy-of-holies where there are six statues. These are the four gods of the Great Temple, Ramses II and Nefertari, his Queen, and they all sit on their thrones carved in the back wall waiting for dawn.

The temple was aligned in such a way that on 22 February and 22 October every year, the first rays of the rising sun reach across the Nile, penetrate the temple and move along the hypostyle hall,

through the vestibule and into the sanctuary, where they illuminate the figures on the wall. The temple was moved in 1964 to save it from the rising waters created by the building of the Aswan High Dam, and the creation of Lake Nasser. It took four years to build a manmade mountain and then painstakingly cut the great temple into two thousand blocks and carefully re-erect it in a new position on higher ground. But, when the project was complete, the alignment was out by one day and the sun now hits the sanctuary a day earlier than originally designed! It goes to show that, despite modern technology, we were unable to align the temple as accurately as the ancient Egyptians who had built it over three thousand two hundred years earlier.

There is a second temple at Abu Simbel, also cut into the rock, the Temple of Hathor, dedicated to Queen Nefertari, Ramses' wife. It is a smaller version of Ramses own temple and is fronted by six standing statues, each about ten metres in height. Four of them are of Ramses and the other two are of Nefertari, who is shown as being the same height as her husband. This is unusual as normally the Queen's statue would just come up to the knees of the pharaoh, as most consorts are depicted. Inside the temple are pillars with capitals in the bovine shape of Hathor and the walls are adorned with reliefs.[3]

We spent several hours at the site, both with a guide and on our own. It is amazing and its location by the lake in such a far-away place in the desert, makes it even more enticing – a must for anyone visiting Egypt for the first time.

We spent two nights in Aswan before flying back to Luxor where we then boarded a coach which travelled in convoy with an armed guard to our next destination, Hurghada, located on the Red Sea. Hurghada is a beach resort, similar to Sharm el-Sheikh, where you are able to go diving and snorkelling amongst the coral and tropical fish of this region. We had a four-night stay at the Marriott – a nice hotel with good restaurants and ideally located for all sorts of excursions into the desert and onto the sea.

Our final stop on this tour of Egypt was three nights at the Sheraton in Cairo, where we had a Nile view room and in the distance, we could just see the pyramids. We did quite a lot of touring whilst we stayed in the capital city of Egypt and the most populated, busiest city in Africa. A must is the Egyptian museum, where some of the treasures found in King Tutankhamun's tomb are displayed. The artefacts are just wonderful and there are lots of photographs showing you how it was laid out when they opened the tomb. The highlight is the gold death mask used to cover the mummified face of the young king and the gold sarcophagus where his remains were originally laid to rest. But there is so much to see and marvel at in the museum, including several mummies and statues and remains from both the old and the middle kingdom. We also went to the Coptic Church in Old Cairo, also known as the Hanging Church, as it is suspended on old columns that are under the flooring and cannot be seen; the Citadel and the Mosque of Muhammad Ali where the clock stands, a gift from the King of France, in exchange for the Luxor obelisk. The clock was damaged on delivery and has never been repaired, so I think that the French got the best in that exchange deal! We passed the City of the Dead which is the old Islamic cemetery in Cairo. At this time, it was being used by the homeless as a place to reside and many had made their homes in the crypts and even houses had been built between the mausoleums. I thought that it was rather creepy! We also had a day trip out of the city to see Memphis, the ancient capital of the Upper Kingdom and to Sakkara to see a stepped pyramid.

But, of course, the highlight of our trip to Cairo was our excursion to the Pyramids of Giza number seventeen on our list, and the sole survivor of the Seven Wonders of the World.

Built over four thousand years ago, there are three main pyramids at the site; the Great Pyramid of Khufu (Cheops), the Pyramid of Khafre and the Pyramid of Menkaure; the Sphinx and the Funerary Temple of Khafre, plus a number of smaller pyramids, mausoleums and temples. Richard went into the Great Pyramid. I thought that it would be too hot and too claustrophobic, so I stayed outside in the heat and wandered around taking photos and being hassled by the local hawkers. Yet again. I was conned by a young boy who gave me a small bronze cat as a "gift". At first, I refused, but he seemed to be really hurt by the fact that I had refused this offer of a gift from him, so reluctantly I took it. As soon as I did, he started to demand money in exchange, and got quite hostile when I said no, and wanted to hand back the statue. In the end, I threatened to call the police over, who were standing nearby and in the end, he took back his "gift" and he wandered off mumbling.

The pharaoh was seen as the intermediary of the gods and was their representative on earth. As such, the pharaoh was worshipped in life and in death. The Egyptians believed in the afterlife and the pyramid was a perfect structure to act as a mausoleum for their pharaoh, a symbol of his power, and a vessel for entering the afterlife.

The funerary temple, which is built and attached to each tomb, is where the people could worship and give offerings to the pharaoh after his death, and each has a long, covered causeway that leads down to the swollen, flooded Nile River. It is believed that the mummy of the dead pharaoh was brought down the Nile in a solar barque (boat) and then brought up the causeway to be laid to rest in his tomb in the pyramid. One of these vessels was excavated in 1954, and has been restored and is now encased behind glass in a small museum, which can be visited at the Giza complex.[3]

The mystical sphinx is a wonderful sight — smaller than I had expected, but it still provides you with the thrill that you are looking at an object thousands of years old, which has stood the test of time except for the bit that was blown off by the cannon practice of Napoleon's army! The face is supposed to be that of Khafre, as it stands at the head of Khafre's Funerary Temple, and it is believed to have been carved from a solid rock at the same time as the Great Pyramid and the temple were being built.

We went to the Sound and Light show at the pyramids. Although it is at the Sphinx rather than the pyramids, as it is the Sphinx that speaks and tells you his story, it is much better than the one at Karnak and it is really good to see the pyramids lit up against the night sky. When you see pictures of the pyramids, it appears that they are far away in the desert, whereas they are actually right on the edge of the city of Cairo. As such, the light pollution at night does not help the Sound and Light show, but it is still worth a visit.

On a cruise in the Mediterranean, we stopped for two nights in Egypt, at Port Said and Alexandria. This overnight stop gave people the opportunity to visit Cairo and to stay for one night in a hotel in the city, as it is a long drive from the Mediterranean to the capital. I did it the first time that I went to Egypt when I was on a mini-cruise from Cyprus, stopping in Tel Aviv and Port Said. We did not bother doing this expensive extended tour, as we had both done Cairo in-depth in 2001 so we walked around Port Said and did a tour of Alexandria. To be honest, there is nothing in Port Said of any interest at all and when we were there the city was filthy, as the refuge collectors were on strike and the roads were covered with garbage. Alexandria was home to one of the other Seven Wonders of the World, the Pharos of Alexandria, which is no longer standing. This city, the second largest in Egypt, was very different from Cairo as it is strictly Islam and has an air of unfamiliarity. But we did see the fort built on the ruins of the lighthouse and some of the other key sites, albeit that these were not that interesting.

I doubt that we will ever return to Egypt due to the unrest and the fact that we have seen the majority of the wondrous temples, pyramids, museums and sights of this wondrous country. It is a pity that things are so bad. I know several people who have cancelled Nile cruises or are not inclined to visit this amazing place. I am sure that the Egyptian economy relies heavily on tourism and as a result of the decline, it will be the Egyptian people who will ultimately suffer.

CHAPTER 4

Las Vegas, USA (7) – November 2001

Not only was this my first time to Las Vegas; it was my first time in the USA. This was one country that I had not wanted to experience on my own. I wanted to share the sights and thrills of this huge nation and this was what I was doing with my fiancé Richard who had proposed to me on my birthday in October, and of course I said yes! On this occasion we were doing Vegas in a weekend! Yes, that's right, we were flying from the UK to the western state of Nevada for just four nights plus an overnight flight on our return journey. You'll be surprised what you can do over a weekend, wait until Chapter 25, then you'll see that this trip was not so fantastic! Our flight was on Delta and we flew from Manchester to Atlanta, where we changed planes to then stop at Phoenix before landing in Las Vegas.

We stayed at the Monte Carlo, which lies towards the top end of the Strip, the main thoroughfare that runs through Las Vegas. Because of the time difference and the length of the journey, when we arrived it was eleven p.m. but we weren't tired at all, so we went for a walk along the Strip. Richard had been to Vegas before and he loved it, calling it Disney World for adults!

At this time of night, even in November, it was reasonably warm and so quiet. It was a Wednesday night so obviously too early for the weekenders, and too late at night for the locals, so we had the Strip to ourselves. As we came to the Bellagio Hotel which had been under construction the last time that Richard was here, we decided to go in and get the little shuttle train that transported grownups between the two hotels. I don't think that it is there anymore. As we walked up the path around the lake, the lights came on, the fountains started to dance and this heavenly music filled the air. We were both awestruck as we had no idea about the famous dancing fountains at this wonderful five-star hotel. We stood and watched with our jaws open as the spectacle of this watery ballet entranced us for five minutes. We were the only ones watching and it felt so special, as though they were performing just for us. The music played was Andrea Bocelli and Sarah Brightman singing "Time to Say Goodbye". It was beautiful and so mesmerising. I didn't want to move, even when it was all over! From that day, that song has had a very special meaning to both of us and I refer to it, even now, as "our song".

Do not think of Las Vegas as just a gambling city. It is SO much more than that – you don't even have to set foot in a casino if you don't want to! The highlight of this city are the wonderful hotels. Everyone is different, and has something to offer the sightseer as you enter through the doors. The Venetian is remarkable. As you enter Saint Mark's Square, you will see the Grand Canal with singing gondoliers prepared to ferry you around the sites and even to go outside onto the canals that are located to the front of the hotel. The clouds float overhead on the ceiling that looks so much like the sky that you forget that there is a multi-story hotel above you. The shops are beautiful and offer everything from designer clothes, jewellery and watches to souvenirs and mementos. There are lots of street cafés and ice cream parlours and performing musicians waiting to bring this Italian paradise to life. We have been to Vegas several times now and the Venetian is always my favourite hotel shopping experience.

Caesars Palace takes you back to the glory of Rome and the arcade is yet again a shoppers' paradise. Taking centre stage is the story of Atlantis, which "erupts" into action at certain times of the day. The toy shop in Caesars is also a fabulous place to browse for the inner child in you. I was amazed at the window display of teddy bears in togas, all moving and performing for the onlooker. The Bellagio is mainly an external show with the fountains, which perform every half hour during the day I think and hourly at night. I can never get enough of these and when we stayed at the Bellagio, we booked a suite that was located on

the central spine of the building and we had views over the lake so as to be able to watch them all day, had we wanted to; with a dedicated channel on the hotel television system that would relay the music to accompany the dance, so we could watch and listen to our hearts content.

The New York Hotel has an interior to represent Times Square, even with grills letting steam out from the fake subway below. This is one of the hotels that has a fairground ride – a roller coaster that starts inside the hotel but then runs around and around the outside of the building. We could see the coaster from our bedroom window at the Monte Carlo on the thirty second floor, as this was the same level where the ride reached its peak! We went on this ride and I screamed the whole way around. I was shaking when I got off, but at least I can say that I did it! Outside there are small replicas of the Statue of Liberty, the Chrysler Building and other landmarks of NYC. When we were there it was only two and a half months after 9/11 and there were lots of flowers and memorials to those who had died in the Twin Towers, especially the brave New York Firemen who gave their lives to try and save those trapped in the shattered buildings.

There are so many grand hotels in Vegas that you need to see them for yourself and make your own decision. Luxor is a pyramid and treats you to an Egyptian feel; Excalibur is supposed to be the legendary castle of King Arthur and everything here is aimed at the stories of the Knights of the Round Table, Merlin and King Arthur – great for children. Sadly the Aladdin is no longer standing, knocked down to make way for the unsightly Planet Hollywood Hotel but when we were there you were taken back to the tales of the Arabian Nights and you even had a rainstorm inside the hotel at certain times of the day, including thunder! There is the Paris Hotel with its Eiffel Tower standing atop the building. Inside there are lots of little boudoir type shops and French cafés.

The Stratosphere Hotel, at the other end of the Strip has more fairground rides, set high on top of its tower, which is the tallest freestanding observation tower in the United States; home to Big Shot, X-Scream and SkyJump Las Vegas. There is also a wonderful revolving restaurant, which gives you magnificent views of Vegas and the Strip, especially at night when the city lights up like a Christmas tree.

Back on the Strip, another hotel, Treasure Island, has the pirate show at night when a French frigate is attacked by a British galleon and on this occasion, the French always win! But this is a great show free to everyone every night with gun fire, cannons roaring and ships being blown up and sinking! Only in America! Outside the Mirage there is an erupting volcano, a very timely one as it erupts at the same time every night!

Along with the amazing themed hotels, Las Vegas has some wonderful restaurants and of course it is famous for its shows.

Every hotel has a choice of different eateries from fine dining, like the steak restaurant in Bellagio, to buffets, where you can eat as much as you want for a fair price. Breakfast at the Monte Carlo was really special when we ordered steak and eggs. Accompanied by a big glass of fresh orange juice and as much steaming coffee as we wanted, this set us up for a day of sightseeing and made us feel like we had really hit America running! You can find out what is on offer by going to their websites. Every hotel will feature their dining options and most will have a sample menu so you can see the price before you book, and also get an idea of what they are offering. You can normally book a table through the website too, and it is wise to do this to avoid disappointment and to make sure that you get a table before you go to a show.

Each hotel normally has one show on offer but some may have several theatres like the Venetian and Luxor, so you can take your pick, from musicals, star attractions, cabaret, magicians, burlesque, cirque du solei, impressionist and so much more. We saw Cher at Caesars Palace the third time we went to Vegas and stayed at the Luxor. We came back to Vegas six days later and stayed in a huge suite at the Venetian to celebrate Richard's sixtieth birthday. We have only seen one cirque du solei show and that is Love at the Mirage. It features music by the Beatles and is a collaboration between Paul McCartney, Ringo Starr, Yoko Ono and Olivia Harrison. It is wonderful and moved me to tears! It was so good that when we returned to Vegas for our fifth time, we saw it again! If you are not bothered as to which show you see or where you sit, then you can probably get some good discounted tickets when you get to Vegas, but, if you are like us and are very particular about your seat location and your show, book well in advance, either through your hotel concierge or via the show's website.

Another evening of entertainment is to go Downtown to Freemont Street to watch the overhead laser show. This spectacle causes a sore neck as you are continually straining to take in all the colour, movement and effects, but it is worth every aching sinew! Set to great modern music, the moving picture show depicts the feeling or meaning of the song in action and covers a great expanse of ceiling that covers the street. It is well worth a visit. It also gives you the opportunity to see Vegas the way it used to be before all the modern building took place along the Strip. Here the hotels are a lower key and the casinos are the main focus. It feels a little bit seedy and I would not like to stay here, preferring the glitzy hotels on the Strip, but it is certainly worth a visit.

We did a helicopter trip while we were in Las Vegas, to fly over the Grand Canyon, which is number one on the fifty list. Although this was the first time that we had seen the canyon together, (Richard had been to the West coast before we met doing Vegas and the canyon), I am going to go into detail in Chapter 18 as that was when we stayed at the canyon. But the helicopter flight from Vegas is fantastic as you get to see how big this natural wonder is and it is almost like a fairground ride as you fly over ridges and drop down into the deep canyon. We stopped at the bottom of the gorge by the river for a little drink and a snack before flying back over Hoover Dam and up the Strip, which, by the time we returned, was lit up in the dark. I need to add a little titbit here; we had to wait for our helicopter to return with the previous group and when they disembarked and walked back through the reception area, we were gobsmacked to see that it was no other than the Bee Gees!

Another trip we did was taking a small plane to the North Rim to visit a ranch. We had a tour of the ranch where they had a little menagerie of local reptiles and insects, including snakes. We then went to the North Rim, which is an area of the canyon that is less visited, and not as popular as the South Rim where the main Canyon village is located. We had the option of going by ATV or in a jeep. There were six of us on the tour, four young Italians and Richard and me. To our surprise, the Italians opted for the jeep, which was the easy mode of travel, whereas we went for the ATV. A little frightening at first, as the ground was rough and trying to control these four wheelers was difficult for me. But once I was used to steering and revving the throttle, not going too fast but enough to keep up with the jeep, I really enjoyed it – in fact, it was quite a thrill. We stopped for photos on the rim, looking down on the Colorado River below, amazed as to how this small waterway had carved through the rock to create this wondrous colossal river. My only problem with this trip was that the flight was very rocky due to the thermals over the canyon and surrounding plateau, and I felt quite ill on the return journey.

Las Vegas is in the middle of the desert and you can do lots of adventurous excursions. We have done many as we have been to Las Vegas on numerous occasions. We love it so much that we would always try and include it on any itinerary to the West coast. We have done quad biking into the surrounding barren hills and driven a dune buggy through the sand dunes of Nevada. When we had a car, we visited Red Rock Canyon and took the scenic circuit around this mini-canyon, stopping for sightseeing and photographs – well worth a trip.

We did a tour to go to Hoover Dam, booking through Viator.com on a tour that offered us something different, as it focused on it being a humorous trip! It was, and great fun, certainly different from just a normal visit to this manmade structure. The coach occupants were all given fake moustaches and glasses with "wobbly" eyes – we were told to put them on as we reached the security gate at the dam. When the military security guy came on board he was greeted by thirty people wearing these comical disguises. He took it in his stride and commented that he had a bus yesterday with a similar looking group! The dam tour is very interesting and it is good to see it close up. We drove over it the next day when we continued with our Parks and Canyons drive in 2008.

We have stayed in quite a few of the hotels in Vegas – the Monte Carlo, Stratosphere, Luxor, Venetian and Bellagio. We stayed in the Venetian for Richard's sixtieth birthday, and upgraded to a suite, which was huge with four televisions, including one in the bathroom! We had a bar, a lounge and a dining area where we enjoyed a champagne breakfast on the special day. But our favourite was at the Bellagio where, as I mentioned, we had a suite located in the central "spine" of the hotel, overlooking the fountains. The benefits of booking a suite started at the airport when we were met by a chauffeured limo, complementary with our booking. As we arrived at the hotel, we were greeted, by name, and escorted to the concierge lounge where we had a drink in comfort whilst waiting to check in. The suite was beautiful with his and hers bathrooms, located on opposite sides of the room. I had a huge Jacuzzi bath and Richard had a spa shower. The TV was hidden at the bottom of the bed, rising up only when required, so as it did not block the view of the fountains and the Strip, which we could look out on whilst lying in bed and gazing out through the huge, floor to ceiling, panoramic windows. It really is a case of – you get what you pay for in life!

    I do hope that we will have the opportunity to return to Vegas again. It is always changing with new facilities, hotels and experiences, and I am sure that when we go back there will be a whole new encounter to recall.

CHAPTER 5

Rio de Janeiro, Brazil (31) – March 2002, Our Honeymoon

On 22 March 2002, Richard and I were married at Whitley Hall, Grenoside. The day was chosen as it was also my parents Golden Wedding Anniversary and we had a double celebration. It was a wonderful day. I know that I'm bound to say that, but I had waited such a long time for this day and I thought that I would never walk down the aisle. Richard said I had a silly grin on my face all day. The wedding photos bear witness to that! Even though it was March, we were lucky enough to have sunshine, and we were able to have the champagne reception outside in the gardens and most of our photographs were taken in the hotel grounds.

But enough of the sentimentality – back to the travels! We had booked a long weekend over the Easter period in Rio before we got engaged, but Richard had contacted Kuoni and upgraded it to be our honeymoon. The upgrade was free and it meant that we had access to the Varig lounge at the airport, and an upgraded room at our hotel, The Luxor Continental. We flew from Heathrow direct to Rio, six days after our wedding and arrived at eight thirty in the morning to a temperature of thirty two degrees. On the flight our name was called out as we landed and we were told we had a private transfer to our hotel – obviously another "upgrade" benefit that we had not been aware of, but we were certainly not complaining! John, our driver, informed us that for a little extra we could have him drive us around on all our excursions that we had booked through Kuoni. This sounded like a wonderful luxury and at a reasonable price, so we agreed. On our drive from the airport to our hotel, we had many of Rio's sites pointed out to us and everything was exactly how I imagined it would be — photographs just don't do the city justice, it is beautiful and so green.

Our hotel was set one street back from Copacabana Beach, and this was our first stop after we had unpacked. The beach is fabulous — very, very long with pristine white sands, aqua blue sea, a walkway/promenade that runs the full length of the beach, the road that is wide and busy and then another footpath where the restaurants, bars and hotels are located on Atlantica Avenue. It is absolutely perfect for strolling along and enjoying the sights of Rio. We did not hit the sands on this first day. We just stopped for a pizza and a beer for our lunch and returned that evening for a great steak.

The following day we had our city tour. The first stop was Corcovado, the mountain that dominates the coastal area of Rio as it is two thousand seven hundred and twenty-six feet high with the thirty metre high statue of Christ the Redeemer on the top. You can ascend the mountain using the colourful funicular railway, but John drove us to the top, well as far as he could go. We walked the last two hundred and fifteen steps which was exhausting but worth all the effort. We were lucky, as it was such a clear day that we could see for miles and the view from the top of the mountain is spectacular. It was busy but not too bad, even though it was Easter Saturday.

From Corcovado we drove to Sugarloaf Mountain, which stands at the top of Copacabana Beach. It is around half the size of Corcovado at thirteen hundred feet, but the experience and views were no less spectacular as we could see the main city of Rio, some of the other beaches and islands in the bay. You reach the summit of Sugarloaf by cable car — there are two cars, one goes up while the other comes down, crossing half way along this incredible, thrilling ride. We were lucky yet again, as the following day they were closing the cable car to have the cable replaced, and it would not be running for the rest of the time we were in Rio, so it was a good job that John took us on this day — and the queues weren't bad either!

That evening we went on an organised event to have a Brazilian barbecue, followed by a Samba show. The barbecue offers so much meat, it was a good job neither of us are vegetarians! It is accompanied by salad and vegetables, so your meal is not a hundred percent protein, but there is certainly enough! The waiters come around the table with huge skewers containing all sorts of roasted meats – beef, lamb, and pork, from which they carve slices of hot, juicy meat onto your plate, as well as chicken pieces, sausages and steak. Fabulous meal! It certainly left us fat and fulfilled! The Samba show is a way of showing off some of the carnival costumes that are used just once for the Mardi Gras Carnival that takes place in February each year. This is Rio's busiest time and is, of course, famous around the world as being the largest street carnival anywhere. Each Samba school has its own float and theme each year, and they practice the dances and prepare their colourful and spectacular costumes months in advance. How the girls manage to dance and move around with the head-dresses made of feathers and material that rise probably two feet from their heads, I'll never know. *(In January 2014 we did a cruise along the Amazon and went to Parintins, a small village where they have an annual festival called La Bamba and they have two teams who dress up with similar outfits as those worn in Rio at the carnival. We had a chance to get up close to them and even try them on – they were not light and very cumbersome to move around in.)*

On Easter Sunday we went to the Maracanã Stadium to see a football match! Not something you would normally expect to be doing on a honeymoon, but this might be the only time that we go to Rio and, being the largest stadium in the world (at that time) with a capacity for one hundred and sixty thousand people, it was a site that was worth a visit, even for a non-footie person like me! We went to see Botafogo play America; two local sides competing in a cup match. It was not well attended, as there were only five thousand there on this occasion, but the Brazilian fans were still loud, rowdy and very active, waving their flags, banging drums and cheering their side-on. Botafogo needed to win to get through to the knockout rounds, but America scored a late goal and won one-nil. There were not a lot of westerners or tourists at the match. It was attended mainly by Brazilians, but everyone made us feel very welcome and allowed us to keep changing our seat to get to the shaded areas as the sun moved around the stadium.

We are not beach people and even when we do stay at a coastal hotel, it is quite rare for us to actually spend time on the beach, but in Rio you MUST lie on Copacabana Beach. It would be unforgivable not to. As we collected our umbrella and chairs from our hotel concierge, we were warned not to take anything to the beach – no camera, wallet, bag, jewellery, watches, anything. This was the first time where we felt nervous about the infamy of Rio and the crime that it is known for. Until then, we had not felt threatened at all and had not witnessed any problems, but after this warning we started to be very cautious about where we walked and what we were carrying. Needless to say, on our morning at the beach, we had no problems at all. I sat in the shade and just enjoyed watching Brazilians enjoying the sun, sea and sand. The girls that parade up and down in skimpy bikini's do their best to get noticed and the boys aren't much better, being macho, playing beach footie or volleyball. The breeze from the ocean kept us cool and we stayed for a few hours just letting the sights pass us by. When we got up to leave, we dipped our feet into the cooling water and then proceeded to walk up the beach, barefoot, to the promenade. Well, we ended up running in a most undignified manner – the sand was so hot it was burning our feet! Talk about a mad dash for freedom!

In the afternoon we had a tour all around Rio, going to Ipanema Beach, through the park where we had wonderful views of the beaches, up through the Saint Theresa district, where we saw the trolley bus climbing slowly up Corcovado. We then went into the city centre where we saw the cathedral, library, opera house, state buildings, red beach and finally the harbour.

The location of our hotel was perfect for finding somewhere to eat. Just around the corner and along Atlantica Avenue are all sorts of eateries from fine dining to pizza and snacks. We enjoyed the seafood at Mab's where the prawns were served on skewers that were so big they looked like small swords! Probably the best meal we had was at the French restaurant on the thirty-seventh floor of the Meridian Hotel overlooking Copacabana. The meal was fabulous and is the birthplace of the dessert "St Honore", which was created by the restaurant's chef, Paul Bocuse. He came out to ask us what we ate and whether we had enjoyed the meal. This was my first time in a really high standard restaurant with a renowned chef, and for him to greet us in such a way was certainly a "wow" factor for me. The meal, including wine, cost us around one hundred pounds and was worth every penny. It is probably a lot more expensive now, but I would not hesitate to go back there again. As Richard and I have travelled more, we have enjoyed many more fabulous meals at some highly recommended restaurants, some of them Michelin starred, and, with age, our palates have become a lot more discerning, and we now really do enjoy fine food and wine.

The next day, we returned to Ipanema Beach using the free shuttle service from our hotel. We had to pay a visit to the workshops and the store of H Stern first, as they were the ones organising the transfer, but, with a guided audio tour it was quite interesting to see the fine workmanship that was taking place behind the glass windows of the workshops. I succumbed to the wonderful pieces on display and purchased a blue topaz ring set in yellow gold. I still wear it to this day, so the one hundred and seventy pounds that it cost was a fair trade. Jewellery and shopping in general is my biggest weakness when I am on holiday as I think that the designs, the quality and the price, are so much better than at home in the UK.

In Ipanema we found the bar where the song "The Girl from Ipanema" was written. Inside are photographs and newspaper cuttings of "that girl", and also the score is plastered all over the walls of the bar.

There is so much to see in Rio and it is developing all the time. Having hosted some of the World Cup matches in 2014, including the final and being the hosts of the Olympics in 2016, there will have been a lot of changes since our holiday in 2002. I hope that we can go back to this vibrant city and see it again to relive some of our honeymoon memories.

CHAPTER 6

Paris, France (27) – June 2002

The City of Lights, Gay Paree! We had six nights in Paris to celebrate Richard's birthday. You will find that a lot of our holidays coincide with our anniversary on the 22nd of March, Richard's birthday on the 6th of June or my birthday on the 10th of October, as we try to celebrate these special occasions away from home. In fact, until 2017, the only anniversary we have had at home was our first, which we celebrated with Mum and Dad at Whitley Hall, where we were married.

I had been to Paris three times before, but this was Richard's first time, so we did everything suggested in the guide book, plus a bit more! I don't know how many times I book holidays which coincide with the Olympics or the World Cup, and this year was no exception – at least we saw England's opening match against Sweden before we flew out (they drew 1–1 by the way).

Our hotel in Paris was not good – the location was perfect, very close to the Arc de Triomphe and a stone's throw from the metro station, but the room was *very* small, even by European standards. We had a sliver of a window, that looked onto an internal patio area; not that we could see it as it really was so narrow. It let in no light and offered very little in the way of a view. You could not have the bathroom door and wardrobe door open at the same time, as they clashed – so one of us had to sit on the bed whilst the other washed and dressed. Breakfast was dreadful too, the worst continental breakfast we have ever experienced. There was so little to choose from, and one morning, when we were down late, all the cheese and ham had gone, so we were left with a bread roll and jam!

Paris has been the capital of France since 987, and, as with all capitals, it was expensive! But I would say that Paris is even more expensive than you would expect – we are talking 2002 here and it cost us twenty-four euro for a stein and a pint of lager, which at that time was sixteen pounds!

On our first full day in Paris we went to the Louvre, which is one of the largest museum/art galleries in the world. It is located at the end of the Champs-Elysees and through the Tuileries Garden, in the former royal palace built by Francis I. It is so big that you need to limit yourself to certain areas to view particular works of art or select your era or artist and plan your visit around this itinerary. The Louvre is home to many masterpieces, including the Mona Lisa, Venus de Milo and Winged Victory. If you are a fan of Dan Brown's fictional books featuring Professor Robert Langdon, then you will know that the book, The Da Vinci Code, starts and ends at this museum.

Paris is such a beautiful city to walk around in, with the Seine running through the centre and lots of leafy roads and boulevards. Originally, the city was organised into three parts, the Ile de la Cite, the Right Bank and the Left Bank. It offers many modern buildings but also aged crumbling edifices that are both romantic and an eyesore at the same time! The neoclassical architecture dates from the Napoleonic era and it was Napoleon III who built the bridges and boulevards of the modern city.[1]

From the Louvre, we walked along the Seine to the Ile de la Cite, an island on the Seine where the first signs of habitation date back to two hundred and fifty BC. We went to the Sainte-Chapelle, a thirteenth century chapel that lies within the Palais de la Cite, the former residence of the kings of France. This gothic building was truly beautiful, with wonderful stained-glass windows and wooden interior. It is only small and may not be on everybody's hit list, but I found it more enchanting than Notre Dame, which is where we went next.

On both my previous visits to Paris, the cathedral was covered with scaffolding, but today it was clear of any obstruction, and we could see this infamous building in all its glory. As it had been

cleaned recently, the towers, built from sandstone, gleamed in the afternoon sun. Inside it is very austere and not as decorated as the exterior, but the stained glass window in the nave is a real treat.

We did so much on this first day. We really packed everything in as we continued our sightseeing, by taking the metro to Champs de Mars for the Eiffel Tower. As it was such a clear day, and there were no queues, we took the elevator to the top of the tower. The tower was built from wrought iron in 1889 for the World Exhibition. It was meant to be a temporary structure, but it was so popular that it was decided to leave it in place and it has now celebrated its hundred and twenty-fifth birthday! It is nine hundred and eighty-four feet tall and it was the tallest manmade structure for many years. Designed by the French engineer Gustave Eiffel; he was also responsible for being the architect of the inner structure of the Statue of Liberty in New York, and a little steel bridge that spans a river in the middle of the rain forest in Venezuela!

The views from the top of the tower, on a clear day, are magnificent, as all of Paris lies before you. There are maps and drawings to help you to identify the streets and the buildings that you can spy from this birds-eye vantage point. The elevators in the tower are split into three. The first one goes at an angle up one of the four slanted legs of the tower, where you reach a big, flat level where the shops are, and also the queue for the next elevator, which goes through the main centre of the structure. On the next stop, where you have to alight, is the Michelin Restaurant, Jules Verne. We have never eaten there but my brother, Gareth, and sister-in-law, Terry, have said that it is absolutely wonderful; expensive, but a fabulous fine dining experience. The final lift takes you to the viewing platform near the top of the tower. This last one is totally enclosed but from memory I think that the first one is open to the elements, and you can walk around the outside of the platform. The upper level used to be open-air, but it was a favourite spot for people to leap to their death, so; to avoid further tragedy, it was closed in.

The tower is open both day and night and the evening view is just as spectacular, as you realise why Paris is called the City of Lights. It is like a fairyland, all lit up in the dark sky and is just as picturesque as during the day.

To get the best view of the tower, for a photograph, you need to be at the top of the Trocadero looking down the avenue of fountains leading to the tower. Of course, you can get some wonderful quirky photos of the steel structure from close-up, but to get the full tower into a picture, this spot is by far the best.

The very first time I came to Paris I was on a tour of Europe with an Australian tour company called Kontiki, and the group was made up of many different English speaking nationalities, many of whom were also on their first visit to Paris. Our guide told us that the best way to see Paris was to have it "jump" out at us!

We were all bemused as to what he meant, but we followed his instructions and when we left the camp site to do our first night tour of the city, those who were on their first visit to Paris, obediently used the coach headrest cover as a blindfold, putting it over our head and eyes whilst we were driven into the city centre. The remaining few passengers watched with amusement at our plight! Our guide relayed to us that we were driving past Notre Dame, the Louvre and Arc de Triomphe, but we could not see a thing as ninety-five of us were blindfolded. Eventually the coach stopped and we were all taken off; each of us led by the hand by someone who had been to Paris before and was not blindfolded. We were lined up against the coach and on the count of three, we removed our eye-covering. There before us lay the fountains and the Eiffel Tower all lit up against a jet-black, clear night sky. THAT was my very first sight of Paris and it still lives with me to this day!

Back to our 2002 visit; on the following day we went, by metro, to the Cimetiere du Pere Lachaise, the oldest and the largest cemetery in Paris. You may think that this is a rather morbid sight to see on holiday, but it was fascinating, as there are so many tombs and graves where the famous and the infamous are laid to rest. The cemetery is broken up into different sections where you will find the graves/tombs of musicians like Chopin; authors, including Oscar Wilde; artists and entertainers including Edith Piaf and Jim Morrison of the Doors. His grave was very simple and had no fresh flowers placed on it at all, but many people were posing for their photograph by his resting place, which we thought was quite disrespectful. We did stop at Chopin's tomb, but it was only in 2016, when we went to Poland, that we discovered that his heart was not interred with him. This was taken to Warsaw and is entombed in the walls of the Holy Cross Church at his bequest, as he was Polish by birth but left before the 1830 uprising when he settled in Paris.

There are many art galleries and museums in Paris, some of them dedicated to a particular art form. We went to two of them, d'Orsay Musee and the George Pompidou Centre. The former has art from the late nineteenth and early twentieth century, including works by Van Gogh, Monet and other impressionist artists. The latter is a very strange building, very modern in its design, which was reflected in the art inside which was very much twentieth century up to present day. All of the buildings "workings" are on the outside – the pipes for water, electric, sewage etcetera, as well as the escalators. It is made of scaffolding and glass and is a work of art in itself albeit not to our taste!

Our next stop was Montmartre, the artists quarter, located on the hill overlooking the city, crowned by the gothic masterpiece or monstrosity depending on your opinion of this white marble edifice which gets whiter with age, the Sacre Couer **(Picture 8?)**.

This building can be seen from all over the city and is more visible than the Eiffel Tower. You can climb the hill by funicular railway and the views from the summit are wonderful, as, from here, you can see the Eiffel Tower. This area in Paris offers small, leafy squares and avenues, where there are lots of cafés and bars. It is my favourite spot in the city. In the centre of the Place du Tertre, many local artists display their works that can be purchased at a reasonable price. From classical views of the city to modern three-dimensional works, there is something to please everyone's taste. There are some artists who will sketch your portrait or produce a caricature while you wait. There are museums around the area dedicated to the artists that are synonymous with Paris and Montmartre, including Salvador Dali.

The Arc de Triomphe is a huge structure lying at the centre of probably the largest, and busiest, roundabout in Paris. It is also the location of one of the main metro stations, Charles de Gaulle. One of the roads leading off from the roundabout is the Champs-Elysees, probably the most famous street in Paris. It is very long and very wide and has some wonderful and expensive cafés and restaurants on both sides of the avenue, with outdoor seats and umbrellas where you can sit and watch the world go by, as you sip a glass of wine in the wonderful Parisian sunshine! There are not many shops along this road, mainly car sales showrooms and offices, but it offers a wonderful stroll from the Arc de Triomphe to Place de la Concorde. This is the location of Cleopatra's Needle that was given to the French as a gift from the Egyptians, in exchange for a clock which has never worked and is located in Cairo.

On 6th June, Richard's birthday, we left the city and took the RER to Disneyland Paris! If you want to feel like a child again, then this is the place to be! A small replica of the theme park in the USA, this was the first one to be built outside of America.

Of course, now there are others in the Far East in Japan and Hong Kong and probably other locations that I am not aware of, but in 2002 this was new to us. We went to Phantom Manor, Thunder Mountain, Pirates of the Caribbean, Honey I Shrunk the Audience and Star Tours. We ate at the Blue Lagoon, which was nice and watched the parade. A few years later we visited Disney World in Florida, which is one of the fifty, and we then realised just how small Euro Disney was and how understated the whole razzamatazz, was in comparison to the original, and the best, of these theme parks.

Other sights to see in Paris include Les Invalides, the domed church where Napoleon's tomb is placed. It is very imposing and certainly worth a visit. The Latin Quarter, which lies on the Left Bank of the Seine and has some wonderful restaurants, cafés and bars where you will get something good to eat and drink whilst gazing at the Notre Dame Cathedral, or watching the street entertainers that frequent this area. And, if you are adventurous, an evening around the Pigalle, the red-light district of Paris, which can be both entertaining and thrilling; it depends on your tastes and how far you want to stretch them! The Pigalle is the location of the infamous nightclub Moulin Rouge, with its windmill on the roof, setting it apart from the other burlesque shows in the area. This was where the Can-Can was created and was also the place where Toulouse-Lautrec painted his famous pictures of the dancing girls. It is expensive and you don't really get value for your money. They obviously rely on its notoriety and fame, as the food is mediocre, the show is burlesque with topless dancers, and drinks are VERY expensive – but it is an experience and part of the Parisian tourist trap.

I like Paris as there is so much to see and to do. It is easy to walk around and the metro is easy, and safe to use. The recent terrorist attacks in 2016/17 on innocent people will have marred it as a popular weekend destination, but these days, anywhere in the world could be a target. You just need to be careful, keep your wits about you, and hope that you are not in the wrong place at the wrong time. The only problem with Paris is that it is full of the French, who are not the friendliest people around. I have found that if you try to converse with a little French, even if you make a mess of it, the locals appreciate the effort, and will assist you.

We returned to Paris in June 2018 for a short break, to celebrate Richard's seventieth birthday. He knew we were going away for five nights but he had no idea where we were going. I obviously managed to keep the secret up to the last minute, as he thought that we were going to drive to the airport and catch a flight and on the morning of our departure I had to call him back to stop him from putting our cases into the car!

On this occasion, we didn't fly – I booked Eurostar from Saint Pancras to Paris, as this was on my wish list – Richard had been on the train, but so far, this trip had eluded me. We took a train from Sheffield, first class, as it was a special occasion, and we then transferred two hours later, onto the premium section of Eurostar. I was impressed with the check-in, the arrangements for boarding and the seats, but the waiting area at the station left a bit to be desired, and the meal was not very good.

When we arrived at the station I had arranged for a transfer through our hotel, the Balmoral, located near the Arc de Triumph. Our suite had a very small balcony, but it was too small to use and there was no view. I wish that I had done a little more research and had found a hotel with an exceptional view, but the location was good for bars and restaurants.

As this was a special occasion, I had wanted to arrange for something different, but also for it all to be spectacular. So the day after we arrived, we took a taxi to the Eiffel Tower and had lunch in the Michelin Star Restaurant on the second level – Jules Verne. I had prepaid for a celebratory lunch, which included a glass of champagne on arrival and wine with each course. You are also guaranteed a window seat. You use a private lift that is exclusive for the restaurant. The food was fabulous, the service was exceptional and the views, despite it being cloudy and grey, were still amazing.

But this meal was surpassed by our excursion the next evening on one of the famous Parisian floating restaurants. I used viator.

com to book the premier service on Parisiens Seine Bateaux River Cruise, which departed from the Eiffel Tower. This consisted of champagne on arrival and a six-course meal with wine. There was entertainment during the evening, but the star of the show was the views we encountered, as we sailed along the Seine, going past Ile de la Cite and returning to our departure point three hours later, to see Tour Eiffel illuminated from top to toe. The food was good and there was plenty to eat and drink – it was a very memorable evening.

The next day we left Paris and took a private transfer to Versailles, where we stayed for two nights at the fabulous Trianon Palace. We have been watching the French-Canadian TV series of the same name and enjoyed the story of its expansion and place in French history, under Louis XIV. It is only forty-five minutes by car, and I had organised a private tour of the palace and the gardens through Tours by Locals. This was an expensive break, as the hotel is five-star and one of the best in France, with a price tag to match, and our tour was over five hundred pounds, but it was worth it. Gustav, our guide, was young, energetic and very knowledgeable. His enthusiasm was infectious and we were both completely enthralled by his tales of the courts of the French kings, the collapse of the monarchy after the revolution and the decline of its magnificent, huge palace. We were very lucky to have beautiful weather to wander around the gardens, before we entered the palace to see the Kings' apartments including the Hall of Mirrors, which was spectacular. It was very busy, but with having a guide we were able to go through the no-queue entrance, which avoided the long lines at the main entrance.

I am certain we did the right thing with having a private guide, as a lady came up to Gustav and asked how she could join a guided tour, rather than listen to the headphones that can be hired. She was told it was not possible to organise this at the Palace. It was necessary to arrange this prior to entry. She had then wanted to join us, but I am afraid I was rather mean and declined; we had paid a lot for this luxury and didn't want to share the experience with anyone else!

This was a fabulous, five-star experience – definitely champagne and caviar, rather than the beer and popcorn one from our previous stay in Paris. We were also blessed with some beautiful weather and we took the open-top bus tour around the city, to be able to see locations we had never visited before, and get some great photographs with blue skies. Paris is an expensive city. Accommodation, food and drink can certainly set you back a bob or two, but there is so much to see and such a lot to experience, I would certainly recommend a visit, but look for something different on Viator and try to see the alternative sides of this wonderful capital city.

CHAPTER 7

Machu Picchu, Peru (14) – January 2003

Our tour of Peru was booked through Voyages Jules Verne, a tour company that offers different holidays to destinations which others do not seem to cover. They are now part of Kuoni, but cater for a traveller on a lower budget, more of a three/four-star travel option. Their vacations are very well priced and they sometimes offer an upgrade, at a cost, to better hotels – if you want to take up this option. They can be found on the internet, www.vjv.com, and they also have a number of brochures available to download or to have them delivered. We had been with them on a tour of South Africa and Swaziland in 2002, and we found them to be competent, well managed and the three-star hotels that they offered in Africa were good, so we stuck with basic accommodation in Peru.

We did have problems with our flight though. The British Airways flight was delayed coming from Miami back to the UK, which had a knock-on delay with the return leg, which was our flight, but due to bad weather in London, as there was ice on the wing of the plane. We had to wait for that to be removed before we could fly – ah, the joys of travelling in the winter! It takes a long time to de-ice a plane and as a result, we were parked on the runway for over an hour before we eventually took off. Due to high winds, the plane also took a slight detour to avoid them and this delayed us even more. By the time we landed in Miami, we were two and a half hours behind schedule.

Everyone has to go through immigration in the USA, regardless of whether you are staying in America or flying on. Any seasoned traveller who has hit United States Immigration will know just how bad that can be, and by the time we had got through, we had missed our connecting flight to Lima. *Since this holiday, we have been to Miami airport on many occasions as we have done quite a few Caribbean cruises which have sailed from Miami or Fort Lauderdale. The new immigration machines have made it a little easier, but the queues for the passport control are still horrendous and I cannot see this changing in the future.* In January 2003, due to our late arrival, we had missed our connecting flight and there was some confusion, as we tried to find out which flight we had been transferred to. British Airways had taken care of our luggage and we were told that we would be on the next American Airlines flight which was at eleven forty-five p.m. and the time now was seven thirty p.m. We were on standby and we would maybe be put on the flight after, which was at five to four p.m. the next day!

When we checked if we would have a hotel for the night, we were then told that we were actually booked on the Lan Peru flight at eleven fifty-five p.m. and there were no issues with this transfer, we would be in Lima the next day. Some of our tour group did fly out on the American Airlines flight, but their luggage was on our flight – we were very surprised that this was allowed after 9/11, but as this flight landed just ten minutes before ours, we were all together again for our holiday to begin. But, one further problem was waiting for us!

Our tour guide, with coach and driver, came out to meet the group at the expected time of arrival the night before, as the company had not been told about everyone being delayed in Miami. When no-one showed up, they went home! So there we were, a group of around twenty-four British tourists stranded at the airport with nowhere to go! It wasn't too bad though, as after about half an hour, a coach came and picked us up to take us to our hotel, the Sonesta Posadas del Inca in Lima. This was a different hotel from the one we had expected to stay at, but it was modern, clean and well positioned for local restaurants. After some breakfast, a shower and a quick nap, we were ready for our tour of Peru's capital city.

Our first stop was the old town and the Plaza des Armes, which is the main square in Lima. With all main squares in South

American cities or towns you will find the cathedral or the main church, the town hall, and other government buildings, which make up the surrounding sides of the square and then a green area in the centre with a statue and this is likely to be of Simon Bolivar (1783–1830). This Venezuelan patriot was known as The Liberator, and succeeded in driving the Spanish from Venezuela, Colombia, Peru and Ecuador. Upper Peru was renamed Bolivia in his honour, and the currency of Venezuela is the Bolivar. [1]

We went into the cathedral, which was on the square. It was painted pale yellow like most of the other government buildings located here. Pizarro's tomb lies in the cathedral – he was the conquistador who conquered Peru for the Spanish. We then went to the Museum of Peruvian Gold, where there are a lot of local artefacts including the strange mummies of ancient Peruvians. The body was put in a sitting position and then wrapped with bandages, which created a huge conical "bundle". This was then buried in the ground where the bandages became rock solid and acted as a coffin for the deceased. A number of these had been found totally intact and were on display – some of them cut partially open, to show the skeleton and the remains of the person inside.

The next day we took a flight to Cusco in the Andes. The flight was great as we flew over the beautiful mountain range. As you approach the airport, you can see the ancient city of Cusco spread out along the valley floor before you at eleven thousand feet above sea level. It is a lovely old city and the central square, although large and oblong, is the same layout as the one that I described in Lima. We were staying at the San Agustin International Hotel and this hotel was built in a similar style to the buildings we had seen in Cusco with plastered, curved walls and decorated internally with local décor, including dark wooden stairs and banisters that twisted through the centre of the building to the bedrooms on the upper levels.

We started off with a city tour where we went to the Inca Temple of the Sun, the cathedral in Plaza des Armes, the temple of Sacsayhuaman and an alpaca shop where they were selling rugs, shawls, hats and scarves made from the wonderful soft wool from this animal, which is farmed on the highlands surrounding Cusco. The cathedral is very old and was one of the first Christian Churches to be built in Peru. It does offer a few interesting elements though – firstly, there is a statue of Christ on the cross, but his image is that of a Peruvian man rather than a European; and secondly, on the picture of the last supper which adorns one of the altars, on the table in front of Christ is the local speciality, laid out exactly how it is served in Cusco today – guinea pig! We had read how this local dish is served with the head removed, fried crispy, and then put on a plate, on its back with the four little legs pointing skywards! We never tried it, but two girls from our group ordered it in a restaurant, and screamed when it was served as they did not know the custom for the preparation of the dish. I don't think that they enjoyed their meal that night! Back to the cathedral, the décor inside is much more elaborate than the one in Lima, and it is large, dominating the square where we found lots of fine restaurants, bars and shops.

The next day we had an optional excursion to go to the Sacred Valley. This was named by the Incas as they had many settlements in the valley that offered shelter for their villages and good fertile soil for their crops. The Incas used to farm on the slopes of the mountains building terraces for their grain and vegetables. The views as we drove into the valley was spectacular, even though we had low clouds spoiling it slightly.

We went on to Ollantaytambo (pronounced Oy-an-tie-tambo) where the terraces were still intact and in use and rose high into the mountains. We went into the old town on foot which consisted of narrow streets and mud brick houses. We were invited into a house where everything was in one room, including the guinea pigs, which were running around our feet and scuttling into a little hide close to the fire grate. They were being raised for food, to eat on special occasions. Back in our coach, we followed the course of the Urubamba River (which created the Sacred Valley) to Urubamba where we had lunch at a Hacienda before moving on to Pisac where we went to the local market. This was not just for the locals, although there were lots of stalls selling beautiful fresh fruit and vegetables, others were selling pots, pans and clothes, but it also offered souvenirs for the tourists.

The next day we started our journey into the Andes to head for Machu Picchu. It was an early start as we took the train from Cusco to Aguas Calientes. This train is owned by the Orient Express and the route is considered to be one of the best train journeys in the world. To leave Cusco, the train had to get over the mountains and this was done by an ingenious English system known as "switchback", where the train goes forward and then backward up sloping tracks, until it clears the mountain peak. It is a slow process, but it works perfectly and offers superb views of Cusco, waking up to a new morning, in the valley below us.

We were soon running quickly along the line, going through the Sacred Valley stopping twice, once at Ollantaytambo to take on some more passengers and in a small place in the mountains close to the path that makes up the Inca Way. The journey covers just a hundred and ten kilometres, but takes three hours and forty-five minutes. We stayed overnight in Aguas Calientes at the Machu Picchu Inn, which was the reason for us choosing this particular tour as we had two days to view this wonderful site. Many of the tours to Machu Picchu return to Cusco on the same day, which does not give you a lot of time, and if the weather is bad, it could be really disappointing.

After checking in, we took the bus that climbs the winding road to Machu Picchu. Until then, we had not been able to see anything of this city that was lost in the Andean mountains for many years before being discovered by Hiram Bingham III, who made public his discovery of the Quechua citadel at Machu Picchu in 1911.[2]

As we entered the site, Enrike, our guide, advised us to take the path immediately to our left and to climb the hill close to the entrance. This leads to the Watchman's Tower. We could not understand his reasoning for this, as the main path leading to the village lay before us, but we did as we were told. Now the altitude here is not as bad as in Cusco, which is a lot higher than this region of the Andes. We were given Coca leaves to chew in Cusco if we felt ill with altitude sickness and the coach had an oxygen tank in case of emergencies. It was still pretty exhausting climbing to the top, but oh boy, was it worth it! It offered us one of those memorable sights that we will never forget!

Laid out before us were the ruins of Machu Picchu and towering above was the pyramid shaped peak of Waynu. Surrounding this ancient town were other similar Andean peaks which were all considered to be sacred to the Inca's. The view was breath-taking and, believe me, photographs do not do it justice; you have to see it with your own eyes!

The Watchman's Tower is the entrance to the town if you walk the Inca Way. If you are fit, this would probably be the best way to approach Machu Picchu, but we took the easy option and

enjoyed every minute of our journey to get to this point. Enrike took us around the ruins and told us all about the individual temples and theories of the mystery behind Machu Picchu, as to why it was built in this high place and also why it was abandoned.

One of the benefits of staying over in the local town is that while we were visiting the site, there were hardly any people there, as most of them had already left to return to Cusco on the three p.m. train. We spent hours walking through the ruined buildings and temples that had been rescued from the overgrown vegetation that kept it hidden from modern man for hundreds of years. The views were amazing and to this day, whenever we are asked which our most favourite sight has been from all the places we have travelled to, we still say that that first sight we had of Machu Picchu was the best. Just to add, we also say that Sydney is our favourite city and the Iguazu Falls the best natural sight.

We returned to the site on our own the following day, and took time to take photographs and to enjoy the complex on our own. It started off very misty and you could not see the main peak, Waynu, as it was lost in the Andean clouds. But this made for fascinating viewing as we watched the mist twist and swirl around the buildings and the peaks. Eventually it did clear and it got very hot. A word of warning, at this altitude you can burn very quickly and you don't need much sun to get badly burnt – take it from someone who suffered for several days afterwards!

There is a fabulous market in Aguas Calientes with lots of souvenirs for tourists. I am a big collector of items to commemorate our holidays and, of course, I needed to buy the plaque for Mum as none of the family had been to Machu Picchu before. It was here that I started my collection of Christmas ornaments, as I was able to get a Peruvian nativity scene with a lama instead of a cow, and all the figurines have Peruvian features.

We returned to our hotel in Cusco on the three p.m. train and we enjoyed those fabulous views of the Andes and the Sacred Valley once more. As we approached the station, night had fallen and we were treated to a fabulous view of Cusco all lit up at night – it was like a fairy tale!

The next day we had to ourselves in Cusco, and we took the walk suggested in our guide book which took us from the Plaza des Armes by the side of the cathedral, past the Temple of the Sun and climbing the hill to San Blas. It was a pleasant walk, taking us past a convent, through the Artisan section of town with art galleries and shops, to another city square which offered us great views of the mountains that encircle Cusco. It was a little overcast but still very warm and a nice way to spend our last day in this city of the Incas.

We returned to Lima by plane the following day for our last night in Peru. In the afternoon we took a walk from the hotel to see the Pacific Ocean which laps the shores of Lima. We enjoyed a drink and a bite to eat at Café Café located close to the ocean, and we returned to our hotel by taxi after walking for a long time. This was an end to a perfect holiday with awe-inspiring sights, wonderful people and memories to last a lifetime.

I would love to return to Peru and have a chance to see Machu Picchu again and take a trip to Lake Titicaca, and fly over the Nazca lines. But, as time passes, it is less likely that we would be able to return to any of our more exotic holiday destinations due to time and money. There are still many other places that we want to see and experiences that we want to discover which take precedence over return visits, but wherever we can include a side trip, we will always do our best to add them on to our current holidays. If you have paid all that money to fly to the other side of the world, you need to make the most of it. One of those places which has been on my personal bucket list for a long time is to see the giant heads on Easter Island. These islands are part of Chile and you get there from Santiago de Chile. I have found a cruise which travels from Chile, along the West coast of South America and you can visit Easter Island as a pre-cruise vacation. The cruise stops in Peru which allows you to do an excursion, flying out to Cusco, taking the train to Aguas Calientes and having time to visit Machu Picchu for a few hours. It will be an expensive excursion with flights, train and hotel accommodation, but it will mean we can revisit this remarkable Inca site.

CHAPTER 8

San Francisco (36) and Hawaii (24), USA – September 2003

This was a four-centre holiday that included either transfers or a car at each location. We started with three nights in San Francisco before flying to Hawaii for five nights. This was followed with three nights in Las Vegas for our second visit and three nights in Los Angeles. We flew directly into San Francisco from Heathrow but we had a bit of a scare on the flight. Richard had got up to stretch his legs as he didn't feel too good – suddenly he leaned forward over the seat towards me and even though I called his name, he did not respond. He had blacked out – only for a moment, but it really panicked me. As he came round, he had no idea what had happened, all he knew was that I was yelling at him! The crew rallied round and gave him some oxygen, a drink of water and an ice-pack for the back of his neck. He felt fine, but it was such a shock for me – talk about panic!

As we flew into San Francisco the visibility was perfect and we flew straight over the Golden Gate Bridge. It was a fabulous sight with the buildings of the city rising in front of us – our pilot told us we had a eighty mile visibility and I would not doubt that! We were collected from the airport and transferred to the Hotel Cosmo for our three nights. The location was okay, but we had lots of walking to do to get around the city to see the sights. On our first night, as we were tired from the long flight from the UK and the eight-hour time difference, we just strolled to Union Square where we saw our first cable car.

The next day we picked up a car from the rental offices, which were located close to our hotel. We had the use of a car for twenty-four hours, which, as I said earlier, was part of our holiday package. We upgraded to a cabriolet as the weather was perfect for us to have the hood down, sunglasses on and enjoy the West Coast air. Being from Britain, it does take a little getting used to – driving on the right (we drive on the correct side of the road in the UK, not the right side!) and, as with all American cities, you need to know which roads you can turn down, as they use a grid system where there are lots of one-way streets and avenues – San Francisco is no exception. As soon as we left the rental offices, we had to turn left and ended up in Union Square, following a cable car up a very steep hill. I was glad it was Richard driving and not me!

We drove over the Golden Gate Bridge, well you have to do that, don't you? On the opposite side, we stopped at a viewing point where we were able to get some great photos of the bridge and the skyline of San Francisco. We returned and took the coast road, stopping at several spots for more photos.

We went to Seal Rock and we could hear the seals but we couldn't see them, they were too far away. We drove to Lombard Street, the most crooked road in the world – it took us a long time to find it, but it just seemed to appear in front of us as we were following a main road up a hill! We drove down it, very slowly, and then headed for Fisherman's Wharf. Parking was not difficult and we found a spot to leave the car while we had a wonderful fish lunch. This area is great for restaurants and shops and is a real tourist hot spot. We spent some time wandering around and went on a submarine before returning for the car and driving back to our hotel.

On our third day in San Francisco we had an included tour which would take us all around the city. We were picked up from our hotel and taken to see all the districts of the city – Chinatown, Little Italy, the Castro, the Mission and Pacific Heights. We stopped at Twin Peaks for a photo shot of the city and also at Golden Gate Park. We crossed the bridge again, but this time Richard could enjoy the view instead of concentrating on the road.

We then took the ferry across to Alcatraz. We made a mistake here of not opting for a guide or using the head phones to inform us of the route to take and details of what we should be looking at. We did see the cell of Al Capone and the Bird Man of Alcatraz, but other than that, we didn't do much else. Our tour returned us to Fisherman's Wharf where it ended. We walked to the cable car terminus where we boarded a car and took the line to Chinatown – this was great fun! We wandered around the shops in the area, which offer some great souvenirs and gifts and then had a meal in a Chinese restaurant to finish off our exhausting day.

The next day we were picked up early at eight thirty a.m. for our transfer back to the airport and our flight to Hawaii. It took us four hours and forty-five minutes to fly to the fiftieth American state, as it is that far away from the mainland. Our watches went back another three hours, so we were now eleven hours behind UK time. Our friend, Sue Stringer, was in Nepal while we were in Hawaii and she was six hours ahead of UK time – it took some getting used to, realising that there was a seventeen-hour time difference between us!

As we came out of the airport at Honolulu, we were greeted by our guide, who handed us garlands of fresh flowers, kissed us on each cheek and greeted us with a loud "Aloha"!

We were staying at a hotel at Waikiki Beach. Unfortunately, we were not in one of the big hotels that are located right on the beachfront; we were set back one street. But we did have a small balcony from where we could sit and enjoy our Cuba Libra's while we watched the sun set over Waikiki Beach.

We had expected Waikiki to be like Copacabana in Rio de Janeiro, but we were disappointed as it is very commercial – that's the beach as well as the town! The hotels go straight up to the beach with no walkway between them – this was so as they could take "ownership" of a certain area on the beach, to be able to service the people staying with them, whilst they lounged on the sand.

The city of Honolulu was like any other city in America – busy, noisy, lots of Seven Eleven shops which sell everything and seem to be open for very long hours, designer shops and American style diners/bars. There is a small area of the beach that lies in front of some of the shops and the main coastal road, but this gets very busy and is not really a pleasant place to walk, as the road is quite narrow and always full of traffic. Further along the road, past this open beach area, are more hotels, bars, shops and restaurants.

As we said, our hotel was quite central and close to Waikiki Beach, and our first impression was not a good one. However, we discovered that by walking the other way, basically to the right along the beach, it was much quieter and there was a lovely park edging the footpath and sands. Here, there was a public area of the beach where you were able to hire an umbrella and chairs.

We took the trolley bus to the Ala Moana shopping centre. This is a typical American Mall with shops selling clothes, shoes, jewellery etcetera. There was one floor at the top where there were several restaurants, but they were mainly fast food, nothing really special.

In the evening we went to a place called Shorebird that was to the right of our hotel and located on the beach. Here they offered steaks which you cook yourself on large hot grills, enabling you to add your own seasoning and sauce, and to cook them exactly how you like them. This was new to us and we thought that it was great, having a fabulous meal for fifty-eight dollars, including wine. We were so impressed that we went again – twice!

There are a lot of excursions you can take on Oahu Island and we opted for two of them. The first was an escorted visit to Pearl Harbour and the Arizona Memorial. First, we walked around the museum before we went to the theatre to watch a documentary about the attack by the Japanese air force on Pearl Harbour, the US Naval base in Hawaii, on the 7th of December 1941. The film explained the build up to the attack, from both the Japanese and the American sides, and also included many clips of the actual attack. In 1941, Britain and her allies were at war in Europe, Africa and Asia, but at that time the USA were not part of the Allied forces. With this unprovoked attack on Pearl Harbour, America entered the war.

Because America was at peace, the armed forces were not expecting any attack and were not ready for the Japanese bombardment that took place that morning. Many of the sailors and marines were on board the ships that made up the American fleet, resting in the calm harbour on this beautiful island. In the film, we witnessed the actual explosion on the USS Arizona battleship, when a bomb hit the forward magazine, which destroyed the ship, causing it to sink and killing one thousand one hundred and seventy-four of the crew. Many other ships were hit – all eight of the battleships were damaged, as well as three cruisers; three destroyers; an anti-aircraft training ship and one minelayer. Four of the battleships were sunk, including the USS Arizona.

The attack was done by three hundred and fifty-three Japanese fighters, bombers and torpedo planes launched from six aircraft carriers in the Pacific. In addition to the naval fleet that was practically destroyed, the Americans also lost one hundred and eighty-eight aircraft; two thousand four hundred and three people were killed and one thousand one hundred and seventy-eight were wounded.[3]

After the film, which had left us all in a very sombre and reflective mood, we went on a launch to the memorial. This is a floating bridge that can only be reached by sea on a launch, and was built in 1962 as a memorial to the one thousand one hundred and two who lie at rest on the sunken ship below the platform. The bridge straddles the sunken hull of the USS Arizona, without touching it. They have never attempted to raise the ship as it now lies as an eternal epitaph to those who died on board, as well as the others who perished in this attack. The memorial is manned by Naval personnel who watch over the memorial, the ship and their fallen colleagues – this made it all the more moving for the visitors that day.

Everyone was silent, as we walked over the bridge, showing our respect for this haunting memorial. As we walked slowly across the bridge, we looked down into the depths at the wrecked ship which is clearly visible in the clear waters below. One area of the bridge is open so that family, mourners or visitors can throw flowers into the water, as a tribute to those who met their end when the ship was destroyed. There is a marble wall at the end of the bridge, which is engraved with all the names of those who died on the USS Arizona on that infamous day. There is a smaller plaque that is engraved with the names of the people who survived the attack but, when they pass away, they have requested that their ashes be entombed with their comrades on board the ship. The ashes are placed in a canister that is then interred within the wreck by US Navy divers.

From the memorial, we continued our tour and boarded the battleship USS Missouri which now resides at Pearl Harbour as a permanent structure. It is located in such a way that it appears as though the ship is standing guard over the Arizona Memorial, but, if any commemorative event is taking place there, the USS Missouri is not visible from the memorial.

It was on this ship that the Japanese surrendered to US General Douglas Macarthur, the Supreme Commander of the Allied

Forces, on 2nd of September 1945. There were many dignitaries on board to witness the signing of the surrender document on that day and, today, there is a plaque on the ship's deck showing the exact spot where this took place. We were able to walk around the ship to see the guns, the technical equipment, cabins and the bridge. The whole visit was a very humbling and moving experience but it was handled very well and was both interesting and informative.

As part of our holiday package, we were able to have a car for a day in Hawaii and we took this offer up on our fourth day on Oahu. Once again, we upgraded to a cabriolet, so as we could put the hood down and enjoy the scenery around us while we drove along the coastal road.

We went around Diamond Head, stopping at various points to take photographs of the stunning rugged coast being lashed by the relentless waves of the Pacific Ocean crashing against the rocks. We stood at the Blow Hole for several minutes watching this natural phenomenon as the sea rises into the sky as a result of the force of the water being pushed through the hole in the rocks. We saw a turtle swimming in the waters below us, which was so clear and blue, that we could see the turtle's movements very clearly.

We followed the road along the East Coast of the island, which was lovely. It was a lot more mountainous than the West and very green – this was what I expected Hawaii to be like!

We climbed into the mountains and went to see a Buddhist Temple in the Valley of the Temples. It was beautiful and set in a stunning location with amazing views over the rippling peaks and towards the ocean below.

Our journey continued to the North coast which is where the big surf hits the beach and we were not disappointed as there were many surfers riding the waves with such agility and expertise it was a great spectacle to watch. We then continued around the road to return to Honolulu for the evening.

We spent the last day on the beach at Waikiki, relaxing, before our long flight the next day back to the US mainland. In the evening we went to a luau at Paradise Cove where we were shown how they make lei, the flower garlands that are synonymous with Hawaii. We also learnt how to hula well I did, Richard did not join in with this demonstration and we learnt how to throw spears. The location was at the coast and, as the sun started to set, casting pink and gold shadows across the sky, we witnessed a group of Indians launch their big canoe into the forceful waves, where they proceeded to jump in and sail out into the ocean.

We enjoyed a barbecue served with local salads and fruits and then took our seats to watch the show. This was a demonstration of how the Indians first came to the islands and there was a parade led by the chief, his wife and other members of the "tribe". There was lots of music and dancing and the climax was the fire sword dance. We had Mai Tai's while we watched, and we both enjoyed the whole evening, leaving us with lasting memories of our short stay here.

The next day we flew to Los Angeles and then took a plane to Las Vegas where we stayed at the Stratosphere Hotel and we had a car for all the three days. Our holiday ended with a flight back to Los Angeles where we stayed at the Radisson Wiltshire for three nights. We had a car for our whole time in LA and drove around Beverley Hills, Venice Beach, Hollywood and Malibu. The freeways in LA are HUGE – some of them seven lanes each way! It was very confusing, as drivers are allowed to overtake on either side and you have to look all ways before you turn off at an exit – a bit frightening, but very thrilling at the same time. We also drove to San Diego, which is not too far from LA, driving along the Pacific Coast Highway. It was a pleasant drive and, in San Diego, we visited Sea World. This was the highlight of our visit to Los Angeles – I know it is not in LA, but I was not too impressed with the City of Angels; especially in comparison to Las Vegas, San Francisco and San Diego.

We did return to the Hawaiian Islands in February 2012 when we did a cruise of French Polynesia and Hawaii and on that occasion, we went to three other islands as well as returning to Oahu. But I am going to cover that cruise in another chapter, so I will return to this twenty fourth rated place later in the book!

We returned to San Francisco in 2011 after a cruise through the Panama Canal. This was our disembarkation port. We stayed for two nights before flying to Las Vegas where we stayed at the Bellagio Hotel. In San Francisco, we did an evening cruise around the harbour on a catamaran, which offered us lovely views of the Golden Gate Bridge from sea level, and the skyline of San Francisco. On our free day, we took an excursion, booked through Viator.com, to the Californian vineyards where we went to a number of different winemakers and tried many of the superb wines that they had to offer – red, white, rose and sparkling! The prices were very reasonable and many of our fellow travellers bought cases, as they were not flying but would be able to transport their purchase back home by road. We stopped for lunch in a small town where we had a number of options of where to eat, from small café's, buying your own picnic items from a supermarket or full-service restaurants. We opted for the last one, which had been recommended by our guide. I had quiche and salad and it has to be the best quiche I have ever eaten!

On this second visit, we spent a lot of time at Fisherman's Wharf as it was within walking distance of our hotel, and has loads of choice for eating, drinking and shopping. It's a busy place as it is very popular as a destination in San Francisco and, being on the sea front, can offer a cool respite from the heat of summer in the city.

CHAPTER 9

Taj Mahal, India (10) and Mount Everest, Nepal/Tibet (30) – October 2003

I had been to India before I had met Richard, travelling on a Kuoni tour that included Nepal. Coincidentally, one of Richard's friends had done exactly the same tour of the Golden Triangle and we often talked about the trip when we met up in our local. As the Taj Mahal was one of the fifty, and Richard needed to see this major landmark to cross it off his list, we made the decision to do a very similar holiday as I had enjoyed it so much five years earlier.

We booked through Voyages Jules Verne, as it was a cheaper trip than the one offered by Kuoni and it did offer a slightly different route, so there would be something new for me to see rather than just doing exactly the same holiday. This was a BIG mistake! Kuoni are very much a five-star company and, although VJV offer great value and a wide choice of destinations, they use lower grade hotels and my advice would be, with India, do NOT go for a lower grade hotel (three-star). We learnt this the hard way!

We were due to fly to Delhi on Austrian Airlines via Vienna, but with just five days to go, VJV notified us of a change, and told us we would be flying with Gulf Air via Abu Dhabi and would be arriving in Delhi at six a.m. instead of twelve at p.m. Six hours later than we originally planned. We were given the option of cancelling our holiday with a full refund and no compensation, but it was a bit late to try and organise something else with so little notice, so we decided to accept the change in flight.

The flight was not good as not only did we stop in Abu Dhabi for a few hours, but we also touched down in Muscat for thirty minutes. It seemed totally out of the way for a flight from

Heathrow to Delhi. But, when we arrived in Delhi and had gone through passport control and collected our luggage, our small tour group, there were four other couples making ten of us in total found ourselves alone in the arrivals hall – there was no-one from the tour company there to meet us! It was difficult to keep everyone together, as some went to look for the hotel bus. I should add that there is no such thing as hotel buses in Asia – as far as I am aware, only London airports offer this facility. Others wanted to get a taxi. We used a mobile phone to contact the hotel where we were due to stay in Delhi, The Park, but we were told that they had no record of a reservation for our party. At this point, we all started to get a little worried.

We approached the tourist police who were based at the airport and they called the agency, but there was no reply. As time ticked away, we started to get a bit desperate and Richard was all for just going back home then and there!

At nine a.m. a representative from Sita, the local agents, appeared. He was actually there for another tour group and was very surprised to see us. It transpired that Sita had not been informed of our change in flight and had come to the airport the night before, and were very concerned that we had not arrived on the Austrian Airline flight. They were waiting for the VJV office to open in the UK to find out what had happened, and, although they had left someone in the office to man the phones in case we called, they had fallen asleep and missed our earlier call! With regard to the hotel not having a booking, this had been changed without notification as The Park was undergoing renovations and would not provide a comfortable place to stay.

With all the problems sorted, we finally entered India and made our way to our new hotel, The Maidens, which was a beautiful, colonial style hotel located outside of the city centre. I had been worried that with us arriving so late, that our itinerary in Delhi would be affected, but this was not the case. We still visited everything we were due to see, but without any sleep. We just had time to freshen up and unpack before we were out on the busy streets of the capital of India.

On this first day we went to see the government buildings and the wide avenues of New Delhi; designed by Lutyens before going to Delhi's oldest monument, the Minar Qutb. In 1911, George V decided to move the capital of the British Raj from Calcutta to Delhi and ordered that a new city be built. This included leafy imperial avenues and whitewashed residences. It was originally built for just seventy thousand inhabitants – it is now home to over one hundred and seventy times that figure! The Qutb Minar is an Islamic complex dating from 1190 and is dominated by a seventy-three metre high tapered tower and a small iron pillar that dates back to the fourth century, and was taken from a Hindu temple dedicated to Vishnu.[4]

The following morning we toured around Old Delhi visiting Jama Masjid, known as the Friday Mosque, and the Red Fort. The Fort is no longer the lavish set of buildings that adorned the complex in the past, as the marble halls and mosques used to be inlaid with gold, silver and precious stones. These have all gone, pillaged and removed many years earlier, leaving plain structures that can only whisper of the grandeur of the past. We also went to the place where Mahatma Gandhi was cremated, which is now a shrine, located in a beautiful green park in the centre of Delhi, on the banks of the River Ganges.

We left Delhi behind us as we drove to Jaipur to stay at the Clarks Shiraz Hotel. We stopped in a small village on the way, to allow us to stretch our legs and also to witness rural life in India. Our guide led us along the busy street, dodging through the stalls and vendors of this small town. We were fascinated by the locals selling their wares; or cooking food, either in hot oil or over glowing coals, but they were even more bemused as they stopped and stared at our group of ten white tourists. We got lots of hoots from car horns and vans as we wandered amongst the town folk. Indian streets are so different from anything in the west and you need to be prepared for the sights, sounds and smells that you will experience when you climb down from the protection of your vehicle. Cows wander freely amongst the bikes, rickshaws, lorries and crumbling cars, and there is a possibility of seeing camels, donkeys and even the odd elephant strolling along the footpath! As we walked, a man came up to me with a closed box and as I looked at him, he lifted the lid to reveal a black cobra curled up inside. I was so surprised and shocked and I made a dash for the coach with him in hot pursuit, box open in his hand and his cobra just inches from my shoulder! I'm sure that he was very amused by this frightened blonde running away, trying to escape from him!

We arrived at the hotel at around seven p.m. and, after having a drink and something to eat, we were told that there was a wedding taking place at the hotel that evening and that we were welcome to watch the groom's procession as it arrived at the hotel. As we went outside, there was a big crowd in the hotel grounds comprising the bride's family, watching the groom arrive. He was being carried towards the hotel by all his family and his friends, accompanied by lots of music, noise and commotion. All his guests were dancing, clapping and cheering as he slowly made his way up the drive to join his bride. We were invited to join in, and all ten of us became part of the procession, jumping, clapping and enjoying this wonderful experience. The outfits were so colourful and extravagant, especially the bride who had a gold lacy sari with a red silk base that shone through behind the golden material. The hotel was laid out for the wedding and there must have been seats for three hundred guests. We were told that the actual ceremony would take place later and only the immediate family would attend, but the party would go on until five a.m.

The next day we went to the Amber Fort, a huge palace built on the top of a hill overlooking a lake with Jaipur in the distance. The climb up the hill would be exhausting in the heat, but you can take the climb in comfort seated on the back of an elephant. There is a continual procession of these majestic beasts making the trek between the road and the entrance hall. The palace complex is well preserved and offers fabulous views through latticed windows where the Maharajah and his harem once resided. The marble gateway to the palace is beautifully decorated with paintings of the Hindu gods, especially Ganesh, the elephant-headed idol. Back in Jaipur we went to the Royal Observatory, the City Palace and to see the Palace of Winds.

We left Jaipur the next day and headed for Agra, stopping at Fatehpur Sikri along the way. This city was built by Akbar in 1570, but was abandoned within twenty years of it being completed. It has now been restored and this lost city offers an atmospheric, mystical stopover on the long journey between Jaipur and Agra. The highlight is the tomb of the Sufi saint, Salim Chishti, that lies within the Jami Masjid mosque. This gleaming white marble dargah is carved so delicately and has a canopy inlaid with mother-of-pearl; it is quite beautiful.

Our hotel, Clarks Amer, was supposed to have views of the Taj Mahal from the rooftop bar, but unfortunately, the whole time when we were in India the weather was muggy and overcast. It was still very hot, but it seemed like the air was full of smog and visibility was very poor. The following morning we set off to see the most famous building in India at sunrise – a very early start, but we were hoping to arrive before the crowds and also to witness the beauty of this structure in the pale light of dawn. But our plans were squashed as many others had the same idea and, yet again, the light was poor and it was quite misty, giving us a grey background rather than a clear blue sky that would have provided us with that perfect photo.

The Taj Mahal is a magnificent building and gives you pleasure viewing it from a distance as well as close up. It is in perfect symmetry, whatever you see on one side, is mirrored on the other. The red brick building to the right of the shrine had a purpose, but they had to build another on the left and that was never used. It is there just to provide balance. The towers that surround the main building lean out slightly so as if one should collapse, it would fall outwards, away from the delicate marble creation that holds the tombs of Shah Jahan and his beloved wife, Mahal Mumtaz, for whom he built this wonderful edifice as she had died giving birth to his fourteenth child.

The temple complex is surrounded by a wall with an impressive entrance gate that hides the building from view. As you enter, the sight is breath-taking and photos cannot do it justice. It is as though the Taj Mahal has been painted on a blue canvas as it lies on the banks of the river, with nothing behind it to spoil that perfect view. Supposedly, Shah Jahan intended to build a replica Taj in black marble on the opposite bank where he would be buried, but his sons usurped him and had him imprisoned in the Agra Fort where he stayed until his death in 1666, so these plans were never fulfilled.

As you approach the shrine, you begin to see the decoration that adorns the white marble and the closer you get, the more impressive it becomes. The marble is inlaid with semi-precious stones, creating intricate patterns of flowers, birds and calligraphy. In Agra many of the workshops still offer souvenirs where they use the same method and you can witness the artisans creating tables, trays and vases for the tourists. The intricate and time-consuming art is fabulous and is still as colourful and desirable today as it was three hundred and fifty years ago.

The tomb of Mumtaz lies in the centre under the great dome, perfectly aligned with the entrance, while Shah Jahan's tomb, which is slightly larger, is joined to one side. These are the public tombs, their actual bodies lie below in the crypt. Surrounding them is a magnificent lace-like marble screen studded with precious stones.

There is a canal leading from the patio that lies in front of the entrance gate to the shrine, which creates a mirror to reflect the beauty of the Taj Mahal. The canal is bordered by a grass verge, flowers and short trees that help to draw the eye to the building set in the centre. The colours are all very striking and simple, which makes the whole site even more striking.

I remember the photograph of Princess Diana seated on the bench that lies on a bridge over the canal. She was on her own and she looked very sad, even at that early stage of her marriage. Today, local photographers seem to monopolise this spot and it is very difficult to try and recreate this memorable shot, but there are plenty of other places where you can still get your own souvenir photo.

We spent a lot of time at the Taj Mahal, allowing us to have an escorted tour but also free time to be able to wander on our own and take photos. In the afternoon we went to Agra Fort, which is very similar to the fort in Delhi except that from one of the towers, which is where Shah Jahan was imprisoned by his sons, you have a view of the Taj Mahal, through a window. This view is very different from actually being at the site of the mausoleum, as you view it with the river in the foreground and, because of the distance and the poor air quality, the building looks ghostly as it shimmers on the river's bank.

From Agra we took the train to Jhansi where we boarded a bus and headed for the palaces of Orchha. This site is not on the main tourist route and was very quiet in comparison to all the places we had visited so far. Although the buildings here have not had the money spent on them and are not as well restored as many of the forts and palaces in Delhi, Jaipur and Agra, they offered a different insight into the history of India. The murals on the walls represented stories of the Hindu gods and we learnt a lot about the Indian deities and their adventures, that are retold in poems and literature. This was just a short stop as we headed for our next overnight stay at Khajuraho where we stayed at the Holiday Inn, a very pleasant, modern hotel with large rooms and a great restaurant, offering more than curries and an Indian buffet.

We had a full day exploring the temples that are the main reason for any visit to this town. There are lots of them scattered over a tranquil rural landscape, built by the Chandelas around the ninth century. They rise to the skies like mountains and are very lavishly decorated with intricate carvings, many of them offering erotic images of the Hindu gods, princes and their concubines. But even though some of these statues could have been taken straight from the pages of the Kama Sutra, you cannot help but admire the exquisite carvings and delicacy of the garments, the jewellery and the posture of the figures. In some instances, the carvings depict dancing girls dressed in sheer, see-through costumes that are so elusive that they offer just a hint of decency. Youngsters are likely to giggle and blush at some of the sexual positions that are depicted in full glory over all the walls, but the total scene is one to absolutely marvel over, when you consider how long ago they were carved.

The temples were forgotten for centuries and engulfed by vegetation until they were rediscovered by a British engineer in 1835. Originally, there were eighty temples, which adorned these fields but now only twenty-two remain. They are mainly dedicated to Siva and Vishnu, but others are offered to Buddhism, Jainism, sun-worship and animal cults.[4]

Our final stop in India was in the holiest of holy places, Varanasi, located on the banks of the Ganges. The mighty Ganga is India's most revered river. It flows two thousand five hundred kilometres from the Himalayas to the Bay of Bengal. All along its winding course lies India's most sacred pilgrimage spots where worshippers pray to the rising sun and meditate under the last rays of the day. Varanasi is the main place for cremations where Ghats line the waterfront. This city is very old, with many shrines, temples and mosques scattered throughout the tiny, narrow streets that make up the old town. As you walk along the paths visiting the different holy sites you have to dodge the mud, cow pats, beggars and rubbish that is left behind by the thousands of visitors and pilgrims who come every day to witness the religious ceremonies, funerals and the chanting's of the *sadhus* and *yogis*. To me, Varanasi depicts *real* India – everything you have ever imagined of the mysticism of this huge country lies within the small area of the town centre and the banks of the Ganges. The other cities we had visited were modern, with historic areas offering wonderful architecture and culture, but Varanasi is the heart of the country and it beats with vibrancy, spirituality and devotion.

In the morning we rose at five-thirty a.m. to make our way down to the banks of the river where we all boarded a boat and drifted out into the centre of the Ganges just as the first light of dawn was starting to colour the sky, with pale shades of pink and gold. Before us, the banks were already full of worshippers who were submerged in the waters; bathing, drinking and raising their prayers to the new day and Mother Ganga. Smoke was already rising from some of the funeral ghats and we could see the holy men seated cross legged where they meditated underneath umbrellas, accepting offerings from worshippers in exchange for their blessings. We were all given a lighted candle held in a little basket that we placed gently on the river and, as the sun climbed higher into the sky, we watched them float away to meet all the hundreds of others being offered by the multitude of visitors.

I know that this sounds very romantic and as I have said, this was a little bit of the real India, but don't be misled. The Ganges is so polluted and the holy waters are filthy! Not only are the ashes of the newly cremated scattered into the river, but for families who cannot afford to pay for a cremation, the alternative is to wrap the body in linen and just place it further upstream allowing it to float away in the flow of the river. There are dead animals too, bloated and stinking and bobbing along with the boats and pilgrims, all vying for a little bit of the river. Watching the Indians drinking the waters as they carry out their ablutions is gut wrenching, but they are obviously used to it and they are not harmed by the pollution.

When we returned to the banks, we walked through the cramped holy city, visiting a number of temples and shrines, including the Monkey Temple and the Mother India Temple where there is a huge map of India, in relief, on the floor of the temple.

That night we returned to the river to witness the evening rituals. This time, instead of being driven there, we went by rickshaw, which was a real thrill! It was all very different at night, offering more of a party atmosphere than a religious ceremony. All the shops and bazaars were well lit and full of people; a hive of activity. As our little convoy whizzed past them, we were ignored and not treated as tourists, but just as part of the night scene. At the river, we were invited into a house where they had a large balcony offering us great views of all the evening events.

There were five priests addressing the crowds that had gathered and they performed blessings using a bell, spices and fire, turning four times to bless each side. Behind them, hundreds of candles floated past on the river offering an ethereal light and looking like a huge ghostly chandelier. All around us, chants boomed out from loud speakers and the throngs of people joined in. It was an amazing sight and we all felt very privileged to be witnessing it.

Overall, the tour of India offered us so much and we experienced so many wonderful sights and events. But our hotels let us down as they were not as good as my previous stay. We did not have a mattress at the hotel in Varanasi – very uncomfortable, but we were moved for the second night to a better room and a comfier bed. If you visit India, and you enjoy a bit of luxury when you travel, my recommendation would be to stay in five-star hotels and don't even try to do this holiday on a tight budget; you are likely to regret it.

From Varanasi we flew to Kathmandu, Nepal. We stayed at The Grand which was okay but it was quite a long walk to get to Durbar Square, the main focus point of Kathmandu. We stayed here for four nights and during our stay we visited many wonderful temples, monuments and squares. One temple in Durbar Square, the Kumari Ghar, is home to the Living Goddess, and if you are lucky or your guide offers a donation to the temple guards, she will appear at a window, in order for visitors to try and catch her in a photo.

She is chosen from girls aged three to five in the Buddhist Shakya clan. Elders meet with hundreds of girls, approving only those with thirty-two auspicious signs of divinity. The small group of would-be goddesses are then placed in a darkened room with freshly severed buffalo heads and dancing men wearing demon masks. This is certainly frightening for ordinary girls under five years old, but the goddess would not be frightened. Therefore, the girl who shows no fear is likely to be the incarnation of Durga. In one final test, the girl must be able to pick out the clothing of her predecessor. Thus identified, the Kumari moves into the Kumari Ghar and is worshipped as a living goddess. Her needs and those of her caretakers are paid in full by the Nepalese government and she spends most of her time studying and performing religious rituals.[5]

She only leaves the temple a few times a year, during festivals and her feet must never touch the ground. The Kumari's reign comes to an end when she menstruates or bleeds for any other reason, including just a minor scratch. The girl then reverts to mortal status and the search starts again to find her replacement. The retiring goddess is given a modest state pension, but may find it difficult to marry – tradition has it that a man who marries an ex-Kumari will die young.

Besides the ancient capital of Patan which lies in the heart of Kathmandu, we also went to Bhaktapur and Pashupati, and we had a wonderful drive through the stunning Nepalese countryside where we stopped for lunch at a scenic spot, where we had views of the Annapurna range of the Himalayas. We were also very lucky with our morning flight to see Mount Everest, number thirty on the list. Initially, the day was very foggy but as we only had the opportunity to do this flight on this one morning, we were quite prepared to sit around at the airport in the hope that the fog would lift as it started to get warmer. Our patience was rewarded and at eight a.m. we took off on our flight towards the Himalayas and the world's highest mountain.

The plane was small and everyone had a window seat. The flight has to remain on the Nepalese side as the "other" side of the mountain is in China/Tibet airspace and a no-go area. The plane flies in front of Everest and then turns around to fly back, so as it does not matter which side you are sitting on, you will get a good view of the mountain.

I have a confession to make – this was the second time I had done the Everest flight, as I did this on my previous visit which was before 9/11. At that time we were able to go into the cockpit to get a better view from the pilot's larger window. Now, do you remember my blunder in Venezuela when I was looking the wrong way in the cockpit when we flew past Angel Falls? This time, I asked the pilot which one of the peaks I could see in front of me was Mount Everest, and he replied, "the highest!" – dumb question or what!

I was expecting Mount Everest to stand on its own like Mount Kilimanjaro or Mount Fuji, but it is a completely different type of mountain. The Himalayas are continually growing, being pushed up as India continues to "crash" into Asia. Created over millions of years, the huge mountain range, which has several of the highest peaks in the world amidst its ranks, is a majestic sight, even if you only see it from a small aeroplane window.

The photograph does not do number thirty justice as the enormity of the peaks cannot be properly portrayed in a snapshot. We are not climbers, hikers or even serious walkers, so this will be the only way that we will see Mount Everest. But the BBC's programme was "Fifty Places to SEE before You Die", and we have certainly seen this colossal mountain, our photo proves it!

By the way, in the photograph Everest is the one on the left – it's the highest!

CHAPTER 10

Petra, Jordan (16) – March 2005

We flew out on our third wedding anniversary and Richard had pre-ordered a bottle of champagne for us to enjoy on the flight. This holiday was booked through Voyages Jules Verne again and we were going to be in Jordan for a week, staying in Petra, Amman and Aqaba. The flight from Gatwick went into Aqaba and we had a two-and-a-half-hour coach transfer to Petra where we arrived at our hotel, the Petra Palace, late in the evening. This did not leave us with much time on our first day, and all we did was have something to eat and book our additional excursions before retiring for the night.

This hotel was not far from the entrance to Petra, but I had not realised how far we would have to walk. The only thing I really knew about Petra was that it was used as a film location in Indiana Jones and the Last Crusade. You will probably know it as the church where Jones found the Holy Grail, but this building is actually known as the Treasury. I was aware that there was more to see, but I had no idea as to how big the lost city of Petra actually is. The city was the capital of the Nabateans and reputedly dates back to around 327 AD. It was practically unknown to the western world until it was discovered in 1812 by a Swiss explorer and was described as a "rose red city".

As we leave modern Petra behind us and start our walk down the path towards the ancient city, we immediately come across some small carvings in the rock that are remnants of tombs and shrines of the Nabatean people. The path seems to drop down, as the rock walls begin to climb and we enter the sik, a narrow pathway with sheer cliffs on either side, that twists and turns, so you cannot see where it begins or where it ends. The light shines down from high above, but the floor is bathed in shadows and darkness. Our guide stops us at several places to point out reliefs of men and camels carved into the walls, and also the gulley that runs the full length of the sik where fresh water was collected and ran towards the old citadel. There is so much to see and learn that it actually takes us two hours to walk the length of the canyon before we finally come to the end, and we can see our goal in the crack that appears. It looks really narrow at first, as though we will have to slide through sideways, and we can glimpse the upper level of the Treasury through the gap. But as we get closer and the sik takes one last turn, we realise there are no issues with entering into the large open gorge that opens out in front of us and we catch our first sighting of the old city of Petra.

You cannot help but just stand and admire this huge edifice that is so beautifully carved into the rock face. It is actually just a façade; there are no rooms behind that dramatic entrance. It really is a shock to enter the door and see a tiny room with no decoration, just polished rock face. It is a bit disappointing as you expect to see the huge chamber of the church from the Indiana Jones film, but that was done just for Hollywood.

We continued along the path to the open valley, where there are a number of tombs, houses and storage rooms carved into the rock along the sides. There was even a large amphitheatre built in the open area. There are remains of column-lined avenues and various structures that remain from this ancient city. You have the option to climb into the hills to visit the Monastery; another huge façade that is carved into the rock face at the top of the mountain, but in the heat and, after doing so much standing and walking during the morning, I wasn't able to make it all the way. Richard struggled on and was rewarded with this fabulous sight.

If you visit Petra and you think that you may not make the climb, you have the option of ascending the steep climb on the back of a donkey, but you have to take this mode of transport from the bottom. There are no bus stops for you to catch one halfway up! I wish I had taken this option now as I missed out on this building and will probably never return. In 2018, this particular activity was in the news, as there was concern over the welfare of the donkeys, the horses and the camels used to explore Petra, claiming that they had to work all day in the heat of the sun without shade or water and that the animals were beaten to perform their tasks. We did not witness any beatings and the donkeys certainly seemed to be well-cared-for although, with hindsight, it was very hot work for them. But it is similar with all beasts of burden all around the world – donkeys, elephants or domesticated animals. If the local needs them to bring in income, they will be cared for better than an animal that cannot work or is purely raised for food.

We had the afternoon to ourselves and we were able to take our time on the walk back to the hotel, after most of the crowds and day visitors had left the site and it was so peaceful and mesmerising to have the place to ourselves.

Petra is huge and offered so much more than just the Treasury, which is the building synonymous with this archaeological site. The sik is narrow and confined but once you enter the city it is wide and open with all of the aforementioned houses, streets and temples scattered all around. Its age and enormity makes this place all the more astounding and worthier of its place in the fifty.

The following day we went to Beida or Little Petra, which offered us a Nubian settlement that is quite different from the huge open spaces of Petra. You enter through a short, narrow sik, but this time you can see homes, including a staircase and a restaurant/hostelry.

In the evening, we returned to Petra but this time we started our walk down the sik in twilight. All along the narrow path there were torches that lit the way and everyone was silent as we walked along, enjoying the atmosphere and creating a surreal silence. As we approached the end of the sik there was an eerie glow in front of the Treasury and, as we slipped through into the open ground, we saw thousands of tea-lights flickering in the dark. It was a fabulous sight as the whole of the area in front of the Treasury was laid out with these little earthly stars. We found a spot to sit on the floor and listen to a musician who sat amongst the candles in front of the Treasury.

People began to drift away, returning to the modern town of Petra and their respective hotels. When we left, there were very few remaining, and we had the luxury of strolling back along the sik in relative solitude, just enjoying the beauty of this incredible place and the mysticism of the Rose Red City.

The following day we left Petra to drive to the capital of Jordan, Amman. I was surprised that we would have another five days touring around Jordan, as I thought the only site worth seeing was Petra, but I was so wrong. Our first stop was Karak where there is a Crusader Castle, which is in excellent condition. It was once attacked by Saladin during the crusades. We listened to Sami, our guide, relaying the stories of the battles from the middle ages as though they took place just last year. We had a little time to wander around the building before we set off for Mount Nebo, which is where Moses saw the Promised Land over the River Jordan and is supposedly the place where Moses is buried. From this high spot we could see the Dead Sea, Bethany which is where John baptised Jesus, and Jericho and, in the mist, we could just make out Jerusalem. A monastery has been built on this holy site with some wonderful mosaics. Our final stop, before getting to Amman, was Madaba where there is a church with a huge mosaic that dates back to the sixth century, showing a map of the Holy Land. The walled city of Jerusalem, the River Jordan and many other famous sites are very clear to see on this ancient map.

After our first night in Amman we travelled to the East of Jordan into the desert, where we visited three sites. The first was a castle that was used by caravans passing during Islamic times. The second was a bath house, again built during Islamic times where there were some beautiful paintings preserved on the ceiling and the walls, and finally the ruins of the fort at Azrak where Lawrence of Arabia stayed. But it was the afternoon that gave us the highlight, and the surprise, of our stay in the capital.

We went to Jerash, a Greco-Roman town that is better preserved than the Forum in Rome. We had no idea that this place existed, and we were both absolutely awestruck when we saw the size of this place and the beauty of the structures that remain. There is so much to see; you cannot call these "ruins" as so many of the buildings are in almost perfect condition. There are fountains, pillars, arches, gardens, an amphitheatre and much, much more. As you walk up the main street you can see the ridges that have been worn into the stones by the wheels of carriages that ran along them hundreds of years ago. As you walk away from the main street there are the remains of shops and houses where it is so easy to envisage the townspeople living, working and relaxing. The place is just amazing and so large you just can't take it all in.

On our second day in Amman we went to the Great Mosque, which is dedicated to King Abdullah I who was assassinated in 1951. It is a modern mosque and, as the ladies on the tour were provided with hooded robes, we were all able to enter and see the mosaics, whilst learning about Islam. We then went to the remains of the Citadel, where there is a museum and, with it being located on a hill in the centre of the city, the location offers fabulous city views. As we stood admiring the view of modern Amman the call to prayers began to rise up from the mosque below us – it was an eerie sound, as we could not see where the sound was coming from, but the rise and fall of the voice of the Imam was so atmospheric.

We left Amman behind us and we headed back to Aqaba, which is where we started our journey, but stopped at the Dead Sea on the way. We had the opportunity to do a bit of shopping and to float in the waters that are at the lowest point below sea level. It is true that you are able to float and read a book with no effort but beware if you have any cuts or scratches as the water is so salty it will really sting!

Aqaba is located on the Red Sea and is Jordan's only access to the sea. It is here where you can see Eilat in Israel, which is the closest neighbour, but the Egyptian borders are also very close and you can see their resorts from Aqaba. We took an excursion to Wadi Rum where we were transferred from our coach onto the back of trucks for our journey into the desert. This barren area has a very atmospheric presence and, after seeing the wall paintings and a natural spring, we were able to witness the serenity and peacefulness of this place as we climbed onto the rocks to find our own personal spot to watch the sun set. Everyone was very quiet with no-one talking; not even a whisper, as we experienced this wonderful location in pure silence. It was an ideal opportunity to reflect on the amazing sites we had seen of Petra, Jerash and the whole country of Jordan.

CHAPTER *11*

Bangkok, Thailand (42), Sydney (8), Uluru (12), The Great Barrier Reef (2), Australia and Singapore (39) – November 2005

This is going to be a big chapter because, not only did we see five of the fifty in one holiday in 2005, but we have returned to Bangkok, Sydney and Singapore on several occasions and it seems only right that I include details of these other trips in this chapter. Richard had been to Bangkok and Singapore before we met, but he had never been to Australia. He really enjoyed Bangkok and I can understand why – I am sure that we will keep returning to this amazing city, as it is an ideal stopover on the way to holidays down under.

In 2005 we were not quite so adventurous with organising our own excursions and side-trips, so this package was booked through Tradewinds and all the flights, hotels, transfers and excursions were included in the price. Except for Cairns where we were in a four-star hotel, we stayed in 3-star hotels throughout. They were fine, but the locations were not very good, and all of them were a long way from the key tourist areas. Bangkok does not really have a centre to the city, and there are so many things to see that are spread all over the area, but our hotel, the Bangkok Palace, was well away from everything and not in a good location at all. But in Bangkok, taxis are cheap, and tuk-tuks are a great way to get around.

Bangkok: Our first day included a trip to the Grand Palace. This is by far the most visited site in Bangkok and it was packed on the day that we went. You just had to move with the crowd, but it was difficult to take photos and get close to any of the statues or landmarks. They're all very colourful with grotesque animals, gods and icons. We saw the Emerald Buddha, which is actually made of jade and is quite small, but it sits high on an altar made of gold with intricate carvings. The statue wears robes that are changed, depending on the season.

From the palace we visited a jewellery shop, probably the largest I have ever seen! It is not easy to browse as your own personal assistant accompanies you and they are very persuasive; prepared to show you anything that you may just look at for an instant. If you show any interest at all, well that's it. They know that you are hooked and then the hard sell starts! The pieces are beautiful and there is so much choice, but it is not my idea of a pleasant shopping experience.

In the evening we went to the Asia Hotel where we had a Brazilian barbecue and then went to the Calypso Cabaret. This show is infamous in Bangkok as it features the Ladyboys. It is a transvestite show but it is not raunchy or seedy and it is really suitable for young and old. Some of the "girls" are absolutely stunning with fabulous figures that made me quite jealous! They wear some pretty skimpy outfits and you can't help but wonder how they hide their bits! The show itself is a bit corny, with singing and dancing by straight artists as well as the Ladyboys. But it is a bit of fun and as long as you don't take it as a serious show, you will enjoy the evening. After the show, some of the artists will pose with you for photographs.

The next day we went to the floating markets at Damnoen. The day started with an hour's drive as we left the city behind us, and we then boarded dragon boats which are the very long, thin motor boats used throughout Bangkok for getting around on the rivers and the canals. The boat sped off along the waterway through little villages, under bridges and along lovely rural countryside. We eventually arrived at Damnoen where we had time to wander along the banks of the river, browsing the stalls in the normal market, and also watching the small rowing boats vying for space on the crowded river, with women selling their wares. We took one of the small paddle boats in order to be able to get in amongst the sellers. Most of them were selling souvenirs for the tourists but others had food on their boats: some had fresh fruit and vegetables and others offered steaming dishes of rice, soup and other concoctions. We returned to the hotel on the coach, which was a long journey and was broken up with a visit to a teak-carving factory. Some of the large pieces were very beautiful and we succumbed to temptation buying a small bar. It was small by their standards, but it would take two months to make and two months to ship before we would get it delivered to our home. It cost one thousand pounds but it still stands in our living room at home, and takes pride of place when we open it out for social occasions.

In the evening we went to the Banyan Tree Hotel, to their Vertigo Restaurant. We picked it from our guidebook and went by taxi. It was quite a distance from our hotel and we thought

that we were going to a Mediterranean restaurant that was classed as "reasonably" priced. When we took the lift to go to the sixty-first floor, we were stunned to find ourselves on the roof of this huge hotel. The food was international and wonderful; a lot more expensive than we expected, but the view was worth every penny. This used to be the helicopter pad, but had been converted into a five-star, open-air restaurant that totally exceeded our expectations. A perfect ending to our stay in Bangkok.

There is so much to see in Bangkok – temples, statues, sanctuaries, and markets, and there is an abundance of other sights to see on a day trip. This is an ideal city to stay in for a few days to break up the long journey, if you are going on to Australia and there is a lot more on offer than in Singapore. We have been lucky enough to visit it on several occasions and every time we have found something different, and I have detailed these excursions later in this chapter. Even if you just do a city tour from your cruise port, you get to see so many of the beautiful temples and the magnificent architecture of this very Asian city. I would definitely recommend a diversion, as Bangkok is so very vibrant. It is now very modern, but it still manages to maintain some mysticism and intrigue in its back streets and its night markets.

Sydney: We flew from Bangkok in the evening to land in Sydney at six-fifteen a.m. but it was only two-fifteen a.m. in Thailand, and as such, we had not got any sleep on the flight and, when we arrived, we were both tired and weary, but we thought, no worries, we'll get a nap during the day! How wrong we were! We had a transfer to our hotel, the Mercure, and we arrived at seven-thirty a.m., but understandably we could not check in. So, we left the bags and went out to discover Sydney, starting with Darling Harbour, which was about a fifteen minute walk from our hotel. This was our first time in Australia and we were really excited about seeing the iconic buildings that are recognisable all around the world!

I think that I should make a note here to say that we have had issues twice out of the three times we have been to Sydney with our transfers. If you can, book a private transfer through your hotel. It may cost you more, but it is worth it, because on the other occasions where we were sharing, it took ages for us to leave the airport and get to the hotel. Also, book a late arrival and pay for the extra night, so you can go straight to your room to rest. You will be exhausted after travelling through the night. And finally, select a hotel with a good location. The Mercure was nowhere near the city centre and we walked a LOT on this first visit, even though we learnt to take the train from the station near the Mercure to Circular Quay.

When we arrived at Darling Harbour, it was so early that even the breakfast restaurants weren't open for business! So we headed for the Opera House where we needed to pick up tickets we had booked for a performance that evening. By now, the sun had come out and it was getting quite warm and we had beautiful blue skies. On our transfer, our driver had told us that the weather had been very bad in Sydney recently and lots of people had got their fur coats out again! So, we decided not to waste this beautiful morning and we headed back to the Mercure to pick up our cameras and get those memorable shots of the harbour with the sun shining and the blue sky as a backdrop – priceless for any photographer!

We returned to Circular Quay to get those iconic pictures and took a harbour cruise too, so as to get plenty of shots from all different angles, of the Opera House, the Harbour Bridge and the Quay itself. You will have seen so many photos of this area and these buildings and you will not be disappointed when you see them for yourself – it is just wonderful and you feel like you are on a film set!

Eventually, we did go back to the hotel and checked in. At this stage, we were both exhausted and had a quick nap before showering and changing for our night at the ballet, which was in one of the theatres at the Opera House. But it became obvious later that this nap was not enough for us to recharge our batteries, as both of us fell asleep during the first act! Neither of us could keep our eyes open, and when we did jerk awake, our neighbour's faces showed that they were not amused! We left at the end of the second act, as we needed to eat and if we waited

until the end of the performance, it would be very late before we would return to our hotel. At night, when the harbour is all lit up, I would say that it is even more beautiful than it is during the day, if that is possible!

I will admit that we both slept very well that first night, which was a good job because the next day Richard did the harbour bridge climb! I went shopping at the Queen Victoria Building where there are some wonderful shops: big and small; some expensive, some reasonably priced; designer, quirky, touristy and unique; there's something for everyone!

I went to Circular Quay for my lunch at around two-thirty so as I could look at the bridge knowing that Richard was up there! I am very nervous of heights and, as I am not the fittest person around, I thought that I would struggle with such a steep and exhausting climb. But Richard said it was quite easy going and not too exhausting at all. I thought that I would give it a go the next time we went to Sydney, but I chickened out!

The following day we went on a tour of Sydney and the surrounding area, which was part of the package booked through Tradewinds. We were joined by another couple from the USA, who were on their honeymoon, so we were a very small group. Our guide, Tony, was from Italy originally, but has lived in Australia for thirty-seven years. Despite this, he still had an Italian accent! We drove around the suburbs of Sydney, seeing some of the glorious houses and villas that adorn the waterside. Some of them belong to big stars, including Kylie Minogue and Russell Crowe. We also saw the church where Elton John married Renate Blauel in 1984, and we walked through the park where you will find Mrs Macquarie's Chair; a rock formation where Elizabeth Macquarie used to sit to enjoy the views (c1835) – and the views are amazing from this spot, looking towards the Opera House and Sydney Harbour Bridge also affectionately known as the Coat Hanger!

We also went to Bondi Beach, but we were disappointed with this famous resort in the same way as we were with Waikiki. It is a very large beach with white sand, blue seas and big surf, but it is very commercialised in a sort of tacky way. Obviously very popular with young people, and it was really busy during our short stop.

In the evening, we booked on Captain Cook Cruises to do the sunset cruise around the harbour. There are several different levels that you can reserve, and we went for the Gold Dinner, which gives you priority boarding with a champagne and canapé welcome reception; followed by a six-course meal complemented by accompanying wines. It also included a free bar, guaranteed window seat, disco and access to the Star Deck after dinner, for the most spectacular views of Sydney at night. It is worth every penny, as we felt like royalty the way we were treated. Our menu included scallops, baby lobster and Angus steak and it was truly delicious.

Ayers Rock: After three nights in Sydney, we headed for Ayers Rock, Uluru where we stayed for two nights at the Outback Pioneer. There is only one resort at Ayers Rock but they offer three standards of hotel. The Outback was very basic and classed as three stars, but it was adequate for the two nights that we stayed for.

Unfortunately, we then hit a problem; the first of our holiday that we booked through Tradewinds. Our five-centre holiday included flights, hotels, transfers and a lot of included excursions, which covered everything that was available at Ayers Rock. The package included an evening tour of the Olgas and sunset at Ayers Rock; a sunrise tour of Uluru itself; and a Sound of Silence dinner. But AAT Kings, the tour company at Ayers Rock, did not have a record of our booking, and due to the time difference with the UK, if we waited for them to get this sorted out, we would have missed out on the first evening and the sunrise tour. We had a voucher from our agents, showing the booking, but AAT Kings would not accept it as they had no reservation on their books. So we had no option but to pay forty Australian dollars for the package, and then claim it back off Tradewinds on our return. Due to this taking so long to sort out, we did not have time to do any of the other optional excursions which include camel trekking in the desert and a helicopter flight over Uluru. We were not interested in the camels, but we did fancy the flight.

But, at least we were sorted for the main excursions and that night we headed out for the Olgas, which is a rock formation close to Ayers Rock where you can walk into the canyons and clamber over some of the rocks. But this was just the starter before the main course, which was the sunset at Ayers Rock. We were taken to the location where you can get the best views, but at this point, the heavens opened, and we had one of the most torrential thunderstorms I have ever witnessed. Uluru just vanished into the mist and the sky went from very dark grey to black, without any sign of a sunset. We did enjoy our glass of wine under cover, but without a view. There is supposed to be only eleven point two inches of rainfall per annum in the park, but I reckon that more than that fell on this one night!

The next day we had a very early start, rising at three-forty-five a.m. to go on our sunrise tour. The rain had stopped, but it was very dull and cloudy and the sunrise was not very spectacular. We did see the rock change colours as the sun climbed into the sky, but it was not exactly awe inspiring.

We then went on a cultural walk around Uluru, well not all the way round, as this monolith is huge – five point eight miles to be exact. We learnt about the plant life in the desert, and the formation of the rock itself. We were also told some of the Aboriginal stories about Uluru and the dream world, which was fascinating. Uluru is considered to be a very sacred place to the Aborigines and as such, it is now frowned upon to do the climb up the rock. Some people still went ahead and did it, despite the request to respect the local customs, but we were happy to do the circumference tour.

Ayers Rock is red! But, for a desert, there is a lot of plant life. The sides of the mountain are pockmarked and it does have staining when you get close. These marks help to enhance the local stories of Uluru and the gods. Some areas are very sacred and you are not allowed to take photographs of the rock close-up, but you are told where you are safe to snap away.

From the distance, Uluru looks like one huge mountain that is smooth and solid, but as you get close you realise that there is a lot more to it. As well as valleys, peaks and rockslides, there are some caves with various Aboriginal paintings inside. The caves were used by the Aborigines in the past and they actually think that the area has been inhabited for over ten thousand years. In 1985, the Australian government returned ownership of Uluru to the Aborigines, on the understanding that it would be leased back to the National Park for ninety-nine years, and that it would be jointly managed during that time.

We had a siesta in the afternoon, before driving out for our Sound of Silence dinner. This starts with a champagne reception in a location with the most amazing full view of Ayers Rock ready for you to witness the amazing sunset behind the mountain. We sipped our champagne and waited, but there was no dramatic change in the skies; but, as we turned to our right, we could see the Olgas in the distance and there was the most dramatic sunset I have ever witnessed! The sky looked as though it was on fire! The reds, yellows, oranges and blacks lit up the sky with the silhouette of the rock formation and trees in the foreground, which helped to create some of the most dramatic sunset pictures that we have in our library.

We then went for our dinner, which was a barbeque, served in the open air close to our viewing platform, but, it started to rain again! Hey! – we already had a year's rain the night before; give us a break! Our pleas fell on deaf ears; obviously those who had climbed the rock that day had upset the powers that be, and this was their revenge! Our dinner was cut short and we headed

back to the resort where we finished our meal at the Sails in the Desert hotel. A disappointing end to our break at Ayers Rock, but it did not spoil our trip, as the sights of this amazing natural phenomena are just fabulous and I hope to return some day – but hopefully without the rain!

Cairns and the Great Barrier Reef: It is when you fly across Australia that you realise just how big this continent is. It took us a hundred and thirty-five minutes to fly from Uluru to Cairns, where we stayed at the four-star Oasis Resort, which was conveniently located close to the beach, where you will find the Esplanade where all the restaurants are located. We were staying here for five nights, the longest stay of our holiday and we had managed to book quite a few excursions of our own, to make the most of this area.

The following day we went to Cairns Tropical Zoo where we had breakfast with the koala bears. This involved us selecting from the café menu and sitting at a table close to the koala's enclosure, where they were in the tree tops eating their eucalyptus while we dined on our croissants. We spent the morning at the zoo where there were a lot of indigenous animals, including red pandas, crocodiles, snakes, birds, kangaroos and koalas. I had the chance to hold one of these cuddly bears – she was called Winita. I thought that this was wonderful, but I don't think that Richard was too impressed.

We went to the snake exhibition where we were shown a number of different snakes, all different sizes and colours, some of them deadly, and we were given the opportunity to hold them. I did not go near them, but Richard did hold one of these! We went to the birds of prey flight where they had some huge eagles, demonstrating the power of their enormous wings, as well as cockatoos and other smaller, colourful birds.

One of the most interesting exhibitions was the demonstration of the power and speed of the crocodile. They always look so docile and cumbersome when they lie by the sides of the pools in the zoos I have visited before, and this huge Australian specimen was no exception. You could just see his snout above the water level – that is until the keeper put a chicken in front of him. That croc came out of the water so quickly, so that everyone who was watching let out a yell of surprise! The keeper teased him for a while, and we could hear the jaws snap shut as the crocodile tried to grab the chicken that was dangled in front of him. It certainly made me jump and I realise now just how dangerous these reptiles are, and why there are so many deaths caused by these monsters.

In the afternoon we decided to book tickets for a trip on the Kuranda Scenic Railway and Skyrail. Firstly, we asked our hotel about their options, but we could not find what we wanted. We used the internet to try and find a company who offered the Royale Service that we had read about in our guide book, but we had no success. We phoned the actual company who runs the railway and we purchased our package through them for ninety Australian dollars. The hotels package was eighty-eight Australian dollars and was nowhere near as good as the Royale Service. That evening, we ate at one of the many restaurants on the Esplanade and we had Moreton Bay Bugs! These delicious crustaceans are a sort of prawn without pincers and are absolutely delicious! I would definitely recommend them.

The next day we had our included excursion from Tradewinds, which was a balloon flight – my first! We were picked up from our hotel at four fifteen, a.m. a very early start, but balloon flights are always early in the morning, so it is something you have to accept. We drove into the rainforest and it took a long time before we reached our designated launch site. This is picked on the morning of the flight as they have to determine the wind direction and speed before they can start to inflate the balloons. There were two balloons and we went in the second flight, so we were able to watch the first team take off in theirs before we climbed into the basket and took to the skies. The baskets were very big and held twenty people, but we had room to move around and gaze down at the fields and the farms below us. We saw some wild kangaroos hopping around, but they were so far below us that it was impossible to take a photo. We were in the air for around thirty minutes before we returned to earth without too much of a problem. It was a very smooth landing and it certainly did not cause us any problems. We helped to pack the balloons away into the big trucks that follow the flight before going for our champagne breakfast. We spent the rest of the day at rest.

On our third morning in Cairns we had another early start as we needed to be at the harbour at seven-thirty a.m., for our trip out to see the Great Barrier Reef. It was very warm and even at this early hour we were both very hot. We went on the yacht, Ocean Free, which can carry thirty-five, but only twenty-five were on that day's excursion, which was good as it would give us room to move around and to find a sheltered spot to get out of the sun. Our yacht sailed out to Green Island and gave everyone on board the option to go diving or snorkelling. I have dived in both Turkey and Mauritius, but now that I have been diagnosed with Type 2 diabetes it is not advised to go diving. But we both went snorkelling and, as we are both novices and not confident swimmers, one of the crew stayed with us all the time. I am sure that it is much better to have a diving holiday on the Great Barrier Reef to really experience this amazing place, but this was not an option for us, and this was the best way for us to cross it off the list. Even just doing snorkelling around the boat, we saw loads of fish and, of course, we could see the actual reef below us.

We landed at Green Island and we went on the submarine, which submerges into the waters for us to be able to see the fish and the coral all around us. As we returned to Cairns, the wind was up so we were able to travel part of the way under full sail which was a wonderful experience. The drinks flowed, cake, cheese and fruit was passed around, and we just had the most wonderful, and friendly experience.

On our final day in Cairns, we went on the train to Kuranda, which we had struggled to book earlier in the week. An early start, yet again, before we headed for Cairns train station, where we boarded the scenic rail service. Now, as we had booked the Royale Service, we were shown to a designated carriage and given a picnic hamper with our breakfast, which included champagne. The train would make one other stop at Freshwater before going on to Kuranda and, as we were the only ones in our Royale carriage, we thought that others would board there. As we approached the station at Freshwater, the platform was full of people and we thought; 'well there goes our quiet journey.'

But no-one was booked on the Royale service and they all squeezed into the other carriages, leaving us alone in our private car! This was a luxury and was totally unexpected. Many of those who had boarded in Freshwater were young Italians and VERY noisy, we could hear them through the open windows!

The train zig-zagged its way up the mountainous rain forest, using a switchback system. The views were beautiful and we stopped once to see a very dramatic waterfall cascading over the ridge. We were all allowed to climb off the train to view this lovely sight, and, as we re-boarded and people realised that there was an empty carriage, we were joined by a few others for the last leg. Many of them asked why we had the carriage to ourselves and a picnic hamper, and also why the train staff were being so attentive to us – we must have looked like royalty or VIP's at least! When we explained that we had booked the Royale Service, they thought that it must have cost us a fortune and were surprised that it was just a few Australian dollars more than they had paid! It just goes to show that you need to do your research before going on a trip!

Kuranda is set high in the mountains and the rainforest and has a few touristy places to visit as well as some nice shops, restaurants and walks. We went to the Butterfly Sanctuary and walked down to the river through the rainforest before boarding the Skyrail for our journey back down the mountain. This is a cable car that rises from the town, soaring above the huge forest at heights that are mesmerising, before descending down to sea level, just outside of Cairns. There are a couple of stops where you can get out and take a walk around to see the waterfall from a different angle and experience the flora and fauna of the rainforest. The ticket for the Skyrail is included in the initial train ticket, and you have the option of both going to Kuranda by the train or the Skyrail, and then returning via the other. But I think this was the best way of doing this exhilarating trip.

Singapore: We flew direct to Singapore from Cairns. It is a long flight as we have to cross the whole of Australia before landing in this sovereign city-sate which is totally independent and is classified as one of the hundred and ninety-eight countries in the world. We were staying at the Holiday Inn Atrium – a huge skyscraper of a hotel close to the shopping district. We had great views of the modern city of Singapore from our room which was large and spacious. We were only staying for three nights and as we arrived so late, there was not a lot to do on this first evening except to eat at the hotel.

The next day we did our inclusive tour of the city, which, to be honest, was a bit disappointing as we didn't really see much. We went to the quayside, and saw the symbol of the city the Merlion Fountain, and then we went to a Chinese temple that was built by Chinese immigrants without the use of any nails. We carried on to the Botanic Gardens which are immense, but we just went into the Orchid Gardens. These were lovely although Richard was not impressed, as he is not really interested in plants and gardens! We finally went to Little India where there is a market and shopping centre, but we left the tour here and went to Chinatown instead.

Singapore seems to be made up of lots of different ethnic areas, where each one has its own flavour and shopping experience. There are many modern, air-conditioned shopping centres all over the city, and also lots of markets and street sellers where you can buy just about anything your heart desires. There are tailors where you can have suits, dresses and shirts made within a few hours and, as in Bangkok, there are lots of stalls selling replica watches, handbags and clothes. It is a shopper's paradise!

In the evening, we went on a night tour. The city is beautiful when it is all lit up, especially around the river area, where

we ate at one of the street cafés and dined on meat cooked at the table on hot stones. It was great food and a wonderful setting. We tried to repeat this experience when we returned in 2013 but, although the restaurants are still there, none of them offered the experience of cooking on the hot stones, as they had been replaced by Chinese, Thai and steak restaurants. We went to see Raffles and have a drink in the Long Bar. As it was late November, Raffles was decorated for Christmas and it was all lit up against the night sky. The Long Bar is very strange as the custom is to throw your peanut shells onto the floor! Very unsophisticated! We had a traditional Singapore Sling, well you have to have one when you visit Raffles and we went to the night market to end our evening.

The following afternoon we went to the resort island, Sentosa. To get there you have to go on a cable car which offers you fabulous views of the city. It actually goes through a building, which is quite an experience! On this occasion it was very windy and the cable car had stopped at its highest point. I have said that I am quite nervous of heights and I started to panic, as we were so high up and I had no idea how we would be rescued. It felt like it took them a long time to get the problem fixed; whereas it was actually only a couple of minutes, but my life flashed before me during those seconds of terror!

At Sentosa we went to see the pink dolphin display and we also went to SeaWorld where I saw Nemo! We made our own way back to our hotel and we ate at Boat Quay again; only this time we had a wonderful Chinese meal. It had been overcast all day and that night the heavens opened and we had a very dramatic electric storm. The thunder and the lightening crashed around us as we ate, and the rain was torrential, but we stayed dry under the covers of the riverside restaurant.

Our final day involved packing and a bit more shopping in Chinatown before we went on our final excursion, which was an afternoon sailing around the islands of Singapore on a Chinese junk. Although it was still overcast, it was very warm and it was a pleasant way to spend a few hours tripping from island to island where there were very few tourists and certainly no more shops! We stopped at Koso, the turtle island, where there was a little pool with turtles and a temple, but not a lot else.

Details of our return journeys to Bangkok, Sydney and Singapore: Bangkok 2010 and 2012: We returned to Bangkok as a stopover, before going on to Sydney for a cruise. This time we stayed at the Shangri-La Hotel, which was beautiful and in a much better location close to the river. We upgraded to a Horizon Club room, which gave us access to the Club room where we could have breakfast and free drinks and snacks during Happy Hour each evening. The room was large and beautifully furnished with a fabulous view over the river. We went to Vertigo again to the Banyan Tree, as we had enjoyed it so much on our last visit, but this time it was a lot more expensive. It had obviously become very popular over the last five years.

On our second day we took a very action-packed day trip out of the city, which we arranged through Viator.com. It was only a small group; a family of five, a single man and us, but we had a small minibus and it was quite cramped, especially as it was a long day with a lot of travelling. We had many stops along the way, the first being at a food market which was located in a small town away from the hustle and bustle of Bangkok. It was interesting to stroll through and see the produce that they were selling which was all very fresh and clean. Some of the items did not look very appealing as the Thai people do eat some strange things, but it certainly was an interesting interlude.

After another forty-five minutes driving through the countryside, passing paddy fields and small villages, we stopped for a ride on an ox cart. These big beasts had no problems dragging the carts with four people in each, but the journey was slow and bumpy and very hot! We then continued our journey to Koh Samui National Park, where we left the "comfort" of our minibus and took a walk into the park to see a waterfall. It was a pleasant walk, but we didn't actually get to see the waterfall – no idea why! We then headed for the main event which was a hotel complex where they have elephants trekking through the jungle. After lunch, we mounted our elephant sitting in a car seat that was tied to its back with seat belts to provide us with a little bit of a safety strap. Our mahout sat straddled around the elephant's head and encouraged him to set off on our trek. After about ten minutes, our mahout clambered down to lead the elephant down a slope and through a stream and then he motioned for me to climb forward and take his place on the elephant's head. I have ridden elephants in India and in Africa, but always on a seat safely located on their broad back; this was the first time that I would be riding from the front! It was amazing! The hairs on his head were very prickly and coarse, I wished that I hadn't been wearing shorts! But, what a wonderful experience! When we dismounted after our trek, we were given bananas to feed the elephants and to thank them for our afternoon.

It was a very long drive back to Bangkok and we were a lot later than what we thought we would be. The trip should have been eight hours and was closer to twelve. We had booked to do the Horizon dinner cruise as it was Valentine's Day, but we were so late getting back, that we had to cancel. Instead we had dinner at the buffet at the hotel and it was very good, offering a lot of choice – all sorts of local and international delicacies. It was a beautiful evening and we were able to sit outside, where I was presented with a chocolate heart from the hotel and then, to our surprise, there was a huge fireworks display across the river. We had forgotten that it was also the Chinese New Year, and the fireworks were celebrating this Asian holiday.

We then took a side trip and spent the next two nights in Cambodia, but I will cover this in another chapter, as I am concentrating on covering Bangkok here. We returned to the Shangri-La for two more nights and the next day we went on one of our most exciting excursions EVER!

Before our holiday, I had read about a Tiger Temple where monks had originally taken an abandoned tiger cub, who they had cared for at the temple. The number of tigers grew and to keep them semi-domesticated as you can never truly tame a big cat, the cats were fed on cooked meat so that they never got the taste for raw flesh. Tourists had the opportunity to interact with the animals and this temple was not too far from Bangkok.

I had used the internet to find a tour company that could take us to the temple for the morning and then to visit the River Kwai area in the afternoon. It took us two and a half hours to get to the temple, but we were instantly rewarded as we approached the first platform. There were three cubs and a few full-grown tigers lounging around the area. The grown animals were actually tethered to the posts for security as there were a lot of people around. We were the only day tourists, but there were a lot of monks and quite a few young people who were residing for a few days, and who were assisting with the care of the tigers.

We took a seat and watched the cubs rolling around, irritating the bigger cats and scrambling over the visitors. It was just amazing and I never thought that I would get so close to these fabulous animals. We then went through an area where they had some very young newly born cubs, as the resident tigers were now breeding, and into the back where we fed the cubs with cooked chicken, from our hands, and then we washed them with lots of soapy water, rinsing them off with a hose. They really enjoyed the pampering, and of course it was a real thrill for us.

We moved on to another compound where there was a large pool, rocks and a climbing area and some of the juvenile tigers were brought in to play. We had all been given instructions that we should not turn our backs on any of the tigers and always be fully aware of where they were and some of us were given huge black carrier bags on sticks that acted as balls for the tigers. We watched them wrestle, splash around and tussle with the bin bags. They were just like our cats at home except for being fifty times bigger and deadlier!

Then we were introduced to the fully-grown tigers who resided at the temple. They are classed as being fully grown after they are one year old, and these beasts were BIG! They have all their teeth, claws and strength, and we sat with one, very carefully, to pose for our photograph. It was reasonably placid as we crouched behind him, but we were very conscious that he could turn on us at any moment and inflict a serious injury. All I kept thinking of was that they would not allow tourists to visit if it was dangerous, but we're in Thailand not in Europe!

Our morning ended with us being in a cage! We were escorted into an area that was enclosed by mountain walls on three sides with just one way in and the same way out. Here there was an area enclosed by high fencing and we were herded into this space and the circle was completed as the gate was closed, and locked, behind us. The handlers then came into the valley with a number of fully grown tigers who were let off their chains and allowed to fight, swim, run and attack one another to their hearts content. We just stood there and watched these majestic animals who were very healthy, and were well fed, and they seemed totally happy with their life in captivity.

It does appear that initially the monks took in some abandoned tiger cubs to care for, but obviously as the numbers increased and their reputation brought in tourists and money, their good intentions have now turned into a commercial operation. I would have thought that most of these tigers that we saw would have been bred at the temple and would have probably never known freedom. But they were very healthy, they seemed perfectly happy and would probably not be alive if it had not been for the monks, so we do not feel as though we are sponsoring a cruel practice. We are just very pleased that we have been able to experience these incredible big cats in such a way.

From the temple we went to the river to see where they built the original bridge over the River Kwai, and we were told about the atrocious conditions that the prisoners of war suffered at the hands of the Japanese in this area, whilst they were forced to work on the "death railway". From the viewpoint we went to see the Kaset Buddha Cave, where there are a number of Buddhas and temples built inside the mountain. These caves were used as a POW military hospital during the Second World War, and they offer a cool sanctuary against the heat of the Thai countryside. There is also a museum and a cemetery, which is tended by the locals, to keep it in good condition for the hundreds of visitors who come to this place each day. Our lunch was on a river-boat and was very pleasant. It is very hot in this area of Thailand and we were glad for the water and the wet towels provided by our tour guides before we took to our minibus for the long drive back into Bangkok.

On this visit, we returned to Bangkok for another night at the Shangri-La Hotel after our cruise. It gave us the opportunity to relax before the long flight home, which always departs very late to get you back home to England in the early hours of the next morning. As we had a day free, we booked a tour to do some sightseeing by tuk-tuk. But unfortunately this was at the time where the red shirts and the yellow shirts had disagreements and there were demonstrations on the street, and our tour was cancelled as it was too difficult to get around with road-blocks etcetera. So, instead we took to the river and went on one of the dragon boats that zip along the Chao Phraya River to visit some of the smaller canals that create a Venice-like city within Bangkok. As you travel down these narrow waterways seeing the life that exists here, you forget that you are in the middle of a huge, modern metropolis. There are some lovely villas, temples and colleges but also a lot of ramshackle buildings. We stopped at the Temple of Dawn (Wat Arun), which dates back to 1809 and has a tall central tower that is decorated with coloured broken porcelain and glass, which reflects the light making it sparkle during the day. From here, you get fabulous views across the river to the new palace. This was a lovely way to spend our last day of this extensive holiday, as it was both relaxing and very interesting.

We returned to Bangkok in October 2012, where we stayed for a couple of nights after an Asian cruise, travelling from Beijing to Bangkok. Even though this was our third visit, we still found things to do and places to visit that were very different from before. This time we were able to do our tour by tuk-tuk and it was brilliant! We love this mode of transport as you are able to get around the car-blocked city so much quicker than in a taxi, and you experience all the sights, sounds and smells of the capital city while you are whizzing around. We had a convoy of four tuk-tuks and the guide would take it in turns to sit in each vehicle to be able to provide a commentary of what we were seeing. We visited a few temples, including the Temple of the Reclining Buddha (Wat Pho) which offers a lot more than just a huge statue. We also visited various street markets and different ethnic areas of the city, including the flower market and the Amulet Market, and also the fortress of Sumera Phra where you have fabulous views of the city.

The next day we took a coach tour away from the hustle and the bustle to visit the ancient capital of Siam at Ayutthaya. The first stop was the Summer Palace built by King Rama IV and offers a mixture of Thai, Chinese and Gothic architecture, set in beautiful gardens and grounds. We hired one of the little golf carts, to get around, and this was much better than walking in the heat of the day!

From there, we went to the ruins of Ayutthaya, which thrived until they were taken-over by the Burmese in 1767. Some of the temples are still in excellent condition and have some wonderful Buddha statues, including one that is reported to be the oldest in Thailand. We also saw the eerie remains of just the head of a statue that had been taken over by the roots of the trees. Our visit ended with a stop at the great stone reclining Buddha, before we took to the water and returned to Bangkok along the river, passing by the Royal Palace just before our tour ended. This was a very pleasant excursion and we saw a lot in a very short time. It was very photogenic and there was something different to see around every corner. There were around six stops in total, so this is a very extensive trip. We arranged both of these tours through www.viator.com.

Sydney – 2010, 2013 and 2017: We returned to Sydney in 2010 and stayed at the Shangri-La, a beautiful, large hotel near Circular Quay. This time, we booked for two nights and we said that we would be checking in early so that we could go straight to our room on arrival; but there had been a mix up with our reservation and they had us as a no-show for our first night, as they thought that we would be arriving the day before. It got sorted-out, and we were given an upgrade to a Horizon Club room, but we did not have the Harbour View room that we had booked. However, we did get a refund from Thomas Cook when we returned home. This meant we had just the one night before boarding our cruise ship to sail back to Bangkok, visiting Melbourne, Tasmania, Adelaide, Perth, Singapore, Vietnam and Cambodia during the twenty-one day cruise.

We have been to Sydney twice more, in February 2013 before we cruised to New Zealand and again in February 2017 when we drove around South Island, New Zealand and followed this with a Fijian cruise. We stayed for two nights in February 2017 as a break between flights from the UK to Queenstown, so that we could get over the time difference and the long flight time. We enjoyed being in Sydney but we did not do anything out of the ordinary.

We spent four nights in this wonderful city in 2013 and did a couple of remarkable tours during our stay, that I would like to tell you about. On this occasion, we stayed at the Langdon Observatory Hotel near The Rocks – a lovely five-star hotel that just oozes opulence and has an antiquated feel to its décor and its ambience. We made reservations through the hotel for our airport transfer, so we had no problems with shared transport and we were able to go straight to our room on arrival as the hotel had us as a late show. For once, our plans worked and we were able to have a bit of a snooze before we set out in the afternoon to get our bearings. We headed for Darling Harbour as there are loads of restaurants and shops in this area, and we wanted to find a place that served Moreton Bay Bugs – it took time, but we eventually found a place that did a seafood platter – very good!

The next day we did wine tasting in Hunter Valley. We had booked this through Viator.com before we had travelled – it was VERY expensive, as we were going by helicopter! When we arrived at the heliport we had a briefing and then we headed for our chopper with Peter as our pilot. We had expected to be part of a group, but we discovered that we were the only people booked on the excursion and that we had the helicopter to ourselves. The tour started with a flight along the Northern beaches and over towards Sydney Harbour, where we had fabulous views of the bridge and the Opera House.

We then headed out past Manly and Palm Beach before turning inland and heading over forests towards the Hunter Valley. We landed in the grounds of the Bimbadgen wine cellars, where we tasted many different wines before selecting our favourite, which we would have with our lunch. The restaurant, Esca Bimbadgen, was on the upper level, looking out over the vineyards and the helicopter park where our transport awaited our return. We had a wonderful three-course lunch, accompanied by an excellent Pinot Gris, sitting on the balcony enjoying the sunny weather, atmosphere and views. We could hear people from the other tables making comments about the helicopter, wondering which high-flying dignitary was visiting. I think that they were quite shocked when our pilot came to collect us, and they watched us walk out and board the chopper for our return flight. This time

we flew right over Harbour Bridge and Darling Harbour before returning to the heliport. It was a fabulous day out and I would love to have the opportunity to do it again.

We also did a full day trip out to the Blue Mountains, again booked through Viator.com, before the trip. It was a small group tour and there were nineteen in the minibus – not really a small tour, I had expected that there would be around ten people, but it wasn't too cramped and everyone spoke English. It was a packed day with lots of stops and activities. After a coffee stop, we went to the first of two sightseeing spots; one to be able to take photos of the Three Sisters and then at the viewpoint before you board Skyway and Cable Car. From both places we had views of the valley, some rocky outcrops and the surrounding mountains, which are covered in eucalyptus trees; the reason for calling them the Blue Mountains.

This is probably a great trip but the queues were very long and by the time we eventually crossed over the chasm to take the cable car down to the valley floor, we did not have a lot of time to enjoy the area, as we almost instantly had to turn around and start queuing to come back! We went to Katoomba, the chief town in the Blue Mountain area, for our lunch, and then headed for a wildlife park where we saw many of the indigenous animals of Australia. On our way back, we stopped at the Olympic Park where Sydney successfully hosted the Summer Olympics in 2000, and then we boarded the Wild Cat to sail back along the river to Circular Quay in Sydney. A long and busy day – we would have preferred to have had more time at the Blue Mountains, but they obviously try and pack the itinerary with as many activities as possible, to make sure that you get your money's worth.

In 2013 and 2017, we did the hop-on, hop-off bus tour which does a circuit around the city and has a branch that takes you to Bondi Beach, although we did not take this branch. On the first ride, we had beautiful sunny weather and it was really hot sitting on the open-top deck; but in 2017, we had the most awful rain during the whole time that we were on the bus. Everyone was seated on the lower level, as they would have been drenched sitting upstairs. In fact, we still got wet downstairs, as the water poured down the stairs in a torrent when we went around corners! It was amusing at first, as we tried to dodge the tsunami that was being collected on the open upper deck but we would have preferred it to be fine and dry, so that we could have at least seen the sights that we were driving past!

Sydney has some fabulous restaurants, especially open-air places around Circular Quay, where you get great views of the Harbour Bridge. But, in 2013, on our last night at the Langdon, we dined at the hotel restaurant, Galileo, a fine dining experience. We had the tasting menu, expensive at one hundred and ten Australian dollars each, but a wonderful experience. The meal started with a amuse-bouche of toasted watermelon with parmesan, followed by a selection of seafood, which was very pretty and full of many flavours. Our second starter was yellowfin tuna and then the fish course was barramundi served on a mussel volute. We had a palate refresher of strawberry ice before the main course of beef tenderloin, which was really delicious and our favourite dish. The first of two desserts was a strawberry soup with basil sorbet and this was followed by vanilla panna cotta with rhubarb compote. Eight courses later, we were stuffed but very satisfied, although our pockets were three hundred Australian dollars lighter!

Singapore 2010, 2012 and 2013: We returned to Singapore in 2010, during our cruise from Sydney to Bangkok and spent the day in port. At this time the cruise ships docked in the container terminal, which is one of the busiest in the world and it took fifteen minutes to drive from the ship to the main road. As we had been to Singapore before, but we didn't fancy any of the excursions, so instead, we got glammed up and we went for lunch at Raffles. The restaurant was fairly quiet, but the food was delicious and the whole affair was just so decadent. It cost quite a bit as we had champagne cocktails, the taster menu and a bottle of wine, but it was worth it, and it was great to be able to go into this iconic hotel and experience the atmosphere in that way.

We also stopped at Singapore on our cruise from Beijing to Bangkok in 2012, and this time we did an excursion with the ship where we had a walking tour around the harbour, a boat ride in the harbour where we saw the Merlion Fountain again from a different angle, a visit to the same Chinese temple as we had been to on our first visit, and then onwards to Little India to visit some of the temples there, as well as spending some time going around the market. By this time the new cruise port was open which is located much closer to the city centre. There was still a lot of work taking place though, with land reclamation, huge skyscrapers, modern hotels and the concrete forest in the sky.

The best visit we had was when we spent two nights staying at Raffles in February 2013, after our New Zealand cruise. All I can say is WOW! The hotel is perfect; from the way you are greeted at the door by liveried Indian doormen to the attention to detail in your room, which is very large and beautifully furnished. The open corridors outside your room look down onto the numerous courtyards and gardens that make up the Raffles grounds and each bedroom has its own table and chairs on the veranda, where you can enjoy the hot steamy evenings, sipping your ice cold cocktails. The rooms have a feeling of colonial splendour that date back to the time of Sir Raffles himself. I loved it! It was a perfect ending to that holiday.

On our free day, we did a private excursion to cross the border and go into neighbouring Malaysia. There isn't a lot to see, but crossing through passport control was an experience and it was another country crossed off the list, as I had never been to Malaysia before. We were lucky as we were not held up at the border, but there is always a chance that you could be delayed for a long time, as the border control operators work at their own pace! In 2015 we went to Kuala Lumpur for a few nights after our holiday in Myanmar, so I have now been to Malaysia twice.

We returned to Singapore in February 2018, staying just one night, before we boarded our cruise ship to sail to Thailand, Vietnam and Taiwan, ending in Hong Kong. We arrived the day after the Chinese New Year celebrations had begun and everywhere was decorated for this national Asian holiday. Singapore is considered to be one of the best places to visit during this celebration and we witnessed this popularity when we went to the Gardens by the Bay in the evening. Everywhere was so crowded and festivities were taking place all over the city with parades, firework displays and special exhibitions. Luckily, our hotel, the Pan Pacific, was within walking distance of the gardens, and we joined the multitude of people out on the streets enjoying the warm night air and the sights and the sounds of the festival. I wish I had done some more research on what to expect at this new attraction, I just knew that there were a number of artificial trees that rise to the sky, and are spectacular when they are illuminated at night. We saw some of these and I was not disappointed, but there are many trees in the gardens and we only saw a few of them; but I was still able to get that iconic photograph of the newest of attractions in Singapore.

CHAPTER 12

Disney World, USA (3) – April 2006

I can understand Disney World being one of the fifty, but I don't think that it deserves to be number three. But this was a poll of the British public and I would have thought that a lot more people have visited Florida than have seen Angel Falls or travelled to New Zealand! But, it is on the list, so we needed to go there, in order to complete the challenge – and besides, I am such a big kid at heart that I wanted to have the opportunity to see Flipper, Mickey Mouse and Winnie the Pooh!

We flew from Gatwick, which meant a long drive down south from Sheffield but, even though we drove down on Good Friday, going the night before our flight, we made good time and had no issues. On this occasion, we flew out with Virgin and they allow you to check your luggage the night before, using their Twilight Check-in. This was so easy as there were only two people in the queue which meant no waiting or hassle. We were also able to pay for extra legroom seats on the flight out. It cost us fifty pounds, but we knew that we would have a more comfortable flight.

We stayed overnight at one of the airport hotels and the next day, as we had no suitcases, just hand luggage, it was an absolute doddle going to the airport. On arrival in Orlando we had a car waiting for us – we had taken the route of hiring a car and a villa, rather than staying in a hotel. This would give us freedom to go where we wanted and when we wanted. We had found the villa online and booked it independently from a private owner. It had taken us a long time to find the right one, as we wanted a pool with a pleasant sitting area around it, but also, we wanted a view from this area – we didn't want to back onto another villa. We were not disappointed—our villa was beautiful!

It was far too big for the two of us, as it had five bedrooms, two seating areas, a large kitchen and a dining area and a great view from the master bedroom, which looked out over the pool and onto a lake – we were not overlooked by anyone!

Of course, with having a week in Florida, we didn't just go to Disneyland, but we went to most of the theme parks. We did not bother with Animal Kingdom, as we would rather do a real safari than visit a zoo, whether it is Disney or not. We started our week off with SeaWorld. This was on Easter Sunday, so we expected all the theme parks to be packed and that we would encounter queues wherever we went. We thought that SeaWorld might be the quietest and we were right – it was busy, but with going there early we did manage to avoid the really long queues.

We watched Clyde and Seymore, a couple of sea lions, and their show was funny and entertaining, more of a sketch-show than just performing sea lions. The dolphin show was very flamboyant and was real "Disney" in its production. It combined dolphins, whales, Cirque du Soleil type acrobatics, ballet, birds and all manner of story-telling and circus stunts. I am rather embarrassed to say that it moved me to tears, as it was so beautifully performed and choreographed.

We were disappointed with the killer whale show, as they were rehearsing for a new production due to start in May, so it was very haphazard and not as good as the one we had seen in San Diego. There was so much to see – another show involved speed boats, kites, jet skis and high diving – very James Bond!

We had our lunch looking onto the shark tank which was different. I felt as if they were eyeing us up for their dinner treat! We did not stay for the fireworks display, which takes place late at every theme park, we knew that we would catch it on another day.

The next day we went to Universal Studios. We paid forty dollars each for a fast track ticket, which got us to the front of the queue for every ride. It was really busy, so this saved us a lot of time. We went on a lot of rides and saw some of the shows – it is pointless telling you what we did, as they are changing all the time, and as it is now almost ten years since our visit, I doubt that the rides that we did are still there. A word of warning though for people who suffer from travel sickness – if the Back to the Future ride is still in operation, be prepared, as it made me feel very ill!

We were having lunch in the Irish pub when lots of people started to gather around, and we came out to watch the Blues Brothers sketch which is performed on the streets in amongst the crowds. It was great fun and the music was brilliant – everyone was bopping around to the songs! As you walk around, the scenery and the architecture change, so one minute you are in San Francisco and then you move to New York. You go from a medieval area to a science-fiction scene of the future, just by crossing the road. It is great fun and is ideal for adults and children, as there is so much to see and to do.

After a day of rest from theme parks, we went to International Drive and did a bit of shopping. We went to the Kennedy Space Centre, which is about an hour and a half's drive from Kissimmee. We had reserved our tour online before we went and, even though we arrived early before the doors had opened, there was already a long queue, so we were glad that we had pre-booked. We had timed our visit to be able to see an actual launch of a rocket – not the Shuttle, but it was still fantastic to witness this event, live.

We watched this from the visitor's centre, which was a long way from the actual launch site, but we were given the countdown to the launch and then we could hear, and we could feel, the great roar of the rocket as it rose up into the sky for us all to see. There is a lot to see and do at the space centre, so be sure to give yourself enough time to take in all the sites and attractions and check the internet to find out if any events are taking place. Doing this before you plan your visit may give you access to special tickets and shows that might be taking place. We reserved the "Close up" tour, but you can also have lunch with an astronaut. The guides are very interesting and it made a change from the theme parks.

We had decided to save Magic Kingdom for our last day in Orlando, so that day, we went to Epcot as we wanted to stay late and watch the fireworks and we had heard that this park offered the best show. To be able to stay late, we went in the afternoon, spending the morning in Downtown Disney. We were not impressed with this area, although some of the hotels surrounding the lake did look quite nice.

The Epcot Theme Park was very busy and we were not able to get fast track tickets as we had arrived late in the afternoon. There were a lot of queues for the science section of the park and, as we were not prepared to queue, we did not see much of this area. We thought that this futuristic area looked rather "tired" and it did not have a lot to offer, but then we went to the World Showcase and we were pleasantly surprised about how nice this was. We saw a three hundred and sixty degree film of Canada, before going to "England" where they had a small replica of Hampton Court; a few old thatched cottages and the book shop, which represented Christopher Robin's house. As we arrived Pooh Bear was just leaving, but I waited near the barrier to see Rabbit arrive. He took me by the hand and led me into the library to meet Tigger! Now, I need to say that at this point that Richard had disowned me! I was in my element as Tigger is my favourite cartoon character, and despite going to Disneyland Paris twice, I have never had the opportunity to see him.

I was so overcome with glee that I gave Tigger a huge bear hug. I then had to go to the door to lead Eeyore into the room, as he was standing there being very bashful and nervous, as you would expect of this character. Richard took my photo hugging Tigger and with Rabbit pointing at me, as though to say, "We've got a right nutter here!" But I didn't care! My lifelong ambition had been fulfilled – I had met Tigger!

We carried on with our walk with me smiling like a Cheshire cat who had got the cream! We went to Morocco to see belly dancing; and Japan to hear some drums being played, which was great. We did some shopping in Germany; and had a meal in China but most of the restaurants were fully booked, so if you ever want to eat at a theme park in the evening, make sure that you reserve a table earlier in the day.

We found a spot on a grassy bank to watch the fireworks, which were spectacular. The people at Disney really know how to put on a show, and to entertain the crowd. There were thousands of people at Epcot that day and many had stayed into the evening for this display. When it was over, we were surprised as to how quickly we managed to get away from the car park, as the hordes descended on the exits. A really great day and I would thoroughly recommend Epcot Theme Park as a full day's visit, as we missed so much.

Our final day in Orlando and we saved the best for last, as that day we went to Magic Kingdom Theme Park. We went early, as our intentions were to just spend the morning there, so that we could come back and pack to be ready for our departure the next day. This theme park was SO busy – probably the busiest of all the places that we had visited. I assume that this was due to us coming in Easter week, but I am pretty certain that Disney World is always busy. At Magic Kingdom we went for a fast track ticket again, which did speed up our visit.

We started off with an Indy car race and then went on the Buzz Lightyear ride, which was great fun. It is aimed for younger children, but we enjoyed it, zapping the aliens and trying to destroy emperor Zog. We went on Splash Mountain, fantastic! and Thunder Mountain, superb. We had to queue for this ride for twenty minutes and it stopped halfway around, which spoiled the ride a bit, but we still enjoyed it. We watched the midday parade, and had a great view from the front of the line where the parade had started. This theme park is aimed at the younger children and the queues were very long in Fantasyland, but we did see the 3D film starring Mickey Mouse. We had very good weather all week; blue skies, hot days and comfortable evenings. But, as we left Magic Kingdom, the heavens opened and we had one of the worst storms I have ever witnessed. Rain poured down on the car and there was thunder and lightning like I had never heard or seen before! We had to pull over and wait for it to pass. We were lucky it had not started earlier while we were at the park, otherwise it could have been a real dampener on our day!

CHAPTER 13

Lake Louise, Canada (11) and Alaska, USA (28) – August 2006

This was our first cruise. Until now Richard had not fancied cruising, as he did not want to be "trapped" on board a ship with two thousand other people with nowhere to go. But we both thought that the best way to see Alaska was on a cruise. We booked a cruise/tour through Princess where we spent the first week driving from Calgary to Vancouver, before we boarded the Sun Princess in Seattle to do a round trip the next week, doing the Inside Passage. We now know that this does not provide the best views of Alaska as we did not get to see those huge glaciers that you see on all the advertising brochures for Alaskan cruises; so we did another cruise in 2012, travelling from Whittier in Alaska to Vancouver, and this one provided us with some spectacular Calving's. We also preceded the second cruise with an eight-day tour through Alaska, where we got to see some of the most dramatic scenery that we have ever seen and we witnessed the wildlife that this largest state of the union has to offer.

But, I am going to start with our journey through the Rockies in 2006, as this is where we stayed at Lake Louise, the first of the fifty on this holiday. In the new listing it is the Canadian Rockies that are shown in eleventh place, but the original voting very clearly specified Lake Louise as the place to see.

We started our tour after spending a night at the Fairmont Palliser in Calgary. One of the reasons why we booked this particular tour and cruise was because of the hotels that we would be staying at during the tour, as they included some of the best that Canada has to offer, and the Palliser was no exception – a grand, old hotel, right in the centre of town, close to the Calgary Tower and with lots of bars, restaurants and shops. After a relaxing morning, which gave us time to recover from the nine hour flight and the seven-hour time difference, we set off for the Canadian Pacific Highway No. 1 that leads straight to Vancouver.

We started with a tour of Calgary before leaving the city and then stopping at Mount Norquay where we could see Banff in the distance. Banff is only fifty six miles from Calgary, so we arrived at this beautiful town in time for lunch. We had some free time to shop (my favourite pastime), before we continued our tour. Our first stop was Surprise Corner where we had a lovely view of the Banff Springs Hotel, another grand hotel that is referred to as the Castle in the Rockies, as it looks just like a Scottish castle – although a very BIG castle! We continued-on to see the Hoodoos which are weird shaped, balancing rocks carved by wind and rain. The Indians believe that these rock formations are gods. We continued to see Bow River Falls before going back to our hotel, the wonderful Banff Springs.

This hotel is huge! We got lost trying to find the bar! But it was wonderful. The interior was just as elaborate as the exterior, and the views from the terraces and our room were spectacular. There were so many public rooms to lounge around in, and to enjoy the hotel and the surroundings. You could stay there a week and still manage to find something new to see. But we were only there for one night, as the next day we were off to Lake Louise; but first we had a helicopter trip.

Out of the thirty-eight people on our tour, we were the only ones who opted for this extra excursion. We had to be up early to be transferred to the heliport, and we were greeted by clear skies. We both thought that this would be a wonderful trip, but as soon as our helicopter took off, the weather started to change – the skies darkened and there were some very foreboding clouds closing in on us. Although the helicopter could take four passengers plus the pilot, we had it to ourselves. As we sored into the skies, our pilot decided to change the route to avoid the on-coming storm clouds. This meant that we did not get to see the most dramatic views of the Rockies, but we soon realised that it was a necessity, as the pilot started to battle against the winds and the turbulence being created by the approaching storm. Our flight was cut short and, as we returned to the heliport, we discovered that we were the only ones who had been able to take off that morning. All the other flights had been cancelled, so we did feel very lucky that we had not had a wasted journey, and we had seen something of these stunning mountains from the skies.

We returned to the hotel where we picked up all our fellow group members and we set off for Lake Louise. Firstly, we went on the gondolas that took us up the mountain where we had our first sighting of this beautiful lake. We then went to Takakkaw Falls, which were spectacular due to the rains that we had had the night before. We continued our journey and stopped at Maligne Lake, a clear turquoise lake carved by glaciers and surrounded by dramatic mountains.

We were staying at the beautiful Chateau Lake Louise – very different from Banff Springs, but large and opulent. Its location by the lake and beside some high dramatic mountains is exceptional, and it's a fabulous place to spend a night. We had a view overlooking the lake and the next morning we were rewarded with clear skies, sunshine and a wonderful photo opportunity to be able to capture this emerald green lake with its magnificent mountain setting, with a background of clear blue skies. Photos do not do it justice: you have to see it to be able to appreciate the beauty of the setting and the clarity of the waters. But to see the white glaciers reflected in the mirror-like calm water was a sight to behold, and we understood why this particular setting had been selected as one of the fifty.

There are so many beautiful lakes in the Rockies, and I am not sure why this particular lake was selected for the list. Depending on how the lakes are fed, the colours change and create different views for the spectator. Some are green due to the amount of ice-melt and others are a bright blue; especially when the sun shines on the crystal clear waters. Mountains surrounding the lakes can also affect the colour and the atmosphere, as they cast shadows on the water and can be a bit gloomy and foreboding. Maligne Lake was one of these, as there are seven high peaks

surrounding the lake; but with Lake Louise the mountains created a backdrop that made this particular place picture perfect and, in the quiet of the morning before the multitude of day visitors would ruin the calm and the tranquillity, we were totally mesmerised by this beautiful setting.

We left Lake Louise and we continued on our journey through the Rockies. We were lucky with the weather that day, which had been very mixed for most of our journey so far, and had not allowed us to see the glory of this mountain range at its best. But that day, as we travelled along the highway to Jasper, we had some spectacular mountain, lake and glacier views. We stopped at the Ice Field and went on a Snow coach onto the glacier.

We only travelled a short distance, creeping along the solid ice at a slow speed, but we were soon surrounded by this immense whiteness, with a feeling of being back in the ice age apart from the hundreds of tourists and the huge beasts who had carried us there! Our guide, JP, had brought along a bottle of whisky and small glasses, and we all had a tot of newly distilled

Canadian whisky, served with melted glacial ice, that was millions of years old!

We visited the Athabasca Falls which were very dramatic and well worth a visit, before we boarded a raft and floated down the river to Jasper. We were told that this would be a "gentle" ride and that we wouldn't get wet! Needless to say, they were wrong – it got a bit hairy at times, as we went over rapids and Richard ended up completely soaked! That night, we stayed at Jasper Park Lodge, a really pleasant campground where we all had small lodges with an outside seating area. As we went inside and opened the curtains, we were surprised to be greeted by two elk outside. They were very quickly joined by the whole herd, who leisurely grazed away at the grass in front of our lodge.

The next day we headed for Kamloops, after firstly visiting Maligne Canyon and then the town of Jasper, which is not very pretty as it is a railroad town and is one of the places where you can board the Rocky Mountaineer Train that runs through the Rockies from Calgary to Vancouver. We stopped at a roadside café for lunch, where we had a fabulous view of Mount Robson, the tallest mountain in Canada. There was not a cloud in the sky and the view was breath-taking, even from this lowly spot along the roadside.

On this occasion, we did not go to our hotel straight away, but instead we stopped at the location where we would be having our evening meal, the Hacienda Cabella. Although we knew that we were dining here, none of us knew what to expect—and what a wonderful surprise we had! This hacienda is privately owned, but the family, Rick, Donna and Lila, who own it, made us all feel so welcome: it was like we were long lost relatives returning home. We had a free bar, the most wonderful barbecue dinner, all home cooked to their own recipe, served in a marquee, and we were free to wander around the grounds. They had the most wonderful herd of horses that are used by the Mounties; some of whom were there to greet and talk to us too. Even the cat and dog were friendly, and wanted to be a part of the party. The evening was just magical and the four hours we spent there went by very quickly – it was the highlight of our trip so far.

That night we stayed at the South Thompson Inn and Guest Ranch, which was really lovely but we did not have much time to enjoy it, after arriving so late from our dinner at the hacienda. We left early the next day for our drive to Vancouver, stopping at Minter Country Gardens for lunch. Our entrance fees to the garden were included in our tour and at fifteen dollars each, this was more than just a quick place to eat. We had time to wander around these beautiful gardens, admiring the colours and the different arrangement of plants, grasses and flowers. It really was a beautiful place to stop and to spend a couple of hours before we finally arrived in Vancouver where we stayed at the Pan Pacific Hotel, which is located right on the waterfront, next to the cruise port. Not all our tour group were carrying on to Seattle as thirty of them left us there and boarded their ship for a different Alaskan cruise.

We had to cross the border from Canada to America, and at this time security was high, as it was not long after the discovery of the infamous Shoe Bomber, so it took us a long time to go through customs and security. There were a lot of queues at the port. It seemed as though everyone had arrived all at the same time! We have since found out that this is a peculiarity with Seattle, as we have not had any issues at any other port of embarkation and we know of others who had similar problems at this particular port. Our cruise would be calling at Ketchikan, Juneau and Skagway (to be honest, all the Alaskan cruises stop at these locations), before turning round and stopping at Victoria before returning back to Seattle.

After a day at sea and before arriving in Juneau, we sailed up Tracy Arm where we saw the Sawyer Glacier. This was interesting, but we realise now it was nowhere near as good as Glacier Bay. Because of bad weather, the disappointment at not seeing some big glaciers and Richard not being well on the cruise, this was not as good an experience as our return to Alaska in 2012 had been, so I am going to use this second trip to describe the twenty-eighth entry on our list – and besides, we saw so much more of the forty-ninth state on our return visit. But, for now, I will continue with our first cruise.

In Ketchikan, we took a float plane to go out into the pristine forests of wild Alaska, and then we returned to the port by boat, so we saw the countryside from both land, air and water. The views were lovely but the weather was not good, so it did not make for good photos. We did see our first bear though, as he was feeding on salmon remains on the shore. In Juneau we did a photographic tour but we were disappointed with this, as we felt that the guide did not plan the trip very well with all the beautiful mountains and views around Juneau, we went into a park to take close-up shots of fungi! This did not even really help us to understand our cameras better than we already did. We had booked an excursion in Skagway but, unfortunately, Richard was not well, and we had to cancel. He did get a sick note from the doctor on board the ship; so we got a full refund for the trip. He was well enough to have a walk through the town, which is an old miners' post used by the prospectors taking the Yukon trek to look for gold.

After another day and a half at sea, where I suffered from sea sickness, even though the water was not that rough, we stopped in the afternoon in Victoria, which was very pleasant. We do like this very Anglicised island of Canada and we enjoyed a horse drawn coach ride around the town, and the gardens, before we stopped at the Inner Harbour, to enjoy a meal ashore with views of the setting sun over the harbour.

We had booked to spend a month in Alaska and in Canada in 2011 but, two weeks before we were due to leave, Richard had a heart attack, and we had to cancel. He had two stents and he was only in hospital for three nights and, I am pleased to say, he has made a good recovery, allowing us to continue with our travels for years to follow. Our 2011 trip had been booked in sections – the cruise/tour, car hire, Rocky Mountaineer and hotel accommodation had been booked together through Thomas Cook, and we had booked the flights ourselves through British Airways and Alaskan Airlines. I had not known before this occurrence that we were only covered for a maximum of ten thousand pounds on any single insurance policy but, because of the bank account I had, we actually had two lots of travel insurance. Princess and Thomas Cook refunded some of our money and the rest of the trip was covered by our main insurance. We got the tax back from the British Airways flight and we claimed the airfare back from the bank insurance and Alaskan Airlines postponed our booking for us to be able to transfer the payment to another flight; as long as it was taken within twelve months from the original booking. This meant that we only lost out on the first loss of two hundred pounds and, on an eighteen thousand pound holiday, we thought that this was a very good result.

The whole trip was rebooked; exactly the same as before, except for two small changes. Because 2012 was a leap year, in order to utilise the twelve month delay offered by Alaskan Airlines, we needed to fly out one day earlier, and have an extra night in Fairbanks and, because of the timing, we were able to have two nights in London before our trip, in order to attend the Olympics! We purchased a package to include accommodation and tickets for Wembley to see a semi-final Olympic football match, and to attend the athletics at the Olympic Stadium the following afternoon. We saw a number of qualifying races, including the five thousand metre featuring Mo Farah. To be able to experience this amazing event was fantastic! We knew that we would never have the opportunity again, so we were really pleased that we were able to combine this break with our Alaskan holiday.

We stayed in Reading the night before our flight to America, so that we did not have too far to drive the next day and it was cheaper than the Kensington Hotel. We were flying to Seattle with British Airways, so we were able to use the lounge and we arrived at five-fifteen p.m. It was a long flight, but the time difference was in our favour. We had to go through immigration and collect our bags on arrival, and then we transferred these to our Alaskan Airlines flight, which departed from the N gates – three trains away! Our onward flight was at nine-forty p.m. so we had time to have a drink and something to eat before we took the two-and-half hour flight to Fairbanks. As we had to come out a day earlier because of using the previous year's postponed flight, we could not yet join the Princess tour, so we stayed at the Best Western Plus Chena River for one night. All we did that night was to collapse on the bed and sleep!

The next day we took a taxi to the Princess Riverside Lodge and checked in with the tour organiser. We would be staying there for two nights, but this first day was being used to meet and greet people arriving for the tour, so we had a very pleasant leisurely day, giving us time to acclimatise and to get over the long journey.

Our Princess tour started early, having a group meeting at seven a.m. where we met our fellow travellers – thirty-seven in total, four others from the UK and the rest were Americans. Once we left the hotel, we headed for the river and we boarded a paddle steamer for our trip down the Chena River. We saw the puppy stables of the famous dog musher, Susan Butcher's, who had won the famous dog sledding race, Iditarod, three times running. We did not get off the boat, but Susan showed-off some of her husky puppies and did a demonstration on a dry sled.

We stopped at a replica Indian village, where we had demonstrations of how these people lived and how they survived in the freezing cold winters. We had lunch at the steamer's dock, Miners Stew, and then we went gold dredging, which included a train ride around an old mining area and stopping to have a go for ourselves. This was our first sighting of the Pipeline Alyeska – over eight-hundred miles long, it is one of the longest pipelines in the world, carrying oil from the north to the Valdez Marine Terminal near Seward. The details of the construction and maintenance of this huge project was fascinating and we continually caught glimpses of the pipeline during our weeks' journey as we were travelling to the coast along the same path, more or less. The Alaskan people did not want it to be built, expecting it to spoil the natural surroundings. For most of its length, the pipeline is below ground, so it is not too much of an eyesore, and with the money that it generates, every single member of the population of Alaska receives one thousand eight hundred and eighty-four dollars every year! There has been one major disaster which was not due to the pipeline being damaged, but was caused by an explosion at the terminal that killed one man, injured five others and caused one of the world's largest oil spills.

The next day we had another early start, meeting at seven p.m. again, to board a coach and transfer to the railway station, where we boarded the Midnight Sun Express to Denali. We were in domed cars to be able to get good views during our journey, and had our breakfast in the lower section of the car. The first three hours of the journey were not very interesting, as the land was flat and had very little in the way of trees and foliage. We certainly did not see any wildlife as we were going too fast. Eventually, when we reached Healy, we went through a river gorge and this was much more interesting, with high cliff faces on both sides and a roaring river below us. We finally reached our destination at twelve-fifteen and transferred to our hotel for the next two nights, the Princess Denali Lodge.

All of the places we would be staying at during this tour were owned by Princess – they were large resorts, all with well furnished, reasonably sized rooms, bars, restaurant and shops, and, at Denali we had a nice view over the Nenana River. Although certain tours were included at the different sites, we had free time to be able to book on other excursions that they offered, at a price, of course. We had pre-booked one of these excursions months earlier, as we had not wanted to take the chance that our first choice would not be available. We tend to always pre-book our excursions on a cruise, as the popular ones can sell out before you set sail, and we don't want to be disappointed and not do a trip that we really want to go on.

In Denali, we did an excursion in the afternoon after we had arrived. We were collected after lunch and, together with eight others on the trip, we were transferred to Healy airstrip where we were given special, reinforced boots for us to wear for our flight, and landing on the glacier. We boarded an Otter plane, which was small, but offered sufficient room for all of us, plus the pilot. Our flight was an hour heading toward Mount McKinley, the tallest mountain in USA, passing over the Alaskan Range.

The views were breath-taking, passing mountains, rivers, valleys, glaciers and finally circling the great mountain itself – turning around and coming back on ourselves, so that both sides of the plane got great views.

Then our little plane descended and we landed on Ruth Glacier, giving us the chance to get out and walk on the glacier, looking back towards Mount McKinley. All I can say is – WOW! The skies were crystal clear and so blue, providing us with the most amazing landscape views. But to add to this wonderful vista was the fact that it was so quiet – eerily so! There was absolutely no life up here on the glacier, and certainly no other humans, and the deep ice and the compacted snow beneath our feet muffled any sound that we made – it was just totally mesmerising. It was so quiet, you could actually here the glacier moving – creaking and groaning like a living thing.

Another day and another early start! Six-fifty a.m. today, for our included tour into Denali National Park. We had a local guide, Clay, and he was really informative, telling us about Denali, the state of Alaska and the wildlife that we might see during our day in this pristine location. We had beautiful weather – blue skies and no clouds, and during our drive we had a continual view of Mount McKinley rising high on the horizon ahead of us.

We were not disappointed with our wildlife sightings either, seeing moose, caribou, bears and Doll sheep – the four main animals of Denali. But we also saw a wolf and a lynx, and a mother bear with two cubs who walked right by the side of our bus. Even Clay admitted that he had never seen so much on a single day in the park – our photos were amazing!

Our tour continued toward the Copper River – the weather was not as good that day with a good start, but clouds developed, rather spoiling our views as we drove through this huge state. Scott, our Princess guide, kept us entertained during our long journey telling us about the history of the place (Russia sold Alaska to the USA in 1867 for seven point two million dollars – they didn't know about the oil when they did; with hindsight, not a profitable deal), how the locals coped during the winter months and other interesting facts. For example, Alaska is so large, twice the size of Texas, but underpopulated, so as most of the area is pristine wilderness with very few towns, there are certain rules when driving in Alaska: firstly it is illegal to drive past anyone who has broken down or needs assistance, you MUST stop and help, and secondly, if there are five or more vehicles in a queue of traffic on the open roads, the front car has to stop and let the others go past.

Our lodge at Copper River was smaller and more rustic, but no less comforting and welcoming than our previous accommodation. We enjoyed a dry dog sled ride there, where we took it in turns to take the sled, mounted on a wheel base, which whizzed around the grounds drawn by a pack of huskies – not the fluffy, curly-tailed breed, but hard-working, rugged dogs who looked more like mongrels than any pure-breed, but they were strong and they did not have any problems pulling two of us around the grounds. We took an extra excursion to go to Prince William Sound and take a cruise out to the Columbia Glacier. We had some good wildlife sightings on this trip – sea otters, dolls porpoises and a bald eagle. It was good to get close to this huge wall of ice – the glacier is half a mile long, and, being in a small boat, we could get quite close. But it was SO cold! You could not stay out for long as your fingers felt frostbitten within minutes of venturing outside. It was a long day – twelve hours in total, with a five hour drive transfer, there and back, and six-and-half hours out on the boat. When we got back to the lodge we were amazed to find out that it was Christmas! Because December is so harsh, the locals cannot celebrate the festive season in the same way that other Americans do so they have their celebrations in the summer – the 15th of August to be exact! There was a huge blow-up Santa by the front door, and the reception was decorated with a huge tree, garlands and fairy lights. It was lovely!

Our last two nights of the land tour were spent at Kenai Wilderness Lodge, and we stopped in Anchorage, the largest city in Alaska. It is not the capital though – that is Juneau, which can't be reached by road; only by sea or air. At this lodge we had log cabins with verandas to sit out-on, and enjoy the view of the Kenai forest which surrounds the accommodation. We were told not to sit out at night as there could be dangerous wildlife in the area, but we felt relatively safe and we ignored this warning as it was the perfect setting for our Cuba Libra's.

On our full day in this location we headed for Seward, to board the Glacier Explorer and head out towards the Holgate Glacier. The wildlife was even better that day and, within thirty minutes from leaving the dock, we saw two pods of orcas (killer whales). We also saw more Dolls porpoises, Stellar sea lions, puffins, sea otters, hump back whales and mountain goats, they were on the cliff face, not in the water! The scenery was stunning and we witnessed a bit of calving, as the ice fell from the glacier into the sea.

After our land tour of Alaska, we started our cruise. We boarded the Sapphire Princess in Whittier, having gone through a huge tunnel on the transfer, which is a one way only and you have to book a slot to be able to drive through in a convoy. This meant that lots of coaches all arrived at the same time, coming from various locations as there are many different tour options you can take before your cruise. Princess certainly seems to have the best options to do some touring as well as cruising, and you don't have to spend as long as we did, but, I must admit, I think that our tour was spectacular giving us a great insight into the size of this largest state in the union.

Our first day was at sea, but we were still sightseeing as we travelled south along the coast of Alaska. We took a detour to go towards the Hubbard Glacier, a huge wall of ice located in Disenchantment Bay. The longest source is seventy-six miles from the sea, and it takes four hundred years for ice to traverse the length of the glacier. Ships going to view the glacier need to be very cautious, as newly calved icebergs can shoot up quite dramatically as most of the glacier is actually below the waterline.[2] The day we were there, we had superb weather and there was very little floating ice, so, very slowly and cautiously, we approached the great wall until finally we were just a few miles away. The captain told us that this was only the second occasion this season that they had been able to approach to this distance away, having previously had to keep well back on other sailings – it is all the luck of the draw or the weather!

Nearly all Alaskan cruises stop in the same three ports, and this cruise was no exception. The difference in itineraries varies as to where you board and disembark from the ship, as this dictates which glaciers you get to see and whether you sail into Glacier Bay, Tracy Arm or another bay to be able to view the glaciers. We sailed into Glacier Bay and very slowly approached one of the larger tide water glaciers, deep inside the bay. A tidewater glacier is one that comes down to the sea. This area is actually a National Park, the largest in area in the USA and part of it is protected by UNESCO. There are several glaciers and we stopped in front of two. The park limits the number of ships and tour boats that can enter each day – cruise ships are limited to

just two, and when you consider how many ships there are that visit Alaska each year, you need to check your itinerary to make sure that this destination is on your cruise.

The views were spectacular in this fiord, with so many mountains and glaciers. We had a suite at the bow of the ship, with a huge balcony that wrapped around the side and front of our cabin. This meant that we could keep popping in and out of our suite during the slow approach, as it was bitterly cold outside! But it was worth braving the cold as the sight, and sound, of the huge glacier came into view. You could hear the ice creaking and groaning, and every so often you could hear a crack before some ice calved away and crashed into the ocean below. You could see chips falling away, leaving larger overhangs and you knew that this would eventually fall. Some of these were huge and when they calved, the ice created huge wave surges and ice bergs that floated away from the glacier. The captain moved the ship very slowly in front of the glacier, so that everyone could get a great view from their balcony. As we started to turn our backs on the view, we left the comfort of our cabin to take in the view from the opposite side and from the open decks. It was here that we witnessed the biggest calving as a gigantic section of the wall separated from the glacier and crashed into the sea. The impact was incredible as some of the smaller boats rocked with the force of the tidal surge this calving created. Unfortunately, we were too late to set up the camera and so missed the epic photo, but we still managed to catch some of the smaller calving's as a memory of this amazing natural wonder.

We continued down the West coast of Alaska and our first stop was Skagway, and on this occasion, we did a tour – as I had previously mentioned. Unfortunately on our first visit, Richard had not been well and we just had a stroll through this old prospector's town. We took a bus tour to the summit of White Pass as we thought that this would give us a better opportunity for photos and sightseeing, as opposed to the more popular train journey. We were not disappointed as there were only six of us on the mini-coach meaning that we could move around to get those enigmatic shots. We stopped several times; once to view a waterfall close to the road and another time to see the train winding its way along the steep track, using a switchback system to edge its way to the summit. Our driver entertained us with stories of the Gold Rush, and details of how tough it was living in the Yukon. We were very lucky to see a black bear, right by the side of the road – perfect for photos, except that the roadside plants were very overgrown and he was hidden amongst large, purple wild flowers. We went to the summit and actually crossed the Canadian border, before turning round and returning to town.

Skagway is a really nice town, with lots of shops selling souvenirs and jewellery. There is a bar – the Red Onion Saloon – which used to be a brothel and the girls serving food and drink still wear costumes that you would link with this profession. It is good fun and you feel as though you have stepped back in time, when you enter. Take care that you don't get on the wrong side of the Madam though, as she will shoot you down in an instant – not with a bullet but with some witty, cutting remark!

There are loads of different tours and excursions available in all of the Alaskan stops – you really are spoilt for choice. Taking trains, buses, boats or even flights in some of the locations gives you a multitude of opportunities to see wildlife and stunning scenery. Juneau is famous for the Mendenhall Glacier and for whale watching. This is the capital of Alaska and can only be reached by sea or air – there are no overland routes at all. On this occasion we decided to go whale watching – and they guarantee some of your money back if you don't get a sighting! The boats that take you out into the bay are still quite large and there were several coaches all piling onto one boat. There was plenty of seating, but the problem with whale watching is that you never know where one will appear and you need to be able to move around to get the sighting. I was disappointed with the number of people on this tour, but there was nothing we could do about it – at least the boat was fast and the captain was obviously very experienced, knowing exactly where to go to find the whales.

After about twenty minutes, there was a sighting – on the opposite side from where we were sitting, so we saw nothing due to everyone standing up to try and get a good view. There was an open deck on the top of the boat, but it was really cold and wet, and was not a suitable place to be with a camera with a huge lens! But, as we sailed on, we came alongside a pod of around ten whales on our side of the boat and we watched them spurt, swim and dive for several minutes – but then we were treated to a wonderful surprise.

One by one, each of the whales dived down, so there was no sign of them on the surface. Very slowly, some bubbles started to appear on the surface, creating a circle and, all at once, all of the whales surged up through the circle, mouths open, catching the fish that had been trapped by the net of bubbles – we could see the smaller fish flying out of their grasp and crashing back into the sea! It was amazing! I had seen bubble-netting on the

TV and heard about the way that whales work in unison to trap large shoals of fish by confusing them with this whale-made net, but I never thought that I would actually witness this very rare event. The pod performed for us, several times, and, although we never knew exactly when or where they would reappear, so that we could be prepared to catch the event on video/photo, it was absolutely amazing to watch – I could have stayed there all day! As the Americans would say – awesome!

Our final stop on the cruise was at Ketchikan, and it was here that we had the best excursion of the trip. We went by float plane out to Neets Bay where there is a salmon hatchery and, as a result of the abundance of salmon in the area, it is also an excellent location to see bears. The flight was around twenty-five minutes long, and the views were fabulous, looking down on the green mountains, fields and inlets. Alaska is so huge, and so much of it is inaccessible by road and can only be reached by air. Once we were all off the planes, our group took a walk of around a quarter of a mile through the woodland towards the actual hatchery. Our guide gave us an explanation of what takes place and the fact that around three and a half million fish are produced each year, that are then released into the sea at different locations. However, only three percent would actually return to this particular stream at Neets Bay.

But we weren't here for the salmon, we had come to see the huge mammals that feed on them! We were not disappointed! During our forty-five minute stop by the small river estuary, we saw many bears fishing for salmon, scavenging on dead fish left behind and strolling in and out of the surrounding wooded area approaching either the river or the sea. One came down quite close to where we were standing on a viewing platform, which caused a little bit of concern for the guide, but the bear was more interested in the smelly, bloody salmon remains than us. Our return flight took a different route and we flew over snow-capped mountains, glaciers and frozen water inlets. This was an expensive excursion, understandably with the mode of transport, but it was worth every penny to get so close to so many bears.

The cruise ended in Vancouver, but we still had another adventure ahead of us. We stayed overnight in the big city, before we hired a car and took four days driving through the Rockies before taking the Rocky Mountaineer from Jasper to return to Vancouver. We arranged our own driving tour through Canada, stopping firstly at Hope to see Hell's Gate – well worth a visit, as you can go on the Aerial Tram down towards the raging Fraser River. Our next stop was in Revelstoke, having driven through some fabulous scenery, past many lakes, stopping at the Blue Heron for lunch.

The next day we drove through Rogers Pass, past Radium Hot Springs and we took the route through Kootenay National Park which was really spectacular, finally ending our journey in Banff where we took the gondola up Sulphur Mountain for the fabulous three hundred and sixty degree views. Our final day on the road took us along the Iceland's Highway to Jasper; the same route that we had taken on our previous visit to the Rockies. We stopped off at Moraine Lake, Lake Louise and the Athabasca Falls but unfortunately, the weather was not good – it was overcast, cold and miserable, so we did not linger. During our journey we did see a bear by the roadside and some moose. If you see bear, you are not meant to get out of the car, but nearly everyone who stopped to view ignored this piece of important advice!

We left the car in Jasper and returned on the Rocky Mountaineer, having booked the Gold Leaf Service, which is the top level, and the most expensive. There were lots of coaches arriving with people transferring onto the train from tours with Titan, Saga and many more. There did not seem to be too many independent travellers like us. When the train came into the platform, a red carpet was laid out for the Gold Leaf passengers and we took our seats in the upper domed carriage, allocated for our two-day journey. The seats were wide and comfy, with plenty of legroom and with the windows being domed, we had good visibility all around. As our carriage was the first of the Gold Leaf group, when we went to the front of the coach we could see over to the other coaches as they were single storey.

We were on the first sitting for breakfast, which was served on the lower floor – it was good, with plenty of food. After that, the bar opened and we sat back with a glass of wine to enjoy the views. It sounds idyllic, but the problem was that the trees rose high above the tracks and, even in a double decker train, we could not see over the tops, so there was not much in way of scenery or vistas. There is a commentary over the loudspeaker and, if we went past something of interest, like a waterfall, the train would slow down to try and give everyone the opportunity to see the feature. You were able to stand on the first deck vestibule where the windows were open, but this area got very crowded. Lunch was again split into two sittings and, once again, the food was good – hot and plentiful and served with wine.

We arrived in Kamloops for our overnight stop in early afternoon, and the passengers on the train, around five hundred, were transferred to different hotels in the town. Accommodation is advertised as being deluxe for Gold Leaf passengers, but the Thompson Hotel where we stayed was basic – it was comfortable and located on the main street in the town, but it was certainly not what we had expected, especially having paid so much money for this first class upgrade.

The next day we were taken back to the station to re-board the train. The weather was so much better on the second day and the scenery was more spectacular as we followed the Fraser River through the mountains to Vancouver. The train went past Hell's Gate where we had stopped earlier in the week, and, as half of the passengers were in the first sitting at breakfast, we had the vestibule to ourselves! We skipped breakfast as we were given Barack Obama coffee when we boarded, and we knew that it would not be long before lunch would be served – you certainly did not starve on this train journey! The final section heading into Vancouver was flat and there was not much to see. We enjoyed the two day trip and it is certainly one of those excursions that we wanted to cross off our list, but the Rocky Mountaineer journey from Jasper to Vancouver was not what we had expected. Personally, I think Calgary to Jasper, stopping in Banff would probably be the better leg.

We spent our last three nights of this mammoth holiday in Vancouver, enjoying beautiful sunny days with clear blue skies. We went to Victoria Island on the float plane, taking around forty minutes. We had pre-booked a whale watching excursion to go out looking for orcas. We were given the choice of either going on a speedboat or a Zodiac. We picked the latter, as we were told that there were only eight people on the trip and the Zodiac could take twelve. All the passengers had to wear special overalls, which were padded and bright orange. The padding and colour were probably for safety precautions, to protect you from bumps and the cold, and to ensure that you would be seen if you fell overboard. We sat near the back, as we thought it would be less bumpy – we were wrong! I don't think it mattered where you sat; you would be bounced up and down in your seat as the Zodiac skimmed over the waves at a high speed. It was actually great fun although a little uncomfortable at times. We headed towards the US coast and we were not disappointed with our orca sightings, seeing several pods from a distance, and one large male who came very close to our boat. I like Victoria Island; it is very English, with some great restaurants at the harbour, and it's well worth a visit if you stay in Vancouver.

During the rest of our time in Vancouver, we mainly went sightseeing, going on the hop-on, hop-off, open-top circular tour bus and we saw all the key landmarks of the city, stopping off and transferring to the Stanley Park loop. In the evening we went to the restaurant at the Observatory, taking the Skyride up Grouse Mountain. Drinks are served in the Altitude Bar and we were lucky to be given a table at the window in the restaurant where we could enjoy the fabulous views, while we devoured our fine dining meal. We arrived in daylight and left in the dark, so we got to see the view in many different lights – a wonderful, final experience on this epic journey.

CHAPTER 14

Reykjavik, Iceland (44) – May 2007

We have been to Reykjavik twice. The second time was in August 2013 on a cruise from Southampton to New York when we stopped three times in Iceland, including the capital. On the cruise we also went to Greenland which is still a territory of Denmark, whereas Iceland gained its sovereignty in 1918 and became a republic in 1944. We have been told that when the Danes discovered Iceland they thought that as it so green and beautiful and they called it Iceland to deter too many people from coming, but with Greenland, which is barren, cold, icy and very unwelcoming, they wanted to try and encourage settlers so that is how this island got named – both names are very contradictory!

But in 2007, we spent three nights in Reykjavik and during that short time we got to see a lot of the capital and the surrounding area. The city itself is quite small in comparison with other capital cities, but there again; the population of Iceland as a whole, is not large it is less than half a million people, but it is an expensive place to visit and alcoholic drinks in particular incur a high tax and are very pricey!

We flew from Manchester on a Friday evening, leaving at ten p.m. The flight was just over two hours and, with a one hour time difference, we arrived in Iceland at eleven thirty p.m. – it was still light! Because of the position of Iceland on the Arctic Circle, it is one of the Scandinavian countries that benefits from the Midnight Sun. I had been to Saint Petersburg during their White Nights Festival in June but at the time when I had visited it was known as Leningrad. During this time it never goes completely dark at night, always staying dusk. But here in Iceland it was actually really light, even at that late hour.

We took the airport bus into the city, which took an hour, and then we walked to our hotel, Bjork, which was located ten minutes from the city centre. By the time we had checked in, unpacked and had a quick drink a Cuba Libra of course, it was two a.m. and it was still light!

We were able to have a bit of a lie in as we had booked a city tour for the afternoon. We had used Viator.com to book all the excursions in Reykjavik and we were not let down by them. Our guide spoke very good English and she was very knowledgeable and informative, telling us about the history of the country; all about its geography and its culture. We went to see the home of the President and the church; the house where Regan and Gorbachev had met and ended the Cold War; the harbour with the fishing fleet; The Pearl, a hill just outside of the city where you have magnificent views overlooking Reykjavik; the cathedral, which, because of its location, can be seen from anywhere in the city; the centre of town and some of the old historical buildings; but we didn't get to see any of the Hidden People!

We were not prepared for just how cold it was going to be at this time of year and our shopping expedition in the afternoon was mainly to try and find jumpers that were not too expensive! That evening we ate at The Lobster House, which, according to our research, is one of the best restaurants in town. Richard had whale, which he said was okay, and I had the lobster feast which was delicious. We even splashed out and had champagne, as it was only slightly more expensive than a bottle of wine. Expensive meal, but, as everything is expensive in Iceland, we thought that it was actually good value.

The next day we did the Classic Golden Circle tour, which took us out of the city and into the Icelandic countryside. There are a lot of active volcanoes and we could see smoke rising from the ground in the distance as we set off on our journey. The thermal activity is utilised by the people of Iceland as they use the hot springs and underground heat to generate electricity and our first stop on the tour was to climb a hill and see one of these factories. The building is set in a valley so as to try and obscure the gruesome features, as the landscape around it is beautiful. All around you can see steam rising out of the ground providing the evidence that this area is high in thermal activity.

There is a natural fault that runs through Iceland and close to this is the location of the first parliament. I would have expected a building, but this is a grassy bank with terraces around a central area and was used by all the people to listen to the speakers. We went to the Golden Waterfalls, which was the highlight of this tour. You had to walk along a pathway to see them but they were really majestic and fell with such force over the break in the rock. I thought that if your foot slipped that you would have stood no chance in the roaring torrent of the water below us, it was so powerful. We went on to see a geyser, which obediently blows at regular intervals soaring into the sky with its jet of hot steam. Finally, we saw an extinct volcano and there are plenty of active ones, especially Eyjafjallajokull which erupted in 2010, and caused chaos to flights in the northern hemisphere.

The next day we were due to fly back to Manchester in the evening, but it still left us the rest of the day to be able to discover more of Reykjavik. In the morning we went whale watching. This was on a big boat and there were a lot of people, but after just half an hour we saw some blue nose dolphins and as we sailed further out, we saw Minke whales. There were a lot of them and they were all around the boat – impossible to photograph as they never stay in the same place for long enough to focus on them, but great to watch. We then picked up our transfer to the airport, but we stopped at the Blue Lagoon first. These hot springs are very famous and although we did not have enough time to go into the warm waters, we were able to see what all the fuss is about. The large pool is actually outside and as it was very cold that day, we had no intention of swimming, but the people who were enjoying the hot spring did not seem to be deterred by the biting wind. We enjoyed a lovely lunch in the surroundings of the complex, looking onto the lagoon that gets its name from the clear blue thermal waters edged by the therapeutic white salts. It's very busy every day of the year so do not expect exclusivity if you ever get the chance to visit.

In 2013 we returned to Iceland and we had three ports of call where we were able to see other parts of the country. On this occasion, we stopped in the north and visited another waterfall and saw some geysers. Our cruise ship, the Caribbean Princess, stopped in Reykjavik and we did a 4x4 excursion into the countryside around the capital. Iceland is a popular location for many film and television programmes and in particular, Game of Thrones. At this time, we had not watched the programme, so when we stopped at one of these locations, we had no idea what it represented. Even now that we are avid watchers of the programme, I can't tell you what part is filmed in the countryside of Reykjavik.

A lot of the scenery is quite barren but still beautiful in a very natural way. The 4x4s that we drove over ridges and through streams, some of them quite deep, made quite a splash! There was no one around, so our motor playtime did not affect anyone.

Reykjavik is named on the list of fifty, but, in my opinion, there are many nicer places which were missed out. You cannot compare this modern city and its sights, with Florence or Istanbul, but it probably entices a completely different set of visitors, and they are the ones who voted for this city to be included. It is worth a visit, but you need to make the most of the rest of Iceland during your visit as there is actually not a lot to see in Reykjavik itself. Of course, being above the Arctic Circle, it is also a great spot to see the Northern Lights but you need to get away from the lights of the city to be able to view this natural wonder at its best. The best time to view this theatrical display is between October and March. We have seen them twice, but not in Iceland; once during a week in Lapland and again on a weekend in Tromsø, Norway. The second showing was by far the best, as we had booked excursions to go out of the town and search for the Aurora Borealis.

CHAPTER 15

Seychelles (40) and Masai Mara, Kenya (32) – October 2007

This holiday was booked through the African Safari Club who owned the plane that we flew with for all the legs of the journey, the hotels and the lodges where we stayed and the cruise ship, the Royal Star. The company, the ship and the hotels came under a lot of criticism in reviews; but overall, we had no complaints and we had a brilliant holiday which lived up to our expectations. The company became insolvent in 2011, after a reduction in bookings due to the financial crash of 2008. I don't know what happened to the ship or the hotels, I assume that they were sold off to pay the debts and they probably now operate under different ownership and have a change of name.

We flew from Gatwick on their DC10 where we had the extra leg-room seats. I would not call this Business Class, but it was certainly more comfortable than being in economy. We arrived in Mombasa early the next day, and we were transferred to the Palm Beach hotel, where we had breakfast before being taken to the port to board the Royal Star.

I need to backtrack a bit here. The African Safari Club offered a number of different Indian Ocean cruises which you could combine with beach stays and safaris. Originally, we had opted for a fourteen day cruise, a four day safari and then three days at a beach hotel, which would have meant that I would be celebrating my birthday on board the ship; but, I decided that other than going to the Seychelles on the cruise, the main reason for this particular holiday was the safari, and I thought it would be better to extend this section of the holiday. So, with three months to go, we changed to a ten day cruise that ended in the Seychelles, a seven day safari staying at three different lodges, and four days in Mombasa. But we also upgraded our room to the Presidents' Suite, which was the best on the ship – well, I was celebrating a landmark birthday! This trip, even with the upgrade, worked out to be cheaper than the original one, due to discounts that were being applied at that time, so we were totally in a win-win situation!

I am so glad that we did the upgrade. There are only two suites on this ship – the other, the honeymoon suite, was already occupied when we looked at changing. But what a surprise we had when we boarded the ship and we were taken to our cabin. It was beautiful and twice the size of the cabin we had originally booked. This was the only cabin on the ship that had a balcony, although it was more of a terrace than a balcony. The furniture in the suite was excellent, mainly mahogany fittings with a drinks cabinet and display stands; there were large wardrobes and two shower rooms—his and hers! This suite is normally used by the owners, when they are on board the ship, and we found out later that it is very rarely occupied by guests.

There was a bottle of champagne waiting for us on our arrival, which Richard had arranged before our departure. He had told me that the company had been very awkward and unhelpful when he contacted them to try and arrange anything special for my birthday, and I believed him. When I saw the champagne, he said that that was the only thing that he'd been able to arrange.

When we went for lunch and ordered some wine, we were asked for our cabin number. When we told them our number they were amazed and said, "Oh, you're the people in the owner's suite!" From that time on, we were known as Sir Richard and Lady Susan by the staff! What a promotion – just by picking this cabin!

We set sail for Zanzibar. Now, we had only been on one cruise before and unfortunately, I had suffered from sea-sickness on our Alaskan cruise. I thought that I might be better on this ship, but we were still in sight of land when I started to feel queasy. I took some tablets and by dinner I felt okay. On this ship there were two fixed dining times, and we went on the second sitting. We had a table of eight and shared it with the couple in the honeymoon suite and two couples who were in deluxe cabins, which was the type of cabin we had originally booked.

Our first excursion took us on a walking tour around Stone Town, the main city on Zanzibar. Our guide, Mohamed, was very good and he took us all around the little streets, stopping at a school to hear the children reciting their lessons; the cathedral; a coffee shop where we had spiced tea, and a market which was very smelly with fish and meat. We went to the Emerson Hotel for lunch, where we climbed to the top floor and sat out under awnings and on huge cushions on the floor. The breeze passed through the four open sides and it was a very pleasant stop after the heat of the streets. We were entertained by the staff with dancing and local songs.

This city commemorates Freddie Mercury, the lead singer of Queen, who was born in Zanzibar. There is a museum in Stone Town dedicated to him and his music, but unfortunately, we did not have time to visit. We returned to the ship at three p.m. and sat out on our terrace to enjoy the sunshine and to gaze back at the city, as we set sail for the Comoros.

This second night was a formal night and we had been invited to dine with the captain. We started with champagne and canapes in the lounge, and then had the top table in the dining room. This event only takes place twice during any cruise, so it was a very special occasion, and the first time for us. I used to watch the Love Boat on TV many years ago and always romanced over the way that they portrayed life at sea, and every episode of this rather antiquated programme had the captain dining with the guests. Well, after many cruises, let me tell you that this does not happen very often, so we really relished the honour on this occasion!

After a day at sea, we arrived at Mayotte in Las Comoros. We went on the whale watching trip and we transferred from our ship on to little speed boats that each took about twelve people. After an hour we came across a pod of dolphins – there were loads of them! Our guide said that there were around two to three hundred, but I thought that was exaggerating quite a bit! They surrounded the little boat and they were jumping and swimming at great speed beside us – it was wonderful! We then came across a female Humpback whale with her calf. They were quite a long way off, and she was not impressed as we tried to get closer, starting to dive and staying down for a long time, when we were too near to her. We stopped at White Sea Island, a little atoll made up of ground coral. Surrounding us was a beautiful clear blue sea with just the occasional sailboat drifting past. It was paradise! We stopped once more on the mainland where we had a picnic before heading to Mayotte for the last tender back to the ship.

The next day we were in Nosy Be, Madagascar. Our excursion was taking us to Nosy Komba or Lemur Island, and we crossed over from our ship in long narrow speedboats. We started our walk through the village and we had things explained to us about the life on the island. It was quite obvious that this was all done for the tourists, as they started to work as we walked by and then stopped after we had passed! They also had a number of tame lemurs that would jump on to your shoulder to eat the bananas that you were holding. At least you got to take a close up photo of a lemur, even though it was a pet one!

As we left Madagascar, the weather started to turn and that night the seas were really rough. During the night, the ship was being tossed around by eight metre waves and gale force winds! Everything in our cabin fell off the shelves. The toiletries in the shower rooms clattered to the floor and we had to put them all into the sinks, to stop them from rolling around. As we lay in bed, it seemed that first the ship would tilt to the left, slowly, slowly, and I thought that we were going to capsize. We had to hold on to the bed so as we didn't slide off! Then we would crash into an upright position for a few seconds before we would start to tilt to the right, and our heads crushed against the headboard. With every second I was thinking, 'this is it – we're not coming back this time, we're going to capsize!' But we did straighten up and it was all repeated again. This went on all night and the next day. It never eased up, and I spent the day in bed as that was the only way I could stop myself from being sick. Even Richard, who does not suffer from travel sickness, was ill, and he spent the day with me. I thought that we were going to die!

The following day we were still at sea, but the winds had eased a little and things got back to normal. We found out that during the night that they had thought about turning around and going back to Madagascar, but by this time we were more than half way there, so they decided to continue on to La Digue in the Seychelles.

When we arrived, the skies were blue and the weather was warm and sunny. You would not have thought that we had just gone through three nights of hell! We took the ferry to Praslin where we went to Vallee de Mai to see the Coco de Mer, an indigenous tree of Praslin and the symbol of the Seychelles. We walked through the forests looking at the plants, the trees, the nut of the Coco de Mer, which is huge, the animals and the insects. We then went to Lazio Anse which has been voted the best beach in the world. I don't know by who, it's just what we were told! It was beautiful with golden sand, clear aqua-blue waters, large grey boulders that were more a pearly pink than dull grey, and palm trees. The waves created crystal white foam horses, that broke on the coral reefs, before gently drifting to the shore. This beach was worthy of this title, as it really was a wonderful sight to see; the only problem – too many people!

The next day we docked in Victoria, Mahe Island, the capital of the Seychelles, and our final destination on the cruise. Victoria is the smallest capital city in the world. We went on a full day tour around the island, as we were staying overnight in Mahe before flying back to Mombasa the next day.

We started with the botanical gardens where they had some of the giant tortoises of the Seychelles, then we went to a market selling fish and vegetables; smelly again! We went up into the mountains to see an early slave settlement, but this location also offered us wonderful views of Victoria below. We stopped at a hotel on the edge of the sea, which had another lovely beach. I can understand why the Seychelles is on the list of fifty, as there

are so many beautiful beaches, scenic vistas and fabulous five-star hotels. Our lunch was served on another beach where we had a Creole barbecue, and had time to stroll along the golden sands before going to a craft village and then returning to the ship.

At this point, I would like to come to the defence of the Royal Star, as I know that it has received a lot of bad reports and was slated by some reviewers. I know that I am biased, as we had the best cabin on the ship and we were treated like royalty during the whole cruise, but there were a lot of good things about the cruise and a few comical events too! The Royal Star used to be owned by royalty and the decoration inside was superb, with a teak deck, mahogany fittings and brass handrails that were polished every night. The staff were wonderful – the managers knew everyone by name, and everyone was so helpful, polite and friendly, they were the stars of our trip. The ship only took two hundred passengers and had a hundred and twenty crew members to service them and to run the ship; so it is tiny in comparison to the normal ocean-going cruise ships and liners. It does not have as much to offer by way of entertainment, but the staff certainly did their best. During the days at sea we had port talks, historical lectures and movies, and in the evening, we always had some form of cabaret show in the Starlight Lounge. The problem was that the stage was very small and the ceilings were low, so the jugglers kept losing their balls in the curtains and the dancers, with their high plumed headdresses, could not can-can properly, as the feathers kept hitting the ceiling! But they tried and we thoroughly enjoyed our cruise!

On our last day in the Seychelles we took a helicopter ride around the shoreline of the island. It was cloudy at first, but this lifted and we had some beautiful views of this tiny tropical island. This included a flight over the island home of Wilbur Smith the author. From the heliport we were transferred to the airport, where we boarded the DC10 again and headed for Mombasa and the Flamingo Beach Hotel, where we would stay for two nights, before the second part of our holiday, a seven-night safari.

Our first game park was Tsavo East National Park, where we stayed at Crocodile Camp. We flew there on a small de Havilland plane, which took off from a patch of scrub land outside Mombasa, which was being used as an airstrip for these light aircraft. There were just three other people on our Best of Kenya trip, and the five of us were together on all the transfers, game drives and shared a table at dinner. It only took thirty minutes to get to the lodge. The flight was a little bumpy, as most of the seats were empty, but we arrived in one piece. Our chalet looked out over the river and, although basic, was reasonably comfortable. That evening we went on our first game drive and we saw lots of antelope, zebra and some elephants. Tsavo East is known for the Red Elephant, due to the colour of the sand found in the area.

After dinner we found out how this camp got its name. The river lies below the camp and is protected by a high wall, so as we could look down onto the banks. As we stepped forward to peer over the ledge, a number of crocodiles had gathered for their dinner. Scraps, bones and chicken carcasses were thrown over the wall and the twelve crocs below us clambered over one another to get to the food. It was surprising just how fast they could move when they wanted to! Spectacle over, we retired to our chalet for a nightcap before having an early night.

The next day we were up at five a.m. You always have early starts on a safari, as that is when the animals are at their most active, as they sleep during the heat of the day. Today, we were on a full day drive, so we went all the way through the park to visit the Masai warriors' village, where they performed a war dance, jumping very high from a standing position.

We went into one of their mud houses, which was dark but cool, and we sat with a mother and her baby, asking questions about their way of life and the hardships that they face. We all felt that this was contrived and was actually all an act for the tourists; as behind the mud huts was a modern settlement with normal houses; all with satellite TV! But the dance and chanting were good to watch and I really would not want to upset one of these fierce warriors!

In addition to the same animals that we had seen the day before, we also saw lion, giraffe, buffalo, ostrich and loads of birdlife. The park is very barren with the red dust everywhere, and it is very dry. The animals rely on the river and a few scattered water holes for refreshment; but the best part of the drive was that we witnessed a kill, something very few people actually get to see, even though it is happening all the time.

We had driven past a zebra that was limping and had been abandoned by the rest of the herd. We all thought that he would probably not survive the night and how right we were. We drove a little further on and saw a small pride of lions – a male, two lionesses and a young cub. One of the lionesses was looking directly at the injured zebra, with such a stare that there was no doubt what was going through her mind. We pulled over and watched as she very slowly crept closer to the limping animal, who was totally unaware that it was being stalked. The other two lions followed her, keeping their distance, lying low in the grass so that they were almost invisible. We had to manoeuvre the bus to get a better view, as all three adult lions crossed the road, followed by the cub, who was keeping well back from the proceedings. It was the lionesses who took it in turns to creep closer and closer to their quarry, and we watched, mesmerised, for twenty minutes, while they got to within attack range. Then, suddenly, the male dashed forward to pounce on the unsuspecting zebra. It had no chance being lame, and the lion soon had it on the ground and the other two lionesses bounded in to help with the final kill. Finally, the cub came running up so that he could get his fill too. It seemed so cruel, but it is either kill or be killed for the wildlife in Africa. The hunters live up to their name – they hunt!

The following day we had another game drive in the morning, before flying on to our next camp in Kimona. As the small plane touched down at the airstrip at Crocodile Camp and people started to get off, it was quite apparent from their white faces, that the flight had not been a good one. We had to wait for the final passenger to disembark, as she was so frightened and so ill from the journey from Mombasa that she would not leave the safety of her seat now that the plane had touched down. She had to be coaxed and led off the plane by the pilot, and she came off looking like a ghost! How they managed to get her back on a plane for the next leg I'll never know! But it did not bode well for us either!

We got to Zebra Lodge in Kimona after a very bumpy flight, with a lot of turbulence. As the plane landed and we were driven to the camp, there were animals all around us, actually on and close to the runway – warthog, a baboon and some birds. We did not have time to unpack. We went straight off on our game drive, and we were not disappointed. We had lots of sightings, including eland, wildebeest and grants gazelle. We could also see

Mount Kilimanjaro as the clouds cleared at sunset and we were rewarded with a golden sky, as the sun dropped below the horizon.

Again, we stayed in small lodges located by a stream and watched over by tall, leafy trees. When we went for dinner we had to wait for a Masai warrior to come for us and escort us to the dining area. We sat out together by the campfire enjoying the clear starry sky and listening to the sounds of the African plains.

A late start the next day, seven am! We went on a walking safari and became park rangers for the day. As we were led into the big bush, we learnt about the plant life in the area, the tracks and other things left behind by the animals, who call this park home. I don't need to go into detail of what else they had left as a reminder that they had walked through this way! After breakfast, we continued our walk and we went to a large waterhole where we saw crocodile and hippos. They were in the water coming up for air and then submerging below the waterline. The noise they make is so loud and almost like a great big belly laugh, but these animals can be the most dangerous to humans in the bush, if you get between them and the water. We had a great sighting of some giraffe, who did not seem to be too spooked by our party being so close. But the warthogs were up and away at breakneck speed as soon as you spotted them – they deserve their nickname of African Express!

The next day we had a seventy minute flight to Mara Buffalo Camp in the Masai Mara. This was our longest flight in the de Havilland, but also our smoothest with no turbulence. But when we arrived and we were transferred to the camp, we were not impressed with our cabin, as it was small, dark and cold, with very little furniture and amenities. This was also the largest of the camps we had stayed in and it was too big and quite impersonal. But this was where we were staying for three nights and where I would celebrate my fiftieth birthday. I could understand now why Richard had not had much luck arranging anything as a celebration before we came away. The staff seemed to be quite aloof and unhelpful! The camp was set on the banks of a river, which was flowing very fast, as there had been a lot of rain in this area the night before. This was apparent when we went out on our first game drive at ten thirty, and our landrover got stuck in a mud hole! We all had to get out and wait while another vehicle pulled us out – luckily, no lions around!

But then we got to see one of the animals that had eluded us so far on our safari. In fact we saw two of them! Cheetahs! They truly are beautiful animals; so majestic and sleek and much more pleasing to the eye than the big, burly lions! We saw lions, more plain animals and a new antelope called a Topi. The game drive the next day, was a long one and we saw plenty of lions, including a lioness devouring a recent kill. The pride walked right in front of our vehicle, ignoring us, carrying on with their search for their next meal. We saw our two cheetahs again and we also saw some jackal pups, just for an instant, before they ran back into their hide.

The next day was my birthday and we weren't on an early start, so I had time to open all my cards and my presents, before we set off on our full day game drive to look for rhino. Now, if anyone who is reading this book has been to Kenya, I bet you're saying, "But they don't have rhino in Africa, they've all been poached!" Well you're right, but they are trying to reintroduce this animal back into Kenya and we went to see two of them who were being kept in a quiet location where they were being readjusted to their new surroundings. Nice idea, but with the number of tourists from all over the park going to see them, it was more like a zoo than a halfway home! Not a good day's game viewing as it was a long drive, with very little else to see except for our two cheetahs, who were being very lazy under a tree!

We returned to the camp and our lodge, to find a bottle of champagne waiting for us, and the room was decorated with flowers and petals, all strewn amongst my cards. It was a total surprise as I had not expected anything. When we went to dinner, our table was also scattered with flower petals so it looked very colourful and just right for a birthday celebration. As we finished our meal, all the lights went out, and the doors to the kitchen opened and a parade of cooks, KP's, and waiters came out banging drums, blowing horns and singing. Leading the line was the chef with a HUGE birthday cake lit with candles. They wound around all the other tables before reaching me, and by that time everyone in the dining hall was clapping and singing too. Philip, the maître d' announced that it was my birthday and everyone sang happy birthday to me, after which they all had a piece of my delicious cake. It was so big that it went around the whole room! I was in tears with joy and happiness. It was such a total surprise and obviously Richard had been having me on all along with the fact that he had not been able to sort-out anything to celebrate my special day. This was all his doing! The next day, we returned to Mombasa where we spent the last two days relaxing at Flamingo Beach.

One of the best things about Mara Buffalo Camp was Amelia! She is a zebra who was rescued as a calf when her mother was killed by lions and has been reared at the camp. She is very tame and wanders around the lodges and tents. She would often poke her head through the dining room window to see if there were any nice titbits for her, and she would drink from the tap outside the WC in the centre of the camp!

This was Richard's second safari. The first one was part of our holiday touring South Africa and Swaziland, and, to be honest, on both of these occasions, the camp sites were not very good as they were not selected by us but were part of a package. I had done a safari in Zimbabwe before we met and this trip was purposely built to include all the lodges and the camps that we had personally selected. We have done many safaris since then in Kenya, South Africa and Botswana. The second time we went to Kenya we stayed at Mara Bushtops, a tented camp in its own conservation area, just outside the Masai Mara Park. Although it was a tented camp, it was very luxurious, as the tents were the largest in Eastern Africa, with stone built showers and washroom, a huge comfortable bed and a large wooden balcony with a Jacuzzi! The camp was built on a hill and we looked out over the savannah of the conservation area, where we could see zebra, elephant and antelope roaming freely.

Each evening, we were treated to five star meals and a good selection of wines from their own wine cellar, which the owner was very proud of, and he would invite guests to visit and enjoy some tastings. Before dinner, we would go on a game drive into the conservation area and, as this belonged to the camp, only other guests were present, so it was very exclusive. We would stop and a table and chairs were laid out in order for us to have our sundowners a Cuba Libra of course! We had the same driver and spotter for the whole of our stay, Daniel and Senna, and they were very good; ensuring that we had a very special stay. One night we did come across a lion, totally invisible in the dark. We were only aware of his presence because of his roaring. Daniel had a spotlight, which he used to light the area where the lion lay – he could not have cared less that we had disturbed his search for a mate, just giving us a rather unwelcoming glance as we looked at him.

The camp was a thirty minute drive from the gates of the park, and we took this route early every morning – there are a lot of camps in the park, which would mean that you avoided this trek each day, but it did not affect our viewing, which was brilliant! Most of our drives were for just half a day, with one being for a full day, when we had breakfast and lunch seated by our vehicle. We were also very lucky that all but one drive was private – just Richard and I, which meant that we could take any route that we wanted, retrace our steps or go somewhere entirely new. Our game spotting was excellent, and we saw a lioness with four cubs, teaching them to hunt, using a flock of guinea fowl as prey; the coupling of a huge lion with his mate – his triumphant roar after the event was deafening! an elusive leopard perched on a high branch who, appreciatively, climbed down for a better view and a cape buffalo cow with a sickly calf who survived a hyena and a lion attack. These were two separate attacks, they were not working together!

On our full-day drive we saw the big five – elephant, lion, leopard, Cape buffalo and black rhino – all within one hour. The rhino was a bit of a cheat, as it was another attempt to repopulate the park with these beasts, reduced by constant hunting for the aphrodisiac properties of their horns. On this occasion, the single rhino stood in a large field, away from the roads, but visible – Daniel did tell us that it was real and a black rhino (the white rhino, which is named because of its "wider" mouth – the South African translation has been misinterpreted, stating white instead of wide); is more common to see on safari, but it was too far away to get a really good sighting, and certainly not within photo distance, even with the size of the lens that we were using.

At the camp, we were able to do a safari on foot, accompanied by a guide, a spotter and a ranger, with a gun. We got up close and personal to termite mounds, but all the animals that we encountered kept their distance. At night, we had to wait to be accompanied by a Masai warrior, when we went for dinner. We thought that our camp was very safe and unlikely to be invaded by any of the wildlife, but one day we came across an okapi on our path, and, after hearing it roaring all night from our tent, we were told that a lion had come into camp in the dark, so this protection was not just a tourist thing! One night, we made the mistake of leaving the exterior light on outside our tent, and when we returned, the light and the entrance to our tent was covered in creepy crawlies – and they were BIG! We had to get inside, so we ran through the opening, closing it behind us as quickly as we could! We did not manage to get inside alone, some of these beasts came in with us and we then had to spray inside with fly killer. The next day, the floor of our tent was covered with the bodies of these gruesome creatures!

On this visit to Kenya, we flew into Nairobi, spending one night in a hotel in the city before taking the small plane which stops at several airstrips serving the camps and lodges in the park. When you land, there are several jeeps waiting for their guests; many of them offering cooling drinks and towels to refresh you after a cramped journey. My main reason for mentioning this is that we had taken too much luggage with us and, due to weight and size, we had to leave some of it at Nairobi Airport for collection on our return. This was mainly due to our camera equipment which is very heavy and bulky. We did not mind doing this, but when we went to collect our luggage, the compound was locked and they could not find the key! It took us about an hour to finally be reconnected with our luggage, and we had visions of having to leave it behind or miss our flight home!

The best safari we had was in South Africa at Ulusaba, Sir Richard Branson's private game reserve. This truly was five-star in so many ways – the camp, the staff, the food, the game and the whole experience. We used our air miles and companion flight, and flew first class with British Airways for about one thousand pounds, as we had to only pay the taxes and this is not much more expensive than economy! We flew into Johannesburg and then took the connecting flight which calls at many camp sites. Our airstrip, about the third stop, was right by the side of our camp. We had booked for four nights. We had paid extra for three of them to do a photographic safari, which meant that we were accompanied by a professional photographer, who would find us the best locations, game and give us tips on how to get the best shots. We had expected to be accompanied by other guests who had made a similar reservation, but we were on our own, and this meant that we had a private game drive every time. But even better, if there was something really worth seeing, the other vehicles had to move out of our way so that we could get the best position for the photograph! We thought that this was brilliant, but I bet that the other guests weren't too happy!

We had great viewing at Ulusaba. This is a private reserve so only the few camps in the area had access, meaning we saw very few jeeps during our game drives. We were out morning, afternoon and evening, enjoying sundowners by the side of our jeep while watching fabulous sunsets. We saw plenty of leopard and they were not perturbed by us watching them; in fact one female walked by the side of our open jeep, so close that you could have stroked her. We didn't of course; not a good idea as we would have likely lost a hand! A huge male was perched on a mound with us parked next to him. It was difficult to take the photo with our long lens, as he was actually too close! We saw all the usual game – loads of elephant, white rhino, prides of lion, and antelope of every description, but some of the smaller encounters were just as memorable. We spent a long time trying to catch images of colourful weaver birds, dangling from their flimsy nests, while they built them up, ready to entice a mate; a dung beetle, rolling his prize possession of a pile of elephant poo; and managed to catch a shot of a chameleon who only comes out at night or tracking George; a lone hippopotamus who would entertain his audience with gaping jaws, territorial protective gestures and the loudest roars and guffaws we have ever heard from these huge creatures.

In the evening, all of the guests would gather at the bar before dinner, enjoying a drink while describing their experiences of the day. It seemed as though everyone saw something different, and we each had a tale to tell. The set meal in the evening was accompanied with wine from the cellar and was really of exceptional quality. All the food, drinks and game drives were included in the price, and of course, when you are paying around five hundred pounds per night, you would expect it to be of the highest standard! This was a fantastic experience and our recommendation would be that, if you want to go on safari, don't try and do it on the cheap – the more you spend, the better your experience will be! Do your research, read the reviews and use an experienced company to help you to plan your holiday as this really will be a holiday of a lifetime – believe me, it's worth it!

CHAPTER 16

New York, USA (9) – New Year 2007/08

This was my first time in New York but Richard had been there before. We arrived in the evening and came out of JFK to get a taxi to the Big Apple. Now, I have got a word of warning here for anyone who is going to New York for the first time, so as you don't fall foul of the same con that we unfortunately came across. The taxi fares for transfers to and from the city and the airport are fixed by the city authorities, and all licensed cab drivers have to adhere to these prices. But, when we left the terminal, we were given a voucher to hand over to the taxis waiting in the ranks, but the person who had given us the voucher then led us out to his taxi which was not actually in the rank. It was a proper yellow cab and we thought nothing of it.

He proceeded to drive into New York City and gave us a commentary on the way, pointing out some of the sporting venues that are located outside of the city. But, when we arrived at our hotel, the Fitzpatrick near Grand Central, he claimed that due to the one way system, it was difficult for him to park in front of the hotel, so he dropped us off at the side, a couple of hundred yards from the hotel lobby. He then charged us two hundred dollars for the transfer! Now at this time, the cost should have been around sixty dollars and it was only at this point that we realised we had been "had". Our driver was a large man and obviously had us locked in his car. It was not the right situation to be in to make a stand and to disagree with his actions, so reluctantly, we paid him two hundred dollars with no tip, of course and we got out of that cab with our luggage intact and put the whole incident down to experience. But it was not a good start to our New York trip.

In the hotel, we found out that the suite we had booked was not available. My heart sank as I thought that we were about to have another disastrous encounter, but we were then told that we had been given an upgrade to one of the penthouse floor suites—the Garden Suite! This was a beautiful room with a bathroom, that was bigger than some of the rooms that we had stayed in in the past! We were told that our neighbouring suite was always used by Liam Neeson whenever he stayed in New York. The suite also had a rooftop garden with amazing views of the city skyline. Unfortunately, at this time of year, it was not a place where we lingered for very long.

We had pre booked tickets to see Spamalot on Broadway, so we did a quick turnaround to get to the theatre in time for the show. It was a rush as we had to walk to Times Square and find the theatre; arriving just in time to order a couple of drinks for now and for the interval and then we sat down and enjoyed this very funny adaptation of the Monty Python film of the same name. We strolled back to our hotel after the show and had a drink in a bar just off Times Square before collapsing into bed, exhausted from our flight and our first day encounter.

The following day we enjoyed a big Irish breakfast at the Fitzpatrick before getting a cab; a bona-fide one this time, down to the pier, where we took the Circle Line ferry around Manhattan. It was cold, and you could only bear to be outside the cabin for a few minutes before retreating back into the warmth of the inside seating area. But even from inside, we had good views as we cruised around Manhattan, over to Ellis Island and past the Statue of Liberty, under the Brooklyn Bridge and up the other side to see the Chrysler Building. The Empire State Building seemed to be visible from every angle, rising above the other skyscrapers that are so synonymous with New York.

It had been six years since 911 when terrorists caused so much chaos and destruction when they brought down the Twin Towers of the World Trade Centre. In 2007, the clearing of the site was still underway – I don't think that they had even decided on what would replace the towers at that point. But we had found a tour on Viator.com which gave us access to the Ground Zero Workshop Museum. This museum is very small and only allowed a small number of visitors at any time – all tickets were presold and were on a fixed time basis. If you weren't there on time, you missed your visiting slot. It was very tastefully done and contained a number of photographs that were taken by the official photographer, who was brought in to record the initial disaster site and the clear-up operation. In addition to the photos there were a number of items taken from the ground zero site, including crushed tin cans that had been melted and welded together as a result of the intense heat generated from the collapse of the building; the clock taken from the subway station located below the World Trade Centre which had stopped at the exact time of the impact of the first plane and other personal items that had been crushed and mutilated during this devastating attack on 9th September 2001.

Many of the photographs had moving stories relating to them, telling us about the searches carried out to retrieve the bodies and remains of the hundreds who had died on that day, including the brave firemen who entered the damaged buildings, without concern for their own lives, trying to rescue those trapped in the upper floors. The stories moved me to tears. One in particular concerned the dogs they had used, to try and find any remains lying in the rubble. These search and rescue dogs are normally brought in to find living people, and as they went through the huge site only finding remains and bodies, the dogs became depressed! So, in order to cheer them up and to motivate them to carry on the search, some of the handlers would lie in the rubble, so that the dogs could get the satisfaction of finding people alive. The sad ending to this tale is that within twelve months of the end of the search, all of the dogs died, due to the toxic fumes that they had inhaled during their hunt.

The following day was New Year's Eve. We had decided not to go to Times Square to see the ball drop as we thought that we would feel a little intimidated by the huge numbers that would be there. We understand that you can expect a million people to fill Times Square and the surrounding streets at midnight, to experience this infamous ritual. But, we still wanted to try and witness some of the atmosphere so we went to Times Square during the day, after a shopping expedition to Saks, Bloomingdales and FAO Schwarz which is a huge toy store where they have a huge piano keyboard on the floor that is played by walking and jumping on the "keys", and was featured in the Tom Hanks film, Big. As we got to Times Square, at around one p.m. it was already crowded as people had started to gather and to claim their space for the night's festivities. We saw the ball held high on its pole on the rooftop of one of the huge skyscrapers and wondered how this insignificant event could cause so much excitement and fervour. We left the crowds and went around the corner to have some lunch in a bar. As we were leaving we heard someone say, "Richard; Richard Battersby?" As we turned around we saw Sarah, the daughter of our neighbour, who had married an American marine, Will, and now lived in Washington DC. She was in New York to celebrate the New Year with her husband, and her sister, Sally, who was standing in Times Square saving their place for that evening. Talk about a small world! Will went to find Sally and held their place, while she came into the bar and joined us for a drink, all of us exclaiming what a coincidence it was and what were the chances of us bumping into one another with all the thousands, if not millions of people who were in New York on that day!

Our celebrations that night would take place on a cruise, sailing past the Statue of Liberty, and then stopping to enjoy the fireworks at midnight. We took a taxi to get to the pier and we made sure that we had given ourselves plenty of time, as the streets and avenues all around Times Square were closed to traffic and we had to take a very long way around, to get from our hotel to the waterside. As we were early, we had a choice of seats and took one right at the front, with great views laid out in front of us as we sailed around Manhattan. The meal was enjoyable and we had plenty of champagne and drinks included in the price, although we did pay for a better bottle of wine to accompany the meal.

At midnight, we braved the cold December night or the January morning depending on how you looked at it and we went on deck to watch the fireworks that lit up the sky of Manhattan. This was a fabulous sight, and we are sure that it was the best location in the city to see this starry spectacular. We returned to the pier at around one a.m. and walked back to our hotel as it was impossible to get a taxi. There were still a lot of revellers out, even at that time, and we had a few issues trying to cross the police barriers that had been set up to help manage the massive crowds that had enjoyed the New Year celebrations. We got back to our hotel at two a.m. and we went to bed exhausted but also exhilarated at being able to experience such a fantastic evening in such an iconic place.

We did not get much of a lie-in on New Year's Day, as we had booked another excursion through Viator.com and we needed to head for Times Square to meet up with our photographer/ guide who would be showing us around the city, taking our photo while we toured. This was an expensive excursion, but how many times do you go on holiday and all of the snaps are of views, of other people or of just one of us ending up in front of the camera. With this tour, we would have some great memories of our holiday TOGETHER!

We started in Times Square and then took the tube to Central Park. We walked through a section of the park and visited the Strawberry Fields memorial, designed and donated by Yoko Ono, in memory of John Lennon who was shot in the Dakota Building that was close by. We proceeded to walk to Little Amsterdam, where we saw some typical brownstone buildings which are so famous in New York and who can forget Rosemary's Baby!

We took the tube again and headed for Brooklyn Bridge, where we walked part way across the huge steel structure to enjoy a different view of Manhattan. From here, we walked to Soho, this actually stands for "south of Houston" and Greenwich Village. So many of the district names we knew from TV, film and news and to visit them all on one morning was quite a challenge. The weather was not kind to us on that day, but the rain had stopped at the start of our walk and although it was grey and chilly, we remained dry for the whole of the morning.

We were exhausted after doing so much walking, so we rested in the afternoon, before our evening excursion out to the Rockefeller Centre and the Top of the Rock. The views from there were fabulous, as you actually get to see the Empire State Building in all its glory. We walked all the way around, enjoying the view of the city at night and then we proceeded to the Rainbow Rooms where we had a table booked. As we entered and we were shown to our table, we had a magnificent view of the Empire State Building again, all lit up, and looking like a shot from "An Affair to Remember" – I could almost imagine Cary Grant sitting at one of the tables! Outside the Rockefeller Centre there is a skating rink and the tallest Christmas tree I have ever seen. The decorations around this area were wonderful, and gave you a real feeling of Christmas in the Big Apple.

On our last day we went to the Empire State Building itself. There were huge queues and we paid to jump the outside queue, but we still had to wait our turn on the inside. There was a lot of maintenance work taking place, which did not help. It was very crowded and it took us an hour to take the two sets of elevators up to the roof balcony. Once we were there, you could not move, as there were so many people cramped, pushing and shoving their way to try and get that iconic shot from the top of this infamous building. And it was so cold! The wind was frosty and chilled you to the bone even though the day was bright and sunny, with wonderful blue skies. I don't know whether it was the crowds, the queues, or the building work that was taking place, but I didn't like the building and I much preferred the Top of the Rock. Besides, you could see the Empire State Building from there, which makes for a much better view.

We strolled back to our hotel, enjoying the last sights of New York including Grand Central Station and the Chrysler Building, which had just missed out on being the tallest building in the world when they put the radio mast on top of The Empire State Building at the last minute, after the Chrysler had been completed.

It is a pity that it never achieved the accolade, as it is a much more beautiful building and is worthier. The ESB is a concrete monstrosity in comparison!

Since this first visit, we have been to New York quite a few times, as we have cruised into the Big Apple and cruised out, twice! The views of Manhattan from the deck of a big cruise ship are magnificent, much better than from the small harbour boats which are a little too low in the water for you to get a great photograph.

During this time, we have seen the development of the World Trade Centre site and we visited it twice – the first time was a walking tour which, we took after the site had been cleared, and they had started to build the memorial and to construct the new surrounding skyscrapers. Our guide was a lady who was working

in the city, close to the World Trade Centre on that fateful day, and had witnessed the effects of the event itself and the aftermath. She took us to the church where the firemen had rested in between searches and was, at that time, a shrine to those who had died in the catastrophe, with letters of thanks, love and despair still on show. We went into one of the repaired buildings close to the site where there was a memorial to the people who had worked at that particular building and lost their lives in the incident, but the small museum that was located at the site was far too busy and not a pleasant stop at that time, so we avoided it.

We walked past the building site that used to be the location of the Twin Towers, and our guide told us about her experience of the day and how people who were not directly affected by the disaster had coped. All of the people in the surrounding buildings had to evacuate and, as there were no buses, taxis or trains running, they all had to walk home that day. She described how everyone walked in silence, with their heads down in sorrow; each person immersed in their own thoughts of remorse, as though they were alone in the world, whilst they were actually surrounded by thousands of people, all reacting in the same manner. She relayed her feelings, her thoughts and her experiences of the event with emotion and empathy, and the tour was very moving. This tour probably sounds rather grim and macabre, but it wasn't. It was tastefully done, informative and has helped us both to really understand what the New Yorkers have gone through.

We have been to New York since the ten-year anniversary and the memorial has been completed and opened to the public. There was still a lot of building work taking place in the surrounding area, but the submerged granite water features and gardens were complete. We queued with many others to enter the memorial gardens and to walk around the two deep pools that have been built on the foundations of the Twin Towers; water cascading over the sides, and disappearing at the centre with the names of all those who had died engraved around the edges. There were roses placed by the side of some of the names, and as we looked, we discovered that today would have been their birthday and this small gesture was a way to personally remember those who had lost their lives in the terrorist attack. The museum was still under construction, so maybe this will be a place to visit on another occasion.

Central Park is a destination that must be visited during a visit to the city. The first time we had a stroll around a small section of the park which was deserted at the time, due to it being very cold, wet and early on New Year's Day! The park is huge and, on a map, it looks like it is the heart of the city. We returned on another visit, to try and see more of this iconic park, and we took one of the horse drawn carriages on a tour around the park. Even using this faster mode of transport we still did not see all of the park, but we did go a lot further than our previous visit, viewing fountains, statues and gardens.

We have taken the open-top bus tour all around New York without stopping, as well as using it as a hop on hop off; stopping at various locations. One location we love is Little Italy, especially in September during the celebrations that take place for the Feast of San Gennaro. The little streets are closed to traffic and are full of stalls, selling food, drink and delicacies – they are crowded with tourists and locals alike, revelling in the atmosphere of this popular festival. We have been able to experience this celebration twice and eaten in different Italian restaurants on both occasions, sitting out and enjoying the chaotic events surrounding us.

On our most recent visit in 2016, we finally went over to Liberty Island to visit the Statue of Liberty. We booked a tour through Viator.com and we were accompanied joining the ferry at Battery Park, visiting the museum and the statue and then crossing to Ellis Island. Cory, our young guide, was very enthusiastic and knowledgeable, and certainly made this a very good way to see, to hear and to understand the history of this iconic structure. We were very lucky as it was late September but we had beautiful clear blue skies and it was warm too – a perfect day to visit and to get some great photos. On Liberty Island, which is in New York State, we went into the museum first, where you learn all about the initial conception and plans for building a memorial statue on this land that would greet ships sailing to the New World. This was followed by photos and descriptions of the design, followed by details of how the platform and the statue were built.

Her full title is actually – the Statue of Liberty (Liberty Enlightening the World), and was designed by Frederic Auguste Bartholdi and was built by Gustave Eiffel – a gift to the people of the United States from the people of France. The statue is made of copper, which is why she appears to be green in colour. The building was completed in 1886 and is a hundred and fifty-one feet tall – the total height, including the plinth, is three

hundred and five feet. During the building, they ran out of money and turned to the people of New York for donations. They had over a hundred and twenty thousand contributors, many of whom gave less than a dollar, but it was enough to get the project completed.[2]

The museum is fascinating and can be visited without a guide, but it was easier for us to have Cory provide all the details while we gazed on at the photos, the plans and the memento's that are on display. From the museum, you start the ascent through the first section of the platform to the viewing platform. There is a lift for those who can't face the climb, but it is small and slow. We only had a short time to walk around the crowded terrace to get views looking up at the statue and over towards Manhattan before we returned to ground level to take photos and to catch the ferry to go to Ellis Island and the National Museum of Immigration. This was the gateway to the United States and, from 1892 to 1954, saw over a hundred and twenty million immigrants enter the country through the nation's busiest immigrant inspection station, now restored and is now a museum.

We have sailed out of New York before on the Queen Mary, and this has to be one of the best sail-aways, as the sight of Manhattan from the Hudson is iconic and this is followed by Lady Liberty raising her hand in a farewell gesture. Of course, you get the same view arriving in New York too, but this is normally very early in the morning, and you need to rise while it is still dark to see this magnificent sight. In 2016, we sailed from the port in New Hampshire which is located by the side of Liberty Island – depending on the side of your cabin, you get great views of the statue, but our ship sailed past Liberty Island towards New York so everyone had an opportunity to see this world famous icon. Once we turned, we sailed out of the Hudson and headed north to cruise the Atlantic and to visit coastal cities in New England before heading for Canada. This is a lovely cruise as we had an overnight in Quebec City, and had stopped in Nova Scotia, Prince Edward Island and Boston. We continued our journey after the cruise, hiring a car and driving through the North-Eastern states that make up New England, leaf-spotting! The colours of the Fall were so dramatic and we had a fabulous ten days staying in some beautiful hotels and admiring the scenery, the sights and the visions of this lovely area.

There is a lot to see and do in New York, and it has to be the most iconic of cities in the USA. But I have heard some people say that they hate it! I love it! There are so many sights that are iconic and known around the world, and seeing them yourself is like being on a huge film set! In fact, you can do a tour with Viator.com to visit locations that are used in TV series like Sex in the City – we've not done this, but it is an option. New York certainly deserves to be on our list, and in its lofty position in the top ten.

CHAPTER 17

Barcelona, Spain (37) – March 2008

We flew to Barcelona on EasyJet from Liverpool Airport. For Europe/short haul holidays the cheap, budget airlines are fine – we have flown on EasyJet and Ryanair many times. But in our view, you should never leave it to the last minute to arrive at the airport for check-in. There can quite often be queues and awkward passengers who seem to take ages to check in. We would recommend that you allow as much time as you can if you are flying on a scheduled flight, allow at least two hours before your flight.

On this occasion, when we arrived at John Lennon Airport, there were huge queues as the computers had broken down and no one was able to check-in. With EasyJet, there is just one queue for all flights and it stretched all the way along the hall and had started to wrap around itself too. There was panic on everybody's face as it became clear what chaos was being caused by this IT malfunction, including ours. But we had no need to be worried; the staff obviously had things in hand, even though they did not make the passengers clear about this.

As we were queuing, they started to call forward everyone on the Barcelona flight and obviously this is what they would be doing for each flight in turn, until they had got the queue down to a manageable size. We checked in and headed straight for the plane, no time to shop! But it did mean that we were in our seats and the flight took off on time, despite the pandemonium in the terminal!

This holiday, over the Easter weekend, had been done on the cheap and, once we had gone through immigration, collected our bags and gone through customs, we took the airport bus to the main square that lies at the top of Las Ramblas. I had selected a hotel, the Continental Palacete, also known as the Pink Palace, as I had understood it to be located on Las Ramblas. It was on a street off the square but in the opposite direction, and it ended up that we had a long walk to get to our hotel and an even longer one every night when we came out to eat.

The hotel had looked wonderful on the internet – really old and grand and it included breakfast and a twenty-four hour buffet, which included wine and beer. I had booked a "sol" room as in the pictures it looked as though this had a balcony overlooking Las Ramblas, but when we entered we discovered that we had a very small room with a large window that didn't open properly because of the tiny railing cage outside the window. This made the hotel look pretty from the outside, but was totally impractical in the room. Although we were disappointed with our room, the staff had provided us with a bottle of champagne as a gift, as it was our sixth wedding anniversary.

Las Ramblas is wonderful and I would recommend that anyone going to Barcelona must walk down this street at least once during their stay. It is a very wide street with cafés, stalls and entertainers down the central pedestrian, tree-lined avenue and lots of restaurants and shops lining each side where the road runs. It has to be one of the most famous streets in the world, and it certainly deserves this accolade. You will find all manner of food and hospitality along here or in one of the plazas or streets that run off the main thoroughfare.

It is so entertaining walking down the street as firstly you will see living statues, then we found stalls selling pets, yes, live animals including small rabbits, birds, fish, hamsters, mice, weasels and lizards; followed by flower stalls and finally crafts and souvenirs. We walked all the way down until we reached the sea wall, where we stopped and found a Tapas bar to enjoy some lunch over a nice bottle of wine.

We went through the old quarter on the way back to our hotel. This is where the cathedral is located, but on this visit, it was being cleaned and repaired and was covered in scaffolding and a tarpaulin so it did not look very pretty,

At the hotel we tried some of the free wine on offer but it was warm; not good for a white wine and it did not taste good at all. Most of the snack items from the buffet were also unavailable; the only things left on offer were the things that nobody wanted to eat – including us! We tried the buffet for breakfast the next day, and it was not good. It was like a self-service shop where you picked items from containers and it was not at all appealing, so we did not bother again after this first attempt. Our second day in Barcelona fell on Easter Sunday, and the city was packed! We queued for a long time to get an upstairs seat on the open-top city bus tour. Luckily it was sunny, but it was bitterly cold with a chill wind blowing in our faces as we drove along. The open-top buses are a great way to see the city and you have a running commentary in English through your headphones. It is timed perfectly with the sites as you drive past them. We admired many of Gaudi's weird

and wonderful buildings with roof tops that look like the backs of dragons, and curved walls that are brightly coloured and look so amazing compared with the solemn brick architecture back at home.

On this first day, we stayed on the bus and did the full circuit, passing the site of the 1992 Olympics; the government buildings;

Barcelona's football stadium; the beach and the port. But the next day we took the bus again and this time we got off twice, firstly at the infamous Gaudi designed church of Sagrada Familia.

After a hundred years, it is still under construction and there is no estimated completion date. It is obvious that they have concentrated on getting the outside of this monumental project done first, and although this is not quite finished, it is well on its way to being completed. The intricacy of the detail on the towers, the walls, the doors and the arches is quite remarkable. I loved it, but I am sure that this is a matter of personal taste and you either love it or you hate it. It is a huge building and photographs do not do it justice, you have to see it with your own eyes. It is very modern and so different from anything that I have seen before.

Inside it is still a building site, and it is here that it is apparent that the church will not be complete in my lifetime. Inside the pillars are made of different types of stone. Some of them resemble trees rising high into the vault of the church, splitting like branches, as they reach up to the sky. Others are twisted and they look as though they are moving as you walk around this wondrous sight. The time it has taken to get this far and the expense of the ongoing building is immense, but it is good to know that those continuing with Gaudi's vision are not taking any shortcuts to complete the project quicker but are sticking to his original dream structure.

We continued our bus journey and went to the Parque Guell which was another area designed by Gaudi. Located at the top of a hill, the views from the park are spectacular and worth a visit just to see them. But the main reason for coming is to see Gaudi's playful visionary architecture in all its glory. From the moment when you enter and see the fairy-tale, almost gingerbread-like houses at the gateway to the pavilion and raised viewing platform, you realise that you are somewhere very special.

We returned to Barcelona in June 2013, and came back to this park as we both enjoyed it so much. They now have a Gaudi film show in 3D. This stop in Barcelona was after a cruise on the maiden voyage of the new Royal Princess, sailing from Southampton to Barcelona.

On this second visit, our hotel was located close to Las Ramblas, which was very convenient for finding restaurants in the evening. We were there on the eve of the festival for Saint John, a big night in Catalonian tradition, when they celebrate the summer solstice. There are fireworks and groups of people, clothed in fancy dress, parading through the streets with lighted torches, all with police escort to ensure that the party mood does not get out of hand. Our room at the hotel, the Catalonia Ramblas, had a rooftop terrace, and that night on the 23rd of June, we enjoyed the fireworks that lit up the night sky all around us.

In 2015 we had another short weekend in Barcelona, and this time we did a Segway around the Gothic area and the beach front and a day trip to France and Andorra, which meant that we had another country crossed off our list. The Segway was fun, although marred by a fellow passenger who fell off twice, due to not paying attention and clipping the kerbs of the narrow cobbled paths in the Gothic area. She was not badly hurt; more embarrassed than injured, but it did put a dampener on the trip. The trip to Andorra was long and not very exciting. We had three stops on the way, one in the Spanish hills, another in France and then finally Andorra, which is pretty much just a duty-free shopping town, albeit located in a very nice valley amongst high mountains.

There is such a lot to see in Barcelona and, with its location on the Mediterranean; it normally offers good weather to be able to spend a very nice weekend there. If you time it right, you may be able to see a football match at Camp Nou (the New Camp), Barcelona's home ground – try Viator.com!

CHAPTER 18

Yosemite National Park (23), The Grand Canyon (1), USA – May 2008

This tour was organised to celebrate Richard's sixtieth birthday, and we selected to do a fly drive through the parks and canyons of Western America. Most of the trip was done through Thomas Cook, but there were a few places where we wanted to stay in specific rooms at our choice of hotel, so we organised these ourselves. We find this to be a great option, and our Thomas Cook agency in Meadowhall, especially Jane Gill one of the travel advisors, is very accommodating in adapting their tour around our precise requirements. We have got to know Jane very well over the years we have been travelling and she is always eager to hear about our latest adventures on our return.

On this trip we were flying from Manchester to San Francisco via Chicago, as Manchester was a convenient option for us as my parents lived just ten minutes from the airport, so we could park the car outside their house and take a taxi – much cheaper than airport parking. When we arrived though, there was chaos, as the luggage belt had broken down and although they were checking people in for their flights, we had to then carry our own luggage to another area, for them to carry it out to the planes.

Our check-in queue had three flights allocated to the same desks, which meant that we had people going to Barcelona, Barbados and Chicago, all creeping along a very, very slow check-in line. Just as we got to the front, they called forward everyone going to Barbados; obviously they were due to leave before us. So we had to wait as many people filed past us to the front of the queue to check in for their flight – very annoying: just five minutes later and we'd have been through!

But once we did check-in, we then took our luggage around the corner to the designated site where we had been told to go, and could not believe the pandemonium that greeted us! There were cases everywhere, just dumped where people had left them, in order to board their flight. We were criss-crossing people and bags, trying to find others bound for the Chicago flight. We did not take any chances and we stayed with our bags until we knew that they had been taken through for our flight. I am sure that a lot of people in Barcelona and Barbados were disappointed when they were waiting at their carousels, as there was no way that they could have sorted out that mess to get the right case on the right flight for every passenger!

The flight to Chicago was around nine hours and in Chicago we had to go through immigration, collect our luggage and transfer it to the San Francisco flight, which meant that we had to go through security again and then face a four-hour wait at O'Hare airport. Now, anyone who has flown through or out of the USA will know that their airports are not very accommodating. Before 911, the turn-around time was very quick at airports, and the Americans used air transport like buses, due to the country being so huge. But after the terrorist attack this changed travel in the USA, and now security is a lot stricter, you have to arrive early and prepare to queue for security checks and be at the airport for a lot longer than you used to be. But they have not changed the layout or facilities in the airports and LAX is the worst by the way! They only offer fast food take-away stalls or commercialised restaurants, with very little seating and limited menus, and the bars are mainly sports joints with stools at the counter and the odd seat here and there. You do not have a choice of a nice meal and a bottle of wine seated in relative comfort, while you wait for your connection. But in Chicago Airport, we managed to find a seat in a bar and had a few drinks to while away the time. As a result of this, we slept on the second leg that took us four and half hours to San Francisco.

On arrival, we had to wait for our luggage, but it did all arrive, which was a blessing. We took the monorail around to the car hire location, and had to queue again for our Alamo rental. So far, all we seemed to have done on this holiday is queue for everything – is this the way it's always going to be now when we travel? We had a nice large 4x4 car and we took the thirty-minute drive to stay at the Hilton Garden Inn on the outskirts of San Francisco. We decided to stay close to the airport on our first night, as we knew that we would be arriving late and would be tired, so this was a very much deserved stopover after almost twenty-four hours travelling.

We set off for Yosemite stopping in Groveland for lunch. The day had started dull and overcast and as we approached Yosemite National Park it got even worse! We drove through mist, low clouds and pouring rain! We stopped once at a photo spot to take a picture of the vistas that were supposed to lie before us but, to be honest, we couldn't see a thing, and got soaked in the process. We drove past Bridal Veil Falls, and had intended on stopping there for a photo, but we would have got wet for a very dreary snapshot, so we didn't bother! We were using the GPS to get to our hotel, the Tenaya Lodge, which was located just outside the National Park, but the navigation system was sending us up a dirt track and saying that we had twenty-five miles to go! We knew that this was wrong, so we turned around and headed back to the park to retrace our tracks.

We eventually found the hotel and were very pleased with our choice. This was a huge hotel but the public areas were cosy and beautifully decorated and it felt like a large hunting lodge. Our room was lovely, with a view onto grassland and a wooded area. We ate in the Sierra Restaurant and I had elk, which was very tasty.

We decided to do an organised tour of the park, arranged through the hotel, as this would provide us with information on the park and an expert's eye if we saw any wildlife during our drive. It was very cold that day, not what we had expected for the end of May. There were only seventeen on the trip, a nice number for getting on and off a tour bus. Glacier Point was closed due to bad weather, so we spent a bit longer at Mariposa Grove with the giant redwoods, which, by the way, are huge!

We were then told that they had opened Glacier Point, so we made a mad dash to get up there before the crowds beat us to it. There was no point, as we were met by thick, icy fog instead. It was so thick, that you couldn't see any of the valleys below us, in fact, we could not even see the edge of the path in front of us – very disappointing. We drove back down into the valley where we had some lunch.

From the café, we walked to see Yosemite Falls which were actually visible and quite spectacular as with the rains and the recent snow melt, they had quite a volume of water falling over the precipice. Because of the mist that lingered during our whole day in Yosemite, we did not see anything of Half Dome and El Capitan kept playing a game of now you see me now you don't! We did get a good view of Bridal Veil Falls before we left, which was a small consolation. Although we did not get good views of the key features in the park, we did find it very interesting, and we realised how beautiful this place could be in the right weather!

The next day we were leaving to drive to Death Valley, and we were concerned as we had been told that Tioga Pass had been closed due to snow, and that was our planned route. Luckily, as we checked at reception on the driving conditions for the day, we were told it had opened that morning and was just passable. We faced a long drive today, so we set off early, retracing the route we had taken on arrival, to find the pass that would take us past the Sierra Nevada, and on to Death Valley. We left at eight-twenty, and stopped in Yosemite Valley for breakfast. We also stopped a number of times to take photos, as the weather was so much better than the day before, and we were able to get a few shots of El Capitan and the falls, before we started our long journey east.

The Tioga road was surprisingly quiet and we were not held up by slow moving traffic, in front of us. We still had a very heavy mist on the journey, so the views were not as good as they should have been and there was still a lot of snow at the side or the road creating four to five feet deep drifts in some places. At one point the fog was so dense that it was difficult to see just five feet in front of us, which made our going very slow as we compensated for the poor visibility. The temperature dropped to thirty-five degrees, but, after we had taken a break at Whoa Nellie Deli which was at the edge of the park, it started to rise and the skies cleared, to offer us beautiful views of the mountain range and the wide open desert plain in front of us.

We stopped in Bishop for lunch at a real American deli and had a sandwich – there was so much choice, just the way you see it on American TV shows. We carried on for almost four hours, without stopping, to the Furnace Creek Ranch where we were staying for one night. The rooms at the ranch are basic but large and clean. We had a patio door which led out onto a seating area, where we had some chairs, to be able to enjoy our sundowners in relative luxury. The temperature now was ninety-five degrees – it seemed crazy that we had gone from winter to spring to high summer in just a few hours.

Our neighbours at the ranch were bikers – Pam, Roger, Jenny and Dave, from Nevada, all retired and were enjoying travelling around on their Harley's. We joined them in the steakhouse that night and had a great meal with really good company, chatting about life, the universe and everything.

The following day we did some sightseeing around Death Valley, going to see most of the sites that are highlighted in the guide book. We then continued to our next stop, which was Las Vegas where we stayed at the Luxor Resort for two nights. I have covered Las Vegas in Chapter four but it is worthwhile telling you about the excursions that we did while we stayed there on this occasion.

We went to Hoover Dam with a tour company called Comedy on Deck. Our guide was called "Uncle George" and he was really good – very informative, but also very entertaining and funny. When he asked us for our names, he asked Richard if he could call him Dick, and that was what he was called all day, whether he liked it or not! As we headed for the dam, he handed out fake glasses and moustaches to everyone on board, and told us to put them on when we reached the security check. Since 911, the USA has taken the threat of another terrorist attack very seriously and the possible damage and devastation that would result if there was an attack on the Hoover Dam does not bear thinking about. So the security checks for cars and coaches approaching the dam and crossing the highway that sits on top of it are manned by the military, and are obviously a very serious inspection. But today, when the guard climbed aboard the bus, he gazed on thirty people all wearing pop-out, wobbly-eye glasses and moustaches and his response was, "This lot all looks familiar!" It was all done with good humour and was certainly a memory of the day.

We had a walk around the dam and went down into the workings of the hydro-electric plant. I can't tell you a thing about what we were told as, in my personal opinion, this was a man's thing! We walked across the road over the dam, and looked on to Lake Mead and down into the deep valley below, where the Colorado used to run before it was harnessed by this colossal, monumental construction, that defied all the limitations of similar structures at that time. Our tour continued to Boulder City, where we had some lunch and then to Ethel M's Chocolate Factory before returning to Vegas by two p.m. I would certainly recommend this tour as an alternative for visiting Hoover Dam, as it was quite different and amusing but still very informative.

It is difficult knowing when and where I should be putting entries into this book, as we have returned to quite a few of the fifty places several times, and I never know whether I should put all the entries together in the chapter when we do the first visit there, or come back to them again from time to time when they are part of other trips and holidays. The first time we went to the Grand Canyon was in 2001 when we had a weekend in Las Vegas (Chapter 4), but, as that was only a short stop, I decided to wait until this chapter to cover our main visit there, because the Grand Canyon was voted number one on the "Fifty Places to see Before You Die" list. And, this was also the third time that we went to Vegas and we did it twice during the holiday, returning at the end of the tour for four nights for Richard's sixtieth birthday. So, I apologise if this is confusing and seems a bit haphazard, but I hope you will understand the reasons for this.

We left Las Vegas for our drive to the Grand Canyon. This took us over the Hoover Dam and we were surprised that this was still allowed, with the fear of terrorist attacks. The view while driving over was wonderful, and we stopped in a parking layby on the other side, to take photographs of the dam, Lake Mead and the valley below the dam. From this spot, you got a much better view of the dam than the day before, when we were actually on it. You could clearly see the high water mark against the walls when they have to open the dam and let some of the water escape into the valley beyond. With global warming and the demand on the water catchment from the dam, I don't think it reaches this height very often.

We continued our drive through Kingsman and Williams, taking a little bit of Route Sixty-Six, which still runs through Williams and is commemorated in this smart little town. This is where the railway runs from, that takes you to the Grand Canyon and it is a popular overnight stop for those visiting the canyon who do not want to pay the price of staying in the National Park itself. We had booked to stay at the El Tovar Hotel and had made a point of booking it very early, so that we could have a suite with a partial canyon view. There are quite a few different categories of accommodation at the canyon, including Bright Angel and the El Tovar Hotel, which is by far the most luxurious of them all, with a price to match!

We arrived at the canyon rim at around four p.m. and the first thing that we did was to stop at the ridge before going to the hotel. We parked and walked the short distance to find ourselves standing on the edge of the Grand Canyon with the huge ravine laid out before us. To say it was a jaw-dropping sight is an understatement – all I could say was "WOW!"

This was not actually my first sight of the Grand Canyon. In 2001 we had done a helicopter flight from Las Vegas and we had actually landed on the bottom of the canyon by the Colorado River. This trip is a very popular excursion from Vegas, and can be done with lots of different experiences including just a flight over, river rafting on the river, or, as we had done, a touchdown with snacks on the canyon bottom. The flight was amazing and we had front seats coming back, as we sped along the top of the canyon to have the floor disappear from under us as we leapt over the canyon ridge. It was like a roller coaster as we twisted and dipped into the canyon and over the rim. As we returned to Vegas and flew along the strip, it was night time so we had the added bonus of seeing Vegas from the air lit up like a fairyland. I need to add, that when we were waiting to board the helicopter, that the Bee Gees came through the door, having just taken the same trip that we were going on. So it could be that my bum touched the same spot where Barry Gibb had just been sitting! What a claim to fame!

Back to 2008, Richard had said that the helicopter flight did not give us the best view of the canyon and now I could understand exactly what he meant. The Grand Canyon village, is the main site for all activities and accommodation, including the station for the Williams train, the hotel, El Tovar and all the shops and the cafés, and certainly offers magnificent views across the chasm. This is where you can walk down the canyon walls and it is also the starting point for the horse treks that take you to the bottom of the gorge, allowing you to stay overnight if you want to. We took the easy option of just staying at the village and enjoying that fabulous view, along with hundreds of others, as this is a very busy spot.

We checked into our hotel and our suite, which had a huge balcony that looked out over the Indian range that is based at the hotel and had a view of the canyon beyond – a great location for our Cuba Libra's that evening. The hotel is lovely and luxurious with a fine dining restaurant, as well as a bar that serves as a café too.

The following morning we had booked the sunrise tour and we had to be up at three-forty-five a.m. to get to our departure point at Bright Angel. We arrived early, and it was still dark when our bus came to pick us up and once the entire group were on board, we headed for Powell Point. I should add that there were not many on our tour, so we had the sunrise almost to ourselves. As we arrived, it was starting to get light but it was a good few minutes before the sun actually started to peek above the rim. The colours on the canyon sides reflected the rising sun, changing with every moment as it took its daily route high into the sky. I don't think that our photos did it justice, as the scene was just so wonderful to watch and, of course, the view from this spot was amazing.

We returned to the hotel for breakfast and then went on the Desert Tour which took us to lots of different viewing points along the rim, as well as the Watch Tower – a modern building that has been built in the Pueblo Indian style. You can climb the tower for views of the canyon, but it is not necessary as you can see just as well from ground level. There is also a small museum in the car park near the tower, which can while away a few minutes. Some of the paintings done by children are really pleasant to see.

After four hours, we returned to the village where we had a drink, a stroll around the shops and stopped at the replica Indian settlement where they had some souvenir shops and also were entertained with an Indian ritual, including dancing, singing and chanting.

We would recommend that you stay in the National Park for at least one night, so as you can either do the sunset or the sunrise tour. There are a lot of choices for accommodation that is right for all budgets and although it is probably more expensive than staying in Williams, you cannot enjoy the views at all times of the day if you are not actually staying at the canyon.

We went back to the Grand Canyon in 2014, when we did a tour with Titan called the Awesome National Parks of the USA, but on this occasion, we just had an afternoon at the Grand Canyon and, in total honesty, we saw very little of the canyon, as the coach could not find a parking space at one spot and so drove on to the village and, if this was the first time for anyone

on our tour, I'm afraid they did not really get a good opportunity to see this remarkable and mesmerising natural monument in all its glory. Both Richard and I agree that the Grand Canyon deserves its number one spot in the fifty places list – it has to be the most wonderful natural wonder anywhere on earth!

On this tour we stayed at Williams, which is a really lovely town, and certainly makes the most of having Route Sixty-Six still running through its centre. Some of our tour did the morning flight over the canyon, but they had to be up very early, as they had a long drive back to the canyon to pick up their plane, retracing the route that we had taken the previous day. This was not ideal and if the weather had not been good, they would have been very disappointed.

Back to 2008; from the Grand Canyon we drove on to Monument Valley. It did not take too long, about three and a half hours, and that was after we had stopped at a lookout point as we approached the end of the canyon, which offered us a different perspective. We stayed at Goulding's Lodge, which, I think, is the only place to stay that is close to the National Park. The rooms are nicely furnished and are quite large, but the main bonus was a little veranda that looked out onto Monument Valley.

Goulding's Lodge is a famous location in its own right, and there is a museum on the grounds telling you the story of Harry and "Mike" Goulding. Mike being the nickname for his wife, but everyone called her this. He set up the trading post by working with the local Indians and it became a very popular place for movie stars, directors and camera crew etcetera to stay, while they were on location filming in the National Park. John Wayne was a regular guest and there was a shack on show, which was named after him, and used as part of a movie set. Even if you don't stay at Monument Valley and have a day visit only, it is worth visiting Goulding's for the gift shop and the museum; the restaurant is good too.

You cannot drive yourself around Monument Valley; you have to take an organised tour using old school buses. It can be uncomfortable and dusty, but the guides are very informative and we stopped at several locations learning about the geology, the Navajo Indians and the locations that are most recognisable from many Hollywood films, especially cowboy epics directed by John Ford.

Many of the buttes and mesas have names depending on their current resemblance to day to day objects like Left Mitten (and Right Mitten), the Cockerel, the Spear, John Wayne's Boot, the Window and many others. I bet you can guess the names of some of the photos on this page? But you do need quite a vivid imagination to see all of the links.

The tour started at four p.m. when it was a little cooler, as during the day the temperature can soar. We went into a Hogan, a typical home of the Navajo Indians, and I had my hair tied into an Indian bun. We ate at Goulding's and then spent a long time on our veranda looking at the night sky. There was so little light pollution here, as Goulding's is the only place for miles around, that the sky was a myriad of twinkling jewels and the constellations stood out like signposts in the clear dark sky.

We set the alarm the following morning to be able to get up for the sunrise. But, and here is another word of warning for anyone who may visit Monument Valley in the future, when they say that the sunrise is at six am, the sun will be up at that time and gone five minutes later! We set our alarm for five forty-five, and when I got up and looked out of our window the sight was breath-taking with so many colours and the buttes silhouetted against a perfect orange glow. I went to the bathroom, washed my face, got dressed a matter of maybe ten minutes at the most and that golden hour had gone. Should I say it was more a golden five minutes than a golden hour, which is what they say all photographers should look for! Richard never even saw it as he always rises after me. Never mind; a reason to return some day!

We had a very early breakfast at six thirty, and we set off for our next destination at eight, driving to Page and then stopping at Kanab to go to the Frontier Movie Town museum, a bit of light hearted fun to break our journey to Bryce Canyon National Park. Because we were early, we drove into the park and went to a couple of the sites to look at the Bryce amphitheatre and the Hoodoos. We stayed at Bryce Canyon Lodge which is located in the park and had a log cabin at the site. Another option is to stay at Ruby's Inn which is located just outside the park gates. We stayed there on our Titan tour in 2014 and it was very nice and certainly close enough to the park entrance to get an early start if that is what you want to do. Bryce is very different from the Grand Canyon, as it is a huge crater into the earth, full of hoodoos, spires and windows and it is very beautiful to view. It is so big that you cannot capture it in a photo that gives it the justice that it deserves, but it is well worth a visit. Just give yourself enough time to explore the different viewing platforms, and maybe even walk down to the bottom of the canyon.

The next day we headed for Zion National Park, which is about an hour and a half from Bryce Canyon. We stopped in Springdale for lunch, which is the closest town, and the main spot for hotels and motels if you are not staying in the park itself. This is a nice town with lots of shops, bars and restaurants. To get to Springfield from Bryce you have to go through a mountain tunnel that only allows for one-way traffic, so you may have to queue before being allowed through. The scenery along this route is stunning; not in the tunnel of course, but when you come out the other side, and it has to be one of the most beautiful I have ever driven along. We were staying in Zion Lodge so we had a permit to drive into the park and use the car park, but otherwise you have to use the public shuttle bus to actually enter the park.

In the park there is a bus that takes you down the single road deep into the valley, and stops at several scenic points. As our room wasn't ready, we took the bus and we went to Big Bend National Park and the Temple of Shahavar. This park is very different from the Grand Canyon and Bryce, as you are on the valley floor, looking up at the huge mountains that surround you. This park is a must for any trekkers or serious walkers as the treks up into the heights would be amazing. We stayed on terra firma and enjoyed the views from ground level.

The following day we did something neither of us had ever done before – we went mule trekking! We went to the coral where we were allocated a mule or a horse, depending on your experience. I had Buckstop and Richard rode Bridie. We had to hoist ourselves up onto the saddle, which is no mean feat, and then we trotted off, in a convoy, on our half hour ride into the Valley of the Patriarchs. It was not a long ride and the scenery was not spectacular, but it was good fun and certainly different.

We then took the road back to Vegas, having done a very big loop to see all these wonderful National Parks and Monuments. It took us two and half hours to get to the Strip, which we drove down in relish, enjoying the sights on either side. On this second stop, we stayed for four nights at the Venetian which has to be one of my favourite hotels in Vegas. The pure luxury and extravagance of this mega– hotel is something to behold. I believe that you either love Vegas or you hate it, and we LOVE it! We left our car with the valet parking and went to check-in, which did not take long. We paid for a room upgrade as this is where we would be staying to celebrate Richard's sixtieth birthday on the 6th of June. Our suite was absolutely amazing. I have never stayed anywhere that is so large and opulent as this!

As you walked through the door we had a bar with seating. This led to a huge open-plan lounge and dining room with an enormous TV and there was a TV at the bar too. You then went through to the bedroom and finally the bathroom, which, by the way, was bigger than our bedroom back at home. We had a huge walk-in shower, an enormous Jacuzzi bath, a dressing table and another TV. That made four televisions in total, including the one in the bedroom! How much television can you be expected to watch on vacation? The total size of the suite was around fifteen hundred square feet.

The following day, we returned to the Grand Canyon! But this time we flew to the North Rim, which is the less visited area. The Grand Canyon Village is on the South Rim. We were picked up from the Venetian at six oh five a.m. to check-in at the private airport for our seven-thirty flight. The views from the plane were fabulous but the turbulence was really bad; the worst I had known, up until that point anyway! We were picked up from the landing strip and taken to the ranch where we all received a briefing about the events for that day. There were six others on the tour. We had booked the ATV adventure, another first for this holiday, and we were surprised to find that the other six younger members of our group opted to go in a jeep to the rim – very much the easy option! At first, even after the instruction briefing and the fact that we started slowly, I was very nervous, and when we actually set off on the tour and went at some speed, I was in even more fear for my life. I could not control the ATV, and it seemed to go in every direction other than the one we were supposed to be following! But, once I got the hang of it, it was great fun, and I really enjoyed our little adventure. In fact, since that time we have done quite a few ATV rides, and it is certainly something that I would recommend for anyone with a taste for adventure.

We were out for a total of two hours, and we went right up to the ridge, which offered us amazing views of the Colorado River and the canyon, from a totally different angle than we had experienced before. We even saw some rafts going down the river. At South rim, the canyon walls are so steep you can't see the river down below, but here it was quite clearly visible. When we returned to the ranch, my arms ached from controlling the ATV, but the pain soon subsided after a good lunch and a stroll around, before taking the flight back to Vegas.

Now, as I said, the turbulence was awful going out to the ranch, and almost the worst I had ever known – well, that is because the flight back was even worse! I suffer from travel sickness and although I have found that the wrist bands help me with motor travel, they did not help me with this return flight. Oh my God! I felt so ill! All I could do when we got back to our room was just to lie down for a few hours and let it pass!

By the evening, I had recovered, and we went to see Love at the Mirage. This was a Cirque de Soleil production using the music of the Beatles as a backing for their acrobatics and dance. It was one of the most amazing shows that I have ever seen! It was so good that when we returned to Vegas in 2010 we went again, and if we ever return to Vegas, we plan on going to see it for the third time – it was that good!

The next day was Richard's birthday. We could not start with champagne as we were going on an excursion to drive a dune buggy, but we had breakfast in our room; laid out on our beautiful dining table in our luxurious suite, and there was certainly enough to eat! We were picked up and taken to an office, where we were fitted out with our helmet and we picked up the buggy. We were the only ones on this excursion – very private! From the minute we left the office, we had a forty-five minute drive to the Valley of Fire where Richard had a quick lesson on how to drive the buggy and then we were off, following our guide around this barren landscape. I was the passenger, and held on for grim life! It was very hot, dusty and bumpy, and there were some difficult climbs and descents that Richard handled really well. We drove through sand dunes, very quickly, skidding along the way but, miraculously, we stayed upright! It was great fun, and I am certain that it made Richard's day quite special.

Back at the hotel, we had champagne waiting for us and then in the evening we went to the Country Club at Wynn's for a meal, where I had arranged for a birthday cake to be presented to him for our dessert. It did not go quite to plan, as they came up and asked me when we arrived about when I wanted the cake to be delivered, rather spoiling the surprise, but, as we were able to sit outside for our meal, it was a lovely experience. After dinner, we went to the Playboy Club at Palms and the Moon Night Club. I had arranged this as a surprise, but it was not as exclusive, as I thought it would be, but we did have some magnificent views of Vegas from the balcony at the night club. I think, all in all, it was a special day for him and one that he would remember.

Our final day in Vegas started with steak and eggs in our room – something you have to try in the USA, as it is just an amazing breakfast and certainly sets you up for the day. We spent the rest of the day walking around the city, visiting many of the hotels and shopping malls. Before we set off, Richard gave me one thousand dollars in cash, for me to spend in the shops on anything that I wanted. I could not believe his generosity and his thoughtfulness; after all, this was his special holiday! Needless to say, I did not struggle to spend the money as the shops in Vegas are wonderful with so much to offer, and at great prices, as they are all in competition with one another.

Our holiday ended when we returned the car to the airport in Las Vegas, and flew home to Manchester, this time flying directly with no stopover or changes. This was a great holiday and, except for Yosemite, we had great weather. The parks and canyons are all so different and are just awesome!

On our tour with Titan in 2014, we also went to Arches National Park and Canyonlands National Park. We started in

Denver and the coach tour took us through the Rockies National Park before stopping in Rapid City where we went to Mount Rushmore National Monument and the Crazy Horse Monument. We stopped at Devils Tower in Wyoming, which is well worth a visit, before going to Yellowstone National Park. This was the first national park in the USA, but on our visit, we had miserable weather and we were staying outside the park, which meant that we had long drives on arrival, during the tour and on leaving. We stopped for an hour in Salt Lake City, before moving on to Bryce, Zion and the Grand Canyon. The tour finished in Phoenix. It took fourteen days and we travelled through seven states. Our guide who accompanied us all the way was so informative and we learned so much about American history; the story of the Red Indian and details about the geology, flora and fauna of the region. The hotels where we stayed were a bit mixed, but, as you expect of the United States of America, all were large and comfortable, and we certainly could not complain.

CHAPTER 19

Dubai, United Arab Emirates (38) – November 2008

Now at this point I am not saying that we were going away too often, but over the summer, after visiting the USA, we went to Egypt (Nile cruise), and had weekend breaks in Denmark (Copenhagen), France (Carcassonne), and Italy (Pisa) and now we were at the new Terminal 5 at Heathrow to fly to Dubai. As Richard looked at the screen to see where we should check-in, he stood staring for what seemed like several minutes. When I asked him what was wrong, he said, "I can't remember where we're flying to!" – in his defence, it was very early, and we had been on the road since three a.m.!

When we went to check-in we discovered that Elegant Resorts, our agent for this weekend break, had not reserved us our seats and, as a result, we were not sitting together on this very long flight. This was the very last time that we ever left it to chance on seat selection and since this date we have made sure that we have seat reservations, to ensure that we are seated together and, wherever possible, we get extra legroom! Needless to say, it was not a pleasant flight, as we were both in middle seats on opposite sides of the plane. To make matters worse, it was a very bumpy flight and at that time, I was very nervous whenever we went through turbulence, and I did not have Richard to grab hold of every time the plane jumped and swayed! I have now read that turbulence should be seen as a hole in the road, if you were driving. As an experienced driver, you go over the bump but you keep control of the car, and that is just what the pilot does, possibly trying to manoeuvre the plane to avoid too big a bump. I'm not so nervous now.

We arrived in Dubai, almost an hour early, but our transfer was waiting for us and we were very quickly through with our luggage, through immigration and security, and off to our hotel, the Al Qasr. Our room was nicely decorated, it was a reasonable size and it had a beautiful balcony that looked onto the Gulf and across to the Palms, where we could make out the new Atlantis in the distance. The Al Qasr is part of a resort complex which has two hotels, villas, shopping mall and many restaurants, as well as a canal that connects all of them. We took one of the dhows that transports you along the canal, dropping you at the different sites along its banks including the spa, shopping mall, a market place and the restaurants. They are only available to residents staying at the resort. It was very warm, as you would expect for the United Arab Emirates, with clear blue, cloudless skies. On this, our first morning, we went to the souk, which was surprisingly quiet, but all of the restaurants were very busy.

There are also paths and walkways that wind around the resort, connecting all of the key sites and from these you had a fine view of the Burj Al Arab, the tallest hotel in the world, and the first if not the only seven-star hotel too. Set against the blue sky, it really did resemble a huge sail, and was a beautiful sight to see. As it stands on its own promontory, there are no other buildings close to it that could spoil that spectacular, iconic view.

In the evening we had dinner at MJ's Steakhouse, which was located at the Al Qasr. It was a lovely warm evening and we sat outside. We enjoyed an excellent meal with wine, but it was very expensive. When we were in Dubai, the exchange rate was not too good and where holidays here in the past were good value and you could get some really good bargains, this was not the case when we were there. A bottle of mediocre wine cost around fifty pounds! But this was our first chance to try Wagyu Beef, the famed Japanese beef that is known for its tenderness and marbling. It was very tasty and had a superb flavour, but is it worth all the fuss and the extortionate costs that goes with it? Not in my opinion, but then, I am not a steak connoisseur.

The next day we used the hotel shuttle bus to go to the Mall of the Emirates. This is a huge shopping mall; it even has a ski slope inside! It is full of very expensive designer shops that seem to cater for tiny, super-slim people. It was very interesting to see a shop that sold designer veils, headdresses and burkas for fashionable Muslim women. Some of them were very beautiful, albeit quite simple but tasteful, with edgings in gold and silver and with the fabric containing the same colour motifs.

Back at Al Qasr, we went to Kabbeahs, which was located on the canal edge, and we had a waterside seat, so that we could enjoy the views of the Burj while we had a drink. In the evening, we came back to try and dine at the Chinese, but it was full and it would be too late if we waited for a seat. So instead, we dined at the Meat Co. and we had a wonderful Steak Rossini, so we were not disappointed that our first choice of restaurant was not available. But it did make us realise just how popular the area was for dining and that if we wanted to eat somewhere specific, it would be better to book rather than to just turn up.

We did an organised tour the following day, which was called "Dream Dubai", and it took us to some of the new buildings that have already been completed in Dubai, as well as others which are still in the design stage. We were amazed as we drove along, as to how many cranes are being used in the city for building purposes and there is so much construction going on that you could not say that this was a nice looking city. Maybe when it is complete you could say that – if it is ever complete! We were in Dubai towards the end of 2008, which of course, was when there was an economic crash that was felt around the world. It took time for Dubai to be affected, but we have learnt since that many of the projects that we visited that day have either been downgraded or scrapped completely.

Our first stop was the Palms, which is an area that has been reclaimed from the sea and is designed to look like a palm tree with each of its "throngs" having many beautiful villas and apartments built along the length. Atlantis, which only opened the week before we arrived with a fanfare of fireworks and celebrity guests, including an exclusive performance by Kylie Minogue, was located at the far end, sitting on top of the tree. We then drove to the new harbour area, which has so many skyscrapers, that you would think that you were in New York; except for the fact that they are all shiny and new, and mainly made from steel and reflective glass, rather than concrete.

Our next stop was Dubailand which was very much a place or a dream of the future. When we went it was a building site, but they had a large exhibition hall called the Dubailand Experience Centre which had various models, films, diagrams and designs for this huge complex, that would consist of several huge parks or "lands", each devoted to a particular subject. There would be theme parks, historical centres, replicas of major landmarks like the Taj Mahal and the Eiffel Tower, and sporting venues. At the time, this included an eighteen hole golf course and a hotel resort designed and named after Tiger Woods. But it has opened as the Ernie Els golf course, presumably after the disgrace that Tiger Woods faced in the years in-between. It was such a huge project. Only Dubai could even dream of such an extensive visionary complex, and it is only Dubai who could pull it off. Although the 2008 crash has probably slowed the construction down, I know that some of the dream venues are now operating, including a twenty-five thousand seated cricket stadium and the motor city, where they hope to hold the grand prix in the future. If you look up Dubailand on the internet, it certainly gives you a perspective of their plans for the future.

Our tour stopped for some shopping (don't they all), but on this occasion it was a small complex dedicated entirely to jewellery shops, in particular focusing on diamonds. I was in my element! I love buying jewellery on holiday, as the designs are so much more ornate than at home, and, normally, are excellent value. As we wandered around, admiring everything on display, I succumbed and purchased a solitaire diamond ring. Set in eighteen carat gold and holding a stone of one point two carats with other diamonds in the bars, it cost two and a half thousand pounds – but when we returned home and had it valued, I was pleasantly surprised, and delighted, when we were told that the insurance and the replacement value was seven thousand pounds – a good investment.

Our final stop was the Burj Dubai, which is now called the Burj Khalifa. When we were there, this building had only just been completed and was not yet open to the public, so we viewed it from the outside. It stands at two thousand seven hundred and twenty-two feet tall and is by far the tallest building in the world. Second is the CN Tower in Toronto, Canada which, as a free standing building, and stands at one thousand eight hundred and fifteen feet. The Burj Khalifa was actually opened officially on the 17th of January 2009, two months after our visit.

The next day, we went by taxi to the Gold Souk. Oh My God! Every window along the streets of this shopper's paradise were just laden with gold, and it is very yellow! The Arabs love their jewellery and they like their gold to be big, heavy, high carats and yellow! We wandered around, and I managed to find some earrings that would fit the bill perfectly, matching a necklace that Richard had given me for my birthday the month before. Even though we had found Dubai to be a lot more expensive than we had thought it would be; especially for food and drink, the gold and the jewellery was very well priced and, as I found out on my return, I certainly managed to find two bargains that were worth a lot more when I had them valued in the UK.

But, and here is another word of warning for anyone who might visit the Gold Souk independently as we did, we had real difficulties in trying to get a taxi back to our hotel, which was a thirty minute drive away. Every taxi that pulled up was already reserved and they did not have anything that even resembled a taxi rank. We ended up walking a long way, under the creek, past the Dubai Museum, and towards a more central part of town and even then, we could not find a taxi. In the end, a man agreed to take us back to the hotel for eighty dirhams – a little risky as you hear so many horror stories of fake taxi drivers, but he seemed very genuine and, to be honest, we were desperate at this point! We gave him one hundred dirhams to show our gratitude at this kind gesture, but it would be better to organise a trip like this through your hotel, so that you have a guaranteed return driver.

In the afternoon we were told that the QE2 was due to sail past our hotel to its mooring place on the Palms Jumeirah as it had been sold to a Dubai businessman who had bought this iconic liner to turn it into a floating, but static, hotel. Richard said that he saw it in the distance, but with my eyesight, I had no chance. We later found out that it had actually sailed into the port which was close to the Gold Souk where we had been that morning. We should have stayed there to see it sail in after its last cruise as a commercial liner for Cunard.

That evening was probably the highlight of our stay in Dubai, as we went to the Burj Al Arab for drinks and dinner. The Al Qasr is part of the same resort that owns the Burj Al Arab, the Jumeirah Beach and the Wild Wadi. We were taken around from our hotel on a golf buggy – not quite the grand entrance that people staying at the hotel usually make when they arrive from the airport in one of the hotels many white Rolls Royce's; but it was fun going under the roads and walkways in our little buggy.

The opulence of the entrance to this huge hotel is jaw-dropping! The inside of the huge structure is completely hollow with all the rooms having outside positions and the corridors and the halls facing inwards, down into the lobby area. The escalators to the main lobby floor had dancing fountains running along the central divider and the furnishings were all so bright and gaudy. We went up to the Sky Bar for a pre-dinner drink on the twenty seventh floor. We were seated by the window, where we had wonderful views over the beach area towards the Jumeirah. We then came down into the basement of the hotel, where we had reservations at the Al Mahara Restaurant, which is located below sea level. There is a huge fish tank in the centre of the restaurant, and seating is placed in a circle surrounding this tank, which holds many colourful corals and large marine fish. This was a *very* expensive restaurant, but certainly an experience that we will not forget.

The following evening we dined at the Pierchic Restaurant which is actually a part of our hotel complex. It is listed as one of the top ten restaurants in Dubai, and is a dedicated fish restaurant. You get to it by walking through the gardens, past the villas and the pool and along a pier, which, if you look back the way you have come, offers superb views of Al Qasr, Burj Al Arab and Jumeirah, all lit up against the jet black sky; a pleasant ending to our weekend break.

We returned to Dubai in December 2014, where we did a cruise in the Gulf. Starting from Dubai, we visited Oman and Abu Dhabi before returning to Dubai. We stayed for one night after the cruise at The Palace, which was right next to the now fully completed Burj Khalifa and the Dubai Mall, the largest shopping mall in the world.

We did an excursion from the ship to tour the city, which has now got even more building work taking place than when we were there in 2008. And this gave us the opportunity to go up the Burj Khalifa. The views were amazing, even with all the pollution caused by the thousands of motor cars. The horizon was very hazy and did not make for good photos. But we were so amazed by the solitude of this huge building, which stands so much higher than anything around it, that we made the decision to return that evening and take the VIP trip to the higher viewing platform, that is limited to only a certain number of visitors at any one time. We were not disappointed!

Greeted with a drink and the chance to go on to an outside platform that was very well screened and not dangerous at all and the views of Dubai at night were even more spectacular! You could look down on the dancing fountains which lie in front of the Burj, Dubai Mall, and The Palace Hotel and although there was no sound this high up, you could still make out their mystical dance, with lights emblazoned all around. It felt quite exclusive due to minimising the number of people allowed to go to this upper level and not at all crowded, unlike the daytime visit where you were vying for good spots to view and to take your selfies!

Dubai is a very cosmopolitan city but still has very strict Muslim laws, and you do need to be cautious to ensure that you do not fall foul of them. It will not be to everyone's taste either, as, after all, it is a concrete jungle, but so very different from all the big cities in the western hemisphere. But it is quite amazing, with all its huge skyscrapers, imaginative malls, parks and thrill-seeking adventure sites. It breaks so many world records and yet still wants to achieve more. You can understand why it is a must on so many bucket lists. I would not say it is a beautiful city, but it certainly is a fascinating one and well worth a visit; an alternative for a stop off on the way to Australia.

CHAPTER 20

Iguazu Falls, Argentina/Brazil (26) – April 2009

We had a very long journey to get to Buenos Aires for our holiday in South America, as it consisted of three flights – Manchester to Heathrow, Heathrow to Madrid and then Madrid to Buenos Aires. We left home at ten a.m. and arrived at our hotel, Melia, in Buenos Aires at nine p.m. With a four-hour time difference – this meant that we had been travelling for a total of twenty-seven hours!

We had managed to get some sleep on the plane, so once we had unpacked for our two nights in the capital of Argentina, we went out to explore. Our hotel was located in downtown Buenos Aires and was very close to the main pedestrian shopping area. We had a light lunch with a bottle of wine an Argentinian white, of course, and it cost us fifty three Argentinian pesos, not US dollars which at that time was around twelve pounds – very good value!

In the afternoon, we started our tour, which was all included in the price. We had booked this holiday with Royal Caribbean through Thomas Cook, and it consisted of two nights in Buenos Aires, flights to Iguazu for two nights, return to Buenos Aires where we would board the Radiance of the Seas for a fourteen-day cruise around South America, ending in Santiago de Chile for one night before flying home. Our tour this afternoon was of the city and we went to Recoleta, Palermo, La Boca and Puerto Madera.

The main square, which is the same as all town and city main squares in South America, included the cathedral, the police station and the main government house. In this case, this was Casa Rosada, made famous as this was the place where Eva Peron gave her renowned speech to the people when she was dying of cancer, made equally famous in the Andrew Lloyd Webber musical, Evita, with the song "Don't Cry For me Argentina". The colour of the building is as a result of adding bulls' blood to the paint, which gives it this mysterious rose colour, hence its name and it is known as the Pink Palace in English.

El Boca, an area near the old docks, has two claims to fame. Firstly it is the home of the Argentine Tango and secondly, this is where you will find the home of the football club, Boca Juniors. Football is an absolute passion for the Argentinians, as with the Brazilians, and Buenos Aires has two clubs, and understandably, they are big rivals. Boca Juniors are sponsored by Coca-Cola but, as the colours of the football club are royal blue, the logo of the famous drink has been changed from red to blue, to match the team that they support. We were told that this was the only place where Coca-Cola did this, but in 2014 we did a cruise on the Amazon and went to Parintins where they sponsor the carnival which is made up of two teams: one red, one blue, and yet again, the adverts for Coca-Cola appear in both colours.

In Ricoletta we went to the cemetery which houses the tomb of Eva Peron, a shrine to those who loved her, and many Argentinians still do – or they love her legend at least. The cemetery is full of beautiful and poignant mausoleums, and is worth a visit to see some of the masterpieces carved out of stone and marble that decorate the monuments and the tombs. Peron is entombed in a family tomb and there is just a simple brass plaque, marking her presence. It is so simple, you could easily miss it if it were not for the hundreds of people all queuing to catch a glimpse of her final resting place.

There are many fine districts in Buenos Aires with beautiful tree-lined avenues, designer shops, trendy apartments and villas, parks and wide, busy streets. One is the widest street in the world, and in its centre is an obelisk.

That evening, we went to a restaurant recommended by our tour guide, Alex, which was located on the newly refurbished port in Puerto Madero, now home to lots of trendy bars and restaurants and up-market shops. The Cabana las Lilas did not disappoint, as we both had wonderful steaks that were tasty and very tender. The meal included some antipasto and breads, which were more than enough for an appetiser. In fact, this restaurant was so good that we returned there six years later, when we did a cruise to the Antarctic, which started and ended in Buenos Aires.

The next day, we had a late start for our full day excursion to the Estancia, stopping en-route at San Antonia, a small town, two hour's drive from Buenos Aires. We had a stroll around the main square, which included the police station, main government office and cathedral – it was very pleasant as the weather was nice and the square was very quiet.

When we arrived at the Estancia, we were met by a group of gauchos on horseback who escorted our coach to the main house. We then met the owner, Francis, his wife and their grandsons who greeted us like family members. One of the younger grandsons went up to Richard and shook his hand and then he came to me and shook my hand and he kissed me on the cheek! It was just so sociable! We had a drink of wine and we all sat chatting with the family around the barbecue. Francis had actually met Peron and his father was second in command of the coup that overthrew him. It was really interesting talking to the family for a good hour. The Estancia raised polo ponies, but they also grew crops, raised cattle for beef and they had a hotel.

We then went to a show stand and we watched the gauchos perform. Their riding skills and agility in the saddle were amazing to watch and we were there for probably an hour, while they competed amongst themselves to ride around poles, spear a ring with small sticks, used the boleros balls to bring down a log and various other riding stunts. Only one of the four gauchos succeeded in spearing the ring, and he presented it to me in return for a kiss! Very exciting!

Lunch followed the show where we had plenty of wine, champagne and a delicious barbecued meal of steak, chicken and sausage, served with salads. This was followed by strawberries and ice cream, Argentine cakes, pastries and black coffee to help compensate for the amount of wine we drank! We took a stroll after lunch to see the new hotel that they are building to increase their guest capacity. It did look really lovely and it would certainly be a pleasant place to stay in the future.

Francis had six sons and three daughters and the second son, Marcel, was with us, chatting away during dinner and telling us that he played polo in England and that he had fifteen polo ponies in the UK at his home in Windsor. At the age of just twenty-eight, he obviously had an extremely good life style, but he sat chatting to us and making us feel so welcome, as though we were family, or friends at the very least. There was so much respect from all the family for their father and us, their guests. It was a strain to leave them and return to Buenos Aires. It really was a very magical afternoon.

In the evening we went to a tango show that was wonderful. The venue was very large and it had a lot of tour groups, but we had excellent seats near the front of the stage. We were entertained with tango through the ages and our expectations were exceeded by their agility and expertise at dancing this most sensual of classic dances. The food was wonderful too, as we both enjoyed steak, again! But this is Argentina and they probably produce the best steak in the world – well in our opinion, they do!

On the following day we left early and went to the airport where we had a charter flight on a small plane to take the fourteen of us on the tour, plus Alex our guide, to Iguazu, the airstrip on the Argentine side of the falls. It took us just under three hours and we landed at around midday. We went straight to the national park to see the Devil's Throat, which is probably the most dramatic section of these wonderful waterfalls. We had to get two trains to get to the location and then we walked quite a long way over bridges and paths to finally reach the most dramatic waterfalls I have ever seen. Because we were just coming out of the rainy season, the falls were at their most dramatic and, with it being Easter too, they had opened-up the dams upstream, to provide the full flow of the Iguazu River as it fell over this huge chasm into the valley below. I cannot explain to you just how wonderful this scene was, even though it was so crowded. We had to fight our way to the front to get pictures, but this was Easter Sunday so many Argentinians had come for the day.

The Iguazu River forms the border between Argentina and Brazil and Paraguay also has a border further along from the falls. On our return, the queues for the train were very long, so we took the train for the first leg and then walked the second leg, through the forests that surround the falls, which took us about ten minutes. We stayed at the Panoramic Hotel, which is located in the town of Iguazu. It was a pleasant, modern hotel, but well away from the falls. There are a couple of hotels located in the park with views of the falls. If we ever get the chance to return, this would be our choice of accommodation so as to be so close to this wonderful natural wonder. It would be nice to stay on a night with a full moon, as on those evenings, the park opens in the evening, for you to be able to view the falls by moonlight. But, it gets booked up very quickly and, even though we were lucky to be there on a full moon in 2009, the tour was already fully booked, so we had to settle for dinner at the Sheraton instead, taking a taxi with two others from our tour group, Larry and Carrie.

As we were staying for two nights at Iguazu, we had plenty of time to look at the falls in a leisurely manner. They do day trips from Buenos Aires, but there is no way that you can get to see the full majesty of this wonderful natural wonder in a few hours. Our second day started early and we went to a different part of the falls – no trains this time, just walking. We walked along the upper circuit where we could see the main section of the falls. They were stunning, and there was just so much water cascading over so many ridges. The falls are made up of a number of waterfalls, each having its own individual title including Adam and Eve, Brocetti and Chico. Many tumble directly into the valley but others fall into canyons and crevices before they topple over the main ridge and continue, to join the river. These create beautiful small lagoons that are so quiet in comparison to the main falls. There's lots of bird and wildlife too in the forests, and tropical flora in the park.

These falls are so big, and there are so many separate cascades and waterfalls that it is impossible to see it all from ground level. It is only from the air that you can really appreciate just how huge these falls are. We have been to the four major waterfalls in the world; the Victoria Falls in Zimbabwe; the Angel Falls in Venezuela and the Niagara Falls in Canada, but Iguazu Falls are by far the best and the most dramatic.

You have an option to take a zodiac out onto the river to get closer to the falls. And when I say closer, I mean closer! You actually go under one of the larger falls that topples from the upper level to a ledge and then crashes down into the river below. We didn't take this ride. I used the excuse of getting our camera equipment wet, but in total honesty, it was due to having to walk down two-hundred slippery steps to get to the river, and then take the same number back to the top! But we watched the zodiac disappear under the spray and could hear the screams of the passengers from our upper circuit walkway! We also took the

lower circuit and from there you look up at the falls and get a completely different prospective of this wonderful phenomenon.

The next day we had another early start, as we went across the bridge that creates the border crossing between Argentina and Brazil to view the falls from the Brazilian side. This meant we had to go through passport control and we had our passports stamped for entering Brazil. When we returned, we got another stamp for entering Argentina – an easy way of getting your passport filled quickly! We headed for the park on the Brazilian side of the falls, but had an option to be able to take a short helicopter flight over the falls.

Richard and I decided to do this. The others on our tour declined the offer but we could not miss this opportunity to take this flight that lasted about ten minutes. We are so glad that we did. What a view! I can definitely say that the only way to see all the falls in one go, is by flying over them and we had the most wonderful view with clear blue skies and amazing visibility. On this, our third visit, I think they had closed the dam upstream, as the water was not as ferocious as it had been over the Easter weekend. But it was still well worth the two hundred dollars.

We continued into the Brazilian National Park, walking the full circuit. This gave us the chance to look at the falls on the Argentinian side as the day before, we could see the Brazilian falls and look down and up at the Argentine Falls. This circuit in Brazil was not as good, but the views of the Devil's Throat were much better, as you almost looked straight down into the mouth of the Devil. They had elevators to take you to different levels, to get great views of this most dramatic section of the falls.

We crossed back into Argentina and we were taken to the airport where we had our charter flight waiting for us, to return to Buenos Aires, where we would be boarding our ship for our South American cruise. But, when we had all taken our seats ready for the flight back, there was a problem as the door of the plane would not close properly. We all had to leave the plane through the emergency hatch at the back of the plane, clambering over all our luggage on the way!

We were told that there was an issue with one of the sensors on the door, and the plane was secure but with the sensor malfunctioning, the safety systems had taken over and would not allow the pilot to start the engine. A bit of duct tape did the trick, but an elderly couple on our tour then refused to fly, saying that the plane was not properly maintained for this fault to occur! Alex, our guide, was doing his best to persuade them, as the alternative option of taking the scheduled flight was not possible as that was already fully booked, and the next flight was not until the day after that, and would arrive after the ship had sailed! We eventually persuaded them that everything would be okay, as the pilot would not risk his own life in a plane that was not safe.

But, as a result of the technical problem and then the delay due to our reluctant passengers, we were late getting back to Buenos Aires and when we arrived at the pier, all the porters had finished for the night and we had no one to transfer our luggage from the coach to the ship and the main check-in had closed. In the end, we had to sort our own luggage out, helping others who could not handle this themselves, and check-in on-board, but at least it meant we were able to board the ship as we had nowhere else to spend the night!

We had an Owner's Suite on the ship and it was beautiful – the best cabin we have had so far on any cruise. This has been surpassed now on three occasions – in August 2013 on the Caribbean Princess, on our sailing from Southampton to New York, we had the Grand Suite which lived up to its name – very grand indeed! In June 2016 when we were able to upgrade to a Grand Suite on Cunard's Queen Victoria for our four day cruise in the English Channel we had a huge cabin and an enormous balcony; and, most recently, the top suite on the Celebrity Reflection in November 2016, on a Caribbean cruise. The Reflection Suite has two bedrooms and a shower that extends over the side, with views of the sea through its floor! It was very modern, luxurious and came with lots of trimmings, including dinner one night with the captain, a cabana by the Lawn Club for us to use during the week, unlimited access to all the speciality restaurants and free drinks anywhere on the ship; this is definitely the way to cruise!

We were not sailing until the next day, giving us time to enjoy the shops of Florida Street, which was a short taxi drive away. The leather shops in Buenos Aires are wonderful, with so many colours and designs. But the Argentine women are very petite and none of the jackets I tried fitted me. Then I was told that a jacket could be made in six hours and would be ready for us to collect at four p.m. plenty of time to board our ship before we sailed at six p.m. that evening. I thought that this would be extortionate but at that time it cost me just six hundred and ninety five dollars – approximately one hundred and forty pounds per jacket! When I picked them up, I was really pleased with the quality and the fit, and the price was an absolute bargain!

Our first port of call was Montevideo, the capital of Uruguay, which lies on the opposite bank of the River Plate, but closer to the ocean than Buenos Aires. The River Plate is the widest river in the world, and ferries take three hours to make the crossing between the two capitals – but our cruise ship took all night! We went on a tour to see the main attractions of the city before going into the countryside to Juanico for a tour of the vineyards, some wine tasting and lunch. It was a good wine tasting as we had six wines, marking each for colour, scent and taste, the last one being an after dinner liqueur which was very nice. After lunch we were entertained with a tango show and the audience were invited to join in. I was picked by one of the professional dancers and I actually danced an Argentine Tango – definitely the highlight of the day!

We had another stop in Uruguay at Punta del Este, a pleasant seaside town, but not much in the way of sightseeing. This was followed by a day at sea, before we docked in Puerto Madryn in Patagonia, Argentina. This port is very close to Peninsula Valdes, which is very famous for its wildlife and is a UNESCO heritage site. We went on a full day excursion to Punta Norte and the Estancia San Lorenzo Penguin Colony. It was a long drive, but we saw sea lions and elephant seals on the beach, and in the sea at Punta Norte and then we took an army truck to take us over the rough terrain to San Lorenzo. We were late in the season, so most of the penguins had already "flown" the nest, so to speak. But there were still a few remaining, waddling around us, and nesting in their burrows.

After a day at sea we arrived at Cape Horn. We did not get off the ship, but we did scenic cruising going around the island that lies at the end of South America. It was nothing like I imagined that it would be. The sea was so calm! It was like a millpond. We had blue skies and sunshine, but it was bitterly cold.

Our next port was Ushuaia, named the city at the end of the world! We left for our tour at eight a.m. and it was still quite dark. But, as we got off the ship and walked to our catamaran, it started to get a little lighter, and I was blown away by the scenery that greeted us. The town, which was just waking up and had just a few lights on here and there, is set against a huge mountain range, capped with snow that glistened in the early morning light. It was beautiful!

We sailed along the Beagle Channel, viewing sea lions and the birds that call this bleak area home. We then boarded a coach and went to the Tierra del Fuego National Park. We had clear blue skies and the scenery was just wonderful with the snow-capped mountains reflecting in the clear, still lakes. We saw a red fox too, just sitting in the car park of all places. This is where you will find the post office at the end of the world and you can mail back your post cards with especially designed stamps to state this.

We left Argentina at this point and sailed on to Chile, stopping at Punta Arenas. This was the first bad day of the holiday and it was raining heavily so we just had a walk around the town, as none of the excursions interested us. This port day was followed by a couple of days at sea where we had scenic cruising. On the first day we sailed through the Magellan Straits stopping to view a glacier, and the second day was through the Chilean Fjords, but the weather here was not good and the scenery, which should have been beautiful, was quite insignificant.

Our next port was Puerto Montt and we went on a tour which took us to the Osorno Volcano. Unfortunately we had mist and low cloud which spoilt this very dramatic scenery. After visiting Petrohue Falls, which were quite spectacular, we had lunch at a spot which overlooked a lake and the volcano. Luckily, the clouds lifted and we eventually got a clear view of this perfectly conical shaped volcano topped with deep snow. It was quite stunning. We were lucky on this tour as it did not rain and we were told that it almost always rains in this area. That's why it is so green and lush!

Our cruise ended in Valparaiso, which is the port closest to Santiago. We should have been going on a city tour of the Chilean capital, but it was cancelled. This was unfortunate as we had added an overnight in Santiago in order to do this and, as we did it after the original holiday was booked and confirmed, it cost us quite a bit to make the change. Now we were left at our hotel in limbo with nothing to do for the day, but we found a shopping mall and we had a wander around there for a few hours. Not ideal, but it was better than just sitting in the hotel. In the evening, our hotel, the Kennedy, arranged a special dinner for its guests and we went to see Chilean dancing and have a typical local dinner. It was quite nice and a good way to end this amazing tour. This South American cruise is definitely one to take. We returned to the area in February 2015 when we went to Antarctica for an amazing adventure, but that is not one of the fifty, so I won't go into detail.

CHAPTER 21

Venice, Italy (18) – June 2009

Richard and I had been to Venice before 2009 but this was the first time that we had been to this wonderful city together. I love Venice – it is my favourite European city and comes second only to Sydney as top cities of the world. On this occasion, we were staying for a few days to celebrate Richard's birthday at the beginning of June. I chose the Best Western just off St Mark's Square. Superb location but the hotel itself left a lot to be desired. Our room was small and high at the top of the hotel, with just a small window offering us a view of the rooftops of Venice with no pleasant outlook whatsoever. I was very disappointed as this was not a cheap choice of accommodation, but we were not able to get an alternative room as they were fully booked. But on this occasion, we certainly did not spend a lot of time in our room, so we did not suffer the inadequacies for too long.

Anyone who has been to Venice knows that St Mark's Square has a dog leg, or is L shaped, with the entrance to the Grand Canal and the quayside where many waterbuses, taxi's, gondolas and vaporetti stop to take the eager sightseers to one of the most beautiful sites in the world. Napoleon referred to it as Europe's Drawing Room, and I don't think that he could have described it better. With the Doge's Palace to your right, St Mark's Basilica beside it, the bell tower to the left and the astronomical clock with its archway and road leading to the Rialto in front of you, entry to our hotel was through an archway in the very left corner of the Piazza when looking at the clock. As I said; a great location just a shame about our hotel.

On this first occasion in Venice we took a water bus from the airport to St Mark's Square. This is probably the easiest method of getting to this watery city, but as we learned on our next visit, it is certainly not the best way to arrive! There is something very different about staying in Venice rather than visiting it for a day on a tour or on an excursion from a cruise ship. In the evening, so many of the thousands of day visitors vanish and the narrow streets become quiet, mysterious and offer an adventure, while you wander around staring into the gaily decorated shop windows, passing small cafés offering up delicious aromas of Venetian cuisine and criss-crossing the canals, large and small, getting lost the further and deeper you go into the narrow streets of Venice. It really is a wonderful place to just wander, and to stroll around, not really knowing where you are going or where you will end up. We have found so may wonderful restaurants, cafés and bars doing this, knowing that we will never find them again as we had no way of knowing which way we went in the first place!

One nice thing about our hotel was the bar on the ground floor. It had small balconies that looked onto a canal where many gondolas lined up, waiting to ferry passengers on their romantic excursion into the little inner canals of the city, whilst the gondolier recites tales of the past, of Casanova's nightly rendezvous with his many mistresses, and the rise of this amazing city. If you are lucky, he may even sing an Italian love song to you, which echoes eerily against the tall, ancient buildings that rise up all around you. The intricacy of the manoeuvring of the gondola around sheer corners and under low bridges; dodging others coming to meet you in the narrowest of waterways, really does beggar belief, and you cannot help but be amazed at the mastery of this strange, long craft, and why it was designed in such a manner to make this method of travel so difficult. And when you leave the solitude of the small canals and enter the huge Grand Canal, the hustle and the bustle greets you as if you have just emerged from a B road and onto the M25 motorway! I am sure that you can tell by these ravings of familiarity, that we did take a gondola ride, although we took ours from the pier on the lagoon at Piazza San Marco – St Mark's Square to you and me. I loved it, although I think that Richard was not too keen on the romantic connotation attached to a Venetian gondola ride!

Although Richard had been to Venice before, the last time that he was here he was with a group of lads and in his early twenties, so he had other things on his mind mainly beautiful Italian girls, rather than the major sights of Venice, so he had not been inside the Basilica, up the bell tower or into the Doge's Palace, whereas I had done all three! On this occasion we decided to go into the Basilica which is a jewel to the beholder. The décor inside is just truly magnificent with every inch covered with decoration – frescoes, paintings and statues. You do not know which way to look. The problem is, neither do all the hundreds of other visitors who are meandering around the building at the same time as you! Venice is a very popular city and the population swells by many thousands during the day and, on this occasion, many of those seemed to be in the Basilica! But we still managed to see everything that we wanted to see, including the choir screen, which costs extra, but is well worth seeing as it has to be one of the masterpieces of Renaissance art; and the bronze horses stolen from Constantinople and mounted high on the front porch of the Basilica, as proof of the might of Italy and, in particular, Venice. The statues are now a copy of the originals, which stand in a museum in the attic of the Basilica, badly damaged and weather-beaten but now protected against the elements and the millions of tourists traipsing by them in their original location.

The weather was kind to us during the day, and we were able to enjoy the beautiful view of the Piazza from one of the restaurants, whilst we enjoyed a chilled bottle of wine listening to the orchestras play. This is an expensive option – the prices of the refreshments in the numerous restaurants in St Mark's Square are renowned and, yes, a coffee will set you back seven pounds or so and probably more now, seven years later and an ice cream sundae is ten pounds plus – our wine was around fifty pounds for just a basic Pinot Grigio including the service charge and the table fees, but where else can you enjoy a view like this, I ask you!

It just so happened that my brother, Gareth and his wife, Terry, were also in Venice at the same time as us, as they were going to board a cruise ship from this popular European port. So we met up with them at a wonderful restaurant called Mercanti. Terry's birthday is just four days after Richard's so this was a nice way to celebrate the double occasion. It felt so cosmopolitan to be meeting up with others from overseas for dinner! We had a wonderful evening; the wine flowed and much merriment was had by all, although I am sure that other diners around us thought that we were a little too loud for the pre-show meal, as the restaurant was very close to the Phoenix Theatre.

After dinner, we walked to St Mark's Square to find that it had been flooded and the duck boards were out. It had rained very heavily that afternoon, but as the restaurant was in the opposite direction from the square, we had not realised the plight until we tried to enter it later. St Mark's Basilica was surrounded by a small lake and people were wading through the ankle-deep water, going about their business as if nothing was wrong. Many of the shops that were close to the Basilica and the astronomical clock had been invaded by the rising waters and the only bar open was the one furthest away at the top end of the square. We had a nightcap watching the soggy passers-by, amazed at how quickly the flood had happened and wondering how long it would last and what lasting damage was incurred by those affected. As we parted and returned to the Best Western Hotel, we realised that we were going to suffer ourselves from this calamity. The archway and the bridge that we would normally take to return to our hotel was completely underwater and, unless we wanted to get very wet indeed as it was over knee deep, we had to find an alternative way around. When we entered our hotel, the ground floor was submerged in about two inches of murky water – the bar was closed, and everyone was walking around either in wellington boots or with their trousers hitched up high, to avoid the soggy surroundings.

By the following day, all the water had resided. We had sunshine again and all the hotels, restaurants, shops and bars were back to normal. As we were early, many of the shops were sweeping out the remains of the water and any debris that had been left behind from the flood, but there was certainly no lasting damage and you could tell that they were used to it – a common occurrence that they just accepted as though the wind had blown in a few loose leaves.

At the designated time, we went down to the lagoon, close to Harry's Bar, where we watched Gareth and Terry's ship sail by, ready for their Adriatic sojourn and we waved like mad, knowing that they would not see us, but in the knowledge that they would be on the deck somewhere, sipping their sail-away cocktails, looking down on the crowds that were lining the lagoon and the Piazza San Marco, while their ship sailed past us and into the main shipping channels, heading out to sea. We got to do the same thing several years later; twice in fact, but there was no-one to personally wave us off when we eventually cruised out of Venice.

In October 2010, we returned to Venice, this time to stay for two nights at the Gritti Palace located on the Grand Canal. I had no problems with the view from our window on this occasion as I had made a point of booking a Grand Canal view room. I also arranged for transfers by the hotel, from the airport. We were met after customs and taken to a van to transfer us and our luggage. I got quite a shock as I had expected something a little more glamorous to get us to our five-star accommodation, and a minibus is not my way of arriving in Venice in style! I was mistaken – the van just drove us the short distance to the airport pier and I mean short, it took a few minutes – you could walk it in ten minutes. Here we boarded a private taxi, just the two of us, and departed for our journey to the hotel. This is the way to arrive in Venice! We were served champagne as we sat in the back, in the open air, speeding along past the busy public waterbus, towards our destination on the Grand Canal. It was wonderful! Call me a snob, but I felt like a million dollars, it was a great experience.

As we arrived at our hotel, at their own private jetty, we were met by the hotel staff and escorted to our room. And the view from our little balcony certainly met my expectations. We looked onto the Santa Maria Della Salute, which stands at the entrance to the Grand Canal and we were surrounded by beautiful buildings, hotels and museums that line this grandest of all the canals in Venice. All were coloured cream, pink and green, and offered just a magical, mesmerising view, as the canal bends around towards the Rialto Bridge. We had a complementary bottle of champagne and strawberries waiting for us, and we sipped this while we enjoyed the wonderful sunset reflecting off our surroundings, bathing the buildings in a glow that mesmerised you. As the light slowly vanished from the sky, it became dark, and all the lights of Venice at night changed the scene to another, more melancholy visage.

This trip to Venice was for my birthday, and, to celebrate our return, we dined at Harry's Bar located on the spot where the Grand Canal merges with the lagoon. This famous bar and restaurant was a haunt of Ernest Hemingway and many other actors, writers and singers in the past. We enjoyed a meal in the restaurant upstairs it was very expensive, but also very nice and, of course, we enjoyed the famous creation that Harry's Bar is renowned for – a Bellini!

The next morning, when we tried to get the lift to go down to the ground floor for breakfast, we found that it was not working. We could not understand why, no matter how many times we pressed the ground floor button, it did not move! We decided to walk down and we then found out the reason for our plight. The ground floor was flooded! The waters from the Grand Canal had risen overnight, and the whole of the ground floor was under water, and there were duckboards throughout reception and a doorman was assisting guests around, bedecked in large, glossy, wellington boots! Breakfast was being served on the first floor and, as a precaution, the lift had been taken out of action, rather than letting it be flooded and damaged, if anybody had descended to the ground floor.

When we emerged, balancing on the duck boards, we discovered that all the paths around us were under water and duck boards were the manner of getting around this morning! The nearest bridge, which crossed over a canal offering gondola rides, was in pure chaos, with gondolas on either side, unable to get under the bridge due to the height of the water! Many of the small squares and piazzas were also under water and the shops were closed, to try and avoid too much damage from the dirty canal water. St Mark's Square was really badly affected and duck boards were raised high over the murky water. Many people were trying hard to keep away from the invading onslaught, but it was very difficult to pass one another on the narrow boards and it was like watching a particularly intricate dance, as tourists interacted with one another, keeping their balance, while going about their day to day business.

As it was so difficult to try and get anywhere around our hotel, we took a water taxi to Murano to see the glass blowing. This was complementary, arranged by our hotel concierge, and we knew that there would be a price to pay, as we were likely to undergo a hard sell at the factory, to purchase some of their glassware. We knew what to expect, but it was actually fascinating watching them make the baubles for a huge glass chandelier that had been commissioned. As this was a private visit, we were given a detailed explanation as to what they were doing, and how they managed to achieve the intricate patterns, colours and designs of the glass. Afterwards, we were taken around the museum and the gallery, to see some of the magnificent sculptures made from glass – they were breath-taking! Finally, of course, we were taken into the shop and at this point we had decided that we wanted to take home some of this craftwork, as a reminder of our holiday. We decided on six champagne glasses that are tall and delicate and cost us six hundred and ninety euros.

Our host at the factory suggested that we have lunch across the canal in a wonderful little outdoor restaurant that looked back onto the glass makers. He walked us over and told the owners to look after us, and for us to return after dinner to the glass makers by return taxi. We did return, and bought six wine glasses, to go with our champagne flutes and a glass tray to display the decanter and the glasses that we had bought on our previous visit to Venice! Our host was obviously delighted at such a gesture, and ensured that we had a private return taxi, with champagne, and instructions to take us on a scenic return journey to enjoy the sights of St Mark's from the lagoon. A very pleasant day!

The following day we departed Venice by water taxi, to head for the train station where we would be boarding the Orient Express for our journey back to the UK. This was the main reason for our holiday on this occasion. Our stay in Venice was just a taster of the finesse and luxury that was to follow. We could have arranged a transfer from our hotel to the station through Orient Express, but it was expensive, and would have been shared for forty-nine euros each, whereas we paid sixty euros for the two of us in the water taxi. I don't quite know what I was expecting at Venice train station, but the chaos that greeted us certainly did not come anywhere near my vision of this enigmatic, legendary service. We have travelled on the Orient Express in the UK, departing from Victoria, where you are formally greeted and provided with a very nice waiting area, before you board the train. But in Venice it was a bit of a free for all and you just had to join a throng of people all vying for the attention of the officials. We had expected guests to be smartly dressed to match the occasion, but most were quite casual. Once we had checked in, we were escorted to a hotel for drinks, before finally boarding the train at five thirty p.m. and we headed for our cabin, G5.

It was very small and had very little storage space. A word of warning – if you ever decide to go overnight on the Orient Express through Europe, pack lightly! We had three smallish cases with us; not realising how cramped we would be, and it took some work to get our stuff hung, sorted and in some semblance of order. We had not gone for the larger compartment, which is quite a lot more expensive, so our cabin offered us a comfy settee during the day and then was converted to bunks for the evening. We had a small basin in the corner for washing and refreshing in the evening and in the morning, but the toilet was shared and at the end of the carriage.

Once unpacked, we went to our normal haunt whenever we go on holiday, we found the bar! It was very busy, but we managed to find a seat when people started to leave, and attend the first dinner sitting at seven thirty p.m. I was disappointed to see that many of these had not followed the custom of dressing for dinner, and were very casually dressed. A journey on the Orient Express is one of the fifty things to do before you die, and I had read so many details about this trip with yearning; never expecting us to have the chance to actually experience it for ourselves, so the fact that the train was crowded, noisy and full of underdressed Japanese, was a let-down! But we did not let this spoil our adventure, and we returned to our cabin, adorned ourselves in our finery, bedecked ourselves with gold and diamonds and headed for dinner at the second sitting at nine-thirty p.m.

The dining cars are very lavish and beautifully decorated; each one having a different name, theme and colour scheme. The meal was fine dining at its best! We shared our table with a couple from Dover, who were also dressed for the occasion, so we had a very pleasant exchange of conversation over our meal, before departing for our cabin at midnight. Getting ready for bed in such a confined space was no easy feat, as the bunks took up even more room than before. The bunk was surprisingly comfortable and once you were able to get used to the noise of the train, the rocking motion eventually lulled you to sleep.

We did not rise until nine a.m. so you can see that the cabin was extremely comfortable for a good night's sleep. Breakfast is served in your cabin, but you attend the restaurant cars for lunch. We opted for the late lunch at one fifteen p.m., which was fine dining yet again, and this time we sat with a couple from Alberta. At three p.m. we rolled into Prague station, where we were transferred to the Mandarin Oriental Hotel, for our two-night stopover on this amazing journey. Prague is a beautiful city. We have spent time here before, and we were very much looking forward to seeing some of the sites that we missed the last time. The excursion we had the following day, was arranged by Orient Express, we went to Prague castle initially, and then to a monastery, where we had a musical recital in one of the ornately decorated libraries. This was arranged purely for us, and it was a wonderful experience.

After spending two nights in Prague, we were collected at one fifteen p.m. to board the train again for our next leg to Paris, and this time, as we knew what to expect, we packed much more efficiently. Your main luggage is stored in a different compartment and delivered to your destination for you. Only the things you need for your journey are packed into the small carry-on luggage you keep with you in your cabin. We went to the bar car early, to get a seat, having learnt from our first leg, and as it started to fill with those coming from the early dinner sitting, we departed to change and go for our second sitting dinner; this time sitting with a couple from Kent. Another lovely meal was served, with wine, of course, and we retired to our cabin at twelve-thirty a.m.

The next day was my birthday, and, as we arrived in Paris at around nine a.m. our steward suggested that we have a walk on the platform, whilst he prepared our room for our breakfast. When we returned, there was a bottle of champagne and a bunch of roses waiting to greet me, arranged by Richard, and a complete surprise. We enjoyed the bubbly, over our simple breakfast and then at ten thirty a.m., we departed Paris and headed for Calais, where we were called for brunch, which would be our last meal on this fabulous train. At the port, we sadly left our cabin and boarded a luxury coach for our transfer under the English Channel through the Eurotunnel to Felixstowe. We passed through passport control and re-boarded the coach, which then made its way onto the transport train carriage for our short journey under the channel.

In Felixstowe, we boarded the British Pullman and set off for London. Yet more food and wine was served on this leg of the journey and we arrived in Victoria Station at around five p.m. and transferred to our final destination of this trip, the Ritz Hotel, London. This five-star luxurious hotel is fabulous. Whatever expectations you have of the hotel, the rooms and the service, you will not be disappointed. We had stayed here before in December 2009, the last time that we took the British Pullman, and enjoyed a Christmas lunch, treating my parents to a weekend they had never experienced before. We had enjoyed every minute of our stay, and it seemed fitting that this was where we would celebrate the evening of my birthday. The whole experience of our stay in Venice, Prague and London and the two nights on the Orient Express was wonderful, and it is certainly a trip that I will remember all my life. It was such a classic journey and everything about it was superb – the food, the accommodation, the service and the atmosphere. I hope that we will get the chance to do it again some-day, maybe heading for Istanbul instead. But one thing I have learnt – pack light!

I have gone off the beaten track a little here, as I am supposed to be writing about Venice and we have been back to this city on two other occasions. I am not going to go into a lot of detail about these other trips, as the first was in June 2012, where we stayed for a couple of nights before we boarded a cruise ship and sailed down the Adriatic and into the Mediterranean, visiting

Israel and Egypt and the last time was in August 2014, when we stopped overnight in Venice during a Mediterranean cruise. But on the second occasion we did do a very interesting tour. We had been told about certain places where you could do "secret" tours and the Doge's Palace in Venice is one of these.

There are many tours taking you around the Palace and across the Bridge of Sighs, the little bridge that connects the palace to the jail, which can be seen from the lagoon, and is a must on your sightseeing in Venice, but this particular tour takes you into the secret parts that are not open to the regular tourists, and can only be accessed if booked on this particular option. You start your tour in the dungeons and learn all about the suffering of those who had inhabited these rooms during the might of Venice and of the Doge himself. And the most famous of these was Giacomo Casanova! Our guide told us about his dastardly salacious life and his capture, imprisonment and escape, bringing it all to life, as we went through room after room. Our journey took us from the dungeons to the court rooms and even to the attic, where we were able to see the intricate eaves of the struts that hold up the ceiling of the great hall below us. We crossed the Bridge of Sighs, which offered us that last fleeting glimpse of Venice and the lagoon; witnessed by hundreds of poor souls in the past, who were sentenced to imprisonment, torture or even execution; being taken from the court room to their final destination.

Finally, we were allowed into the wonderfully decorated rooms and corridors of the palace itself, to see how the other half live. The splendour of this museum is breath-taking and I would definitely recommend this tour whilst in Venice. We booked through www.ticketitaly.com but there are others offering the tour. Search the internet by putting "doges secret palace tour" in your search engine.

There are many places to visit in Venice besides the Basilica and The Doge's Palace. You can go up the bell tower by lift for fabulous views over St Mark's and the city; there are many art galleries, museums and churches, all offering fabulous pieces of art and sculpted tombs; and a walk over the Rialto Bridge with its wonderful shops and views over the Grand Canal is an absolute must! There are signposts all over the city, pointing either towards the Rialto or towards St Mark's Square, so it is difficult to get completely lost. But part of the charm of Venice is wandering around the little back alleys, where you are likely to find charming restaurants that are less frequented than those lining the main streets. Viator.com have a number of tours that will take you to see some of the lesser points of interest that you may not be aware of, as well as offering boat trips to some of the neighbouring islands, that offer something a little different from busy Venice.

It is a photographer's paradise as there are so many iconic sights – the beautiful buildings, the quiet enigmatic small canals, the gondolas and the people. We were lucky to actually see a wedding party board a decorated gondola on one occasion, before it sailed away with the happy couple. At sunset, the buildings along the Grand Canal are bathed in a magnificent golden glow, that captivates the heart and soul.

There are many wonderful hotels in Venice, but there are some bad ones too, so always do your research before you go. We found this out in 2009! Location is the most important thing to consider, but price will probably be the overriding factor. You have to always pay extra for a hotel on the Grand Canal or the Lagoon, and to get a room with a view costs you quite a bit extra. But, believe me, it is worth it as you will never tire of the beautiful architecture of the city, and the view that you have paid for.

I don't think I will ever tire of visiting Venice and part of me would go back year after year except that there are so many other places to see, that we have not been to yet, so the adventurous part of me searches for new destinations and experiences.

CHAPTER 22

Cape Town, South Africa (5) – January 2010

This was the first time that we had ever booked a flight using our Avios points. We flew direct to Cape Town on British Airways from Heathrow, Terminal 5. We only had enough points to go economy, but it is a great deal as you only have to pay the taxes – and we got bumped up to World Traveller Plus on our outward journey! It is a long flight from the UK to South Africa, and both outward and inward flights are overnight, so a five-night break very quickly becomes a weeks' holiday; but there is only a one hour time difference, so it is actually a good place for a short break as you don't suffer jetlag. We have used air miles so many times since this first trip – world traveller plus to Mauritius; business class to Kuala Lumpur, New York and Miami, and even first class to Johannesburg! We use One World affiliate airlines whenever we can, in order to earn Avios points on all our flights. By using the American Express British Airways card we get double points for all bookings done through British Airways, and we can earn a companion flight every year too. I know that Star Alliance offer similar rewards, and it is a great way of making the most of your flights, knowing that you are earning miles to go towards another holiday in the future.

We had arranged for a pick-up and transfer from the airport, and we were staying at the Holiday Inn Express; a basic hotel near Greenmarket square, but it was ideally located for the restaurants we had pre-booked. On our first day, we strolled around the afore-mentioned market, had a beer and found the restaurant where we had booked for that evening – The Five Flies. Unfortunately, I understand that this fabulous restaurant is now closed, but please take my word for it, the food was wonderful – prawns the size of lobsters! And great service from very friendly staff.

We had checked the weather forecast and, as the prediction was not good for the following day, we booked a tour to take us out of Cape Town and down the peninsula. After picking up all the passengers we headed out of the city, taking the coast road, which was a very pretty route. The clouds were low so we did not have a good view of Table Mountain, but we still stopped to get some photos of the mountain range. We continued our journey to Cape Point, where we went up a funicular to the top of the point, where there was a visitor centre, restaurant, lighthouse and a very windy promontory, looking out at the Atlantic Ocean and back towards the Table Mountain National Park. We then descended to the Cape of Good Hope, and had our ubiquitous photo taken, standing behind the sign bearing the Cape's name, looking very windswept! This site is the most south-westerly point of the African continent – it is not the most southerly point as that is around a hundred and fifty kilometres further on at Cape Agulhas.

We took a different route back to Cape Town, driving through Simons Town, where we stopped to look at a small penguin colony, small being the key word, as there were not a lot of these unusual flightless birds and they were certainly of the diminutive variety! This colony is a permanent resident of the area and can be found at this location all year round; they do not migrate. We asked to be dropped at the V&A Waterfront (Victoria and Alfred), as this seems to be the most popular location for shops, bars and restaurants in Cape Town. It is clean and modern, with lots of choice of eateries, and the shops offer recognised names, souvenir shops, and designer fashion houses, as well as unusual arts and crafts. There is something for everyone. We arrived in time for lunch and sat outside, listening to a street band play local music, while we dined and had a very nice bottle of South African white wine!

That evening we ate at the Savoy Cabbage, which, at that time, was voted the best restaurant in Cape Town and the Tomato Tart had been listed as one of the fifty things to eat before you die (when will these lists end!). We had the tart, which was okay, but we have both certainly eaten better, and overall the meal was fine, but we much preferred the Five Flies and actually returned to this restaurant on our last night. When we returned to Cape Town in May 2014 I booked a table at the Five Flies online, but when we arrived having taken a taxi we found it all shut up and deserted, which is why we know that it is closed. It also says so on the internet too so I checked in April 2016, just to make sure that we did not just have a bad encounter.

The next day we had booked to go to Robben Island, but when we arrived at the ferry port we discovered that it had been cancelled, and that no ferries were crossing that day. This is a problem with so many places, and you cannot do anything about the weather, but luckily, we had built in extra time on this holiday to be able to, hopefully, overcome these situations. We were back at the V&A Waterfront area and from there you get the most fabulous view of Table Mountain and, from what we could see, it was clear of clouds. So, we jumped into a taxi and were whisked off to take the cable car up the mountain. We had been told that weather conditions can change very quickly, and if you see a clear mountain, take the opportunity while you can. This advice is very true – by the time we arrived at the cable car station (luckily no queue) and paid to go up, the clouds started to descend. When we got to the top, after quite a rocky ride in a big glass car that was being buffeted by the winds, the clouds were so thick that you could not see a thing! It was a real pea-souper and it had turned very cold too. We had a coffee, waited a while to see if it would clear, but we soon realised that if we did not make a break for it now, that the cable car might stop running altogether, and we could be stranded. There is a path that can be used to climb up, and down, the mountain, but we were not properly dressed to do this, and, although Richard would probably make it, I didn't think I was fit enough to be able to achieve the mile walk downhill!

So, a quick turnaround was the answer, and we went back down in the cable car and returned to our hotel, to get ready for our dinner later that evening. Not the most successful of days, but we had photos of a clear Table Mountain taken from the Waterfront, and we had ridden the cable car. Our meal reservation that night was at Harvey's, a restaurant located in a hotel on the seafront, next to the beach area of Cape Town, which specialises in seafood.

Another day and another tour. This time an organised tour of the city, and our first stop was Table Mountain (no cloud, so go while you can!) This time we had success and as we disembarked from our cable car, we had fabulous views down onto the city and out to Robben Island. Lion's Head and Signal Hill, the two peaks that lie beside Table Mountain, were now visible, whereas they had been shrouded in thick white cloud the day before. Lion's Head is named because it looks like one, and Signal Hill, or Lion's Flank as it is sometimes known, is famous, as being the location of the noon gun which still fires daily on the stroke of twelve midday. We had a walk around the top of the mountain enjoying the flora and fauna of the national park and we went to the far side to be able to look over the range which eventually leads to Cape Point in the distance.

Returning to our tour group we went to a museum where they had a display of the finalists for Wildlife Photographer of the Year. The winner in 2009 became quite infamous – the photo, of a grey wolf jumping over a snow covered gate, was fabulous – it was there in the museum: but it was discovered that the wolf was actually tame, and was trained to do this feat whilst the photographer just had to set up his camera exactly where he wanted it, and took his time to get that perfect shot. It was a great photo, but was not of real wildlife, and certainly not the chance encounter that everyone had been led to believe. We continued on for a stroll around the Company Gardens, where we had another great view of a cloudless Table Mountain, and then we went to the castle, looking on to the square which is where Nelson Mandela gave his speech, after being released from prison.

On our final day, we managed to book the tour to Robben Island for the morning, leaving Mandela Gallery for our one hour sail from the V&A Waterfront to the penal island, giving us another wonderful view of Table Mountain, set against clear blue skies, with just a bit of a table cloth cascading down its side! When we docked, we were taken on a prison bus, on a tour around the island with a guide who was very informative, animated and emotional. We went to Irish Town, the quarry and the lepers' colony before going on the tour of the actual prison itself. This was done by an ex-prisoner, who could feel and relive the pain of those who suffered in this place. We saw Nelson Mandela's tiny cell, and heard all about how he and his fellow political prisoners managed to communicate with the outside world and to cope with being interned for sixteen years on this island. He was in prison for a total of twenty-seven years before finally being released and eventually becoming the president of South Africa. Like Alcatraz, this prison was so cruel, offering those locked away a glimpse of what they had left behind, freedom was so close, but unachievable, as dangerous waters lay between you and your goal. You can certainly understand why nobody escaped from Robben Island and lived.

We returned to the waterfront and dined al fresco on prawns and chips. The prawns were just medium sized, but five were enough for a very filling lunch – a very pleasant end to a wonderful short break.

As I mentioned, we did return for a couple of nights in Cape Town in May 2010, where we boarded a cruise ship which took us up the west coast of Africa and Europe, back to Dover. It took thirty days and we stopped in Namibia, Tonga, Benin, Ghana, Senegal, Cape Verde Islands, Tenerife, Morocco, Spanish Morocco, France and Belgium before arriving in England.

On that occasion our hotel was located very close to the V&A Waterfront, so that we could enjoy the bars, restaurants, shops and sites of this iconic location. We rested on our free day during our stay but were booked on an excursion from our cruise ship in Cape Town, and we went to a vineyard for a tour and a wine tasting as South Africa is famous for its wines; and, in particular, for holidays taking the Garden Route.

We like Cape Town. The tourist areas are very clean and, from what we witnessed, safe. There is a lot to see and to do. You can also swim with sharks; do a safari from there; go whale watching, visit a township; cycle, fly and surf – just to name some of the things listed on viator.com and the scenery is stunning. The food, especially the seafood, is fabulous – I have never seen prawns as big as those in Cape Town, anywhere else in the world. They have good beer, great wine, and a very nice climate. I know there are issues and you hear of horror stories that have struck tourists in this city, but that can happen anywhere in the world – look at the events in London in 2017, with the random terrorist attacks. The key thing to travelling to places like this is to be aware of your surroundings, don't go out brandishing lots of gold and expensive jewellery. Don't flash your money around. Only use registered taxi's and keep to the tourist areas, unless you are on a tour or with a guide. That way, you should have a peaceful and relaxing holiday, enjoying the sights, tastes and sounds of slightly more unusual places.

CHAPTER 23

Angkor Wat, Cambodia (29) – February 2010

We started this holiday in Bangkok, and it was destined to be our longest holiday so far; the 12th of February to the 15th of March. I have covered our stay in the capital of Thailand in detail in Chapter 11; so I am going to skim over the details, and just provide the important parts, which are relevant to this chapter. We flew direct from London to Bangkok, and booked into the Shangri-La hotel, which is close to the river. This is a beautiful five-star hotel, and we upgraded to a Horizon Club room, which gives you access to the lounge, where you can have breakfast and, in the evening during happy hour, complementary drinks and snacks and the snacks are quite substantial and would satisfy a small appetite very adequately. Our reservation was for six nights even though we were only sleeping in the hotel for four – we just thought that it would be easier for us to leave our main luggage in the room, and take a small bag with us for our two night side trip into Cambodia. We never travel light, and as we had a three week cruise following our stay in Bangkok, we certainly would not have been permitted to take all our cases on the economy flight we had booked to fly us to Siem Reap.

I had organised this excursion independently from home. We do a lot of our own planning and reservations, as our holidays can become quite complicated and I like us to be in control, over these add-ons. In this instance, I had made reservations with Dragon Air to take us from Bangkok International Airport to Siem Reap in Cambodia, the site of the famous Angkor Wat temples; and the flight was a short one, just forty-five minutes. I had also arranged for a transfer from the airport to the hotel, Angkor Palace Hotel, but made a mistake here, as I had inadvertently arranged for the hotel to pick us up, as well as our tour organiser Buffalo Tours – oops! When I had made the hotel reservation online, the hotel had accepted the booking to include transfers and charged us accordingly. It was they who met us at the airport and a quick call had to be made to the tour company to recall their agent, and to bring our tour guide to meet us directly at the hotel. There was no harm done – we still had to pay for the error, but it was not expensive, just twelve dollars, but I was embarrassed about this mistake; I am not so good at organising our own extensions after all!

The hotel was very large and pleasant and had a wonderful large pool; if you were prepared for this, which we weren't. It was also very full, with many different tour groups. But, when we went to the restaurant that evening, it was quite empty. We can only assume that the tours were dining elsewhere or had gone to see a show at a different location. I had a Khmer dish to start, pork parcels, which were very nice, but the Nasi Goreng was mediocre. Richard stuck to western cuisine, as he does on most occasions, ordering mushroom soup followed by steak – the former was a bit bland, and the latter was not very hot, but overall the meal was fine, costing eighty-seven dollars, including a bottle of wine.

The following day we had to be up early, as our tour started at eight a.m. We had booked this through Viator.com and we had reserved a private tour of the Angkor temple complex. This was being run by Buffalo Tours, the local operator. Our guide went by the name of Tom, but I am sure that this was a name that he had selected for himself. He was very good and spoke really clear English, which made him easy to understand and a pleasure to listen to.

Our first stop was at Angkor Wat itself. Our driver dropped us at the back of the complex near the lake, and we walked around it to enter the temple in the opposite direction from the normal tour groups. This meant that we had a view of the temple, without any other people, and we got wonderful clear photos, unencumbered by tourists. I have seen many photos of Angkor Wat,

and I always wondered what the balloons were, towering above the tallest temples – now that we were up close, I could see how stupid I had now been realising that these high suspended balloons were actually a type of palm tree, with very long trunks and bushy upright palm fronds – duh!

Once we had taken all our photos of the temple from a distance, we proceeded to go inside. The temples are ruins, but are still quite intact in places, although the stone is pitted and dark. There are many statues and reliefs throughout the building, which we walked through without any restrictions at all. With the number of visitors now going to Siem Reap, I am sure that this open invitation to clamber over the fallen stones and get up close and personal to the monuments will not continue. If it does, there won't be much for future visitors to see! Our guide provided us with detail after detail of the Khmer race, who had built the temple and had worshipped here, as well as some of the stories of the Hindu gods and goddesses, demons and devils; mythological creatures that adorn the buildings and the stories of the creation of earth and other interesting anecdotes. We were there for most of the morning, wandering in and out of the temple, before finally leaving from the main entrance, where, after crossing the bridge, we were able to see the recognisable front view of the complex over the lake, with the towers rising in the background.

We had lunch at a café on the temple complex. This is the only public place to eat, and was very busy, but it also offered just one option, a yellow curry. Needless to say, Richard did not partake! I think that you are able to take a picnic with you to be able to eat in a certain area within this public rest area, but it is not practical to carry anything bulky, whilst walking around the temples – other than your camera of course!

After lunch, we continued with our, tour going to the Elephant Terrace, which is a huge platform area used by the Khmer royal family to watch processions and entertainment and it is decorated with a number of varying sized elephants. We drove on to see the temples at Banyan and Bhajan – our favourite being Banyan. This complex has hundreds of four-sided temples; each one decorated with a face of a Buddha. We were told that the image of the Buddha on each side was modelled on the king, who had ordered the construction of this temple complex. We climbed up, in and around each of the towers, taking so many photos, as it was such a memorable and wonderful building. Neither of these complexes were in as good condition as Angkor Wat, with many of the towers having collapsed, leaving the ground littered with stones and gravel, making it quite difficult to get around within the site. Our final stop was by far in the worst state, but, nevertheless, as a result this made it an absolutely wonderful place to visit.

Ta Prohm had been one of the last sites to be discovered and rescued from the jungle. This complex was a ruin, with very few standing buildings of any note. But what made it so enthralling was that the jungle had grown in and around the ruins, almost capturing the relics for itself. The way that the trunks and the branches of the trees had twisted and entwined themselves around doors, collapsed roofs and images, was absolutely mesmerising and the photo opportunities were tremendous. This was probably the busiest site we had been to, as there were so many local families climbing around and posing in front of the most dramatic buildings, that it was difficult to get a picture without people in it. But, we had time and the patience to wait for our turn, and then we quickly captured the dramatic site of nature conquering man.

Whereas many of the other sites in Siem Reap have been rescued from the encroaching jungle and restored to some of their former glory, it was decided to leave Ta Prohm in this semi-cleared state. It certainly makes for an unusual visit and is just so dramatic. This complex was used as a backdrop for the film Tomb Raider. The huge cave in the film does not exist. That was pure Hollywood effects, but the jungle scene and the overgrown relics were real, and were quite a spectacle to behold.

We left Siem Reap the next day, leaving the hotel at eleven a.m. The local airport was fine and quite modern; we even enjoyed a bottle of wine there before we boarded the flight back to Bangkok where we re-joined the rest of our luggage in our room at the Shangri-La. We stayed another two nights in Bangkok and visited the Tiger Temple which is covered in detail in the chapter on Bangkok.

We then flew to Sydney where we would be boarding a cruise ship to head back to Bangkok. At this point, I would like to give any reader a word of advice. Do not book a shared transfer from Sydney Airport to your hotel! As we had arranged this first part of our holiday ourselves, we did not have any arranged transfer so we booked through Viator, and this is probably the only time where they let us down. We were off the flight, through immigration and had our luggage collected very quickly – probably just thirty minutes from the wheels hitting the tarmac! So when we came out to look for our pick-up, they had not yet arrived – we were too quick for them. This wasn't too bad, as the guide arrived within thirty minutes at seven a.m. But other people on the flight were not so lucky, and it took another hour for everyone to come through and we eventually walked to the coach at eight twenty a.m. – almost two hours after we had arrived! We were staying at the Shangri-La in Sydney and as a courtesy to us, with having to wait the longest, we were dropped off first, although some of the other passengers did comment that they could not understand why our driver drove past their hotels to do this!

After our last visit to Sydney, we knew how early we were likely to be arriving at the hotel, and, when we were not able to check in last time, we took the precaution of booking a room for two nights so that we could check in straight away. But, our travel agent had booked us for an early check-in, and the hotel had expected us to be checking in early the day before. As we had not arrived, we were down as a no-show and they had released our room! This meant that our harbour view room had gone, and unless we were prepared to wait for the normal check-in that day, we could not have this standard of room! I was outraged at this as it was not our mistake and we had paid a lot of money for a room that we could not now use – our plans to be able to rest for a few hours and then enjoy Sydney in the afternoon had been scuppered! But to appease us, they gave us an upgraded room to a Horizon Club room but with a view of Darling Harbour, instead of Sydney Harbour. We accepted this, as they also promised us a full refund of our original booking for the previous night. Although we did not have the view that we wanted from our room, we did have a great view from the lounge, where we were able to enjoy all the amenities that we had been given in Bangkok.

The cruise that we took on this occasion was for three weeks on the Diamond Princess. We sailed along the south coast of Australia, calling at Melbourne, Tasmania, Adelaide and Fremantle. We should have stopped in Geraldton but due to high winds, this was not possible. We then sailed through the Indonesian Islands, crossing the equator, so we were no longer pollywogs but had then become shellbacks! This is a tradition on-board cruise ships, to celebrate the crossing of the equator with King Neptune and Queen Aphrodite – the celebration involves a lot of slapstick torture of volunteer passengers who are tried by the court and then covered in jam, beans, flour, eggs or jelly! It is all in the name of fun, and quite a laugh the first time that you experience this ritual. We have now crossed the equator four times, so we are well and truly shellbacks for our efforts. The cruise continued to Singapore, where we had a wonderful lunch in the grill at Raffles, and then we sailed on to Vietnam.

We docked at the port of Phu My where we went on a long excursion to Ho Chi Minh City or Saigon as it used to be called. It is not the most beautiful city we have seen, and there is not a lot to capture the imagination of the visitor, but it was another country ticked off our list. Our final stop before reaching Bangkok was Sihanoukville in Cambodia, a rather insignificant beach town. It was a good cruise with plenty of time for rest and for relaxation, but with enough interesting stops to inspire and to remember.

We have every intention of returning to Angkor Wat as we thought that the whole area was just wonderful and offered so many sites, excursions and activities. There is probably so much more to see and to do, and on this short two day excursion we were a bit limited regarding doing anything else, except to visit the main sites. There is a very good Viator tour listed which includes accommodation, a private guide for three days, an extended itinerary to include more temples and a visit to a lake with a floating village. I hope that we will get the chance to do this at some point, but, as we have been there, done that and bought the T-shirt, this second visit is quite low on our list and, as we are now doing our own bucket list, there are other places that are likely to take precedence.

CHAPTER 24

Golden Temple of Amritsar, India (6) – May 2010

When we went to India in 2006, Richard hated it so much that he vowed never to go back again. My problem was that this was another of the fifty in India and I was not sure how I was going to get him to return for us to visit this site. I had visions of going on my own, but that would defeat the object of us doing all the fifty places together. But then I had an amazing idea. What if we did this trip in a weekend – literally in and out and fly back home! Richard agreed, but I don't think that either of us realised what a feat this would actually be.

I found a company on-line who would organise our excursion to Amritsar from Delhi, so all I needed to do was to book the flights and everything else would be taken care of. We decided to go over the bank holiday weekend at the start of May 2010, and, as our flight was leaving early on the Friday morning, we stayed at Heathrow the night before. We had reserved Premium Economy with British Airways, and we were given the option of paying a small fee to upgrade to Club World. This was my first time in business class, and I liked it! At that time we were not Silver Executive members of the British Airways Club, but it was thanks to this upgrade, which enabled us to get the tier points we needed to take that extra step up. To move from bronze to silver the first time takes a lot of flights, but as you get more tier points for your flights and once you are silver, it is a lot easier to maintain that level. The increased level means that you have access to lounges, if there is one, and you are on a Oneworld flight; increased luggage allowance, regardless of what class you fly (very useful with economy flights to Europe) and express check-in. As you can use the Club World check-in at the airport; you can reserve your seats free of charge at any time before your flight, through the Executive Club internet site; you can board the plane at the same time as Club World, and you get extra Avios air-miles and Tier points on all flights. These benefits are available on all the Oneworld alliance airlines, so it is a really useful benefit to have and we make sure that we earn enough British Airways flights and tier points each year to keep these privileges.

But back to our flight to Delhi – the flight was probably only at seventy-five percent capacity, which was the reason why we were able to upgrade at such a reasonable price, so we received excellent personal service on-board. We were given papers and a glass of champagne when we boarded, and then we had drinks before our meal so we both had Kir Royals, and wine with our meal, which was scallops, lamb, ice-cream and cheese and biscuits, which was accompanied by a nice glass of port. Now, if you fly business class all the time, you are probably thinking – so what? But this was my first time and I had just got used to the few extra benefits you get from flying premium economy. Richard had been upgraded to business class once before, when he had missed a connecting flight due to fog and had a very long wait for the next one. It certainly gave me a taste for the high-life, and, although we did manage to get a few upgrades on other flights after this, we now prefer to book business class if we can, and enjoy this luxury on all our long haul flights – it is certainly a better way to travel.

We were an hour late taking off and we were late landing due to thunderstorms in the area around Delhi, but our tour operator was there to meet us in the arrivals hall with a clear sign and a pleasant greeting, and we were whisked off for our first night at the Grand Hotel, Delhi, which was not too far from the airport. This is a very modern hotel with a large foyer and nice, good sized, rooms; but we were late arriving, at around eleven p.m. and there was no opportunity to eat, so we just had what was in our room. Because of the time difference, neither of us was particularly tired, so we had a drink from our duty free drinks purchased on the flight out, and we talked until almost one in the morning.

The problem with our late night soiree was that we were being picked up the next day at six fifteen a.m. to be taken to the train station in Delhi to catch the seven twenty a.m. train to Amritsar. We were both exhausted as we had had so little sleep, but it was still an exhilarating experience to drive through the crowded streets of Delhi at this time of the day. At first, the roads around the hotel and the outskirts of Delhi were not too busy, but the closer we got to the train station, the crazier the traffic became. There were cars, trucks, buses, bikes, tuk-tuks and people everywhere, all going in different directions, but all heading for the same place – the station. It was chaos! Horns were going, people were shouting at one another, and at one point no-one was moving, as all the traffic was at gridlock, due to many vehicles not following the traffic regulations and going around roundabouts the wrong way, or not giving way, and going through red lights in order to jump the queue. How we got through I don't know, but our driver pulled up in front of the station, and we were escorted through to our carriage by our guide, who assisted us in finding our seats, storing our luggage and speaking to the guard, regarding our six-hour journey to Amritsar.

We were in first class, but the carriage was very basic, with very little room to move or to stretch out. We were on a forward-facing bench seat for three, which was well padded and comfy and, thank goodness, the air conditioning was very good and working, as it was very hot. We were given a bottle of water and a pot containing hot water; a small thermos flask really. This enabled us to make our own tea on the journey, as we were given tea bags, milk and sugar. There was a cooked breakfast provided on the train, but we both skipped this just to be on the safe side. With such a long journey, I could not cross my legs for six hours, so I had to pay a visit to the toilet. At least it was western style, not a squatting design like most are in India, but it had open plumbing, so everything just falls straight through onto the rail track! What made it worse, was that the catering area is located right by the side of the WC and it did not look very hygienic at all – very small too; so how they managed to cook anything amazed me.

There were several stops along the way, but Amritsar was the final point of call and the Indian who was sitting by my side made sure that we got off at the right stop. We arrived at one forty p.m., so the journey took six hours twenty minutes, a lot longer than I had expected. Our guide was waiting for us on the platform and he took us to our hotel, the Ista; a very nice five-star hotel in the city. We had time to freshen up and to have lunch which included a reasonable bottle of Indian wine before being collected and taken to the Pakistan border to witness the closing of the gates ceremony.

I knew that this was included in our tour package, but I had no idea what it would involve. As we left the comfort of our car, we walked with thousands of other locals and tourists towards the stands that surround the gates, which act as the barrier across the border between India and Pakistan. We had to go through a security check and then we were herded into the VIP stands, where we at least had a seat while we waited for the ceremony to start. I cannot express how shocked we were at the number of people attending this nightly ritual – there were thousands, most of them locals, and this number helped to generate a real party atmosphere. While we waited, there was music being played over the loud speakers, and people were dancing either in their seats or along the barriers that lined the path leading to the gate. People were running up and down waving the Indian flag. There was shouting and cheering and it was a total cacophony of noise. We knew that it was all good natured – if we hadn't, it could have been quite intimidating as there were very few westerners in the crowd.

Through the open gate we could see that a similar party was taking place on the Pakistan side and as time went on, the shouts from the crowd provoked the Pakistanis and similar shouts from them did the same to the Indians. The whole idea was to try and show which of the two were the proudest of their nation, by trying to be the most raucous and patriotic, and fifteen thousand people every night do the same thing. At a certain point in the proceedings, the Indian guards left their building and lined the street performing a military parade for those on the Indian side. Then one of the senior offices strutted towards the gate, goose-stepping with as much pomp as he could muster. He shouted through to the replicated officer on the Pakistan border and then returned to his troop.

This was repeated several times, accompanied by cheers for our side, and jeers against the others. There was more dancing and partying taking place, as the whole audience got more and more animated, until eventually, the officer returned to the gate for the final time and literally slammed it shut in the face of the Pakistan officer and the people on the other side. Although we could not see, we were pretty certain that the same thing happened to the Pakistan gate, so as by the end of the day, both gates were securely closed and locked, and no further border crossings would be taking place that day.

This event has to be one of the most bizarre proceedings we have ever seen and the number of people attending was quite astounding. It is also one of the most memorable and even now, seven years later, I can remember it with clarity. In August 2017, there were celebrations recognising seventy years since the independence of India, and the division of Pakistan, which resulted in a mass migration of Hindus and Muslims moving between the newly created countries to be on the "right" side. During this time there was rioting, murder and rape happening, and many thousands lost their lives. I remember this being portrayed in the film "Gandhi", as well as the massacre in Amritsar, and, knowing that the border ceremony still takes place every night and attracts so many people is evidence of how raw feelings still are.

We returned to the city centre, and made our first visit to the Golden Temple. This site is the most sacred place for the Sikh religion, and there are a number of rituals that have to be followed to pass through the corridors of the surrounding buildings to enter the site. We had to cover our heads – of course all Sikh's wear turbans. It is part of their religion; but anyone visiting had to ensure that their hair was not visible and we were given rather small headscarves to cover our hair, and tie underneath at the back. They were so small that they were almost comical – if they had been blue instead of white, I would have felt like a Smurf! But I had not come all that way to not see that wonderful religious building, due to being too vain to be seen in a silly hat! We then had to remove our shoes and socks and bathe our feet, before we finally entered the grounds of the Golden Temple. What a spectacular sight greeted us!

It was nine at night, but the site was very busy, with pilgrims' bathing in the lake that surrounds the temple, praying and worshipping Allah in the way they wish to. Many were clothed in simple loincloths as they entered the water from the steps that were strategically located along the sides of this manmade lake. The water comes from a natural source, a river inlet, which pours into it and purifies the lake, which is actually eighty feet deep.

At that time we just walked around the circumference of the lake taking in the sights and the sounds and gazing at this beautifully decorated golden building, set in the centre of the water with just a single causeway leading from the marble surroundings to the entrance of the temple. The shrine was lit by bright lights but was done in a way that dramatically enhanced its appearance, rather than being showy and Disney-like. The gold shimmered and the colours of the jewels, marble and decoration were reflected in the water, to provide an ethereal mirror of the temple itself. It was a remarkable sight, and as we walked around in the warm night air, we were mesmerised by what we were witnessing.

We returned to our hotel at around ten p.m. and we went to a restaurant in the hotel, the Tai Chi, where we enjoyed a very nice Chinese meal.

The next day we were picked up at nine a.m. after breakfast, to take our official tour of the temple and the surrounding complex. It was very hot and the site was even more crowded than the night before. We followed the religious process of removing our footwear, washing our feet and covering our heads with the scarf again, and then we entered, to be able to see the site in its full glory. Our guide explained about what it means to be a pure Sikh – you must be a vegetarian, not eating any meat at all, and must carry the five keys of Sikhism at all times, which are – wear a bangle; have long hair, carry a wooden comb, have a beard and carry a sword or a knife. An un-pure Sikh does not carry the keys and eats meat, but it is an individuals' choice, as to whether they are pure or not.

The site does not just consist of the temple, lake and surrounding palaces, but there is a canteen that can feed sixty-thousand people per day. It is mass catering on a grand scale! There was a chapatti making machine, that churned out four thousand chapattis an hour, but this was not enough and there were women sitting cross-legged on the floor, making many more by hand. The vats containing vegetarian curry, rice and dhal were huge, and being stirred with, what looked like, enormous canoe paddles, by barefoot, scantily clad, volunteers. Thousands of people sat on the floor, with a tray containing their meagre meal of curry, rice and bread, while other volunteers passed around them with huge pots of tea, to provide each person with a hot drink to accompany their meal. As each person finished, they took their own tray and mug to an area to wash them and then stacked the utensils, ready for the next person who would already be waiting to take their place. This feeding of the hungry takes place continually throughout the day, offering a free meal to anyone who requires it. Whether you are a beggar, a businessman or a prince; no matter what religion, colour or caste. Every person is entitled to a meal here. There is no hierarchy, no VIP seating – everyone sits on the floor amongst their fellow diners, and enjoys the same meal in the same manner, provided by philanthropic people, and prepared and served by volunteers. It was very humbling.

As we continued with our walk around the lake towards the causeway, it became very evident just how popular a site the Golden Temple is. There were very few western tourists at the complex when we visited. All the visitors and worshippers were Indians, and the queue to enter the temple itself was enormous. There were hundreds of men, women and children packed onto the bridge that connected the temple to the complex; all of them crushed together in the heat of the day, patiently waiting their turn to enter the holy building. I thought that we had come all this way and would not be able to enter the inner sanctuary, but our guide spoke to the security personnel and we were allowed to pass, by all those waiting and to enter through the exit in order to gain a speedy access. Our guide was not able to accompany us, but he told us what to look for, and where to go, once we entered the building.

The base of the building is formed by decorated marble, and it is the upper level that is covered in gold. We climbed to the uppermost part of the temple to touch the gold domes, and, as we climbed, we were able to see inside. There were so many people on all the levels, praying and chanting. As they approached the main shrine and the holy-men, they knelt and bowed, similarly to Muslims, and after they touched the steps of the shrine, they retreated backwards so as not to turn their back on the holiest of holies. There were a number of collection boxes located throughout the shrine and these were stuffed full of money; alms from the pilgrims and the devotees. This had to be the holiest site that I have ever visited, as there were so many people praying, prostrating and humbling themselves before the holy-men and the shrine; and there were hundreds more to follow, which meant that as one person left, they were replaced by many more – a continual procession of devout worshippers, taking this holy route through the Golden Temple and around the complex, where there were so many more alcoves and places of worship. It really was an amazing sight, and it offered so much more than either of us had expected, and is so worthy of its place in the fifty, and, at number six, it truly deserves to be in the top tier.

We left the temple complex and we went to the nearby memorial gardens where, on the 13th of April 1919, the British Indian Army, under the command of Captain Dyer, opened fire on a crowd of nonviolent protestors, consisting of men, women and children, and massacred them.

The civilians had assembled to participate in the annual Baisakhi celebrations – both a religious and a cultural festival for the Punjabis. The Bagh-space was walled on all sides, with five entrances. On Dyer's orders, his troops fired on the crowd for ten minutes, directing their bullets largely towards the few open gates, through which people were trying to flee.[2] It is estimated that over a thousand people were killed, some of them jumping down a well; to try and escape the bullets but dying instead from the impact, or crush of others following them – a hundred and twenty bodies were eventually pulled from the well. You can still see the bullet marks on the walls surrounding this, now, tranquil garden. The site is now a memorial to those who died in what came to be known as the Amritsar Massacre. A central, tall pillar-like temple records the details of what happened that fateful day, in the hope that this will never happen again.

I was ashamed to be British at that moment, as we were told about the massacre and the aftermath – it was hard to believe that anyone could carry out such orders against the innocent, but while we were in Amritsar, the Indians were so friendly to us – children shaking our hands, youths wanting their photo taken with us, everyone making us feel welcome. It was worth going all that way for this wonderful and this spiritual experience.

We had time to shower, change, pack our cases and have lunch, before we took our return train to Delhi. There was a mix-up over our seat numbers, but yet again, the Indians were so understanding and amiable, that they moved around to accommodate us, as we had no idea where we were supposed to be sitting! On the six hour journey, a three course meal was served. Having seen the kitchen conditions on our journey to Amritsar, we just had the soup and the ice-cream, missing out on the main meal, which was curry anyway. At Delhi, we disembarked off the train, and headed for the arrivals lounge, but there was no sign of our guide. We waited for thirty minutes walking back and forth, dodging people asleep on the floor waiting for the early morning trains, but no-one showed. We decided to get a taxi to the hotel as it was so late, and we were going to be leaving early the next morning. I was nervous about taking a strange car with a driver that we did not know, but we both decided that we didn't really have much of a choice.

When we arrived at the hotel, we were met at the gate by people from the hotel and from our tour company who were mortified that they had missed us at the station. Supposedly, someone had been standing on the platform where our carriage was due to pull up, but we missed one another, even though we were both walking around trying to locate one another, we never once crossed paths. But there was no harm done, we were just a few rupees out of pocket about nine hundred to be exact, about fifteen pounds, due to paying for the taxi.

The next day we were picked up early and taken back to the airport, where we were now in premium economy for our return flight. As it was a morning flight and we had the five-hour time difference, we were back at home the same day. This meant that we had been in India for just three nights, but had been on two ten-hour flights, had two six hour train journeys, very little sleep but we had an amazing weekend in Amritsar, staying in first class hotels, and actually enjoying some pleasant meals with good wine. Not one of my brightest ideas, but certainly one of our most enthralling holidays ever. The tour company who we used for this excursion was Cosmovision, and I found them on the internet.

CHAPTER 25

Barbados (43) – November 2010

This is one of the rare entries that we do not agree with. There are so many sites, cities and countries that, in our view, deserve to be on this list, and Barbados is not one of them. We can only think that a resort destination needed to be added, as most British viewers, understandably, would be voting for the places that they have visited, and the Caribbean Islands would probably be a main holiday destination for many UK tourists. I think that I have mentioned that Richard and I are not resort people. We like to travel and to visit places and sites, rather than to relax on a beach all day. We could manage a few days relaxing, but we wanted to see a lot more of a country than just its beach. And besides, if that is all you want to do, why pay all that money to fly for eight or nine hours to see sand that is exactly the same in the Mediterranean! But, Barbados is on the list, so one way or another, I needed to find a way for us to visit this Caribbean Island.

In 2006, we discovered cruising – our first cruise, which went to Alaska, forms a chapter earlier in the book. But the benefits of cruising are that your hotel moves around with you, and every day you can wake up in a new location, with lots of opportunity for you to discover new sights and sounds. Our second cruise was in the Indian Ocean, which was on a very small ship, the African Star, with a capacity of around two hundred – very different from the cruise ship we used, to sail to the Caribbean which was Cunard's beautiful Queen Mary 2. This mammoth of the seas, launched in 2004, has a capacity of two thousand six hundred and twenty passengers – small by the standards being set by Royal Caribbean nowadays; both the Oasis and Allure of the Seas have a capacity of six thousand two hundred and ninety-six, but at the time we started cruising, this truly was a huge ship. Cunard specialise in "the voyage" – they don't cruise. Their itineraries are a journey and you use their ships to travel from continent to continent. They are built for ocean crossings and, the Queen Mary 2 in particular, is the only vessel that still does regular Transatlantic crossings between Southampton and New York and back again with no stops or detours, just seven days at sea. Many other cruise lines will do what they call "repositioning" cruises where they cross the oceans on a single trip to move for the new season. We did one of these cruises in August 2013, going from Southampton to New York on the Caribbean Princess, stopping in Norway, Iceland, Greenland and Newfoundland before arriving in New York. We should have called at the Shetland Islands and the Faroe Islands too, but unfortunately, bad weather prevented us from doing the full itinerary. This ship had been sailing around the UK and Northern Europe during the summer months and was now heading to America, to complete the short Canadian season, before heading down to the Caribbean, during our winter months.

We also did a crossing in April 2016, on the Celebrity Eclipse, leaving Miami and sailing to Southampton, calling at the Bahamas, Lisbon and Le Havre en-route. Unfortunately, we missed our stop in Bermuda; again due to bad weather. It is a problem that you have to accept when cruising, as the captain will not put the passengers or the ship at risk if bad weather is reported; especially for any tender ports; these are when the ship is not able to dock, so small boats are used to ferry passengers back and forth from ship to pier. We had an issue with the tenders in Greenland, as the weather was not good when we went ashore – very wet and misty, and, as the weather worsened, one of the tenders got lost, returning to the ship! They stopped more people leaving the ship, and suspended the return service until the fog lifted, and it was safe to resume the transfer of passengers.

In the same way that we do not like a long stay at a beach resort, we did not like to have too many days at sea, so the classic Transatlantic voyage did not appeal to us. However, I really wanted to have the experience of sailing into New York on a cruise ship, and the cruise that we booked for in November 2010, did exactly what we wanted. It would be our first time to the Caribbean, but we would stop in Barbados, and we would be doing a return journey to New York so that I could fulfil my own bucket list wish, of sailing past the Statue of Liberty, viewing the Manhattan skyline and sailing into New York. On this occasion, I had received an email from Cruisecritic.com, offering some exceptional bargains for sailing on the Queen Mary, and this particular itinerary was amongst the offers. We booked a Queens Grill suite at an exceptional price, and arranged our own flights to New York, flying with British Airways in Premium Economy class. Whenever we could we would take this class of seat, as they offer more legroom, a slightly larger seat, a cabin just for this class with service being provided before economy and, most importantly, we were rewarded with extra tier and Avios points, which helped us to maintain our silver executive status for many years. We would have liked to fly business class all the time, as this is the way to travel – comfortable, fully reclining seats; priority boarding; a glass of champagne as soon as you board; personal service and you are normally first off, the plane on arrival; But the price of these tickets can quite often be extortionate, and, as the flight is just a means of getting to your holiday destination, we would rather spend our money on the holiday.

Whenever we cruise, we will always build in at least one night prior to boarding, just in case something happens and you are delayed in arriving at the departure point. If you book flights through the cruise line, they will normally guarantee your connection, and will get you to the cruise ship whatever happens as long as it is not your fault of course. Similarly, if for some reason the ship is late returning to port and you miss your flight, if the cruise company has booked the flights for you, they will rearrange the flight, and if necessary, put you up overnight in a hotel, at their expense. This happened on a cruise we did to the Caribbean in 2013, with the Princess. We did a seven-day return cruise from Galveston, Texas calling at Cozumel, Honduras and

Belize. On our return to Galveston, we were met by thick fog, and we were unable to dock. All of the passengers had to vacate their cabins so that the ship could prepare for the next guests, but it was impossible to leave the ship, as we, along with several other cruise ships, were all hovering outside the port. We should have been on a tour at eight fifteen a.m. which was immediately cancelled, and we sat for several hours in the lounge just waiting for the fog to lift. The ship provided us with drinks, breakfast Danishes and sandwiches for lunch, as well as some very quickly arranged entertainment; until, eventually, at one thirty p.m., we started to move and finally docked at two thirty p.m. Many passengers had missed their flights and announcements were being made, telling people what they needed to do. All those with flights arranged by the Princess would be staying in airport hotels, and booked on new flights the next day, but those with their own flight reservations had to sort things out for themselves. To put it bluntly, for these passengers the view of the cruise company was – tough! It would be a case of make your own arrangements and then try and claim from your insurance, for the extra costs! On this occasion it did not affect us, as we were staying for two nights in Houston. It just meant that we missed out on the tour of the city, which was no hardship to us.

But, let me get back to November 2010, and our Queen Mary 2 cruise. We flew from Manchester to Heathrow and then on to JFK. At Manchester, we had issues with trying to reserve our seats on the next flight, and had a few anxious hours thinking that we had been bumped down from our premium seats. When we arrived at Heathrow and we went to customer services, they ripped up our boarding pass and upgraded us to business class – result! This is one of the best reasons for being a member of the airline's frequent flyer programme, as Silver Executive members, we are first to be considered for any upgrades available, and at no cost!

We arrived late in the evening in New York, and just had time, and enough energy, to have something to eat and to drink before we collapsed onto our bed, exhausted from a long day's travelling and the five-hour time difference. Our routine for travelling over time zones is to set our watches to the destination time as soon as we board the plane, and then do everything in line with that time – eat, sleep and stay awake. When we arrive at our destination, even if this is returning home, we very rarely will have a sleep, regardless of how tired we are – we instantly try to get into the routine of that time zone. It works for us and we rarely suffer from jet lag, but this may not be the case for everyone.

The next day we were awake at a reasonable hour and had time for breakfast and some relaxation before we checked out of our hotel and took a taxi to the pier in Brooklyn. Even though there were a lot of passengers on this ship, the queues were not bad at all and, with being suite guests, we skipped the lines for our priority check-in.

Cunard are quite different from many of the other cruise lines, as their cabins are allocated depending upon the grill level you select. The full suites are classed as Queen's Grill; which is the top dining class, and has its own dining room, in a preferred location on the ship – on the Queen Mary 2 this was at the back of the ship, on a very high level. The mini-suites have the Princess Grill and all other cabins dine in the main restaurant. The Britannia Grill, which is the largest, all passengers are able to dine in the speciality restaurants or at the buffet, but only those assigned to the three classes of grills can dine in that location. This can be seen as a class system, but basically, you get what you pay for! The more expensive your cabin or you suite, the higher the grill class. I don't know if the menu is the same in all of the restaurants, but certainly in the Queen's Grill, there was excellent choice. It was beautifully served and tasted delicious – probably the best food we have had on a cruise ship.

Cunard do not offer flexible dining – you are allocated a table for your cruise which can be for two, four, six or eight, and an allotted time. We were on a table for six, with Don and Chuck from America and Simon and Alison from the Isles of Scilly. Our suite was also very well-furnished and a good size, with a balcony, a bar, a walk-in wardrobe and plenty of seating. With Cunard, suite passengers are provided with their choice of a bottle of spirit in their cabin, together with mixers, beers and water. The bar is only stocked up at the start of the cruise, but it is a much better offer than most cruise lines except for Celebrity, who we discovered in 2014. With their full suites you get the same package in your cabin but also a premium drinks package; access to Michael's Lounge for free drinks between eleven a.m. to eleven p.m. and so much more!

This particular cruise was ten days – once we left New York, we had two days at sea before we docked at Saint Thomas in the US Virgin Islands and then we went to Saint Lucia, Grenada, Barbados, another day at sea, then Grand Turk and a final two days at sea before returning to New York. Personally, I thought that each of the islands were very similar except for Grand Turk which is quite barren and there is very little to see and do there, but they each offer something unique, that contributes to the enjoyment of a Caribbean cruise. There are many itineraries for cruising this area and, although you may duplicate some of the islands, more often than not, you will always be able to find a new destination, as the routes and the ports of call are changing all the time. We have been to Saint Lucia and Saint Thomas three times, Barbados twice, and the other Caribbean islands we have been to are Cuba, Sint Maarten, Aruba, Grand Cayman, Haiti, Puerto Rico, Saint Barthelemy, Antigua and Barbuda, Saint Kitts and Nevis, Trinidad and Tobago, and Saint Croix. In November 2016, we should have stopped in Jamaica, but, yet again, due to high winds, we were not able to dock – very disappointing!

But this chapter is about Barbados, and, so far, I have not really written much about this island nation, because, in my view, there isn't really a lot to write about! Let me give you some facts – the island is twenty-one miles long and fourteen miles wide, covering an area of a hundred and sixty-seven square miles. It is situated in the western area of the North Sea, and east of the Windward Islands and the Caribbean Sea. The island was claimed by the Spanish Crown in the fifteenth century, before being possessed in the name of King James I and the English in 1625. In 1996, Barbados became an independent state and part of the

Commonwealth, with the British Monarch as hereditary head of state. The population of the country is around two-hundred and eighty thousand and it is a major tourist destination in the Caribbean, with about forty percent of its visitors coming from the UK which explains why it is on the fifty!

During the time it was a British colony, cultivation of tobacco and cotton were the key exports, followed by sugar cane from the 1640s, which completely transformed society and the economy, mainly as a result of the slave trade bringing black Africans to work in the industry. By the year 1700, there were fifteen thousand free whites and fifty thousand enslaved blacks. [2]

We booked to go on a photographic tour in the afternoon, as we thought that this would give us a good, overall view of the island. In the morning, we took a taxi transfer into the capital, Bridgetown, and had a look at some of the shops, before we decided to head back for something to eat before our tour. As we were waiting, a rickshaw stopped and offered us an alternative way to travel. As we thought that we would have to wait for a taxi to fill up with other passengers, we thought that this might be the quicker option. But we were quite wrong about that! We had done a cycle rickshaw in Varanasi, and that was in a convoy of six. This time we were on our own, and our guide or driver took his time, continually stopping to chat to people who he knew which seemed to be the whole population of Bridgetown, and by taking the back route, obviously to avoid the traffic and causing problems due to him going so slow. We thought that we would miss our tour, but we got back in plenty of time and, I must admit, it did create a very colourful photo opportunity!

Our tour was disappointing – we did not learn any photo tips from our guide as he was more interested in talking about himself, and showing off his own work which was for sale! But we did get to see a lot of the island, stopping firstly at an old sugar plantation, then seeing some "chattel" houses, small, moveable wooden houses. The plantation owners bought them to house their workers and then would move them from one property to another. We continued our journey and we went to the western

part of the island that faces the North Sea. The waves were very rough and crashing onto the shore and the beach which made for a dramatic sight, but was certainly not a good advertisement for beautiful, calm, Caribbean beach life!

We drove through a number of little towns, past rolling green hills, stopping to see goat herds and learning how to make rum punch, which, at our final stop, a little bar close to where our guide lived, we did sample some and I must say it is delicious – very refreshing, fruity, but with a real punch to it. I can only assume that the pristine beaches and the famous resorts of Barbados are on the eastern coast, and it is this area that is popular with the British tourists; unfortunately, this is an area we did not visit on this occasion or on our second visit in November 2013.

This second time, we were on the Emerald Princess, sailing out of Miami, we booked a ship tour again, to go to the centre of the island to visit Harrison's Cave. The area is very touristy but, as we needed to wait for our allocated slot, to descend on the little train, it was rather pleasant to enjoy a rum punch in the village that lies at the base of the chasm, where the caves are located. We boarded our train, and journeyed deep underground, going through lots of caverns and viewing stalagmites and stalactites, as well as numerous rock formations, vanishing streams and disappearing waterfalls; what I mean by this is that the streams dropped out of sight behind walls of rock, only to reappear further on crashing over the granite walls. We had two photographic stops, and the whole journey took about forty-five minutes. Overall, this was a very enjoyable tour, but we did not see a lot of the island, so it was a good choice, as a second visit to Barbados, but I would not recommend it for a first-timer.

In recent years, we have both changed our view of resort holidays, as we now quite enjoy the relaxation of a week in the sun at a good, adults-only hotel. As a result of this, we are more inclined to stay a week on a Caribbean island or a resort, to enjoy some quality downtime and in the future, we may consider Barbados as a destination for this type of holiday. But, as there are so many other islands to enjoy which we have not yet visited, I think that they might take precedence when we make our choice – in particular Jamaica, seeing that we missed out in 2016, and that there seems to be a lot of sights and activities to enjoy on this larger island. But, you never know – as they say, the world is our oyster!

CHAPTER 26

Victoria Falls, Zimbabwe and Zambia border (21) – January 2011

This was another one of our "long" weekend trips, where we travel a long way for a very short time. On this occasion, we flew to Victoria Falls, Zimbabwe via Johannesburg for four nights! I had been to Zimbabwe in 1998, before I met Richard. On that occasion, I was travelling with a friend who had wanted a spectacular holiday, to celebrate her fiftieth birthday, and we stayed at the Kariba Breezes Hotel on Lake Kariba; Ruckomechi Camp in Mana Pools National Park; the Elephant Camp and Safari Lodge at Victoria Falls; Camp Amalinda in Bulawayo and finally at the Hide in Hwange National Park. This was organised for us by a specialist African holiday company, but all of our accommodation was selected after careful research. When we were in Zimbabwe, we found out that Ruckomechi had won Safari Camp of the Year three times in the last four years, losing out once to the Hide, so we had certainly picked the best places to stay. At this time, Robert Mugabe was the president of Zimbabwe, but had not yet started his regime of total domination or repression of white people, residing and working in Zimbabwe. It was awful seeing the news in later years, and learning about the demise of many of these camps, and the decline in this country, being a great place to visit for some of the best camps, lodges and viewing in Africa.

Back to 2011 – This book is about Richard and I seeing the fifty places together, and this was his opportunity to see Victoria Falls, one of four waterfalls listed, and, as we had already seen Angel Falls and Iguazu Falls, after these in Africa, it left us with one more – Niagara Falls, which, incidentally, Richard had seen but I hadn't! We flew to Johannesburg on Avios points in business class with British Airways, and then connected with a Comair flight direct to Victoria Falls. Comair is a British Airways franchise, so that meant that we got all our silver executive perks on the connection, including the use of the lounge at Johannesburg airport. It didn't help us on our arrival in Zimbabwe though, as it took a very long time for us to go through passport control and to obtain our visa to enter the country. But we were soon on our way to our hotel, and I had insisted that we stay at the iconic Victoria Falls Hotel. On arrival, we were greeted with cold towels and homemade lemonade, before we were given a tour of this amazing hotel.

It was built in 1904 and it is considered to be one of the best in Africa. It was originally conceived as accommodation for workers on the Cape-to-Cairo Railway; Cecil Rhodes's dream of a railway line that stretched the length of Africa. It was Rhodes's friend and colleague, Sir Charles Metcalfe, who started plans for the first bridge across the mighty Zambezi River, but it was Rhodes who insisted that the bridge should be built in a place where the spray from the falls would fall on the passing trains. The site chosen was just a little below the Boiling Pot, at almost right angles and in very close proximity to the falls. The hotel was operated by the railway administration until the early 1970s when it was leased to the Southern Sun Hotel group, forerunner of today's African Sun Limited. Today, the property itself belongs to the National Railways of Zimbabwe and there's a 50/50 partnership operation between African Sun and Meikles Africa Hotels. Steeped in history and one of the oldest hotels in Africa, the Victoria Falls Hotel serves as a reminder of the distinguished and elegant era in which it was born, and it has earned its status as the epitome of grand luxury travel.[6]

The hotel is not high-rise, built in the colonial style, and I think it is just two stories high. It only has a hundred and sixty-one rooms and suites, but it is spread over a large area, which includes gardens, restaurants, bars and verandas, and is in easy walking distance from the actual falls. It is a beautiful place, and it was really pleasant to walk around and to explore.

We had been travelling for a total of twenty four hours, so, after we had been shown to our room, had unpacked and freshened up, we went for afternoon tea on the terrace at Stanley's – how very English! This offered us a view of the aforementioned bridge, which spans the gorge connecting Zimbabwe and Zambia with the spray from the falls, rising up to meet the crossing railway line, just as Rhodes had wanted. This first day was used just to get over the flight, and acclimatise to the heat of Africa, and to get our bearings around the hotel. After a restful afternoon, we had dinner in Livingstone, the luxurious restaurant at the hotel. We had a beautiful meal, which cost us one hundred and forty dollars, including a generous tip and a very nice South African rosé wine.

We had an early start the next day as we had booked some tours prior to our arrival. At six—twenty a.m., we were picked up by minibus and taken to Elephant Camp for our elephant safari. In 1998, Elephant Camp was a small, luxury camp, only accommodating eight people in four chalets. They had four African elephants – Jock, Jack, Jumbo and Miss Ellie, all rescued and trained to be able to offer elephant back safaris, the idea being that animals are less likely to run away from these natural residents. I rode Jock, with Wellington as my guide, and I sat astride the elephant's back, legs spread wide, on a blanket, to protect my skin from the rough hairs that line an elephants' skin. In 2011, Elephant Camp no longer had any accommodation; it just offered the elephant safari and this was our reason for visiting that day.

On arrival, we were given coffee and a safety briefing before the elephants arrived. There were five elephants prepared for us to ride, and two young ones that were coming along for the walk. The camp then had a breeding programme, and was not just a rescue site. This time, the elephants had comfy saddles across their backs, which took two riders, the handler still rode at the back of the head behind the ears. Richard and I were given Coco for our outing, and Richard was our handler. The saddles had stirrups, and with the addition of a padded seat, this made for a much more comfortable ride than it had thirteen years before! During our walk, I had a chance to chat with our handler, Richard, and he confirmed that this was the same camp where we had stayed in 1998, but that it had had to move location, due to the problems created by Mugabe. The number of elephants had increased by taking in abandoned orphans, and injured animals and three of the four residents from 1998 were still part of the troop. Only Jack had been released back into the wild, as he got too feisty and hard to handle. Even Wellington still worked for the company.

We did not see much on our ride, just a few birds – to be honest we had not seen much the last time. I think that the theory is good that other animals are less likely to run away from the elephants, as they do not see the humans on their backs, but due to the area being used every day and for several times, the concession is probably bereft of wild life anyway. Back at the camp, we had an opportunity to feed the animals, including the babies, who had been so cute, walking behind either their mother or their sister. We also got a very pleasant surprise, as the camp had another resident, a rescued cheetah called Sylvester, who was used to human company, and we were able to stroke this beautiful big cat. The camp was much more focused on the work that they were doing to save animals, and showed us a film that highlighted the plight of the elephant in Zimbabwe, with poaching, farming and loss of habitat. It might be a tourist trap to offer these rides to visitors, but it is a worthwhile cause, and we hope that our donation has helped these docile giants to live a long and contented life.

We returned to the hotel and changed – elephants can be very muddy creatures – and then we walked to the falls, for Richard to get his first sight of this magnificent natural wonder. There is an easy path to follow straight from the gardens at the Victoria Falls Hotel, that leads directly to the entrance of the National Park. The problem is that the traders know this, and our journey was fraught as we tried to dodge locals selling carvings, souvenirs and even Zimbabwean dollars, which are completely worthless. Most of the time they took "no" for an answer, but some were really persistent and said that they would see us on our walk back.

There is a charge to enter the park that surrounds the falls, and at forty pounds per person, it is not cheap! But we were not coming all this way just to see the spray from a distance; so we paid our money, and entered the park which does have some wildlife, as well as access to the falls. Some baboons blocked our path, and, knowing that these can be vicious, we took a wide detour around them, to head for the statue of David Livingstone, which is located near the Devil's Cataract.

Born in Scotland, David Livingstone arrived in Africa in 1840 at the age of twenty-seven, as a missionary and a physician. He spent most of the remainder of his life on the continent; his exploits making him the most famous explorer of the century. An encounter with a lion in 1843 cost him the use of his left arm but, undeterred, he continued with his exploration of the African interior; in particular, the Zambezi River area in 1852–1856. It was during this expedition that he became the first European to witness the magnificent Victoria Falls. It was 1855 when Livingstone travelled down the Zambezi to see for himself the area that the natives called Mosi-oa-Tunya, translated as "smoke that thunders". On seeing the columns of spray and hearing the thunderous roar of water from miles away, Livingstone's canoe approached the falls, and he commented on the beauty of the place, with its lush vegetation, islands, ridges and the rising spray, that mingled with the clouds above. It was this sight that prompted him to state "scenes so lovely must have been gazed upon by angels".[7]

Victoria Falls is classified as the largest waterfall in the world, based on its combined width of one thousand seven hundred and eight metres and a height of a hundred and eight metres, resulting in the world's largest sheet of falling water. The river upstream flows over a level sheet of basalt, in a shallow valley, bounded by low and distant sandstone hills. The river's course is dotted with numerous tree-covered islands, which increase in number as the river approaches the falls. These are formed as the full width of the river plummets in a single vertical drop into the chasm below, carved by its waters along a fracture zone in the basalt plateau. There are two islands on the crest of the falls, which are large enough to divide the curtain of water, even at full flood.

These are Cataract Island near the western bank and Livingstone Island near the middle – the point from which Livingstone first viewed the falls. At less than full flood, additional islets divide the curtain of water into separate parallel streams and the main ones are called Devil's Cataract, Main Falls, Rainbow Falls and the Eastern Cataract.[2]

On our visit in January 2011, the river was almost at full flood, and we soon found out what this meant on that first visit. We walked from the Devil's Cataract, which is the western start of the falls and walked towards the Main Falls. The amount of water falling over the ridge was tremendous, and the noise was thrilling – we could almost feel the ferocity of its passing, as it reverberated through our bodies. And the spray rose high above us. But as we approached the Main Falls it got worse. We put our macs on, but they were useless against the volume of water that was raining down on us from the spray of the waterfall. The further we walked, the worse it got, and we thought that it was raining, as the water falling on us was so torrential and we were soaked to the skin – our light rain macs offered no protection against the torrent. Our cameras were getting soaked and we were concerned for their welfare, so we decided to abort our visit, and return to the hotel to dry off. As we walked away from the gorge, it stopped raining and we were surprised to see the path as dry as a bone. It had not been rain that had soaked us; just the sheer volume of water rising above the falls in clouds of spray, created by the mass of water cascading over this huge cliff face.

Returning to the hotel was even worse than before, with vendors waiting to catch us at every turn. They all said that we had said that we would buy from then on our return, even though we had promised no such thing. I did buy a couple of carvings as souvenirs, and I took pity on their sorry plight of claiming starvation, by making a general donation of ten dollars, on the understanding that it would be shared amongst those who we talked to.

We had lunch on Stanley Terrace and rested in the afternoon, before our next adventure, a sunset cruise on the Zambezi. We booked this excursion through the hotel, and had taken their recommendation to partake in a small cruise, rather than the large dinner ships that crowded the upper part of the falls. We were collected from the hotel and taken down to a quiet part of the river, where we boarded our little boat, to find that we were the only passengers. We pushed off from the shore, and sailed out onto the great Zambezi, enjoying our Cuba Libra's as we watched the sun set. There were plenty of crowded sunset cruisers on the river, but we did not see any other "private" boats like ours, and, as the sun set and it started to get dark, the big boats all had to call it a day and return to shore while we continued on, having our dinner lit by candlelight, with the river to ourselves – and the hippo's and the elephants which we knew were out there in the dark, somewhere! We ate well – minestrone soup; fish, potatoes and vegetables and fruit salad with cream, served with a reasonable bottle of wine and more drinks after dinner if we wished. At a one hundred and fifty dollars we thought that it was worth every penny!

The next day we had another early start, six-thirty a.m. – one of the drawbacks with African holidays is that all trips, whether it is a safari or not, all seem to start VERY early in the morning! This time, we were headed for the Lion Encounter and this was a very popular excursion with over twenty-five on our bus, from various hotels around Victoria Falls and made up of many different nationalities. We were split into three groups, to take it in turns having breakfast, seeing the lion cubs and walking with grown lions. We managed to get onto the first group, which was the smaller one, with only seven people. We had to sign indemnity forms before we could start anything – the normal event when doing anything that is remotely dangerous and I suppose being in close proximity to lions does fit into this category! We were given a stick to protect ourselves against the lions – not a big stick, just a normal, run-of-the-mill little branch fallen from a big tree, and we started with a visit to see three young lions.

They were older than I had expected, as I thought that we would get to see some very young cubs, but even so, these three youngsters were very cute and were quite active. We posed for photos with them, were able to stroke them and then we walked with them, basically following where they wanted to lead us, which was not very far, as they were reluctant companions, continually wanting to stop and to lie down, and they needed quite a lot of coaxing from our guides to encourage them to walk with us.

The Lion Encounter has been set up to actually help the lion population in Africa and there are several of these in different African countries. The plan is that they take young lions from the wild and bring them to the camp where they are cared for until they reach maturity and are then released back into the wild, but in a different location from where they were originally found. This means that animals from different family groups will form new prides, so as to improve the gene pool and lead to stronger animals as a result of not having continual inter-family breeding. Although the young lions are in contact with humans, it is kept to a minimum, and once they are over one year in age, they are withdrawn from the interaction element in order to learn to hunt and to fend for themselves under protection. The proceeds generated from the public encounter funds this project. To us, it sounded like a good cause – we had seen it featured on a television programme, and it seemed to be getting a thumbs-up by environmentalists, so that was why we decided to go along.

We had breakfast and then we went to meet two older lions, both of them around fourteen months old. These were BIG and almost fully mature. The male was kept away from us, as he was quite temperamental, and not calm enough for interaction with the public. Do you remember that I said that we were all given a stick? I didn't explain what we were supposed to do with it. We were told that if the lions get a bit jittery, to present the stick to them as that tells them who is boss! A stick?

Well, our group was invited to pose for a photo with the lioness; she was lying down and waiting for someone to step forward – and I went first. She was a bit nervous, so I used my stick to show her that I meant business, waving it in front of her head. Please do not be concerned about the lion's welfare, the stick was not used to rap the lions, it was just meant to be waved at them to show them that we were armed and dangerous – WITH A STICK! The guide suddenly shouted at me, "Don't use the stick!" I had not heard the handlers say that the stick should not be waved near her head. Due to the tone of his voice and the increase in volume, the lioness got even more nervous, and very suddenly she turned around to face me. I was crouched down behind her waiting for the photo to be taken. This change in her attitude and the fact that I was now looking straight into a man-eater's mouth full of very sharp teeth, rather upset me a bit too, and in that split second, I jumped and, clumsily, I fell backwards. We had been told not to make any sudden movements ourselves, to be slow and gentle in our mannerisms, and tumbling backwards onto the floor did not comply with these instructions.

It all happened so quickly – as I went down, the lioness got up and stared straight at me, with a look of "dinner-time" in her eyes! All the guides jumped forward shouting at me, the lioness and anyone else who could hear them and to get involved. The lioness retreated, with her haunches down, obviously thinking that she was in trouble, and would be reprimanded. I felt awful as it was my fault for being so clumsy, but I was glad that I was not mauled as a result of this little incident. The lioness settled and the others, hesitantly, stepped forward for their photo opportunity. I thought that I would leave it after my liaison, but they insisted and they set her up in a different location, for me to move in again. This time, I was further back and I made sure that I had a firm footing before I crouched down.

I did not really enjoy the Lion Encounter. Not because I almost ended up as lion food, but because I thought the welfare of the lions was not high on the agenda. The intention seems to be sound, to stop this magnificent creature becoming extinct as a result of inter-breeding, but this was not the way to do it. It is an excuse to make a lot of money on the back of us wanting to have a close encounter with the king of the beasts and, at one hundred and twenty dollars per person and three or four visits per day, they are certainly raking it in. They also pushed to get you to sign up to be a donor to the cause and to get involved in other charities relating to schools and education and this was not what we wanted.

We returned to the hotel and attempted another visit to the falls. This time we bought some of the rain macs that they sell at the entrance to the park. They were really long and we thought that they would keep us better protected than our little foldaway jackets. But they leaked, and we ended up just as wet as the previous day! This time, we started at the centre of the falls and walked to the eastern border. We could hardly see anything because of the spray, and had no chance of peering down into the gorge below, as it was lost from sight in the rising mists created by the torrent of water crashing over the ridge. The last time I came to Victoria Falls was in October 1998 and the river was not as high as it was now in January. It was great to see this spectacle in all its glory, but I think that it is better in the dry season, as you can see so much more of the ledge, the gorge and the ravine than we could view now. The path to and from the falls was guarded by tourist police that day which made our trip much more comfortable and we certainly had less hassle from the vendors.

It was our final full day in Zimbabwe and we got a lie-in. At eight forty-five a.m. we were picked up and taken for our helicopter flight over the falls. This is the best way to see Victoria Falls, from the air, peering down on this wonder of nature and viewing it as "angels in flight". It is a short flight, just fifteen minutes circling over the falls. There were four of us in the helicopter – one in the front and three in the back, which means that the person who is in the middle does not get the best view – and that was me! I had done the flight in '98 and on that occasion I had sat by the window and seeing that this was Richards first, and we thought, last time, I thought it was important that he got the window seat. Besides, he had the better camera! This time, I looked more at the geology and the surrounding area not just the falls. This was fascinating, as you could clearly see the previous fault lines of where the falls used to be in the past.

Victoria Falls is continually changing and moving. The volume of the water crashing over the ridge gradually erodes the basalt away, and creates cracks along the ridge, which will eventually fall away, and a new edge will be created. From the air, you can see the zig-zag of the previous locations of the falls and it is an incredible sight. The full details of the geology of the area and the formation of the falls are on display in the National Park, and are well worth checking out. The erosion line is already visible for the next location of the new falls, but this is likely to take around ten thousand years.

In the afternoon, we walked to the lookout spot, which lies on the edge of the eastern part of the gorge and is easily accessible from the hotel. From there, you could peer down into the gorge below to see the swirling Zambezi as it recovers from its tumble over the ridge, and gathers momentum as it continues its journey to the sea. From the vantage point we saw two African fish eagles soaring high above the gorge – it was a great view.

In the evening we went to the Boma Restaurant, which is located at the Victoria Falls Safari Lodge. This restaurant offers traditional Zimbabwean dishes with a four-course meal made up of a choice of starters, soup from the camp fire and a barbecue buffet of game meat and salads. Partially open air, it offers a unique experience that bombards the senses with the tastes, the sights, the sounds and the smells of Africa. A very strange notion to be eating the meat of the animals that you have come all this way to see on safari, but it works, as this place is always very busy. In addition to kudu and impala, you can also try crocodile tail; it does not taste like chicken but more like a meaty fish, and even Mopani worms.

Normal meats are also available, but I understand that the place is renowned for its warthog fillet! When you arrive you are greeted in a traditional manner and then dressed in 'chitenges' (traditional robes) before entering the main enclosure. You are invited to take part in a hand washing ceremony before having any of the beer and snacks offered as a prelude before dinner.

After dinner, the entertainment starts and includes traditional dancing, singing, story-telling and finally a drumming extravaganza which is the highlight of the evening, and all the guests are invited to participate. We often feel a bit awkward with this sort of thing, and most of the time we don't get involved. But on this occasion, we did join in, and thoroughly enjoyed ourselves. Richard even danced, which is a very rare occurrence indeed!

The next day it was time for us to leave Victoria Falls, but we were not in a rush and so had plenty of time to wander through the hotel gardens, view the wildlife art, which was wonderful, but very expensive, and then mooch around the hotel gift shop. In there, we met a couple from Bramhall, Stockport and we started chatting to them. They were visiting their daughter who lived in South Africa and had come to Zimbabwe as a side trip to see the falls. After we had packed and we were waiting for our transport to take us to the airport, we bumped into them again, and they sat with us. They were telling us how much they liked the place mats that were in the gift shop, that were decorated with pictures of the hotel. She said how reasonably priced they were and what a wonderful reminder they would be of the holiday, but, unfortunately, they did not have the room in their luggage or the weight allowance to fly back to the UK with them as they were flying economy and were at their full capacity already.

As we had only come out for four nights and had extra allowance with flying business class, we had more than enough room and I offered to take them back for her, and then we would deliver them to their home in Stockport on our return. I always remember a "Friends" episode where Phoebe had stated that there is no such thing as a selfless act. She claimed that there is always a reason for doing something, even if it purely makes you feel good about yourself. In my defence, I think that this was pretty close to a selfless act, as we would have to actually go out of our way to deliver them.

It was March when we finally did a detour from visiting Dad in Manchester and called at their home in Bramhall. They were surprised to see us, and we found out that the daughter who they were visiting in South Africa had said how silly they had been, trusting us, and she had thought that her Mum and Dad would never see those place mats again! Well we proved her wrong!

I would like to say that we had become firm friends with the couple in Bramhall, but after our delivery, we never heard from them again! So this really does emphasise the selfless act element of this story.

In September 2015, we returned to Africa, this time visiting Botswana and Zambia – in fact Zambia was our hundredth country visited. We had nine nights in the Okavango Delta, staying at three very different camps, followed by four nights in Zambia, where we stayed at the Tongabezi Hotel just outside of Livingstone. This hotel has two sites and we had two nights in the island camp, Sondabezi, before transferring to the main hotel for the last two nights, where we stayed in the stunning Tree House room. Both of these locations had fabulous views of the Zambezi River, and offered a wilder location than the Victoria Falls Hotel. I am not going to write about the safari, as it isn't really relevant to the theme of this book, but I am including the details, as we had the opportunity to be able to see the Victoria Falls again, but this time from the Zambian side.

There were lots of excursions available through the hotel, including taking a boat over to Livingstone Island and sitting on the very edge of the falls. We were too cowardly for this as it does involve swimming at the head of the falls from the boat to the island. You could get to the park by the falls on the Zambian side, or even walk over the railway bridge which creates the border between the two countries, but we opted for the microlight flight over the falls, as this was something neither of us had done, and it is not possible to do on the Zimbabwean side. We were taken to the aerodrome, signed our lives away, and waited, watching those before us getting strapped in, taking off and returning.

When it came to our turn, I went first. The microlights are small, only taking two people – the pilot, who is well strapped in with belts across his body securing him to his seat and the vehicle, and the passenger, seated at the back, with just a cross-lap seat belt and nothing else! It did not seem very safe, but there was not a lot of time to discuss the health and safety element, as the engine did not stop, and we were very soon taxiing along the makeshift runway, ready for this adventurous flight. The microlights seemed to be pretty flimsy once we were in the air, and were buffeted by the wind that was coming at us from all sides. The pilot explained what we could see on either side, but at this first instance, I was trying to cling to the side frames, to make sure that I was secure, and not likely to slip out of my seat and plummet to the ground which, by now, was a few hundred feet below me.

We approached the falls along the Zambian border of the river, and very soon, I could see the now familiar clouds of spray caused by the water crashing over the ridge. The previous course of the river and the zig-zag of the previous ridges were very visible from this height, and we turned to head directly for our first flight over the falls.

At this point, the pilot said to me, "You need to feel the freedom". My response was, "WHAT?" His reply, "Let go!" I thought to myself, he must be mad! I was holding on for dear life and I did not want to take the risk. But he kept repeating this instruction and, reluctantly, I let go. As I realised that I was not going to fall out, I got more confident, and eventually, I had my arms outstretched on either side, and I was "feeling the freedom". What an amazing feeling – I was whooping like a little kid, amazed at the sights below me, as we flew over and over the falls and the feel of the wind whipping across my hands and arms. I am not saying that I was not frightened – the whole experience left me feeling high on the adrenalin, and I could not stop shaking, even after we had landed and I had been on terra-firma for thirty minutes, but what an adventure! And what a wonderful way to see the falls from above, it was so much more personal than by helicopter.

Richard had taken off straight after I had departed and he was terrified of the flimsy vehicle, the lack of a safety harness, open seating and no handlebars to hold on to. He enjoyed the flight, but had not been told to "feel the freedom". He said that even if he had been told to let go, he wouldn't have done so. He was holding on for dear life!

This excursion left me with one question though. I wondered if those angels that Livingstone had referred to had felt the freedom and whooped and screamed as they flew over Victoria Falls! I'd like to think that they did!

CHAPTER 27

Galapagos Islands, Ecuador (33) – February 2011

Unlike Chapter 25, this location deserves to be on the list. In fact, in my view, it should be a lot higher. Our seven-day cruise around the Galapagos Islands is certainly up there amongst the best holidays we have ever experienced. It is unique and offers so much for sightseeing, photographic experiences, history, nature and geology and, of course, animal encounters! By now, we had completed quite a few cruises and enjoyed the luxury of the big ships, and in particular, the suites and all the benefits associated with this class of travel. We were nervous about selecting a small vessel for doing this particular cruise, as we had never experienced anything smaller than two-hundred passengers, and, with my issues with seasickness, I thought that I would have real problems with rough seas on a boat that only caters for ten to twenty people. When we discovered that Celebrity offered a complete package with flights, transfers, time in Quito and a seven-day cruise on their smallest ship, the Xpedition, we took an interest and investigated further. The ship caters for a maximum of ninety-four passengers with sixty crew members, but it offers all the privileges of a big cruise line, just on a much smaller scale. Everything about the ten-day trip ticked all our boxes, and we booked Cabin 501, classed as an Xpedition suite, which offered us a small balcony and reasonable-sized accommodation. It was tiny in comparison to suites we have had on other ships, but was more than twice the size of the Ocean View Staterooms.

Richard and I are keen photographers and we particularly enjoy "shooting" wildlife. The day before we flew out to Ecuador, we attended a Canon training course on this very subject – the timing could not have been better. They gave us lots of tips for improving our snaps and ensuring that we got the most from our cameras, while we were in this spectacular place. We went straight from the course in Huntingdon to the airport where we stayed overnight before our very early departure the next day. We had been able to check-in the day before and had reserved extra legroom seats, one of the advantages of being silver exec members with One World. As we placed our bags on the conveyor, we were told that we had been upgraded to Business Class on the Iberian flight from Madrid to Quito – for the second time and on consecutive holidays, a definite bonus for this trip.

It was a long day with flights from Heathrow to Madrid, time at the Spanish airport, a long haul flight to Quito, waiting time at the airport waiting for others, transfer to the JW Marriott in Quito and a five-hour time difference. By the time we had eaten and retired to bed, we had been on the go for twenty-four hours!

We had two nights in Quito before we flew to the Galapagos Islands and the Celebrity included a comprehensive tour of the city on the one full day that we were there. We firstly went to the new basilica, before walking to the old town, where we went to the main square. Every main square in South America has the same layout, with the cathedral on one side, municipal buildings along another and a public meeting place in the centre. We have seen this in Lima, Peru and Buenos Aires, Argentina, where the municipal building is the Casa Rosata; famous as being the location where Eva Peron delivered her speech to the people of Argentina.

We continued a little further, to go into the tiny Jesuit Church of Compania de Jesus, known colloquially as la Compania. What a shock! – it has to be one of the most beautiful interiors of any church I have ever seen! It took a hundred and sixty years to construct, and was completed in 1765. Shaped as a Latin cross, it has a large central nave, which leads to a highly decorated altar. The whole interior is so elaborately decorated with paintings, sculptures, plaster reliefs and carvings, many of them covered in gold leaf, so it dazzles you as you enter this spectacular building. I just wanted to sit and admire the richness of the architecture and stunning decorations – it was mind-blowing. I just cannot express how amazing this place was and such a contrast to its austere appearance from the outside. From the doorway of the church, you could peer up El Panecillo, a two hundred metre high hill, where the forty-five metre tall stone statue of the Madonna stands, looking down over Quito in the same manner as Christ the Redeemer does in Rio. It is an unusual depiction of the Virgin Mary, as the statue has wings and locals claim it is the only one in the world that symbolises the Madonna, as an angel. It's quite a new addition to the Quito skyline, inaugurated in 1976. It was inspired by the famous "Virgen de Quito" sculpted by Bernardo de Legarda in 1734, which now stands on the main altar of the Church of Saint Francis, which is where we went to next on our tour.[2]

We were all taken to lunch as a group, to a very nice Italian restaurant on the edge of the city. Traffic was really bad in Quito and we were held up with jams, lights and roadworks wherever we went. Things have probably changed now, as a new International airport opened in 2013 outside the city. When we went, the runway was in the centre of Quito, and you flew into the valley with high mountains on either side – it was quite spectacular. But with moving the main airport for Ecuador to outside the city, I was sure that it would lead to easier traffic issues, just not as interesting an approach. I have been lucky enough to fly into the old Hong Kong airport too, Kai Tak, where the runway ran along the side of Victoria Harbour – the landing there took us in between the towering skyscrapers that lined the flightpath, and it was no exaggeration that you could see into the windows of apartments and hotels along that route!

Ecuador is named because it lies on the equator, and that was our next stop on the tour. They have made a big thing of this location, creating a theme park in order to mark this important point – latitude 0 0 0. They have a line on the floor, similar to the Prime meridian line at Greenwich, and a monument to resemble the mountains of Ecuador. This place is very popular with tourists and locals and was very busy when we arrived. There are lots of shops, cafés, rides and other entertainment at the site, but we were not there long enough to sample any of these – we just queued for our turn to pose for a photograph to show that we had stood on the equator – you have to do the touristy picture sometimes, don't you?

On this day in Quito, the Celebrity had made sure that our day was fully occupied, and we saw as much of the city as we could. Consequently, in the evening, we had a trip organised for us to go for a meal in a restaurant in the opera theatre and for us to be entertained by resident artists after our meal. The opera singer was very good, and sang both opera and popular songs, including "Music of the Night" from the musical Phantom of the Opera and "Time to Say Goodbye", which is my favourite song – it was a very pleasant evening and it gave us the opportunity to meet our fellow cruisers.

The next day we were all able to check-in for our flight at the hotel, and we received our boarding passes for our flight on Air Gal to Baltra, one of the larger islands, where the airstrip is located for everyone travelling to this remote location – a two hour flight from Quito. We were taken to the port by coach and we could see the Xpedition anchored off shore. The only way of getting to the ship was by zodiac, and this mode of transport became our main method of getting around for the next week. This was the first time I had been in a dinghy – a big one, holding around thirty people, and fast too, but that initial step off terra firma and into this flimsy, rocking, unpredictable zodiac was rather unnerving! We all had to wear life jackets, which did not exactly fill you with confidence, but, to be totally honest, it was a piece of cake once you got used to it, and after that first trip, I always felt very safe.

Life on the Xpedition started the way we meant to go on, with a glass of Bucks Fizz being handed to us on arrival, and a meeting to welcome us on the ship and to give us an idea of what to expect over the next seven days. With this particular cruise, not only was all the food included, but also all the drinks, the excursions, the entertainment and the naturalists who would be accompanying us on our voyage. With all the passengers coming on the same flight over from Quito, it did not take long for us all to be allocated our cabins, to get unpacked and to sit down for lunch, while we set sail and headed for our first island, North Seymour. Every day we would have meetings to discuss the different options that were available to us at each stop. I don't know if the smaller ships sailing to this area generally offer this as they may not have enough crew or transport to split the group, but with the Xpedition, every excursion had an easy, medium or a hard option, or you could simply opt out and stay on the ship. We decided on the long walk on North Seymour, as we were eager to see the wildlife of Galapagos and experience this wonderful place we had read so much about.

Every excursion was limited to a small number of participants taking part and all were accompanied by a naturalist to be a guide and a tracker and to provide information about the island and the inhabitants that we were likely to see. Every island in the Galapagos is different, and the wildlife can be confined to just that one location and is often found nowhere else. They have adapted to life on that particular island, whether this is in relation to the food that they eat, the harsh conditions or their fellow island neighbours. This was studied at length by Charles Darwin, when he visited the islands on board the Beagle around 1832, when he came up with his theory of evolution and the origin of the species – basically the survival of the fittest. I can't imagine what criticism and revulsion he faced when he announced his findings as he was denying that God had created man and that life on earth was down to nature and was not as a creation of a celestial being. But it certainly made it interesting on this cruise to be able to see at first hand the differences between birds, reptiles and mammals who had helped him to come to this momentous conclusion.

Our hard walk on North Seymour took two hours and we walked about a mile. It was rough underfoot and there were big boulders that we had to get over or around, but overall it was not too bad. I am not a very fit person, as I do very little exercise and as you will see from the photographs, I am overweight, so if I can manage the walks with relative ease, I hope that this helps to show that these excursions are quite accessible to anyone with the smallest degree of personal fitness. On this occasion we saw frigate birds, blue footed boobies, both land and marine iguanas; land iguanas smile and marine iguanas scowl and seals. The best thing about walking in the Galapagos is that you are able to get really close to the wildlife, as they are not scared of humans – we are not seen as a threat as there are no hunters on these islands, so the birds and the animals just stay put, you have to walk around them, rather than them scurrying away and hiding. This makes for some wonderful photo opportunities and we certainly took many, many photos and some video footage too.

Every evening, when we returned to the ship from our excursions, we had time for a quick drink in the bar before changing for dinner. We would all meet in the lounge, where we would be told about our options for the next day, and asked to complete a form to be handed in to say which excursion we intend taking and to select our meal for the following evening, so this could be prepared and ready when we sat down for dinner. Once all the information is relayed and the forms completed, it was time to go for dinner.

The tables took eight people and you could either sit with your travel companions or move around and sit with different people every night. As there were just the two of us, we moved around and sat with other couples so that we had different dinner companions every night. The food was okay on board the Xpedition – it was not gourmet cuisine and certainly not as fancy as some of the big cruise ships, but there was a good choice – plentiful, hot and quite enjoyable.

The next morning offered an early start for anyone who wanted to go on a zodiac around Kickers Rock at sunrise. We were still getting over the twenty-four hour journey and the time difference, so we did not take this option. Instead, we watched the sunrise from our balcony and watched the little rubber boats going around the remains of this old island in the distance. We had a wonderful view of this monolithic rock formation, as we circled around, giving everyone the opportunity to see it from either side of the ship. The Galapagos Islands are a volcanic archipelago made up of eighteen main islands, three smaller ones, a hundred and seven rocks and islets. They are located on a tectonic plate, Nazca Plate, which is moving east/southeast, diving under the South American Plate at a rate of about two and a half inches per year, and the Galapagos Hotspot, a place where the Earth's crust is being melted from below, by a mantle plume, creating volcanoes. The older islands eventually die and disappear into the sea, but new ones are continually being formed as a result of the volcanic activity. Isabela and Fernandina are the youngest and are still being formed. Kickers Rock is all that remains of an island that has died, leaving just the hard core of the volcano that created it millions of years ago. [2]

In the afternoon, we landed at Puerto Baquerizo on San Cristobal, one of the few inhabited islands, and we went to the Interpretation Centre. This was an excellent showcase, providing us with information about how the islands were formed and how the animals originally arrived on the islands and then evolved, to adapt to their surroundings and to survive. It also explained man's impact on the islands, which is having a serious effect on the delicate eco-system; the visits of Charles Darwin and the problems that are being faced on the islands today. One of these problems is the popularity of tourism and the increase in cruise ships and visitors to the islands. Shortly after our visit, the plans were to limit the number of cruise ships and to ensure that they are not too big or have too many passengers, to try and limit the damage tourism is doing to the islands. They will also introduce a rota system for the islands that can be visited, to reduce footfall on each one, and try to reverse the erosion and harm that is being generated from too many visitors.

After lunch, we landed on Española Island and we opted for the long walk again. This time we saw lots of land iguanas, the very colourful Sally Lightfoot Crab, fur seals, the Galapagos mocking bird which was key in Darwin's research, American oyster catchers, lava lizards and boobies. Española is the oldest island in the archipelago, and we walked to the far side to the cliffs, which offered a spectacular sight with crashing waves below and searing rocks above. There was a blowhole which gave us great entertainment, watching the sea rush through this little aperture and spurting high in the sky with a roar. This was a longer walk than the day before, taking around two and a half hours and covering twice the distance – it was also very hot, which made it just that bit more difficult, but so worth it to view the rugged scenery, and to see different wildlife, from our previous excursion.

Another day, another island. This time Floreana, and we had an early start – eight a.m. This was our first wet landing – at all the other islands, the zodiac had been able to go onto the beach so we could get off on solid ground, and more importantly, do the same when we got back onto the boat. But a wet landing is exactly what it says on the tin; – the zodiac does not get beached, you have to go over the side and into the sea to then walk the last stretch. Needless to say, you get wet feet and, if you have got short legs like me, you get wet shorts too! But with the heat, you soon dry off, except for your feet, as we had to proceed on our short walk, squelching with every step that we took!

There was not a lot of variety of wildlife here, but we did see some flamingos and on another beach, we were shown turtle tracks and we had it explained to us how these giant marine animals lay their eggs and the precarious walk that the hatchlings have to take if they want to reach safety in the ocean. When we returned to the original landing point, we had the opportunity to go snorkelling. Although I had done this previously, it must have been ten years since I had done so and, although I did have a go, I floundered about like a drowning cat and I gave up without any underwater sightings at all! Others in the group had better success, and they were lucky enough to have seals come along and play around them. I was very disappointed that I did not get the chance to witness this, but it was not a pretty sight watching me flapping around and panicking every time I put my face in the water. Richard had gone back to the ship before this exhibition, and I was very glad that he had not caught my diabolical attempt on camera. Even worse was my attempt at doing a wet boarding, as I almost fell onto the floor of the zodiac when I finally managed to climb aboard, causing panic with the crew as these boats are quite delicate and you are not supposed to bring sand in on your shoes or be too heavy footed when boarding. I can honestly say, that watching me board the zodiac on this occasion was not a pretty sight!

There was another visit to a different island in the afternoon, but we opted out as we were so tired from early mornings, long walks, the heat, and the number of activities that we were taking part in every day. We relaxed on board, and saw a huge pod of dolphins swimming, jumping and performing aquatic acrobatics, not too far from our ship. They played for ages and it was great watching them, as there were plenty of youngsters amongst them too. In the evening we had the Naturalists party on deck five, which was great fun! All the senior members of the crew and the team sang and played instruments to entertain us before they switched on the underwater lights so as we could see what was passing underneath us in the dark – we saw sea lions, pelicans and sharks!

The next morning was a special excursion for the snorkelers amongst us and after my fiasco the day before, I did not volunteer for this trip where people went out on the zodiacs to be able to swim amongst the seals and other marine creatures around one of the one hundred and seven rocks. Instead, we relaxed and we enjoyed lunch at the back of the boat in the Beagle Grill, before attending a presentation on the geology of the Galapagos Islands. There were lots of films and presentations being shown during the day or in the evening and you could attend as many, or as few, as you like. Some were a bit too in-depth and you needed to really concentrate on what was being said, but most of them were very enlightening and interesting, they certainly made sure that you got plenty of educative knowledge from participating in the cruise.

In the afternoon, we arrived at Bartolome Island and Richard and I opted for different excursions. He did the hard walk which

took him to the top of the volcano, affording him fantastic views of the island, and especially the leaning rock. I took the easy option and went on a zodiac cruise around the island, hoping to see the little Galapagos penguin. I was unlucky but Richard caught a glimpse of one on his transfer from the ship to Bachas Beach, where he started his walk.

After our dinner that evening we had a party to celebrate crossing the equator. The Galapagos Islands sit astride the equator, so we were continually criss-crossing this imaginary line during the whole week. But tonight was the time to mark this auspicious occasion when all the Pollywogs on-board became Shellbacks! This party is a tradition on the cruise ships and we have now attended quite a few. The one on the Xpedition was not that different, with one of the officers taking the part of King Neptune and members of the crew being his pirates. A Queen was selected from the guests and several victims, who had to impersonate animals of the Galapagos, were presented to the royal couple. It was good fun watching them act the fool, as a blue footed Booby or a marine iguana, and it was all taken in good humour, as it was meant to be.

Our next two stops were on the newest islands, the first being Urbina Bay on Isabela. We took the short walk as it was so hot. We saw many land iguanas which were really large and very colourful, but not the prettiest animal on the planet. We also saw our first wild tortoise – it was only small, certainly not one of the giants of the species, that this area is renowned for, but it was good to see this reptile in the wild. After lunch, which was a very good barbecue on the back deck, we went to Fernandina which is so different from the other islands, as there is very little foliage here, whereas Isabela was abundant with bushes, grasses and trees. The barren surroundings of Fernandina were more like a black, lunar landscape, with rugged lava formations that were jet black, and offered a very hostile environment. This was home to the marine iguanas that are black and ugly, and continuously spit water from their nostrils. There were thousands of them, all around us, climbing over one another, and young ones were crawling out of holes in the rock, looking as though the earth was giving birth to them. They were not a pretty sight, but were totally fascinating to watch. We also saw a flightless cormorant, which is evidence to the incredible way that nature has adjusted to its environment. This bird lives by diving from the rocks to catch the fish that inhabit the seas around the islands and it has no need to fly. It can only be found on this island; understandably, as it cannot fly to populate anywhere else! Like everything else on this island, except for the abundant Sally Lightfoot crabs, the cormorant was black and scrawny-looking.

In Santiago we took the zodiac cruise around the island, to hopefully see some of the marine life of the Galapagos. We were not disappointed as we saw a manta ray, green sea turtles, fur sea lions and a Galapagos shark. In the afternoon, we did the short walk on Dragon Hill on Santa Cruz Island. This was not a pleasant walk as the terrain was difficult; a very rocky trail, but we were pestered continuously by horrible black flies that hurt if they bit you, which they did, often! This was obviously in just one area of Santa Cruz, as the following day, we actually docked in the port and went to the Charles Darwin Research Station, where they have a conservation and breeding programme to help with the continuation of the tortoises on the Galapagos Islands and in particular, to re-introduce them to their original islands where many are now becoming scarce, and, in some cases, extinct. It was here that we saw Lonesome George, the very last of the giant tortoises from Pinta Island. He was in a pen with two females from different islands, but they had had no success in producing any offspring in order to repopulate the island with the original species. George has since died, so yet another species will be seen no more.

The tortoises have adapted, depending on the vegetation on a particular island. Some will eat grass and their shell around their neck is flat, whereas others need to reach up to tree branches and their shell has developed an arch, for them to stretch their necks and to reach up high. Not a nice looking animal at all, but they were fascinating to see, especially with so many different species in the programme.

In the afternoon there was an excursion to go for a walk in the highlands of Santa Cruz, to find giant tortoise that have been released into the area to forage and to live in the wilds on this island. It had been so hot in the morning that we decided not to go, as we felt that we had seen enough tortoises in the morning and we needed to relax before our journey home, and enjoy the air-conditioning in our cabin!

On our last evening, we were shown a video of a compilation of photographs taken by the crew and geologists, who had accompanied us on our excursions. The photos featured the guests as well as the wonderful wildlife we had seen during our week cruising around the Galapagos Islands. The music they used to accompany the show was perfect for the drama of the photos, featuring the scenery, the wildlife and the guests and I used the same piece when I got home, and I prepared my video – it was taken from the film "1492: Conquest of Paradise", a film about Columbus, and the score was written by Vangelis.

The following day we left the Xpedition and we headed for the airport, to get our return flight to Quito, where we were transferred back to the Marriott. Celebrity arranged for us to have a shopping expedition in the afternoon, stopping firstly at a market where they sold lots of local handicrafts and souvenirs, and then to an upmarket gallery, where they had some very nice, although expensive, gifts, ornaments and art. A final dinner was arranged for us at the hotel, which gave us an opportunity to say farewell to our fellow passengers, as we all had different flights the next day, to get us back to our own corner of the world.

Our flight to Madrid and then on to London, was due to depart in the late afternoon, so we had time to pack and to relax at the hotel, before we departed. At the airport, my name was called out and I received an upgrade. I said that we were travelling together and Richard was upgraded too. This was the first time that we had been given automatic upgrades on both legs of the flight, and on our return, we were in business class plus, which was even better, and, as it was a night flight, it offered us very comfortable seating, so we got some sleep on our long flight home.

The Galapagos Islands are absolutely wonderful, and we would love to return, but this is an expensive and an our friends, but so far, we are the only ones in our circle who have witnessed one of Earth's greatest gifts.

CHAPTER 28

Chichen Itza, Mexico (13) – March 2011

This was one of those very rare occasions where we booked a package holiday through Thomas Cook, and added nothing extra to the vacation – we just had seven days in Cancun and it was done for one reason only, to see Chichen Itza. We flew direct from Manchester – an eleven-hour flight; definitely a case of numb-bum syndrome, when we finally arrived. Luggage collection and passport control were very good, and we were out of the airport within thirty minutes from landing. As we were on a package, our transfers were included, so we headed out of the terminal to search for our Thomas Cook representative. Lots of people approached us, asking who we were looking for and stating that they were authorised by Thomas Cook to take us to our resort. We did not fall for this, as it is a common occurrence in Asia and South America for touts to con you into a transfer and then you are charged for it. Our representative. was waiting for us outside, and we boarded our coach to wait for everyone else to clear immigration, and others were not as lucky, as we waited forty-five minutes for everyone to arrive.

We then had to stop at numerous hotels to drop off other passengers, as our resort hotel, Excellence Playa Mujeres, was the third stop after the Aquamarina Beach Hotel and the Temptation Cancun Resort.

Our hotel was well away from the actual resort of Cancun itself, about a twenty-minute drive. From what we saw, Cancun is a very busy place, with mainly high-rise hotels, edged along the beach front – we only caught glimpses of the ocean and beach in between the hotels, where thin gaps separated one from another. A lot of the rooms would have had nice beach-facing windows but many more faced the sides and the back, so all you would see are other hotel windows or the busy back streets, which were full of bars, restaurants, shops and other resort outlets. The whole place gave you a feeling of being a very tacky seaside town, aimed at entertainment and giving access to as many places as possible, to have a good time. I suppose that Cancun is a party place, and it is very popular with younger people, being a bit more adventurous than going to Spain. But, if sunbathing, drinking and partying is all you are after, then why spend all that money and time flying out to Mexico when you can get exactly the same around the corner in Europe? But, each to their own!

Our first impressions of the Excellence were good. The hotel was made up of eight blocks and none of them were higher than five floors. They were placed around gardens and pools, and the public buildings were interspersed between them too. We had booked a Club junior suite, so when we arrived, we were handed a glass of champagne and then taken to the Club concierge, to check into our room. We were taken to our suite, and as we entered I can certainly say that it had the WOW factor – it really was a beautiful, big room. We had decided to come to Cancun at this particular time, as we were celebrating our anniversary on the 22nd of March, and I had made sure that the hotel was aware of this, as there were special privileges included if you were celebrating a special occasion. I had contacted the hotel prior to our arrival to inform them and I was advised that I needed to take a copy of our wedding certificate to prove this. As a result, there was a sash across our door and a bottle of champagne, nicely chilled, waiting for us inside.

The room was really large with a huge bathroom, a four poster bed, a walk-in closet, a Jacuzzi that looks onto the supersize balcony which had a table, chairs and a double lounger. We overlooked one of the pools, but we also had a view beyond of the Caribbean Sea, lined with palm trees – it really was beautiful!

The hotel had several restaurants and you were allowed to dine in any of them as many times as you liked; although it was wise to book in advance as some of them were a lot more popular than others. On our first night, we ate at Tuscani, the Italian themed restaurant, but they also had the Lobster House, the Grill, Chez Isabel, Barcelona and the Flavour Market, where you could get Tapas. This package was all inclusive and the Excellence is also an adults-only resort – these were the two main reasons why we selected this particular hotel from the hundreds that you have to choose from, and, having seen some of the others, as we drove through Cancun, we thought that we had made an excellent choice.

Our club suite gave us access to the private club pool and Jacuzzi, which is reserved for suite guests. We spent most of our free time there, as we had waiters at our beck and call, to bring us anything that we desired. It was quiet in comparison with the beach and the main pool; and it was easy enough to walk around and return to our room. We met up with our Thomas Cook representative to book onto excursions, but we thought that we would keep things simple and actually relax on this break, rather than fill every day with an activity or a visit. So we just opted for two, one being a full day trip to Chichen Itza.

With it being our anniversary, we took up the option to have the romantic dinner on the beach, and this was arranged through the concierge – it was part of the special occasion package. We were taken out to the beach area at the far end of the hotel, which was very private and secluded. There was a gazebo standing on the sand, lit by candles, and after being presented with a glass of champagne, we were served a delicious five-course meal. There was so much food! The main course was veal steak and lobster, so they really pushed the boat out for this special meal. It was windy on the beach, and the gazebo curtains billowed around us, but we had clear skies, so we had a beautiful starry canopy above us – very romantic! We were out here on our own too – another couple had been dining there but they left as we arrived, so we had the beach to ourselves. When we returned to our suite, the bed had been decorated with rose petals and they had run the Jacuzzi, which was full of steaming water and surrounded with scented candles. The doors of the balcony were open, so we enjoyed the extravagance of drinking champagne as we soaked in the hot, scented water, looking out onto the Caribbean Sea – what a wonderful anniversary!

Our first excursion took us to Coba and Tulum, two Mayan ruins close to the coast. We were picked up very early, as the problem with so many hotels and resorts spread out over a big area, is that it takes a lot of stopping to pick up all the passengers on these tours. Luckily, they used minibuses to pick up from two or three hotels and then ferry us to the main coach, but it still takes time for everyone to congregate. The problem was that even after all the buses had dropped off the guests from the Cancun hotels, we then had to drive through Playa del Carmen to call at hotels in this second resort. It ended up that we had thirty-four people on the tour, and, although we had two guides, they did not split us up into two smaller groups with a guide for each, but one of them led us through Coba, and then the other did Tulum. There were too many people, and it was impossible to keep everyone together, and the guide would start speaking before you got a chance to catch up. If possible, it would have been so much better if we had booked a private tour through our rep or Viator.com. These tours can be expensive, but are worth it, to avoid all the wasted time calling at numerous hotels, picking up a couple of people at a time – and you get the guide to yourself once you arrive at your destination.

We went to Coba first, which is a site of ruins contained within a forest. This made it difficult to walk quickly, and to keep up with the guide. There were some dramatic shots with the pyramids rising through the trees, and the bromeliads sprouting from branches, making it look as though a single tree had many different flowers and foliage on the same branch. Richard climbed the hundred and twenty steps to the top of the pyramid at Coba. This is the only place that allows the public to set foot on the steep steps that make up the Mayan pyramid, as they were not covered to make them appear smooth as the Egyptians did. According to the guide books, the view from the top is supposed to be spectacular, but Richard said that it was okay and that the reports are exaggerated. It was very hot and although there was shade with all the trees, the ruins were spread out, and it meant a lot of walking.

Lunch was included with the tour, and we stopped between the two locations for a buffet, which was surprisingly good with chicken wrapped in a banana leaf as one choice.

We continued to Tulum, which lies on top of a cliff with fabulous views out to sea. The forest had been cleared at this site, and the ruins had been renovated so that you could get a much better idea of the layout of this Mayan city which had been completely surrounded by walls. Most of these had been rebuilt and the site was very large but open which gave you a clear sight of houses, temples, walls and roads. But with no trees it meant that there was no shade and, as it was now afternoon, it was very hot and exhausting walking around and following our guide.

Where there are tourists, there are shops, and Tulum did not disappoint. But the area was very pleasant, as it was laid out like a little town with bars, cafés and shops all intertwining around narrow streets decorated with plants and foliage. People were dressed in local costume or wore attire to resemble the Mayan priests and gods. There was also a troop of Mexican acrobats who climbed a pole, hung upside down on a rope and then swung around and around, high above us – not something that I would want to do!

It was a long day, as we didn't get back to our hotel until seven p.m. after transferring from the coach to a mini-bus, that went to six hotels in Cancun, before finally dropping us off at the Excellence.

The next day we went to Chichen Itza. We had our usual small bus pick us up and take us to the main coach, but this time we only picked up one other couple, so it was not long before we were heading inland to the Yucatan, to see the Mayan complex. We had our main guide, Victor, who was easy to understand and very informative. He talked about the Mayan people and passed around maps, tools, books and pictures to entertain us on our long journey, but he also passed on his knowledge of the culture and the history of these people. We had a few stops en-route; the first was a craft market which was expensive and secondly, we stopped for a stroll around a typical Mexican town. The square, which is where we stopped, was so similar to many others we have seen in South America – a central statue, a square park surrounding this, and many municipal buildings including the main town or the city church, the town hall, the police station, the governor's house etcetera. I know that this is Central America but it was certainly more like Argentina than America.

Even when we got to the site entrance, we still had to endure a demonstration on Mayan cartouche making, and this was after we had someone board the coach and give a long talk regarding the Mayan calendar and offering personalised copies to the captured audience. But finally, we made our way through the gates and into the huge complex of buildings that make up Chichen Itza. The translation of this site name means "at the mouth of the Itza well". It was established before the period of Christopher Columbus and it has probably served as a religious centre of the Yucatan for almost a thousand years.

Over this period, there have been many different people who have left their mark, including the Maya and the Toltec and their vision of the world and the universe is revealed in the artistic works and stone monuments that adorn this complex. The complex is split into two sites – the old section, Chichen Viejo, is open to archaeologists only, but Chichen Nuevo is open to the public three hundred and sixty-five days a year. This section, which is referred to as the "new" site, is not that new, as it was started in 850 AD. The first people to build on this site were the Itza people and they characterised the place with images of the god Kukulcan, the plumed serpent. The decline of this great city came at around 1250 AD, with the rise of the nearby rival, Mayapan.

Chichen Itza was one of the largest Mayan cities. The city was built upon broken terrain, which was artificially levelled, in order to build the major structures, with the greatest effort being expended on the levelling of the area for the Castillo pyramid, the central key building on the site. The three best known of the complexes at Chichen Itza are the Great North Platform: which includes the monument of El Castillo, the Temple of Warriors and the Great

Ball Court; the Osario Group and the Central Group. On our visit, we concentrated on the buildings on the Great North Platform, as these are the best preserved and the structures most recognisable from books and pamphlets.

El Castillo dominates the complex, and this is a temple dedicated to Kukulkan. It is a step pyramid that stands ninety-eight feet high, and consists of a series of nine square terraces, each approximately eight point four feet high with a twenty foot high temple on the summit. There are protruding staircases on each of the four faces, which rise at an angle of forty-five degrees and at the base of the north-eastern staircase there are carved serpent heads. At the spring and autumn equinoxes, in the late afternoon, the northwest corner of the pyramid casts a series of triangular shadows against the western balustrade on the north side that evokes the appearance of a serpent wriggling down the staircase, which some scholars have suggested is a representation of the feathered-serpent god Kukulkan. Needless to say, this is when Chichen Itza is at its busiest and thousands of people want to witness this spectacle.

The archaeologists have identified thirteen ball courts within Chichen Itza, but the Great Ball Court is by far the most impressive. It is the largest (five hundred and fifty one foot by two hundred and thirty foot) and the best preserved ball court, in ancient Mesoamerica. At the base of the high interior walls are slanted benches, with sculpted panels of teams of ball players. In one panel, one of the players has been decapitated; the wound emits streams of blood in the form of wriggling snakes!

There are a number of different platforms around the Great Ball Court. Some are dedicated to different animals or objects. Best preserved is the Skull Platform. Some of the others are the Platform of the Eagles and the Jaguars; and the Platform of Venus, dedicated to the planet.

Another famous site at Chichen Itza is the Sacred Cenote or the Well of Souls. This is located at the end of Sacbe Number One; a causeway that is the largest and most elaborate at Chichen Itza, a twenty-minute walk from El Castillo. It starts as a low wall a few metres from the Platform of Venus. This is a natural sinkhole in the limestone plain, two hundred feet in diameter, and surrounded by sheer cliffs that drop to the water table some eighty-nine feet below. This was a place of pilgrimage for ancient Mayan people who would conduct sacrifices during times of drought. Thousands of objects have been removed from the bottom of the cenote, including skeletons of children and men.

Other sites at Chichen Itza include the Temple of the Warriors, a large stepped pyramid flanked by rows of carved columns depicting warriors. A statue of Chac Mool adorns the top of the pyramid. This is a very recognisable design of a statue, with a figure lying on its back, but partially sitting up, knees raised, and with a dish on its stomach. There are other pyramids all over the complex of varying sizes and condition, but the most impressive is El Castillo.[2],[8]

The site of Chichen Itza is huge, and has so much history and culture that you could spend several days here seeing everything and taking it all in. We had only a few hours, so we concentrated on the main areas, and felt that we had a good representation of what it had to offer. We had a very good guide, who always waited for everyone to catch up before he started to speak; he was very informative, but not providing too much detail for you to lose interest and he ensured that everyone knew what there was to see, and how much time we had before we departed.

We had a late lunch back at the hotel, located at the entrance of the site – all of the coach tours seemed to be dining there, but even with it being very busy, the food a buffet again was very good, and the waiters performed acrobatic and balancing feats to entertain us while we ate. On our journey back to Cancun, we stopped at a large sinkhole where it was possible to swim in the deep lake. This was quite a tourist attraction as a whole complex of shops, bars, restaurants and facilities were set up around the deep cavern. There are a lot of these around the Yucatan area, due to the limestone and they vary in size. This natural swimming pool was quite beautiful, with all the hanging greenery and it was very pleasant just to view it, without participating in the activity.

On our final day at the Excellence Playa Mujeres, we utilised the final benefit from our anniversary package and endured a few hours at the spa. This private session would normally have carried quite a hefty price tag, but this one-hour treatment was complementary. Richard and I are not gym or spa users, so we were very naive when it came to this activity. The spa pool had a number of "exercises" which were aimed at benefitting the external body, as well as helping with fitness. It involved a number of apparatus and jets of high pressure water being aimed at us, whilst stretching limbs and cleansing the body.

We then moved on to a sauna and a cold water shower, which was exhilarating to say the least. We had a rather painful massage, lying on a stone bed, but this was followed by another head, neck and shoulder massage in comfortable surroundings, which was a very nice end to the whole session. I thought that this might encourage Richard to utilise spa facilities that are available to us on other holidays, but we still stay clear of them – except for the opportunity for a massage. We both enjoy these relaxing sessions.

Chichen Itza is not the most visited attraction in Mexico. That accolade goes to Teotihuacan; a ruined city with a huge pyramid, located thirty miles from Mexico City, which probably accounts for the numbers of visitors. I am not sure whether Chichen Itza rates high enough to be at number thirteen, on our list, as, in my view, there are more wonderful attractions appearing further down the list, but it certainly does deserve to be on the list. This is down to its size, and its fascinating and mystical history and the location, so close to the Mexican Riviera, giving you a chance to relax, soak up the sun and explore all of this in one holiday.

CHAPTER 29

Hong Kong, China (22) and Bali, Indonesia (49) – January 2012

Richard and I had both been to Hong Kong before we met. I went when it was a British colony, before it was transferred to China in 1997. But, despite us travelling through Asia many times, this was the first time that we had been to this vibrant city together. This trip, booked through Kuoni, consisted of three nights in Hong Kong, staying at the Mandarin Oriental; five nights in Bali staying at the Banyan Tree in Ungasan, Bali; all flights and transfers. We flew on British Airways from Manchester to Hong Kong via Heathrow, and then flew to Bali on Cathay Pacific, all part of the One World Alliance, so we gained Avios points on our flight, and we could utilise the British Airways lounge at all the airports involved.

It is a long flight to Hong Kong, eleven hours and fifteen minutes and an eight-hour time difference, so we arrived mid-afternoon on the next day. Our transfer was waiting for us, and we had a representative from Kuoni, waiting at the hotel to assist with our check-in. The Mandarin Oriental is located on Hong Kong Island, and it is situated in a prime position overlooking Victoria Harbour. The last time I came, I stayed in Kowloon, which is part of the mainland. Well, the Mandarin Hotel used to occupy a prime position – there was a lot of building work taking place while we were there, and land was being reclaimed from the harbour right in front of the hotel. Although during our stay, we had a view looking over to Kowloon, I think that if they were building new high rise hotels and apartments on the plot, that the view will by now have vanished. This is the case with so many Asian cities, the building work is so extensive and so rapid, that the skyline is changing continuously, and if your visits are years apart, then the city may be unrecognisable from the previous time when you were there. But in 2012, we had a great view from our beautiful room, which had a window seat where we spent our three evenings enjoying the view, while we drank a Cuba Libra or two!

We did not have a lot of time to unpack, shower and prepare for our first excursion, which had been arranged by Kuoni – a night time tour of Hong Kong. We met close by at the Excelsior Hotel, to join in with others from different hotels. There were only five of us plus our guide, a very small and intimate group, which meant that we could manage with a minibus, much better for getting around the busy streets of Hong Kong. We drove up Victoria Peak where we firstly had a meal at Bubba Gump and then we had a chance to enjoy the views from the hilltop vantage point. From here you look down on all the hotels on the waters' edge of the island and across to the bustling and colourful metropolis of Kowloon.

The view was not very clear as the city now suffers from really bad pollution, and there is a haze that permanently hangs over the skyscrapers. We continued on to the Temple Street Night Market, great for knick-knacks and souvenirs and I could not let Richard down, so I bought a few bits and pieces for the girls in the office, and a thimble for myself. Have I mentioned that I collect thimbles and Christmas decorations from all the places that we visit? I have six large thimble racks that are almost full; they are categorised into different parts of the world and every Christmas, when we start to put up the decorations, it is like a pictorial map of places we have visited. The tree is full of dazzling baubles, Santas, angels and bells from all over the world, and we have ornaments around the whole house, ranging from glittery trees from Dubai, snowy scenes from Bruges to my favourite, Father Christmas on Boxing Day; a Bermuda-shorts-clad Santa propping up a beach bar with sunglasses on and cocktail in hand, which we brought from Honduras of all places!

We continued our drive through the brightly lit streets of Hong Kong Island before boarding a junk, and sailing out into Victoria

Harbour to enable us to view the light show from the water. It is all so vibrant and all the waterside skyscrapers, whether they are hotels or business offices, seem to be competing to be the brightest, most colourful, creative light display on show. There were just the six of us on the junk, so we had so much space to move around and get the best view of this spectacle – and we had free drinks too! The evening was a great way to experience some of the main sights and see the laser show that takes place every evening after dark.

The next day we had arranged a Viator.com tour to go to Lantau Island. Hong Kong is made up of a number of different islands ranging in size, and many of them have tourist attractions to entice the visitor. Because Richard and I have both been to Hong Kong before, on this occasion we decided to do something different, and as neither of us had been to the outlying islands, this was an ideal trip. We met our tour group at Pier 6 – another reason why the Mandarin Oriental was a good choice; it was located very close to the Star Ferry terminal and the place where piers are located for boat trips taking you all around the area. We took one of these ferries over to Lantau where we boarded a coach which took us around the island.

Our first stop was a beach for the purpose of taking photos. We continued on to a typical fishing village, which we firstly walked around, and then we sailed through the canals on a small boat, looking at the houses, which were built on stilts, and understanding the life of the locals who reside in this little village. This was a fishing village and I would not call it pretty or quaint, but rather a working location with many fishing boats, and the main item for sale on the streets was fish! All types, large and small, alive and dead, whole, or just huge fish heads – all in all a bit slimy and smelly, but it was good to be able to see a little bit of true Hong Kong life; not just the hustle and the bustle of men in suits going about their daily routine amongst the high rise buildings of Kowloon and Victoria Harbour.

Our next stop was the main reason for doing this excursion, as we drove to see the Big Buddha – and it was BIG! The Tian Tan

Buddha is made of bronze and depicts Buddha Shakyamuni seated on a lotus, on top of a three platform altar. This is the reason it is called Tian Tan, as the base is a model of the Altar of Heaven or Earthly Mount of Tian Tan, the Temple of Heaven in Beijing. The statue is thirty-four metres tall and was completed in 1993. The Buddha's right hand is raised, representing the removal of affliction, while the left hand rests open on his lap in a gesture of generosity. This Buddha faces north, which is unique among the great Buddha statues, as all the others face south. There are three floors beneath the statue, which you can visit, all containing Buddhist artefacts, including the alleged cremated remains of Gautama Buddha. The Big Buddha is surrounded by a number of smaller statues which also line the staircase going down.[2]

We were dropped off near the statue itself at the top of the hill, and we all walked around the circumference, before going inside to the museum. We walked down the ceremonial steps, stopping every so often to take photos and to look back at this huge edifice.

We had lunch at the Po-Lin Monastery, which lies at the base of the ceremonial stairway. It was a vegetarian Chinese buffet, and was actually quite good with plenty of choice and lots of it! On this lower level, the area resembled a small theme park, but with a Buddhist feel! There were a few rides and stalls selling souvenirs and snacks – it felt very strange for a religious site. There is a cable car which takes you from the park to the airport and we took this as part of our excursion. You can look back at the Big Buddha behind you, as you soar over the barren hills that lie close by – the cable car runs for twenty-five miles, so it was quite a journey.

Our car stopped for several minutes, probably at the most open stretch of the ride, and the wind blew and rocked us quite severely. I am always nervous of cable cars and gondolas like this. I know that there are very few reports of cars crashing to the ground during slight winds, but there's always a first time! From here, we re-boarded our coach and we were driven back to Pier 6. All in all, a very good excursion, with plenty of different sights to enjoy.

The following day we set off on another excursion, to visit all the different sites of Hong Kong Island. It was an early start, as we needed to meet our tour guide at the Excelsior Hotel at eight-fifty a.m. Luckily, this hotel was just down the road from the Mandarin Oriental – we certainly picked the right hotel for location, as it is so close to everything we needed. The group was too large. One of the issues you can come across when booking with Viator.com. *We like to do their private tours when they're available, but these can be expensive. The more of you in your own group the less it costs each individual, but for two, it can be a pricey event.*

Our first stop was Aberdeen Harbour. Richard and I had both been there before when we came to Hong Kong before we met, but we still did the sampan ride around the harbour. It was very different from our previous visit, which was about fifteen years before. Most of the junks and the floating homes had gone, and, although the big floating restaurants were still there, we felt that it had lost its authentic atmosphere. The jumble of broken down shanty houses and dilapidated junks floating around creating watery streets and narrow channels had all gone, which meant that it had become an orderly journey, sailing through the few remaining smart boats that have been allowed to remain. In 2018, we returned to Hong Kong and went to Aberdeen Harbour again – the area was now an upmarket yacht club, and the expensive boats moored in the harbour offered a total contrast to our memory of the place when we visited in the nineties.

Our drive continued to Repulse Bay on the far side of the island, and we stopped in Stanley to visit the world famous market that is located there. The market is big and claustrophobic, as all the stalls are so close together. They do not sell items of good quality, mainly mass-produced local products, but not just souvenirs – all sorts of paraphernalia for locals and visitors. We continued to Victoria Peak which has to be the highlight of any visit to Hong Kong. Peering down from this height towards Victoria Harbour with all its massive skyscrapers, is the iconic sight of Hong Kong which cannot be missed. On my previous visit, I also spent some time in Victoria Park, which is on the peak – very

nice gardens and an Avery; but time was limited on this trip, so we did not visit on that occasion. After taking photos of the view which was hazy due to the constant pollution that covers the area these days we took the Peak Tram down to sea level.

The Peak Tram is brilliant! This funicular railway was opened in 1888, running from Garden Road, Admiralty, to Victoria Peak. It is one thousand three hundred and sixty-four metres long and rises three hundred and sixty eight metres, and at its steepest, the gradient reaches forty-eight percent. Each car takes a hundred and twenty people, so there is always a queue, top and bottom, waiting to take the journey.[2] And what a journey! – at times you feel as though you are perpendicular to the buildings around you, the gradient is that steep! and you trundle along behind houses, apartments and high rises; so close you can peer into their windows and their gardens. The track is surrounded by dense foliage and the buildings of Victoria Peak, so you don't get any clear views down to the harbour from this ride, but it is still spectacular, and a must for any first-time visitor to Hong Kong,

Our tour ended back at the Excelsior Hotel. It was just a half-day trip that day. We took the Star Ferry over to Kowloon and then had a walk up Nathan Road, infamous for the number of camera and gadget shops along its route. Prices are very good and a lot cheaper than at home; well they were on this occasion, with current exchange rates and the weakening of the pound, this may no longer be the case, so if you are interested in purchasing this sort of item, do your research before you go and take the plunge – you may save quite a bit of money! But a word of caution! – the assistants will always try and convince you to buy something else or additions (cards, extra lenses etcetera), so make sure that you know what you want, and how much you are prepared to pay before you make enquiries. Also, before you pay any money, check that the equipment has the most recent software loaded, and that the instructions are in English – this may sound obvious, but it happened to us in 2018, and we ended up with a completely different camera from the one that we had wanted, and we paid more than it cost in the UK, even though we thought that we were getting a bargain! You can haggle too, and don't be afraid to walk away if the deal is not right!

On our last evening in Hong Kong, we dined at our hotel in one of their restaurants – the Mandarin Grill. I had read that this was a place you should not miss, and with us staying there, it seemed that it was a great opportunity to give it a go – but I wasn't sure what all the fuss was about, as it was a grill! The guide books also warned that it could be expensive – for a grill? How right the critics were, and how wrong I was. This is NOT an ordinary grill! We had the best and most interesting meal we have ever had! As soon as we were given the menu, we could see just how expensive this place was, but the details of the meals were just so unusual and quite mind-boggling! We found it difficult to understand exactly what was on offer, so we decided to opt for the set menu, which was one thousand one hundred and eighty eight Hong Kong dollars around one hundred pounds in 2012 – with the current exchange rates, 2017, this would be one hundred and twenty pounds, but it has probably gone up in price too – that price is per person, by the way.

The five course menu simply offered us: Flower Pot, Scallop, Sirloin, Bread and Butter, Petit Fours.

We had no idea what to expect, as it seemed such an uncomplicated menu for a lot of money! There was no explanation on the menu of what we would be getting, so we sat back and we waited.

We had a little amuse bouche to start, cheese crumble on a wafer, and then we were served with another morsel on a spoon, which was a cheese bite with, what I thought was a green olive, decorated with a real olive tree, albeit a very tiny one! We thought that this was our starter – Flower Pot! It was so small and just a mouthful – I thought 'We're going to be very hungry if this is the size of the portions'. The cheese puff was very nice and the "olive" was actually more of a tablet filled with olive oil, to clear our palate before the actual meal was served.

Our starter arrived, and it was a plant pot – a small terracotta plant pot with a little garden "growing" out of it! It was beautiful – a pleasure to behold. We were told that the soil was edible, made from roasted breadcrumbs, and the dressing for our salad was poured over from a little watering can! The attention to detail was amazing, and the salad was pretty good too. Richard is not a salad person – he says lettuce was meant to be fed to rabbits, not humans, but even he enjoyed this artistic delicacy, although he did find it a little dry. The salad consisted of a number of different types of lettuce leaves; tiny carrots, radish and potato; some vegetables that I could not identify; edible flowers and flowering herbs.

This was followed by our scallop. We were presented with a box and a little jug. The waiters opened the box which held our scallop, seated on a bed of hot stones. They proceeded to pour the liquid from the jug onto the hot stones and we were invited to lean in and smell the rising steam that was created from this action. We could smell the sea! The waiters placed a few delicate leaves on top of the scallop, and we were told in what order to eat them, as the leaves took on the taste of the scallop, through the rising steam. When we finally got to eat the scallop itself, it was delicious – probably the best I have ever eaten. By this time we were getting very excited to know what would follow, as we realised that every dish was not simple at all, but a culinary work of art, designed to excite every sense, through sight, aroma, taste and sound; the liquid sizzled when it touched the hot stones. We were not disappointed with our main course.

The beef was sliced thickly and served on top of glass, on a wooden tray. We were shown where the wood was burnt, from the charcoals used to cook the steaks and that some of the charcoal accompanied the meat. I didn't want to eat charcoal, I thought! It wasn't charcoal – it was actually black vegetables, which tasted really good. The meal was accompanied by two tiny baked potatoes wrapped in edible foil, a little pot of creamed sweet corn, and a pepper sauce. The steak was cooked to perfection, and we both enjoyed this third course immensely.

Then came our Bread and Butter – the bread was two tiny slices of fruit loaf which had been cooked in butter so it was crispy and the butter was actually ice-cream, which had been moulded to represent a little tub of butter to be served with our toast. It was gorgeous! – not too sweet or overpowering and it was perfect to end this delicious meal. There were two petit fours, each served on a shaving knife, which was made from solid chocolate, and made up this final part of the meal. The evening cost us about two hundred and eighty pounds including wine and a service charge, which was impeccable, but it was worth every penny.

The Mandarin Grill is our favourite restaurant in the whole world, and we have eaten in some excellent places. We enjoyed it so much that when we returned to Hong Kong on a cruise, our excursion for the day was to go for lunch at the Mandarin Grill; only this time we selected from the a la carte menu, as we then knew what to expect. Our lunch lived up to expectations, even when I was served a plate of "bones", instead of chicken, being told that my meal had "got away". They weren't real bones but models made from pate, which, when the sauce was added to my dish, dissolved to create the most delicious accompaniment to my chicken. We had hoped to visit again during our layover in February 2017, but I got my timing wrong only to find that we were in Hong Kong on a Sunday; the one day when the Grill is closed!

We did return in March 2018, when we stayed at the Mandarin Oriental for one night after a South East Asian cruise from Singapore. On the cruise, we had been telling everyone how good the Mandarin Grill was and that we had booked a table six months earlier to ensure that we would be able to enjoy another meal at our favourite restaurant. A couple from San Diego were staying in Hong Kong after the cruise and they decided to try the grill for themselves. We arranged for them to join us at dinner. But, when we were given the menu, I could not hide my disappointment. They no longer offered the exciting, unusual food from our previous visits, but they now had a normal grill menu of meats and fish. The restaurant had abandoned that unique showmanship to be just a regular run-of-the-mill grill, and, to be honest, the lack of clientele dining there on that Sunday night was evidence of the fact that it had lost its popularity and place amongst the best dining options in Hong Kong. Luis and Nancy were very gracious after we had been proclaiming the greatness of the Mandarin Grill, and we all enjoyed our meal, but it was not the same and it has certainly lost its spot as our number one restaurant in the world.

But, I would like to add that we have found another amazing restaurant in Hong Kong – Mott 32, a dim sum restaurant of very high calibre and offering fabulous food in very comfortable, classy surroundings. The Applewood Smoked Duck, which is their speciality, has to be pre-ordered and is expensive about six hundred and fifty Hong Kong dollars, but it is worth every penny as it is absolutely delicious! The duck is presented to you whole, and it is golden and succulent. The skin is given to you to eat sprinkled with sugar, and the two breasts are carved and served with pancakes, cucumber, spring onions and sauce. We ordered some fried rice, and they added the rest of the duck meat, chopped finely, to ensure that we got the most out of our dish. We ate there in 2017 and 2018, and on both occasions the restaurant was full. Luis and Nancy tried to book and to reserve the duck, but all portions had been reserved for that day, so that is proof that you must make your reservation, for a table and the duck, well in advance of your visit.

But now back to our first visit – the following morning we were collected by our Kuoni guide, and taken to the airport for our flight at ten a.m. to Bali. All the flights were with Cathay Pacific, so we were earning air miles and we were able to use the lounges at the airport being Silver Executive Members of British Airways. On arrival at the airport, we bought our visa which, at this time, cost us twenty-five dollars, and then we were quickly through immigration and collected our bags, which were already waiting for us. A Kuoni guide met us at the airport and escorted us to the car and then he accompanied us all the way to our hotel. The transfer took some time, as the distance was around thirty-five miles, and we went through a lot of small villages and over some very rough and bumpy roads before we arrived at our hotel, the Banyan Tree.

The location of the hotel was probably not the best choice, as we were miles away from any of the local towns and sights, but when I had seen details of the accommodation at this five-star resort hotel, I knew that that was where I wanted to stay. The greeting we received on our arrival was very welcoming, and we were blessed and given a welcome drink made from honey, before we were transferred to our villa by golf buggy. The hotel site is so big that these buggies are used as taxis, to get you around the place. Our villa, Number 210, did not disappoint. It was HUGE! The area was bigger than our house! It consisted of a large lounge, a dining and kitchen area where the hotel staff can come and prepare meals for you in your villa, a massive bathroom with a television, indoor and outdoor shower, a large bath, a double sink and wardrobes, and then the very impressive bedroom, which had patio doors opening onto steps, that took you down into the pool, directly from the room. Outside, we had the infinity pool, Jacuzzi, a lounge bed, chairs and loungers, giving us three seating options. There was a lovely garden surrounding the outdoor area, and a waterfall cascading into the pool. The ocean views we had just topped it all off. If I said this villa was stunning, it is actually an understatement – it was paradise! We didn't unpack for some time, as we both just kept wandering around, finding new areas, equipment and accessories that would make our stay here exceptional.

After enjoying our bottle of sparkling wine we eventually unpacked, and we ordered a buggy, which would take us for dinner. The hotel had several dining options and tonight we went to Bumbu. The weather and the temperature was very pleasant, so we ate outside. The staff were wonderful and very attentive. I had booked half-board, so our meals were included. We just had the drinks to pay for, and I was glad I had done that, as the food was expensive. I would not have thought that this was normal for Bali, but it was probably as a result of the class of hotel we were staying in. The food was very good – I had Nasi Goreng, which was tasty and not too spicy. We returned to our villa by buggy, and sat outside, enjoying the warm tropical evening over a Cuba Libre.

We stayed in Bali for five nights and unfortunately, most of our days were filled with showers and grey skies. I had not realised that Indonesia has a rainy season. I actually thought that Bali was a year-round holiday location. But it rained a lot during those few days we were there, and when it rains in Bali – IT RAINS! But the temperature was still really nice during the day and at night, although the sea breeze did keep you cool, so it made the intensity of the sun rather misleading, and you needed good protection to stop you from burning. We took the opportunity to relax in and around our villa, and to use the hotel facilities for dining. The staff were wonderful and so friendly, and, even when we came down for breakfast quite late, there was always plenty of freshly made produce and items were topped up, just for us.

We did two excursions during our stay in Bali, both of them were booked through Viator.com before we travelled out. Our full day excursion coincided with the one fine day that we encountered, which was rather convenient. We had booked it as a small tour, but it ended up as just the two of us, plus our driver and a guide. Our intentions were to see a bit more of Bali than just our resort, and we felt that this tour would offer us a bit more of an insight into the Balinese people and their way of life. We were to visit a number of craft workshops and drive through the countryside to a temple. The problem was that the workshops turned out to be a shopping expedition, rather than an opportunity to be able to see craftsmen at their work. The first stop was a silver maker, where we did not see any of the workmanship; we were just taken straight into the shop which was very expensive. I do try and buy something from these local manufacturing craft places to put some money into the local economy, but when they are charging extortionate prices for very simple pieces, it is not easy. I did buy a silver rickshaw, which was intricate and very delicate made from silver wire and not too expensive!

The next stop was wood carving and although on this occasion there were three workers who were plying their trade, when we watched them, we saw that the work that they were doing seemed to be very simple and the pieces being worked on were quite primitive and naive. The pieces in the shop were so much more detailed, and some of them were works of art – but they had a price tag to match! I did enquire about the price of a small mask and was told three hundred and fifty dollars, which was a ludicrous price. I immediately said no, not interested and the price came down instantly to two hundred and fifty dollars. As we left the shop, the price was dropping with every step we took, but by this time I was not interested and even if the price had come down to one dollar, I would not have bought it out of principal. Why do they start at such ridiculously high prices that they know no one would even consider paying? I know that we are meant to barter in places like this, but to offer five percent of the initial asking price and no more, does not seem to be the right way of doing it!

Our next stop was not a workshop but a plantation, where we were able to see the different types of fruit, vegetables and spices grown on the island. We had a pleasant stroll around the gardens, which were not pretty but practical, smelling and tasting some of the items growing. There was a little shop selling different types of tea and we tried a few of these before we continued our journey. By this time, we were well away from our hotel and had entered the true Bali countryside with tiers of rice paddies; workers in wide brimmed straw hats, water buffalo dragging wooden carts and blue skies! I am lying about the blue skies – although it didn't rain that day it was still overcast, with grey skies, but I could always dream of what the vista should have looked like! We continued climbing up the mountain along twisting lanes, which were very rough and unfortunately, despite having my wrist bands on, I started to suffer from car sickness which is the bane of my life! I use the acupressure wrist-bands and they normally work, but on this drive, with all the twists and turns, bumps and constant heavy braking, they were not able to stop me from feeling quite ill.

Halfway up the mountain, we stopped for lunch but I was unable to eat anything due to feeling so bad. Richard had some of the buffet, but it was not his cup of tea as he was concerned that it might be too spicy, and as I could not act as his taster, he was reluctant to try anything that he was not a hundred percent sure of. The views from the restaurant were lovely, looking out over the mountain that was taken over by the tiers of green rice fields, providing us with that perfect impression of Bali.

Our journey continued to the temple, which was disappointing, but was still worth a visit. It was built around the year 1200 AD so it was very old, but it was weather-beaten and unkempt. Most of the relics had moss growing all over them, and there were ferns in amongst the statues and buildings. Maybe I am being harsh about this site, as, if it had been in Angkor Wat you would be praising it as an ancient relic, but somehow here, it just looked sad and neglected. There were several tiers and some of the buildings were in a good state of repair, as it they are still used today for Buddhist ceremonies – in fact there was one taking place while we were there, which meant that we could not

enter a certain section of the temple. There was a big lake in the grounds, which looked stagnant and all I could think about was how many mosquitos were breeding in it! I know this is probably not painting the temple in a good light, but there were very few tourists there, and it was a tranquil, calm place, which offered one an opportunity for reflection, and meandering around the overgrown statues and temples offered us a pleasant respite from the frenzied, crazy roads.

We returned to our hotel at around four p.m. – a long eight hour day, and with the temperature and humidity it made it seem like an even longer one. After relaxing for a while and freshening up, we went to the Tamarind Restaurant at the hotel for a

Mongolian barbecue. The idea of a Mongolian barbecue is that you basically create your own dish by selecting from a number of different meats, vegetables, spices and sauces, putting them in a bowl and handing this over to the chef who cooks your concoction on a large heated skillet. The skillet is supposed to represent the upturned shield of a Mongolian soldier which could act as a cooking utensil when not being used as a defence. Richard and I have had this type of barbecue in many places – there used to be one in Manchester near the Palace Theatre, but I think that it is closed now. You can create as many different types of dishes as you want, either repeating one you really like or creating something completely different. If you don't like what you have invented, no worries; leave it and go and try again. The choice was really good at Tamarind and we started off selecting and cooking outside, but it started to rain, so the whole proceedings were moved indoors – not that it took away any of the enjoyment of the food, just not as pleasant for the surroundings.

The other excursion that we did was an evening sunset dinner cruise, in the harbour at Kato, the nearest town to our hotel. Because our hotel was so far away from the main tourist area, we had to negotiate with Viator.com to pay extra for a taxi to pick us up and take us to our location. I had not realised how isolated our hotel was when I booked it; all I was interested in was the quality. I think if we ever go back to Bali I will certainly do some more research on the area and facilities and not just pick a good hotel.

We were picked up at four fifteen p.m. and taken to the boat, which was large, catering for big groups of tourists from around the area. We were given garlands and when we were invited on board we were given a glass of non-alcoholic cocktail. We were told that the sunset cruise would consist of a drink, dinner and entertainment, but no mention of the drink being non-alcoholic! It was very busy and most of the clientele were from Japan and Australia, with some Russians. We started off by sitting outside but, you guessed it, it started to rain so, everyone moved inside where it was overcrowded and very warm. The buffet was reasonable and was continually being topped up and drinks on board were very reasonably priced about fifty thousand Indonesian Rand, around four pounds at this time. The entertainment was poor, as the stage was too small for the dancing routines that they performed, which consisted of different dances from around the world including Balinese dancers, the Can-Can, Vegas show-time, Flamenco and Indian. Because of the weather, the sunset was a flop, with nothing to be seen – the sun just set behind dark skies, never to be seen again, well not until next day.

The cruise was not much better either, as all we did was go around and around in the harbour. We didn't see anything of interest at all; nothing worth taking a picture of, and nothing to write home about. All in all, for the price we paid including the additional charge for our taxi, it was not money well spent and I certainly would not recommend it as an option to anyone following in our footsteps.

Our final day in Bali was spent at the hotel where, at last, we had some sunny weather, to be able to enjoy our pool and villa facilities. It was very warm and I ended up getting a touch of sunburn, due to not putting lotion on certain areas which were exposed, while I swam in the pool, used the Jacuzzi and relaxed on the loungers – when will I learn that as I am so fair that I burn very easily, and even a few minutes of exposure can affect me very badly.

On our last night we went to the hotel's fine dining restaurant, Jumana, which is reported to be the best on the island. We started with Mai Tai's, which was different for us as we normally have champagne cocktails or Cuba Libra's, and then we selected three courses, allowing us to have another three-course complementary. It was a really good meal, and we splashed out on a good wine for our last night. The staff, yet again, were exceptional; looking after us as though we were family rather than just guests.

We knew that we had a long flight home, having to stop in Hong Kong, London and then on to Manchester. We started the day fairly leisurely, with a long breakfast, where all the staff wished us a good journey home and a pleasant flight. They are all so friendly and conscientious – obviously it is part of their training, but it made it all so personal and it certainly makes you want to return, which is what it's all about. Our Kuoni guide collected us and took us to the airport, accompanying us all the way through check-in, before saying goodbye at security. We were able to use the lounge in Bali and Hong Kong airports and we were upgraded on our leg to London, moving up from economy to World Traveller Plus, which meant that we had better seats for the long flight home.

I am sure that there is so much more to see in Bali, and that we only just touched the surface of what this island resort has to offer. I have always wanted to go to Indonesia, to see the religious structure at Borobudur, but due to unrest and attacks on tourists, I cannot see us ever going there, unfortunately, as otherwise, it would have offered us an ideal opportunity to return to Bali and do some further exploring. I would have liked to go to Komodo too, to see the dragons. I know this can be done from certain cruise itineraries, but so far, I have not found one that appeals to us. Maybe in the future, if things settle, I will be able to find a tour of Indonesia that covers all these aspects, and have more time in Bali, but for now, these five days of very mixed weather, are evidence of ticking off number forty-nine from the list.

We returned to Hong Kong as a port of call on our China and Far East cruise (Beijing to Bangkok), in October 2012. We had lunch at the Mandarin Grill and we went shopping along Nathan Road. When we left the cruise port, which was not pleasant as it was a container port, we sailed through Victoria Harbour at the time that the light show was taking place. Viewing this from our balcony was quite spectacular, as there was nothing obstructing our view of all the buildings lit up by so many colours and dancing lights.

When our ship docked in 2018, we were at the new cruise terminal, which has been built in Kowloon at the location of the old airport. This was a much better location than our airport was in 2012, and a lot more convenient for getting to hotels in Kowloon, and on Hong Kong Island, as well as a rapid departure point for tours. We did a morning tour arranged through Celebrity, taking in the Peak Tram, Victoria Peak (very foggy and hazy), Aberdeen Harbour and Stanley Market before being dropped at the airport. We left our main luggage there and just took an overnight bag into Hong Kong, using the Airport Express. Hong Kong station was just a ten-minute walk from the Mandarin Oriental, where we had a harbour view room once again. The building work was still ongoing but high-rise apartments had not blocked the view, as we had feared that it would, and we enjoyed our Cuba Libras sitting on our lounger in the window that evening.

We have now been in Hong Kong twice on a Sunday, in 2017 and in 2018. We were shocked the first time during our stopover to Sydney, as the streets of Hong Kong Island were taken over by Asian ladies lounging everywhere on cardboard boxes. It looked like a major problem with migration or a massive demonstration. Everyone seemed to be very friendly and either chatting or playing cards or sleeping, but it was all very messy and a little overwhelming. We found out later that these people were employed in household service with families in Hong Kong. Sunday is their day off and they do their best to get out of their employers' home, so that they can get a day of rest and not be coaxed into working. But they have nowhere to go, so they create little pockets around the streets, using cardboard to create "rooms" and "enclosures", in order to meet with friends and to enjoy their day of rest. They are mainly from the Philippines, Indonesia and Vietnam, and together, they make a cacophony of noise as they chat and banter amongst themselves. It is certainly a sight that I have only seen in Hong Kong.

CHAPTER 30

Bora Bora, French Polynesia (50) and return to Hawaii (24) – February 2012

This is a perfect example of how I do not always think things over before I book holidays! I had found a cruise with the Princess, which covered the French Polynesian Islands and Hawaii, and this included a stop in Bora Bora. From the pictures, I thought that this island deserved more than just a few hours, so Thomas Cook arranged for us to have a few days staying in Bora Bora, before the cruise. Everything was booked through the cruise operator including flights, transfers, the hotel and the cruise. Due to the location of Tahiti, which is where the cruise would start, the fact that everything was linked was perfect because if anything went wrong, we would be covered through the guarantee of the cruise company, and they would get us to where we needed to be, at their expense.

We booked this holiday months in advance. It is not the sort of holiday that you leave to chance, as there are very few cruise itineraries that do the trip that we wanted. There was a change to the flight times and, as a result of this, we had a stay in Papeete, Tahiti before we transferred to Bora Bora. We had no problems with this except that when I queried the flights to get us to our next destination, I was told that we would be going on the ferry. I thought that this was strange as it is a long way to Bora Bora by sea; but after checking with the travel agents and them checking with the carrier, everything was confirmed, and I was told that there was nothing to worry about. But, with a few weeks to go, through bloody determination and knowing that there was something wrong, I forced them to investigate further, and that was when we found out that Princess had made a BIG cock-up!

When the international flights were changed and the extra night added in Tahiti, somehow or other our extended stay had been changed from Bora Bora to Moorea, which is the island close to Tahiti and accessible by ferry! I was devastated! Moorea may be very nice, but it's not on the fifty list! Thomas Cook contacted Princess and they said that there had never been a change to our hotel stay – it had always been Moorea! Now luckily, we still had the original documentation from when we first booked and it very clearly stated that we were due to stay in Bora Bora. As a result of this, a very quick check and change in booking took place, which meant that we could fly to Bora Bora instead – problem sorted!

Now back to my original comment. I tend to book main holidays months, if not, years in advance and then I will sandwich in short breaks in between. That is what I did this year, by using our American Express companion flight to get to Zimbabwe in January, and then booking our trip to Hong Kong and Bali on a whim. I never considered the flight times and the distance to these Asian locations, or the fact that two weeks after we returned from Bali, after two flights and carried over a twenty hour period, we would be flying out in the opposite direction to Tahiti. If you look at a map of the Pacific you will see that Indonesia is not actually too far from French Polynesia, and if I had planned these holidays at the same time, we could have saved ourselves a lot of time travelling, and possibly saved some money in the process too. But I didn't, so our holiday started with our flight from London Heathrow to LAX (Los Angeles, USA). We had an overnight stay in Los Angeles, staying at the Hilton – all arranged through Princess.

Getting into America is not much fun as you have to go through immigration, wait for your luggage and then go through customs. On this occasion it took ages, especially waiting for the luggage. Things have improved over the years, as they now use digital entry machines. If they work, they speed up immigration, but so many times we have gone to America and still had to queue to go through. Miami is worse by far, but we have found a great way to overcome this problem – fly from Dublin! In 2016, we did a short cruise out of Miami and flew with American Airlines out of Dublin. The cost for business class flights was around one thousand pounds for the two of us. We had to get to and from Dublin, which we did on a cheap airline from Manchester, and stayed overnight near the airport. The benefit of doing this is that the US border is actually in Dublin airport, and you go through immigration there. No queues, pleasant staff and a quick process. It means that when you arrive in America, you just go straight out to collect your luggage, as it is treated as an internal flight. Definitely something we will do again in the future – business class on American Airlines is not as good as British Airways, but it is not bad, and at the price, it is a great option.

We had a full day in Los Angeles and we had booked a tour through Viator.com for the afternoon. As our hotel was near the airport, we arranged for the hotel to provide us with a car and a driver, to take us into the centre of town, and then to pick us up later. It was a bit extravagant at one hundred and thirty dollars, but it gave us peace of mind. We were dropped off at the Chinese Theatre and we strolled along the Walk of Fame, spotting the names of film stars and artists who we knew. My favourite actor was Tony Curtis and I found his "star" in order to pay homage to him. Our LA tour was a little different from the normal drive around the homes of the rich and famous in Hollywood, it actually covered scandals, deaths and crime in the city!

Our driver or guide certainly knew his stuff, and we went all over Los Angeles learning about murders that took place here and there have been a lot, as well as mysterious deaths that remain unsolved. We learnt about Janice Joplin and Michael Jackson, whilst viewing where they had lived, or died. I didn't make any detailed notes of the tour, but it was certainly interesting and different from your normal run of the mill drive around Hollywood. That is one of the good things with Viator.com. They have all the basic tours that are offered by so many tour operators, but they also have things out of the ordinary, like this one. You can also book private tours which can be expensive but on occasion, can be so much better, as you are not reliant on the timekeeping of your fellow travellers, and, when you've had enough, you can call it a day.

After the tour, our hotel driver was waiting to pick us up, and we returned to the Hilton to retrieve our luggage and, after having time to freshen up, we returned to the airport, for our overnight flight to Papeete, Tahiti. We arrived at five thirty p.m. and we were met by a Princess Representative, who took us to the Intercontinental Tahiti for our one night stay. Our room was quite pleasant, with a view looking over towards the island of Moorea. We unpacked what we needed, and then we took the shuttle bus into town, even though we were tired from the flights and the lack of sleep. Papeete is not at the top of my list for places I would want to return to. It was shabby and fairly run down, and it did not seem to be aimed at tourists at all. I think that if you decide to holiday in Tahiti you're meant to stay at your resort, certainly not take a detour to see the capital of the island. There was a market, but this was selling wares for the locals and the shops had very little to offer.

We found somewhere to have a beer, and then we walked along the sea front, where we found a café to get something to eat. When we arrived in Tahiti it was overcast, but still very hot. Whilst we had our beer, it rained, but only for a short time, and then it cleared until we ate, when it rained again. We returned to our hotel on the shuttle bus, and as we drove back, it rained. We sat out on our balcony having our usual Cuba Libre and – it didn't rain! We ate at the hotel in the evening – they had a fish buffet which offered a huge variety of cooked and raw fish, as well as salads, vegetables and a selection of desserts. During the meal, we were entertained with Tahitian dancing and singing, which was actually very good. We returned to our room for a nightcap and, it rained! Tahiti is certainly very wet!

We were limited by the number of bags and weight of our luggage on our flight over to Bora Bora, but we were able to leave some of our luggage at the hotel, to retrieve it on our return when we would board the cruise ship. We were picked up at nine fifteen a.m. and taken to the airport for our flight at ten thirty-five a.m.

It was a busy flight, as the plane was only small, and it took us forty-five minutes to transfer from Tahiti to Bora Bora. The views were lovely, as we were able to see the island on our approach. It is only small, a lot smaller than Tahiti, and also very green; probably due to all that rain! On arrival, after we had picked up our luggage, we were shown to our transfer boat on the quay. Every hotel on the island picks you up by boat for the transfer – it is obviously a lot quicker than going by land, but then again, many of the hotels are located on smaller islands or sandbars off the mainland.

We were staying at the Hilton Bora Bora Nui and our transfer was on a very nice cruiser, with plenty of room to move around and to enjoy our approach to the resort where we would be staying for the next three nights. And, today, it was SUNNY! We had beautiful blue skies and it was lovely and warm, even with the sea breeze rushing past us, as we sped on our way. As we boarded the boat we were given a garland of flowers, which were placed around our necks, a South Pacific tradition that we had witnessed previously in Hawaii. We then took the thirty minute ride to our hotel, passing many other resorts, and the main island. Moored in the bay was the Ocean Princess, obviously visiting this island, on its itinerary, before we were due to board in three days' time.

At reception, we were given some fruit juice, while we checked in, and then we were driven around to our over-water bungalow, Number 116, which was located not too far from the main facilities but with fabulous uninterrupted views of the ocean – which is very blue, by the way. Our villa was lovely, with a small entrance vestibule, a large lounge with some glass tables, so you can see the fish swimming below; a super large bathroom with walk in shower, bath and double vanity unit, a canopied bed in the separate bedroom area, and a large veranda, with steps leading down to the sea.

Our first day was spent just getting used to our villa and the resort. We had drinks at the pool bar, and collected our snorkelling gear, provided free of charge at the hotel. We both went into the sea for a swim and a splash, and we saw a lot of fish just around our villa – all sizes, shapes and colours. It was exactly how I had expected it to be – glorious blue skies, wonderful aqua blue seas, sunshine, tropical fish and a feeling of pure tranquillity; absolutely fabulous!

Hilton Bora Bora Nui is located on an island. There are other resort hotels on the island, but they were not too close to us so we felt quite independent and isolated, which was lovely. On our first full day, we had a wander around the grounds of the hotel, including a walk up the hill, past the spa, and out towards the little chapel, which offered the most beautiful views over to the main island and back towards our resort. The sea is so blue – aqua, rather than blue, and so clear. The main island has a huge mountain in its centre, with the main town and other resorts dotted all around the island; all at sea level. We could not see any buildings on the slopes of the mountain. We did not go over to the mainland while we stayed at the Hilton, as we knew that we would see more when we returned, as part of the cruise.

In my opinion, Bora Bora was a real paradise. The turquoise sea, abundant green trees and colourful flowers, peaceful solitude away from the madding crowds, the wonderful resort with everything you needed – I was totally blown away with it all. We had some wonderful sunsets during our stay, which we watched from the raised balcony at the restaurant where we ate, for the first two nights of our stay.

There are various excursions you can do whilst staying at the resort. One of them, a Day in Paradise, takes you out to your own deserted island, to relax, to swim and to sunbathe, and includes a picnic lunch. But this wasn't really our scene, so, instead, we opted to have a Tahitian barbecue on our veranda in our villa. In the afternoon, they came to our villa and set the table ready for our banquet that evening – it was all laid out beautifully. Dinner was delivered at six forty-five p.m. and we sat down at seven p.m. to eat. There was so much food! Our barbecue consisted of a lobster and pineapple salad to start, and then swordfish, tuna, chicken and beef to cook on our hot table-top stove, accompanied by corn on the cob and mushrooms. We finished the meal with a fresh fruit platter full of local tropical fruits. We had ordered a bottle of rosé wine which we drank whilst we ate, enjoying the beautiful sunset in idyllic surroundings. The meal was fabulous and it was certainly an evening to remember – very romantic!

After dinner, we sat on our jetty with our legs dangling over the sides, above the water and a huge stingray swam underneath us. It must have been about three metres long! I was so shocked as I had not expected such a big fish to come so close to the shoreline!

The next day, we left the resort at nine a.m. to return to Tahiti, to connect with our cruise ship, the Ocean Princess. It turned out to be an expensive stay, as we had room only and had to pay for all our meals and drinks, but it was worth every penny, as we had had a fantastic stay on the island paradise. We returned to the airport on the same boat, but that time we sailed away to the sounds of a ukulele, having been given beaded necklaces on our departure and all the staff lined the jetty, waving farewell to us. They were all so friendly and helpful from start to finish, making us feel very special, treating us as friends, rather than just paying guests.

The return flight to Papeete took just forty-five minutes, and our luggage came off very quickly. We collected the luggage that we had left at the Tahitian hotel, and then we were driven to the pier, where there was a band playing, welcoming everybody onto the ship. Check-in was very quick, and we were in our suite just fifteen minutes after getting off the plane! We had booked one of the Owners Suites, number 6088, which was at the rear of the ship. It was a very nice cabin – large and comfortable with a really big balcony, that went around the side slightly, so we could enjoy the views from several directions. We had loungers and a table and chairs outside, so we could enjoy the lovely weather we hoped that we would have on our twelve-night cruise.

After we had unpacked and drunk our champagne, we had a walk into Papeete, as we needed to find a plug adapter, as the one we had brought with us did not fit. Luckily, in a small computer shop in town, we found one. This had been left behind by a previous customer and the shop gave it to us free of charge, which we thought was a really generous gesture, and it certainly helped us out.

We had drinks at Sabatini's, which was acting as a lounge for Elite and Suite passengers, in the early evening, and then we had dinner on an open table in the dining room. The smaller ships, Ocean and Pacific Princess only have set time dining, early evening, and then at eight p.m. We had opted for the later slot, as we liked to have a pre-dinner drink and then eat later. We had also requested a table for eight as we thought that would offer a good variety of fellow diners, as we would be sitting with them every night, and the more people at your table would hopefully offer more varied conversation. But, on this first night, obviously because people were arriving at all different times from international incoming flights, you sat with whoever you wanted, and wherever there was space. We were on a table of eight. All our fellow diners were from the USA, but we had a really nice evening with pleasant conversation. We normally find that if you have a lot of Americans sitting at your table, that the conversation can be a little limited, as they tend to talk about where they come from and local news, rather than chatting about things that include us Brits.

The next day we were moored close to Moorea, an island larger than Bora Bora, but smaller than Tahiti. It was very green, but also very mountainous. After our stay in Bora Bora, we knew that there would be lots of beautiful beaches and resort hotels dotted all around the island.

We had booked an excursion with the ship, which involved us driving around the island in four wheel drive vehicles. There was a convoy of four trucks; three of them had eight passengers but ours had just six people, so we had a bit more room, to make ourselves comfortable. We went around the island, stopping occasionally for photos. It was very picturesque, with clear blue skies, turquoise water and green mountains. One member of the group fell ill, and we had to wait for an ambulance which took him to hospital, accompanied by his wife and one of our guides. As a result of this, we lost one of the vehicles that was used to transport the group from the top of the mountain where we were, down to a plateau, which was as far as the ambulance could go. This meant that we needed to squash up more in our truck, to accommodate the others who had been left abandoned, as a result of this, but the vehicle returned after a while, so we were back to normal for the rest of the trip.

We went to a vanilla plantation located on Magic Mountain, and we had to reverse up the steep road, as there was nowhere to turn around at the top. It was quite terrifying as the sides of the road were very steep. The views from the top were magnificent, and we had a nice walk around the herb and spice gardens; in particular learning all about vanilla, which was the key produce of this plantation. Our final stop was a juice factory – not very interesting, but the shop sold some alcoholic cocktail mixes, so we bought a couple for us to have back at home when I would cook a South Pacific meal for friends.

Our ship was moored in Cooks Bay, and it really was a fabulous place to spend the afternoon sitting out on our balcony, enjoying the view of the island. This had to be one of the most breath-taking anchor points that we had ever had on a cruise, and we stayed out on the balcony for a long time when we set sail, in order to watch Moorea disappear from view, as we sailed away and it became just a dot on the horizon.

This evening at dinner, we sat at the table allocated to us for the cruise. But, although I had requested a table of eight so we could have a good variety of dining companions, when we came down, we were at a table for just four, and we sat with Dennis and Carol; French speaking Canadians from Montreal. We immediately had a language barrier, as neither Richard nor I speak French, and they only spoke a little English. This meant that conversation was difficult, and we did not linger long over dinner. We find that if we have good company at dinner and the conversation is entertaining, we can spend all evening there. So, we retired immediately after dinner, as we were too late for the show.

The next day we were back at Bora Bora, moored in the main lagoon, where the only town on the island is located. We booked an afternoon excursion with the ship, to do a full circuit tour of the island, which meant we had a leisurely morning before we took the tender over to the island, and we had time to browse around the shops before we needed to meet up for our tour.

The trucks that day were more like old school buses, and were not very comfortable with a lack of space and hard seats. The trip was not as good as Moorea, as the road stays at sea level; it does not go up the mountain like it had the day before, on Moorea. Bora Bora is also made up of lots of islands and sand bars; we stayed on one just a few days ago, so there was not much else to see. We stopped at a pretty church, a house selling printed sarongs, and we saw some amazing crabs that lived underground eating the foliage that falls from the trees around them. We stopped and watched as our guide threw some leaves onto the ground and the crabs came swarming out of their holes, grabbed the foliage, and then dragged it back into their holes. There were so many of them and they were so quick, it was quite an eerie sight to watch.

We stopped at Bloody Mary's; a renowned cocktail bar on the island. We ordered two of the local cocktails, which were actually quite spicy, but delicious! From the door of Bloody Mary's we could see the island where we had stayed, and just make out the little chapel that was on the top of the hill.

We left the French Polynesian islands behind us and we sailed towards Hawaii. It took five days to traverse the Pacific Ocean between these two sets of islands. The Polynesians believe that the indigenous people from both island groups are related, and that their ancestors also sailed to New Zealand and that the Maori's are descendants of these seafaring people.

I won't bore you with all the details of what we did each day. When we first started cruising we thought that having lots of days at sea would be very boring and monotonous, but this is certainly not the case. There are always lots of things going on all day and in the evening and there is usually something that we would attend like wine tasting, cookery demonstrations, lectures etcetera. These do not fill up all our time on our sea days, but it leaves us with plenty of relaxation time, where we can do what we want to, and we now really enjoy our time at sea. In fact, we enjoy them so much that in 2016 we did a transatlantic cruise from Miami to Southampton comprising thirteen nights, with just three stops en-route.

Our first stop in Hawaii was Big Island, so named because it is the largest of the Hawaiian Islands and has the majority of active volcanoes in the archipelago. There were only five islands on our tour, which was perfect, as it felt very exclusive and personal. Our first stop was for coffee tasting in Hilo, and then we went to Volcano National Park and stopped at the Jagger Museum. The views were really clear, and we had the tallest and the biggest mountains pointed out to us. These are bigger than Mount Everest if you measure them from their base, which is underwater. Both of these mountains are actually volcanoes. We went to the rim of the crater of an active volcano and we could see steam (CO^2) rising from its centre. This last erupted in 2008 creating a magnificent spectacle and a massive lava flow. Big Island is made up of five volcanoes – one is practically extinct, two are dormant, and the other two are active, one of these being the most active volcano in the world.

We walked through a lava tube in the rain forest created by fast flowing lava, that leaves behind an underground tunnel after it cools and has run its journey. Our guide, Monique, was very interesting and knowledgeable. We had some wine tasting on the tour, a picnic lunch and we stopped at the Big Candy store before returning to our ship.

Another day and another island – Kauai. Hawaiian and Polynesian names are very difficult to pronounce. The language has fewer letters than the western alphabet, and you pronounce every letter when you speak. For example, Moorea is pronounced Mo-o-re-a. This knowledge helped us a bit while we were there, but it took us so much time to try and think on how to pronounce a name, that we had already gone past the sign before we could speak!

The weather was not as good as the day before, which was a shame, as that day we had a helicopter ride booked. Yet again, there were very few on our tour; just five of us – a family of three and Richard and I. I don't know why this was the case – maybe, as most cruisers are from the US, they felt that they did not need to book Princess tours, but could do the sightseeing on their own, after all; Hawaii is the fiftieth state of America!

Our driver and guide today was Rick. His commentary during our tour was okay, but he spent a lot of time chatting to the daughter who was young and very attractive, so I suppose you couldn't blame him! We went on the flight first before the tour of the island, and all five of us went up at the same time. We drew the short straw, as we both sat in the back, Richard getting the middle seat, whereas the family had two in the front and the mother had the other window seat. But we still had amazing views, while we flew over the deep canyons that were impossible to reach by any other means; streams that turned to waterfalls, cascading over the steep sides of the ravines; sharp ridges that could only be seen from the air; long, golden sandy beaches, steep cliffs leading down to them and gorges which we flew into, so the helicopter was immersed between these rocky outcrops. We flew below the clouds so, even though it was overcast, we got great views for the whole of our flight, which was a long one, lasting forty-five minutes. On our return to the heliport, we flew over the cruise port, where our ship had been joined by another, and was at rest below us.

We returned to our minivan, and continued with our tour of Kauai, heading to the far side of the island and Hanalei Bay, where we stopped for a picnic lunch. This popular beach location is famous for being the location mentioned in the Peter, Paul and Mary song "Puff, the Magic Dragon, who lived by the sea, and frolicked in the morning mist in a land called Hanalei". They wrote the song whilst visiting this location, as the mountains that fall into the sea at this site looked like a dragon, with its tail curling around and spines along the back of the ridge towards its "head". You needed a good imagination, but I could certainly visualise a dragon sleeping along the water's edge. The rocky outcriop that created the head even had an eye, and a snout – well, I thought that it did!

Our final stop was at a lighthouse before we headed back to the ship. It was a long day, most of which was spent in the van, but we saw a lot of the island, which is used for many film locations, because of its greenery, its beauty and its forest. We got back to the port at four fifteen a.m., with just thirty minutes to spare, before we set sail for our next island, Maui.

Maui is the second largest of the Hawaiian islands and is renowned for being a popular destination for whale watching, as the area around the island attracts these huge beasts as a mating ground, especially at this time of year. As we ate breakfast in the Italian restaurant, Sabatini's, which is reserved for suite guests only, we saw a whale breaching in the distance – this is when they rise out of the water, head first and then crash back, creating a huge tidal surge. I think that this is done to impress the other whales, and we had booked to go on a whale watch cruise in the afternoon, in the hope of seeing this spectacle at closer range. There is something that I should add at this point. Richard and I have been on many whale watching expeditions – in Iceland, Alaska, South Africa and other locations, and whenever we go out on a boat, the whales seem to decide to go on vacation, and we rarely get a good viewing – our only real success was the second time we went to Juneau, Alaska. We hoped that Maoi would be an exception to this rule!

At first, we thought that this was going to be an amazing place for whale watching having seen the breach at breakfast and then when we took the tender to go ashore, two whales came up really close to us, exhaling through their blowholes and coming up just above the surface – it was an amazing sight and really whetted our appetite for the main event at twelve. As we queued to board our whale watching boat, some people we knew were disembarking and said what a wonderful cruise they had had with loads of incredible whale sightings. We were first to board the boat so we could choose what we hoped would be the perfect spot for taking those breath-taking photos of these magnificent beasts.

Fifteen minutes into the cruise there was a shout as a whale was spotted – on the opposite side from where we were sitting: typical! Eventually we did see some whales on our side of the boat, but they were in the distance and these larger whale watching boats are restricted as to how close they can go to the whales, as they were not allowed to disturb them too much during the mating season.

We "chased" a male and a female whale for some time, but all they did was blow and just break the surface, so they were only just visible from our vantage point. Eventually, the captain gave up and started to head for shore. We were disappointed as we had not witnessed anything truly spectacular and, yet again, we thought that this expedition would be recorded as another failed whale watch. As we put our cameras away and settled back for the short journey back to shore, it happened – a whale breached right by the side of the boat where we were sitting. Everyone let out a yell of surprise and amazement, including us! It happened so quickly that there was no chance of catching it on film. This huge whale then stayed with us, swimming alongside – slapping its fin on the water's surface; rising slowly out of the water, nose first, and hovering with its head above the surface, eyeing us up and swimming so close to us that you could see the full length of it along the side of the boat, just under the water. We were told by our guide that this was quite a rare occurrence. This one encounter was truly spectacular and made the trip worthwhile.

On our return to shore, we wandered around the town, which was very nice and better than we had seen on the other islands, with lots of souvenir shops, boutiques, bars and restaurants. We took the tender back to the ship at around three-thirty p.m. as we needed to pack, as we would be leaving the ship the next day. But we still had time to enjoy a drink on the balcony, and, as we gazed back to Maui, a rainbow appeared – perfectly formed and creating a frame over the mountains of the island. It was a beautiful sight and a lovely departing gesture from Mother Nature! But to cap this off, as we started the engines and slowly, very slowly, edged our way on towards Oahu, two dolphins appeared at the stern, right under our balcony – they leapt, swam, clicked and whistled, while I blew kisses at them, before we finally sailed away for the last time on the cruise.

Honolulu, Oahu was our final destination but we had still booked an excursion to while away the morning before going to our hotel, Moana Surfrider, for the last night of our holiday. By doing this, our luggage was taken care of, and taken to the hotel, where we would be reunited later in the day. The coach tour did a circuit of the island, stopping at some of the main vista points. We had done this drive previously when we were staying in Honolulu for five nights, but it was still better than spending the day in the crowded centre of town.

Our final afternoon was spent drinking Rum Runners in a bar opposite our hotel, shopping for a new, super-light suitcase, which meant that we had to repack, and enjoying a pleasant final meal at a steak and seafood restaurant close to our hotel. The next day, we were picked up at four thirty a.m. for our transfer to the airport, where we caught a flight to Los Angeles, and then an onward journey to Heathrow. This was a really long and tedious journey, and with an eleven-hour time difference to cope with too, it was a VERY long day!

This was a great holiday, plenty of variety, restful, fabulous scenery and a wonderful way to see the Hawaiian Islands, much better than just staying in one location in Honolulu.

CHAPTER 31

Matterhorn, Switzerland (46) – July 2012

We had booked a short break in Switzerland for June 2010, to cross the Matterhorn off our list. We were due to fly to Geneva and spend a couple of nights there, before hiring a car and driving to Zermatt to spend two nights deep in the Alps, before flying home. It was all arranged and paid for, but this was the week that we were told that my mother was terminally ill and we cancelled the trip with just a few days' notice. She actually died four days after we received that devastating news, on the 18th of June 2010, the day that we were due to fly out. The hotel were very good and, under the circumstances, they gave us a full refund, as did the car hire company, but we lost the money on the flight and, as we were flying with Easyjet, it was not worth putting in a claim on our insurance for the cost of the flight. I am glad that we took this step though – I would not have forgiven myself if we had not been there when she passed away.

So, two years later, we rearranged a trip to the Matterhorn, but it was a completely different itinerary and this time my Dad was with us. We took him away three times after Mum died, and before he was too ill to travel due to suffering from Alzheimer's and ill health. The first time, in June 2011, was rather special, as we went to Russia and spent nine nights on a river boat, starting in Saint Petersburg and sailing to Moscow along the Neva. There was a lot of walking involved, and Dad was not able to keep up on some occasions, so the next year, we decided to rent a villa for a week in the Italian Lakes, hire a car and drive to Zermatt for a stay in Switzerland. We organised the trip ourselves, booking everything through the internet. We do this a lot, and most of the time we do not have any issues, but there are times when it can go very wrong and you hear so many horror stories of corrupt websites that take your money fraudulently, and you get nothing in return. Even if you are careful and take precautions, there are some unscrupulous people out there, and you do need to be very careful. It is better if you can use recognised sites or companies that are covered by a code of conduct like IATA or ABTA, but, when you find a hotel, deal or villa that you really want, the checks for reliability go to the back of your mind.

We have had three issues that I can recall – when we went to Marrakesh, I had booked a Riad through the internet, but luckily it was through an agency rather than directly with the Riad. I wanted a place that typified the images that you have of Arabian Nights and the mystery of Morocco – brightly coloured tiled walls; central courtyard with fountains and gardens; a hammam (Turkish bath) in your room big enough for two, and hidden away from the outside world. I thought that I had found the perfect place and the location was ideal as it was close to the centre of the city. When we arrived, we were transferred from the airport and we had to walk to the Riad through little narrow streets, our cases following us in a cart! When we arrived and were taken inside, it was beautiful and just as I had hoped – but then we were told that we were not staying there, even though this was the place I had booked, and we were taken across the road to another Riad which was dark, dingy and nothing like the photos on the internet. It appeared that they had overbooked the original Riad and we were shipped off to an alternative, far inferior accommodation with none of the trappings I wanted. I was so upset, as we had paid a lot of money for our intended room and the alternative was awful. Luckily, because we had actually used an agency and they had transferred us from the airport, we had their number and I contacted them to register a complaint. They immediately found us an alternative which lived up to our expectations and we were taken there later that evening – Riad Clementine. It was not as close to the markets and square of central Marrakesh, but this was a small problem compared with staying at the awful place we had been allocated.

In 2017, we went to New Zealand to do a tour of South Island and I arranged everything over the internet, using many different sites to arrange accommodation, tours, car hire and flights. I always shop around to try and get the best deal, and when I decided where we wanted to stay in Franz Josef, the Te Waonui Forest Resort, I used a company called Hoteling.com to make the reservation as they came back with the right price. The room was booked for one night and I paid at the time of making the reservation – I had no issues with this as you have to pay upfront most of the time when you book through Expedia or Hotels.com. But when we arrived at the hotel, they did not have our booking. I gave them our paperwork showing the confirmation and receipt for the payment. We left them to investigate while we did our Air Safari over the Southern Alps, but when we returned we discovered that the company (hoteling.com) had ceased trading, and had not paid the hotel the money that we had deposited with them. As a result of this, they had cancelled the reservation. They still had vacancies, so Te Waonui were able to offer us a room, but we had to pay for it. We had to negotiate a reduced rate, as the first price that they quoted was ridiculous! This was a big hotel and popular with tour companies, but there were other options in the town, and I was not prepared to pay the extortionate rates they were quoting. The price came down to about twenty five percent of the first quote, and this we were prepared to pay.

The reason why I have raised these issues in this chapter is that the third problem we had related to our trip to Italy. I do a lot of research to make sure that any hotel or villa that we book is absolutely perfect for our needs – the right number of rooms, bathrooms preferably en-suite in every room, location, views and facilities. Our week in the lakes was no exception, and I had found a perfect villa on the banks of Lake Maggiore, which was close to the Swiss border and would mean our drive to Zermatt mid-holiday would be an easy one. I made the booking directly with the owner, through the internet, and I paid my deposit – I was early with my reservation, booking around eleven months in advance. We arranged everything else – flights, car hire, hotel in

Zermatt – and waited for the time to pay the balance, eight weeks before we were due to fly. When I contacted the owner to make arrangements to pay the remainder of our rental, she informed me that she had double booked, forgetting all about my reservation, as it had been done the year before. Obviously the second booking was more lucrative to her, as she said it was my reservation that was to be cancelled. I did not know what my rights were, and I thought that it would be too costly and take too long to take legal action, as we already had everything else arranged.

She did have a number of different apartments and villas in the area but none of these alternatives were right for the three of us, so I cancelled. She did refund the deposit in full, but no compensation was offered for the inconvenience that she had caused. With just eight weeks to go, it was back to the drawing board and our dates and area were fixed, with very little room for being flexible, other than which lake we selected. But I found, what I thought, was an ideal place in Menaggio on the Western shores of Lake Como, and I booked this for our stay. It was a case of beggars can't be choosers, and some of the usual requirements did not apply like bedrooms not en-suite, in the town rather than a rural location but the views from the front patio were fabulous. So all's well that ends well!

We flew into Milan – this should have been quite spectacular, as we would be flying over the Alps and, as we would be descending ready to land, we would be quite low as we flew over the mountain range. But it was overcast and, as we were late departing, it was getting dark, so there was no view – pity! We have done this flight before and had fabulous views coming into Milan, but not on this occasion. We hired a car from the airport and then we set off for our drive, which took us along the lakeside road, passing through lots of lovely villages along the route. The road did get very narrow in places, so I was glad that Richard was driving. By the time we got to Menaggio to get the keys for our villa, it was very dark and late about ten p.m., but the letting agents knew that we were coming and had stayed open, waiting for us. Our sat-nav took us directly to their offices, our only problem was trying to find somewhere to park close by, which is always difficult in a strange place, and in the dark – but we managed. The agents advised us to get something to eat in the little bar that was next door to their office, as all the supermarkets and grocery shops would be shut. We took their advice, and even though it was very late by then, we enjoyed three lasagnes with a glass of wine for Dad and I. Richard abstained as he was driving and would wait for a Cuba Libra once we got to the villa.

Yet again, the sat-nav took us directly to the road where the villa was located; it was just a little difficult trying to identify which one was ours, as there were a number of houses or villas on the site. But we recognised the picture, checked the house number and parked, knowing that we were in the right location. We unloaded the car with our luggage, which now included some bottles of diet coke ready for our sundowner, and we checked out our home for the next seven days. It was basic with three bedrooms and two bathrooms, albeit one of these was downstairs which made it pretty impractical for use by us during the night. I did not fancy trying to use the steep, windy stairs in the dark, and it would be dangerous for Dad to do the same. Rooms allocated, clothes unpacked and toiletries dispensed in the bathroom, we sat down and we enjoyed our nightcap before retiring after a very busy and a long day.

It was very warm – no air conditioning, and noisy; even though we were not located on a main road, there was a very busy one which ran past our road and wound around the back of the villa, and it seemed to be active all night long. By the end of the trip I had got used to the traffic noise, but I never got used to the heat in the bedrooms.

The next day, we were greeted by blue skies and sunshine, which was a pleasant sight after it had been so miserable the day before. Our first call that morning was to a supermarket, which was conveniently located a few miles out of Menaggio along the noisy road behind our villa. I know that this probably sounds sad, but I love to go to the local grocery shops and markets when we hire a villa overseas, as the produce always seems to be so fresh and different from what we get back home. Most of the produce is exactly the same, of course, but the fresh breads, cheeses, meats and baked goods are completely different, and, as these become the staple of our diet when we are away, I can spend quite a lot of time, and money, making sure that we have a good variety, and enough to see us through. I never think that we could return and get more each day if we need it, I just load the cart with everything that I want to try, even though a lot of this may end up in the bin, as the bread goes stale and there's too much for three of us anyway. We spent around two hundred euros but this did include quite a few bottles of wine as well as food. As it happened, we did keep returning to this supermarket, stocking up on extra bits that we missed on our first visit, replacing stale with fresh bread, which we needed every other day, and buying more wine!

During our time in Menaggio we certainly kept busy – coming down into town and exploring the quaint shops, finding a very nice place to eat on the lakeside, before boarding the little train which trundled along to Lenno, although we got off at San Lorenzo Church to avoid a long wait for the return journey. Another day, we hired a little boat for a few hours and sailed along the shoreline, enjoying the sight of lots of beautiful villas, hotels and villages that are all situated close to the waters' edge. It was a little choppy and, as passengers, Dad and I got quite wet while Richard, as the pilot, remained dry – I wonder how that happened? We bought Dad a cap as he needed it to keep the sun off his head, and he looked good with a fake captain's hat on! Back on shore, we took a walk along the quayside and found a rather nice hotel, the Bella Vista, where we had a drink and then lunch right on the waters' edge – the meal was really good value as it was a set three-course meal for just twenty six euros each and the wine was only eighteen euros. But, with inflation and the drop in the pound since the Brexit vote in 2016, I am sure that it would be a lot more expensive if we returned now. But the hotel certainly lived up to its name with beautiful views across the lake towards Bellagio.

Later in the week, we took the ferry across the lake to visit Bellagio, which is located at the end of the peninsula, that juts out into the lake. If we had decided to drive there, it would have taken us around an hour and a half, as you have to go the long way around – the car ferry only takes twenty-five minutes, although we went as foot passengers, leaving the car in Menaggio. I really liked Bellagio, but the streets are very narrow and steep and Dad struggled to walk up them, but we took our time, stopping often to window shop, and we managed, eventually, to get from the quayside to the upper level. The souvenir shops are wonderful, full of beautiful pottery, but there were also lots of little boutiques and designer shops offering clothes, handbags, Italian delicacies and designer baby outfits. Fiona, my sister-in-law, was pregnant at the time, and I bought her a beautiful little baby outfit and tiny little slippers to match. I was really happy with my purchase, until the owner asked me if the new born was going to be my first grandchild! I felt really insulted – and old!

We had lunch at a restaurant that was on the lower quayside, sitting out and enjoying the lovely weather and fabulous views, looking back towards Menaggio. We re boarded the ferry and continued on its circuit stopping at Tremezzo and Varenna. There was not a lot to see in either of these towns so, after a sit down and an ice-cream and Italian ice-cream has to be the best in the world, we returned to Menaggio.

Another excursion we took was to the town of Como, the namesake of the Lake and the province where we were located. This is probably the largest of the towns located along the lake, and is situated at the very top, south westerly point, of the lake. On this occasion we took the hydrofoil, which was very quick, even though it stopped at a number of places along the west and east coast of the lake. But, unfortunately, on this day Dad was really suffering with the pains in his legs, and we were not able to walk very far once we disembarked. All we did was leave the quayside and take refuge at the first outdoor café that we could find. After a bite to eat, and a glass of wine, I wandered around the few shops that were close by, while Richard kept

Dad company at the café, and we then returned on the hovercraft back to Menaggio to pick up our car. I am sure that Como has got a lot more to offer, but we were not able to discover anything more on that visit.

The week was broken up with our detour in to Switzerland to go to Zermatt to see the Matterhorn, as this was the choice by the British public who voted this European mountain into forty-sixth place. We packed a picnic lunch, as we knew that we would be on the road for a quite a while, and thought it would be cheaper than paying for lunch in Switzerland, which is renowned as being an expensive country, and we set off, taking the noisy road behind our villa towards the border.

The drive was a very pleasant one – we had expected it to be motorways, but we went along all types of roads, through tunnels, across mountain passes, past Lake Maggiore and continually crossing borders, going from Italy to Switzerland and back again. We did hit some traffic along a narrow stretch of road and took the wrong detour, ending up going through a very long tunnel three times – but overall, we did not have too much trouble. The views were lovely, especially the Simplon Pass – some of the roads were quite amazing, with sheer drops over the side, twisting around mountains and crossing deep ravines. We stopped for our lunch at a picnic spot near a river, and then we continued on our journey to Tasch, which is where we parked the car and caught the train into Zermatt, which is a car- free zone.

We had booked to stay in the town of Zermatt at the Europe Hotel, a reasonably priced four-star hotel, which had its own restaurant. We were met by a representative of the hotel, in a little electric car, which was used to transfer us and our luggage to the hotel. The town was really pretty and had a "chocolate box" appearance with lots of hotels, shops and buildings, all with window boxes full of colourful flowers – especially red geraniums, that spilled over the sides, cascading down towards the footpaths. The whole place was so Swiss – it looked just like the travel brochures and certainly did not disappoint. Our hotel was quite basic, but both rooms we had booked faced onto the Matterhorn. It was six p.m. by then, and there was a cloud obscuring the top of the mountain, but it was unmistakable, as it is a solitary mountain towering above the town of Zermatt.

We had a drink in the bar, which was only small, but we managed to get seats, before eating that night at the hotel restaurant. If it had just been Richard and I, we would probably have found somewhere a little more exotic in the centre of town, but it had been a long day for Dad, and we knew that he would not have been able to cope with walking up the hill back to the hotel if we had gone out. The set menu, which was very tasty, consisted of salmon, cauliflower soup, steak with salad and a strawberry dessert. It cost thirty-five Swiss francs each, which at that time was around thirty pounds. Drinks were expensive, as we had pre-dinner cocktails and that cost nine six Swiss francs and fifty centimes – almost as much as dinner!

The next day, when we woke, all the clouds had lifted and we had the most magnificent view of the Matterhorn. This pyramid-like mountain always has a snowy peak as it is covered in glaciers. We had breakfast and checked out, but left our luggage to be collected later, when we would take the return train to Tasch. We walked into town – it was downhill, so Dad was okay, but we had to take our time, so that he did not have too much pain, but it enabled us to take in the views, admire the lovely buildings and cross the river that runs straight through the town. There is a graveyard with memorials to people who have died trying to climb the Matterhorn, which was not achieved until July 1865. In fact, the North Side was not conquered until 1931, as it is amongst the three biggest north faces of the Alps – the mountain itself is fourteen thousand six hundred and ninety-two feet high.

We took the Gornergrat Railway[2] from Zermatt to the summit of the Gornergrat. The station is located at an altitude of ten thousand one hundred and thirty-five feet and is the second highest railway in Europe after the Jungfrau. It opened in 1898 and is a very popular trip during the tourist season, as it takes you up close and personal with the glaciers and the Swiss Alps, giving you a superb, uninterrupted view of the Matterhorn. We were really lucky, as we had perfect weather for the trip, with clear crystal blue skies and very few clouds. The views on the journey up to the summit were just as breath-taking as the view from the top – you really did feel like you were at the top of the world with three hundred and sixty degree, panoramic views. It cost us eighty Swiss francs each, to go on this railway, but it was worth every penny!

The railway is Europe's highest open-air cog railway, taking passengers from the Zermatt station (one thousand six hundred and twenty metres) to the summit of the Gornergrat, three hundred and sixty-five days a year. The ride takes thirty-three minutes and requires a vertical climb of one thousand four hundred and sixty nine metres. The line leads over dramatic bridges, through galleries and tunnels, across forests of larch and Swiss stone pine, and past rocky ravines and mountain lakes. At the station at the summit there is a small shop, restaurant, restrooms, observatory and Europe's highest-altitude hotel, the 3100 Kulmhotel Gornergrat. There is also a chapel – the Bernhard von Aosta. There are lots of events all year round, but in particular, in the summer, you can do a trip to see the sunrise and have the chance to see wild ibex near the viewing platform and in the winter, you can dine with the stars that is the astral ones, do a moonlight visit and go on the highest sledging slope in Switzerland. [9]

We had a wonderful time enjoying the views, although we did visit the shop to get a souvenir of the occasion, before we re-boarded the train for our descent back into Zermatt. We left Dad to rest at the train station, while we returned to the hotel to pick up our luggage. The little electric car that met us is only available on arrival; you have to manage yourself on departure. But we took our time, knowing that Dad was comfortable, and we did a little more shopping before we joined him and took the train back to Tasch, saying farewell to the Matterhorn, which was still clearly visible on this beautiful day.

We bought a sandwich to eat on our drive back to Lake Como and then we collected the car and started our return journey, taking a different route back, from the one that we had followed the day before. This second drive was probably even more beautiful than the first as it took us high over the tops of the mountain, to a level where there was still a little snow on the ground, despite it being mid-July. We stopped a couple of times to admire the view, taking photographs of this beautiful country, and admiring the small alpine flowers and plants that had a foothold on this high mountain pass.

As we drove over the peak and started to descend into Italy; before us lay the most amazing twisting road I had ever seen. The switchbacks were tight and there were vertical drops along the straights. I am so glad that Richard was driving although both of us could drive the car in Italy, only Richard was insured to drive in Switzerland – I would have been scared witless, going down this fairground-like road! I am sure it has been featured on Top Gear at some point, as being an exciting road to drive. Richard loved it and he put his foot down on the straights, enjoying this race-like descent from mountain peaks to gentle plateau's which awaited us at the end. We arrived back at our villa at seven p.m. and we enjoyed an evening drink on the balcony, on a lovely balmy night, reminiscing about the sights we had seen on our excursion into Switzerland.

There are not many European sites on the list of fifty; the votes went to cities – Venice, Barcelona, Paris, Rome and Reykjavik. I have not seen Mont Blanc, but I have taken the train up the Jungfrau, and stopped at a viewing point on the Eiger, which was a spectacular journey. But for pure majesty and spectacle, the Matterhorn is well worth its place in the list – and a stay in Zermatt is worthwhile too. I am pleased that we included the Italian Lakes in our holiday, as there is so much to see and do around the lakes, and I would certainly like to do this again, maybe Lake Garda next time, for a change.

We lost Dad in January 2017 after he had suffered a heart attack four months earlier and had been diagnosed with cancer, but it was Alzheimer's disease that had made him so weak and fragile that he was unable to battle these ailments. I feel as though I had lost my Dad years earlier, when his memory started to fade and he lost interest in everything that his family was undertaking. He did see us complete our target of going to the fifty places, and he had a plate from every destination on that list, but he never knew that I had written this book and had dedicated it to Mum. Their ashes are now laid together on the hill at Uwchmynydd on the Llyn Peninsula, a special place, where my family would holiday every year, during my childhood.

CHAPTER 32

Terracotta Warriors (45) and the Great Wall of China (20) – October 2012

Both Richard and I had been to China before we met in August 2000, and our tours included stays in Xian and Beijing to visit both of these incredible sites, and so much more that this huge country has to offer. But, as I have mentioned at the start of the book, we wanted to do the fifty together, which meant organising a return holiday to China, but this time add more to the itinerary, so that we would experience something new, as well as re-visiting these two key tourist attractions.

So, our holiday in 2012, was organised through Princess cruises and included a pre-cruise land tour that would offer us extended time in Beijing, to be able to visit all the wonderful places in the capital, as well as time in Xian and a few days cruising the Yangtze River, before we would board a cruise ship and sail to places new, Nagasaki and South Korea, and to places old, Singapore, Hong Kong and, our disembarkation point, Bangkok. In total, we were away for almost all of October, a total of thirty days – a long holiday, even by our standards!

We flew from Heathrow to Beijing on an overnight flight with British Airways. There is an eight-hour time difference between the UK and Beijing, and the secret to overcoming jet lag is to adjust to the local time as soon as possible, even if this means getting very little sleep on your flight, as you are quickly into the time period when you should be getting up to start your day. When we arrived, we had no problems at all with immigration; it was even quicker than trying to get back into the UK, which, these days, can be very slow. Our luggage took its time in arriving, but soon after landing, at around nine a.m. we were meeting our Princess Representative and being transferred with just four others, who were on our flight to The Peninsula. After unpacking just what we needed for our short stay, we went for a walk.

We had no idea of the whereabouts of our hotel, in relation to the centre of Beijing, but we had the cathedral round the corner from us, and a pedestrianised shopping street. The first thing that hit both of us was the decline in the number of bicycles and the increase in cars, motor-bikes and electric bikes. All you could see around us were huge, modern, high-rise offices and apartment blocks – it was as though Beijing had lost its Chinesiness, and become a Western city since the last time we had visited. I felt it worse than Richard, as it was in 1996 when I first came to China, and at that time there was still a rural feeling to this capital city, with four-lane roads – one for bikes and rickshaws, one for horse drawn carts and two for motor vehicles. Not now – you could have been in any city in the world! The people were dressed in Western clothes, driving new, expensive cars, and obviously had money to spend, going by the commercialism in this shopping precinct. It was all so alien; not what we had expected at all.

There was an open-air food market alongside the shopping area and this was where we realised that we were in China – the locals have very strange tastes in food, and in this market, we witnessed some of their peculiar tastes. Many stalls were offering kebabs, but on the sticks were scorpions, seahorses, starfish and centipedes – and they were all ALIVE! These creatures were skewered on sticks and are still wiggling! Another stall offered what looked like cockroaches and another delight on offer was roasted sparrows on a stick. We did not try any of these un-tempting items, we're not that adventurous, but the Chinese were buying and eating with gusto! We found a KFC (Kentucky Fried Chicken) and enjoyed some good old fashioned Western food. We did find a restaurant to eat at in the evening, where we were able to find local food that appealed to our palates – duck, chicken and fried rice. We drank Great Wall white wine, which is not bad, but it wasn't chilled enough for our liking. Not expensive though, the meal and drinks cost us just three hundred and fifty nine yuan, about thirty five pounds.

We had arrived in Beijing on the 1st of October, which is their National Day and the start of a six-day public holiday. We thought that it was very crowded and it was the next day when we were told of this event. It meant that Beijing, Xian and anywhere popular with tourists was going to be extremely busy, as many Chinese people travel within their own country to these popular destinations.

Beijing has a lot to offer the visitor. We left our hotel at eight-thirty a.m. with our fellow travellers on our tour, a coach full of Princess guests and our guide, Fred, who spoke very good English. I found out the last time that I came to China, that all people connected with the tourist industry adopt English names, to avoid any problems with us pronouncing their given Chinese name, and our guide on this occasion followed this routine. Our first stop was the Temple of Heaven, a religious complex of buildings, pavilions and gardens built for the Emperor, to be able to offer prayer and thanks for a good harvest, to the Gods. The main temple is a masterpiece: very colourful, made entirely of wood and not a single nail has been used to hold it together. It was busy here but not as bad as I had thought it would be, and we had beautiful weather too, which was a bonus.

I remember the last time when I visited China, I caused a few people to stare as a result of my blonde hair – Chinese are very dark and many had obviously not seen very blonde hair before. I remember visiting the Temple of Heaven, and I had my hair tied up in a ponytail. I felt someone tug on it and, as I turned around, there was a little old Chinese man standing behind me, with his hand raised. He was part of a visiting Chinese tour group, all dressed the same in grey pyjama-type twin sets, and had obviously volunteered to see if my hair was real – all of his party giggled, when I turned around and gave them a smile. At other places, I was stopped and asked to pose with families for a photograph.

Almost twenty years later, I would have expected it to be a common occurrence now to see groups of Western tourists and white people with strange coloured hair; not that blonde is a strange colour, but you know what I mean! But yet again, our party was stared at and you could see locals pointing at me as I was the only blonde in our group. It was quite amusing seeing them trying to take discreet photos on their mobiles, with friends and family in the foreground, but catching me in the background. I did purposely pose with some of them, which made them giggle and smile – I felt like a celebrity!

After lunch, we went to the Summer Palace, which is the old summer complex of the Emperors of China and located outside Beijing in the countryside, by the side of a lake. It is a popular destination with locals, as it offers a respite from the heat of the city and it is easy for them to get to. But, with it being a public holiday, I think that most of the population of Beijing were visiting at the same time we were there – it was heaving! We did manage to have a sail on the lake in a Dragon Boat, which had been pre-booked for us, but it was so difficult to walk anywhere because of the crowds. There is a very famous long covered corridor or gallery running through the gardens, from the main palace to a smaller pagoda in the grounds. Made of teak wood and beautifully decorated, with thousands of hand painted Chinese scenes, it really is very beautiful, and is worth taking your time looking at the pictures and the workmanship. The last time I was able to walk along the gallery and admire the artwork, but this time there were so many people crowded along its length, that it was impossible to take more than a few steps without coming to a standstill or getting crushed. So we walked alongside the corridor, just peering in here and there, to get a glimpse of the painted frescoes.

It was a shame that it was so busy as it was impossible to enjoy any of the sights at this palace – the gardens were certainly a no-no, and the temples and pagodas were out of bounds, due to masses of people standing between us and the buildings. The visit was a disaster really as, not only did we not get to see anything; it was also very uncomfortable due to the heat and the crowds. When we headed back to our hotel, we drove past the Forbidden City, and there must have been ten thousand people pouring out of the exit gates. This is definitely *not* the time of year to visit Beijing – you need to avoid public holidays! I can imagine the Chinese New Year being even worse! We would be returning to Beijing after our river cruise and the public holiday will be over by then, so hopefully it won't be as crowded when we go to see the Great Wall of China.

The next day we had an early start for our excursion to Xian and the Yangtze – bags out for seven a.m. but not all of them, the bulk of our cruise clothes remained at the hotel and our remaining cases were left out of the room as we left. We had breakfast and by eight-thirty a.m., we were heading for the airport. We were told that they were very strict with the size of our hand luggage for the flight, so Richard just had his camera and I had my tote bag, which is not very secure as it only ties at the middle. I didn't think that this would be a problem as it would be with me all the time and we had locked any valuables into our check-in case. How wrong I was, but I will come to that later!

At the airport, we had no problems with security, even though it was busy as we were still within the Chinese holiday week. Some people were subjected to a random search of their carry-on luggage and I was surprised as to how big the bags were that people were taking onto the plane, we had obviously been given duff information. The flight left on time and it wasn't too long before we were touching down in Xi'an (pronounced ts-yan). Our luggage went in a separate vehicle to the hotel, and we were all loaded on-board our coach and heading to the countryside for the Terracotta Army exhibit. The traffic was total chaos! It was a long drive from the airport, and it was made worse because the roads were so busy. There were road closures and we had to change our route several times; at one point doing a U-turn in the road, which caused havoc. As we approached our destination we could see why the traffic was so bad. There were cars everywhere! They did not care whether they were blocking others in or whether it was an authorised space to park – it seemed as though everyone in China was visiting the Terracotta Army on that day and had just dumped their vehicle wherever they could!

We joined the thousands queuing to get in to the exhibition in lines that were ten people thick and unbelievably long! It was difficult for Fred to keep his group together, but eventually, we entered through the doors, to see this incredible relic which deserves its place on the list. But, with so many people wanting to do the same thing, it was impossible to get to the front of the barrier, to peer down on these statues that are so famous the world over, even being classed as the Eighth Wonder of the World!

The Terracotta Army is a collection of terracotta sculptures depicting the armies of Qin Shi Huang, the first Emperor of China. It is a form of funerary art that was buried with the emperor in 210-209 BCE, and whose purpose was to protect the emperor in his afterlife. Local farmers, who were digging a well, discovered the warriors in 1974. The figures include warriors, chariots and horses and estimates in 2007 were that the three pits containing the army held more than eight thousand soldiers, all life-size and unique. In addition, there were a hundred and thirty chariots with five hundred and twenty horses, a hundred and fifty cavalry horses, and non-military figures, including officials, musicians, strongmen and acrobats. The actual necropolis of the emperor lies under a mound at the base of Mount Li, and the warriors lie east of the tomb, which has not been opened due to concerns over the preservation of its artefacts. [2]

Luckily, Richard and I had both been there before when it was not so popular or so busy. When I came to China in 1996, there were very few tourists visiting the country and the museum at Xian was almost deserted. My problem at that time was that I was suffering from a very bad stomach which I put down to drinking cold milk in foreign countries; obviously issues over pasteurisation that affect me. Now, you can take photographs of the exhibition too, which was not allowed in 1996, but this was so difficult due to the number of people all vying to get a space at the front of the barriers and to stare down at the wonderful sight of thousands of stone warriors standing guard over their ghostly host. We followed the crowd around the exhibit, managing to get a few photos, but they do not do it justice – this exhibit has to be seen to be believed. As we had been before, we did not bother going to the other pits, as we knew that they would be just as crowded, and we went into the museum instead, where they have some solitary statues and relics from the dig. This allows you to get up close to a replica and to realise exactly how large and intricate each statue is. There are a number of photographs showing the original excavation – these seem to be dated a lot earlier than 1974, due to China being under-developed at that time.

We were glad that we left the throng, as we found out that Geoff had had his wallet stolen with one thousand dollars in it, and another fellow member of our group had his camera knocked from his hand and broken. It was a shame for our group, as no others had been here before and it must have been disappointing for them to have to battle thousands of locals just to get a sight of the army.

Our group left the museum and we should have gone to our hotel, the Sofitel, Xian, to change for our evening excursion, but the traffic was so bad and we were running so late. Our guide decided to take us straight to the Tang show, and we arrived there at seven-thirty p.m. just in time for dinner. The meal was good: appetisers, soup, breaded shrimp, beef and rice. For dessert, we had rice pudding and mooncake, and once everything was cleared away, we were entertained by dancers, acrobats, jugglers and instrumentalists. It was actually a good show – very colourful and not too much singing, which was good, as Chinese singing is not our cup of tea – more like cats whining!

Finally, late that evening, we arrived at our hotel and we had a very nice, large room, but just no time to use it! We didn't even bother unpacking as we were only spending one night in Xian, leaving the next day to fly to Chongqing.

We started early, to try and avoid the traffic as there is quite a lot to see in Xian, although nothing else can compare with the Terracotta Warriors. Our first stop was to learn about the city walls which circle the old city and are very impressive – they are high, wide and have garrisons or gates built on them which have a pagoda appearance, albeit very sombre and overpowering, in order to intimidate visitors or raiders in the past. We continued our tour and we went to the Wild Goose Pagoda, a beautiful old, towering pagoda, which used to be higher and now leans ever so slightly. We had some time to walk through the gardens and to visit the new temple which has been built at this location. It was starting to get busy but, as we had arrived early, it wasn't too bad that day.

We left Xian and flew to Chongqing, the largest city in China, with a population of around thirty-two million – and growing. It was not a nice city – skyscrapers, large roads with a lot of traffic and, as it was raining, it seemed very dull and grey. We stopped at the zoo, so those who wanted could see giant pandas to visit for an hour and were able to get a glimpse of these enigmatic and endangered creatures. There were quite a few here in large enclosures, and most of them were quite active – well they were eating mainly, but the last time that I had seen panda's they were just sleeping, so it was good to see some motion.

We eventually arrived at the banks of the Yangtze River at seven p.m. and boarded our boat, the Victoria Katorena, which would be our home for the next four days. We upgraded our cabin by paying one thousand dollars for a suite. We were glad that we did, as the cabins were small and our suite was a little larger, with a small balcony and a seating area. With us being in a suite, we had access to our own dining room that was exclusively for the use of suite guests and we had free Wi-Fi and free evening drinks. We were very late, and we had to be down for dinner at seven forty-five p.m., and then we had a security briefing before we finally retired with our rum and coke and we managed to get some ice and finally we unpacked; the first time since leaving Beijing, before we went to bed.

The next morning, we arose early to have breakfast at seven-thirty a.m., and it was then that disaster struck. Earlier in this chapter I mentioned about us being told that we could only take a small bag on the plane as hand luggage, and, as my daytime bag was not very secure, just tied in the middle, I did not want to carry my jewellery box with me, so I had locked it inside my check-in luggage, thinking that it would be more secure. I was VERY wrong! We had put this little box into the safe the night before without opening it and it was when we were due to leave the suite that I went to put a different necklace on my gold turtle from the Galapagos, but it wasn't there! I then realised that two diamond rings were also missing. one was a one point three carat diamond ring I had bought in Aruba valued at four and a half thousand pounds. I was devastated and gutted. We told Fred, and explained that it could have gone missing any time during our travels from Beijing to the Yangtze, as I had not inspected my box during the whole period. But Richard and I think that these items were taken by security at the airport, as our case had been opened and inspected and even though the box was wrapped inside clothes, they had obviously had a rummage and just taken a few items, so as it would not be obvious that a theft had taken place.

Fred was amazed at the value and other people in the tour group were astounded that I was travelling with something so valuable, but I buy jewellery to wear, and what better place to dress up and show off your gold and diamonds than when you're on holiday! We're insured for travelling with up to ten thousand pounds in jewellery, but I was upset about losing my turtle as it was so unique, generating a lot of compliments; and it was unlikely that we would ever return to the Galapagos to buy another one. I had purchased it from a designer who came aboard the Xpedition during our cruise around the Galapagos in 2011. We were told that we would need to report it to the police when we returned to Beijing, and that I needed to write down what had happened and what was missing.

We had arrived at Fengdu, the City of the Dead, and, even though I felt sick and violated, it was pointless letting this incident spoil our day, so we went on the tour – and I am so glad that we did, as this was the highlight of the river cruise. To get to the Kingdom of the Underworld, you have to climb a mountain – mainly by a steep staircase or by a slightly gentler slope. Twice, I wanted to give up and go back to the boat, but Fred encouraged me to continue, and eventually, out of breath and exhausted, we reached the entrance to this temple complex. There were so many legends and customs relating to the bridges, temples, statues and pathways. It really was an incredible place – and very old! We learnt about a number of the demons, ghosts and devils who haunt the place, as well as Buddha, who guarded you on your journey through the city. It was crowded again, but not unbearable and you just had to wait your turn to cross the crooked bridge together, or balance on the judging stone.

We were back on board at eleven forty-five a.m., ready for a talk about the Three Gorges;– not as dramatic now as a result of them being swallowed up by the waters produced by the building of the great dam that has been built on the Yangtze.

The food on the boat was rather good, and we had quite a decent wine, served with dinner, which was free! The shows on the boat each evening, were performed by the crew. That night we had an exhibition called Chinese Dynasty that featured a collection of costumes through the ages, paraded through the lounge area, accompanied by music and commentary. This show was amusing and enjoyable, and the crew appeared to enjoy themselves too.

The next day, we took the optional tour to go to the White Emperor City – only six of us opted for this, so it was a pleasant, private tour of a very enjoyable site. There were even more steps to climb than the day before – three hundred and sixty-five of them, but we stopped many times to enjoy the views of the river winding its way through the gorge beyond the island, where the city was located. It hadn't been an island before; this happened as a result of the rising waters caused by the dam, and a bridge had to be built to connect the island to the new river bank. The city was a bit contrived, with modern exhibits, but it was an enjoyable excursion. One exhibit was all about hanging coffins which we hoped to see later that day

We set sail and went down the first gorge, which is the smallest of the three. Due to the weather, it was not really an enjoyable cruise, as it was so dull and grey, and we could not see much due to the low cloud. After lunch, we continued to our next stop where we all transferred to a ferry, and we were taken down a tributary of the Yangtze, which took us through a mini-gorge. As the gorge narrowed, the ferry docked, and we were transferred again, this time into narrow pod boats – about twelve people to a boat, and these were propelled by local trackers, who rowed down the narrower river into the deep gorge – five rowers per boat. In the past, when the river was low, this was the only way to get down the river, and the boats were rowed and pulled along by naked tribesmen. We were pulled along by two of our rowers, who aided our passage and we raced against the other pod boats, but now, I should add, they aren't naked! It looked like really hard work, both the rowing and the pulling, and we were encouraged to cheer our pilots on, to get some speed-up, and beat the others in a sort of race through the gorge.

We did see some hanging coffins in the second gorge – these wooden structures, containing a body, were wedged into the rocks along the side of the gorge and we saw a few of these small black objects on our journey.

The ferry returned us to our ship for dinner, and during the evening we sailed through the third gorge, but we didn't see anything as it was too dark, and we still had really miserable weather. Later that night, we arrived at the dam and we went through the locks, in the dark. We did go out onto our little balcony to watch this spectacle, witnessing the ship rise slowly against the sides of the lock until we were clear, and moored for the night, next to this incredible structure, the largest dam in the world.

We were up early to put out our luggage and then visit the Three Gorges Dam Project. It was really wet today, raining very hard, and visibility was really poor at the tourist viewing point. There was an escalator that took us to an upper level, to be able to peer down on the five locks and the new ship lift, which is being constructed. But the fog, the rain and the mist did not make for a pleasurable visit, and we were glad to get back to the ship.

Unfortunately, I slipped on a wet metal grid on the walk back, landing face first, prostate on the soggy concrete; banging my head, grazing my knee, and hurting my right hand in the process. I was knocked out for a few seconds and the Chinese who had gathered around me had to help me to my feet. As I got over the initial shock, I felt very silly and clumsy, and I was even more uncomfortable when they arranged for me to be transferred from the bus to the ship in a wheelchair!

After a visit to the doctor, who cleaned up my grazed cheek and gave me an ice-pack for my knee and my hand, the staff took my trousers to get dried-off, and I felt a bit better when we finally departed and headed for the train station in Yuchang. The train was very modern and clean, not at all like those in India. We spent the night in Wuhan, and by now I had a superb shiner!

A black eye, a swollen hand and a painful knee were my companions for the next few days.

Another early start saw us transferred to the airport for our flight back to Beijing. It was still very cloudy and I thought that our next stop would be very disappointing as you really need good weather to view the Great Wall of China. We had a very nice lunch before continuing our journey through the smog, to arrive at a new entrance gate, which was not here in 1994, the first time that I came to China.

Through the gate, you had a long walk to get to the wall, going along a path lined with high-end souvenir shops. When I came before, there were just little market stalls selling tacky souvenirs – obviously the Chinese realised the potential of making money from the thousands of visitors who come to see this wonder of the world. Fred stayed with us, and talked at length about the building of the wall, the history of the area and a description of what we could do next. We decided to take the easy route, which is to walk part of the wall which is not too steep. Don't underestimate this, as it was still really hard work battling against the incline of this incredible structure which was built almost two thousand years ago and, according to myth, can be seen from the moon; it can't, by the way.

During the hour that we had to ourselves, the skies cleared and we had a background of blue on our photos. The facts relating to the wall are astounding – it is actually a series of fortifications made of stone, brick, tramped earth, wood, and other materials, generally built as protection across the historical northern borders of China. Several walls were being built as early as the seventh century BC, and were eventually strengthened, combined and extended to become the Great Wall. Especially famous is the wall built in 220–206 BC, by the first Emperor of China, Qin, whose tomb is guarded by the terracotta army. Most of the existing wall was built during the Ming Dynasty. It has been measured as being five thousand five hundred miles long, made up of three thousand eight hundred and eighty-nine miles of actual wall, two hundred and twenty-three miles of trenches and one

thousand three hundred and eighty-seven miles of natural barriers (hills and rivers). If you consider all the branches that extend from the wall, the total length has been measured at an astounding thirteen thousand one hundred and seventy-one miles! [2] Richard climbed to the top of one of the garrisons – it was too much for me, so I stayed back, and I watched his efforts from a restful location, leaning against the walls and admiring the view.

The Great Wall is truly a spectacle to behold. It stretches as far as the eye can see and, to be able to walk along this two thousand year-old structure, it has to be the highlight for anyone visiting China. It is actually quite close to Beijing and you can actually see the wall from the Forbidden City – when there isn't any fog or pollution.

We stayed at the Peninsula that evening, and our dinner was arranged for us by Princess, so as to meet up with fellow passengers who had just done a short tour of Beijing before they boarded the ship. The food was excellent, and the entertainment was good too – very colourful, some funny acrobatics and dance, and a really pleasant way to spend the last night on our tour of China.

On our last day in Beijing, we went to the Forbidden City. The weather was beautiful – clear blue skies and very warm. Anyone here just for this one day would be very lucky and get a great view of the Wall. We stopped first at Tiananmen Square which was partially closed due to the parades and decorations commemorating the National Day on the 1st of October, and then we entered the Forbidden City, the former royal residence of the Emperor of China. If you have seen the film "The Last Emperor", it will give you an idea of exactly what to expect. This is not a palace as we have in the Western world, but a series of pagodas, temples, courtyards, and private residences, all held behind high walls where, in the past, the general public were not allowed to enter.

It was still busy but certainly not as bad as we had seen it the week before. It was difficult to see into some of the buildings, even though they are open sided, due to the crowds, and the tour was a little rushed, but as we have both been here before, we were fine just to see the highlights of this ancient city.

Our tour ended with a final lunch, stopping at a Peking Duck Restaurant. There were many dishes served, not just duck, but the highlight of the lunch was LOADS of pancakes with more duck than I have ever seen in my life! Plates and plates of meat just kept arriving at the table so that you could eat your fill of this delicious local dish. The Chinese eat every part of the duck except for its quack (the bill) – even the feet are a delicacy, but not one that I wanted to participate in. Once we were all stuffed and could eat no more, we all made our way to our coaches for the last time, and headed for the port, which is about a two hour drive from the capital.

Once on board the Diamond Princess we enjoyed two weeks cruising the South China Sea, calling at Busan, South Korea; Nagasaki, Japan; Shanghai, China; Hong Kong, Nha Trang; Phu My, Vietnam; Singapore and Bangkok, Thailand. As I have said before, cruising is a great way to tick off the countries visited! We did not find the visit to Nagasaki as moving as Hiroshima, but the museum dedicated to the nuclear blast (9th of August 1945 at eleven oh two a.m.) was very good, although a little gruesome, as it did show scorched human remains and the devastation of the city. There is a statue at Ground Zero, commemorating the blast but the Peace Park is further away, on a hill. Here there are a number of memorial statues donated by nations of the world and a central fountain, where the ashes and remains of those who died in the blast are buried.

In Hong Kong we went for lunch at the Mandarin Oriental Hotel – this has to be our favourite restaurant in the world and we plan on going there again before we fly home after our cruise in February 2018. In fact, I have added an extra night to stay over, so we will be able to enjoy this fabulous place for a third time!

There is so much to see in China, but I will agree that the highlights of any tour are the Great Wall of China and the Terracotta Warriors. I don't understand why they are so low on the list, but my assumption is that this is due to the fact that not many people have been to China on holiday – a lot more have been to the USA, to Mexico and to Barbados. It is worthwhile spending some time travelling around the country and seeing some of the beautiful scenery, gardens, mountains and historical sites. I had no idea about Fengdu, the City of the Dead on the Yangtze, and I thought that was a fabulous place to visit. The architecture, the myths and the legends attached to the site, and the location make this a worthwhile place to visit – pity that the weather wasn't better when we went, as I am sure that the views from this lofty island temple would be fabulous on a clear day – our view was shrouded in mist and you could not see the ships at the pier below.

But, a word of advice, don't go when China is celebrating a major festival – especially Chinese New Year around February each year, – it is not a fixed calendar date, when the country literally closes down for a week. We thought that the number of visitors was bad in October, they would be even worse during this celebration!

I would like to just add a little anecdote at this point. I have said about having some jewellery stolen and on our return home, we made a claim against our insurance and I had the two rings replaced albeit as new designs, but it was impossible to recreate the gold turtle pendant. Over the next twelve months I looked for a replacement, but I was unsuccessful. Then, on my birthday a year later on the 10th of October 2013 Richard presented me with a small box and inside was a new turtle pendant! He had contacted Celebrity to get the name of the visiting jeweller who came aboard the ship during our Galapagos cruise. He then contacted them and sent a photo of me wearing the pendant and ordered an exact copy, which was shipped from Ecuador back to the UK. I could not believe his ingenuity and his generosity, and, once again, my turtle regularly adorns my neck and it receives many complements.

CHAPTER 33

South Island (4) and North Island (25), New Zealand – February 2013

We booked a cruise to New Zealand thirty months before we travelled, as we kept arranging other vacations instead, as we knew that travelling to the opposite side of the world was going to be an expensive and a long trip. As we enjoyed cruising so much, it seemed a good idea to combine a cruise to both islands and then build up the holiday around that. So, we flew out to Sydney without a stopover; had a few days there to overcome the jet lag; then took a fourteen night cruise to Auckland, where we spent a couple of nights; headed for the Bay of Islands for three nights; and finally stopped in Singapore on our return, to stay at the Raffles Hotel. Another long holiday – four weeks, but you can't spend twenty-two hours on a plane, suffer a twelve hour time difference, and not stay long enough to enjoy this incredible part of the world.

I am not going into detail with our stay in Sydney, as I have covered each trip to our favourite city in Chapter 11, but I will say that on this occasion we stayed at the five-star Langdon Observatory Hotel near The Rocks area of the city, and we managed to get our booking right so as to be able to use our room immediately to have a rest, and to get over the flight as soon as we arrived – it means making a reservation for the previous night, and telling the hotel that we would be arriving early in the morning, but it works and we certainly had our best stopover in Sydney as a result of this. It did help with us arranging our transfer from the airport through the hotel too, as this meant that they knew exactly when we would be arriving.

We also did our best excursion EVER on this visit, which was the helicopter trip to do wine tasting in Hunter Valley. We arranged it through Viator.com before we flew out on holiday, and, although it was very expensive, it was so exclusive and we received VIP service throughout.

So this chapter is really going to start at the point where we boarded our cruise ship, the Diamond Princess – again! We have travelled on this ship more than any other, mainly due to it covering Asia and Australia – it is a nice ship with six restaurants for the anytime diners, although two of these do incur a surcharge.

Sydney is a fabulous cruise port, as the ships dock in Circular Quay opposite the Opera House, and by the side of the Harbour Bridge. Wherever you stand, on a balcony or on deck, you get great views. We've been lucky enough to depart from Sydney on three occasions, and we never tire of that wonderful skyline. We had two stops in Australia; Melbourne and Hobart, before we crossed the Tasman Sea to South Island, New Zealand. We had beautiful weather in Tasmania where we went to Port Arthur, the oldest town on the island, and the penal colony, which was very interesting.

We had four days at sea, as well as two days in the ports that I have mentioned, but we actually arrived in New Zealand on the sixth day, whilst at sea! We went through immigration on the ship, as the New Zealand customs officers had boarded in Hobart and, after having our passports checked and scanned, our shoes checked for any nasty attachments (possible contamination from the wildlife park in Melbourne), we were free to continue our journey and, as we left the area allocated to this process, there was a sign saying, "Welcome to New Zealand" – nice touch!

Our first day in New Zealand was spent on the ship, as we did scenic cruising in the fjords of South Island. Unfortunately, the weather was awful – it was cold, grey and very overcast, meaning that the scenery was not very exciting at all. It was so misty that we could not even see the top of the mountains that line the narrow channels of water.

Our first visit was into Milford Sound but it was so dark and dismal that the views were really disappointing. We sailed into the Sound and then did a hundred and eighty degree turn to come back out to the sea. As we left the fjord, the sun shone a little but this was over the sea and not the National Park. A few hours later we sailed into Thomson Sound and came out via Doubtful Sound – the weather was even gloomier here, and it totally ruined the experience of sailing through this beautiful area. Finally, we entered Dusky Sound, but by now it was raining and visibility was even worse. Not a very good welcome to this beautiful country, that had taken so long for us to plan to visit. This scenic cruising, sailing into the different sounds and around Resolution Island, took all day, and it was overnight that we sailed around the bottom of the island, in between Stewart Island and the mainland.

The next day, we arrived at Port Chalmers and we stepped foot on New Zealand soil. But the weather was still poor, the rain and the mist had not cleared overnight. We had opted to take a journey on the Taieri Gorge Railway, which we boarded right by the side of the cruise port. The train firstly went through Dunedin, a large town in the region that has a lot of Scottish connections. The train climbed into the mountains, travelling along a narrow track that wound around the cliff face, travelling through tunnels and over viaducts, climbing higher and higher on this ancient route started in 1890. Even with the bad weather, you could still enjoy the magnificent scenery. We were able to get off at a couple of scenic stops for photos which would have been so much better had the sun been shining.

Our return to Dunedin, along the same track, brightened a little and when we did eventually arrive at the station in the town, it was sunny and warm. We did not return to the ship, but we walked into town to visit the Octagon, where lots of pipe bands were gathering ready to march through the town, playing as they went.

This sight was wonderful – so colourful with all the different tartans, and it was great to hear the bagpipes, fife and drums merging in perfect harmony, as they played Scottish tunes, and marched around the square and away into the town centre. This spectacle really brought home the links that Dunedin has with

Scotland, and you would have thought that we were in Edinburgh, rather than down under in New Zealand – and, of course, the blue skies, the sunshine and the warmth made a big difference to our experience!

The next day we docked at Akaroa in the Canterbury Region of New Zealand, on the east coast of the island, about seventy-five kilometres from Christchurch. In 2011, Christchurch was badly damaged by an earthquake that registered six point three on the Richter scale and it hit on the 22nd of February at twelve fifty one a.m. The earthquake hit Lyttelton, a town just six miles from the centre of the city, and caused mass destruction and loss of life in New Zealand's second city. One hundred and eighty-five people from twenty countries lost their lives. Many homes, hotels, commercial buildings and roads were damaged or destroyed completely – in particular, the famous city cathedral was affected, with the spire collapsing and the tower being very badly damaged.[2]

Two years later, Christchurch was still a no-go area; so all the ships excursions were taking passengers into the Canterbury Region instead of into the city. We opted for a trip to take us to the high country, to view some of the locations used in the filming of the trilogy, "Lord of the Rings". Peter Jackson had originally wanted to base his film in England, because J.R.R. Tolkien had Oxfordshire in mind when he wrote the book; but due to the high population of the area, and the lack of dramatic countryside to match the book, he turned to New Zealand instead. I understand that the New Zealand government were also prepared to work with him and to provide financial investment, dedicated locations and support, as they recognised the effect that the film would, have on promoting the country. Many locations on both islands were used in the film – Hobbiton was purpose-built on the North Island, and can be visited, but I'll talk about this later in the chapter.

Our tour took us to Mount Sunday, which was used as the location for Eldora's in the first film – "Fellowship of the Ring". We stopped at Clearwater Lake, where we had a good view of Mount

Sunday, located on the plain with the mountains of the Southern Alps forming a backdrop behind. But, we had bad weather again, and the magnificent views you see in the film were lost in the low clouds and the dark, grey skies. The one bonus that we had was our tour guide, Hammond Peek, who actually worked on all three films, as a sound engineer and was nominated for Oscars on all three films – he won in 2003 for "Return of the King". His commentary during our tour was fabulous, retelling great stories about the filming and informing us of the legacy that the film has had on the country. His companion on the coach was in the film, acting as Ian McKellen's stunt double, and he did readings from the book during the longer drives. Hammond had brought along some of the props from the film, and we were able to pose for photos holding huge swords and axes.

Another day, another town – this time we were in Picton, a pleasant town at the top of the island, and located in the wine producing state of Marlborough. The ship was able to dock close to the town in the purpose-built cruise port, and it did not take long for shuttle buses to transfer us from the port to the town centre. And, finally, the sun was shining – it was warm and we had lovely clear blue skies. The town is very picturesque, with a lovely harbour, pleasant gardens and low wooden houses and hotels, and we enjoyed coffee and toast before doing a little shopping, and we followed this with a well-deserved bottle of Pinot Gris while sitting on the waterfront, enjoying the view and the sunshine.

Our tour today was just for a half day, to visit two of the wineries in the area, where we would have the opportunity to learn about the wine production of New Zealand and get to taste some of their delicious products. We also went to a chocolate shop, where we could not resist their tempting produce and succumbed to buying some samples. After tasting six wines at each winery, we purchased two bottles of Pinot Gris. The wine for sale was very well priced – around seventeen New Zealand dollars, about ten pounds in 2013. The views were lovely as well, with vineyards stretching as far as the eye could see, but edged by high mountains which created this world famous valley.

We really enjoyed Picton; probably because of the fine weather, but it was so pretty and it felt tranquil and laid-back, and we decided there and then, that we wanted to come back there, as well as travel around the island again, in the hope that we would have better weather when we returned.

The sail away was really special as we sailed through Marlborough Sound and headed towards the North Island. We sat on our balcony, sipping a glass of wine and watched the small islands, inlets and mountains drift past as we slowly headed out into the Cook Strait. Wellington is just across the strait from Picton and it only takes a couple of hours for the ferry to do this journey, but we would take our time, continually turning during the night in order to arrive at our next destination in the morning.

Now that we were further north, the weather had improved dramatically and we were not let down in Wellington, which had moved up the pecking order and was now New Zealand's second city in terms of population, due to people moving away from Christchurch after the earthquake. We did a tour in a 4 x 4 with just five cars in our convoy, starting with a drive through the city; and then we visited a number of locations on the outskirts and the lovely natural recreation area that surrounds Wellington.

Our convoy took a road that twisted around the mountain that overlooks the city. This was too steep for coaches, so only our five cars were able to reach the top, where we were able to enjoy fabulous views of this lovely city, Cook Strait and South Island. We continued around the mountain through this park area, and then we descended down to the beach where we went for a walk by the sea edge to view the leaning lighthouse and to watch some seals swimming and then struggling to drag themselves onto land. They were a bit smelly and noisy, but it was fun to watch the pups chasing after their mothers, as they dashed to get out of our way. We scrambled over some of the huge rocks that were by the sea edge, and had a good time enjoying the sights and the sounds of coastal Wellington.

It took a while for us to cruise up the east coast of North Island, and we had a full day at sea before we arrived at Tauranga, a seaside resort in the top right corner of the island. This stop allows people to visit Rotorua, which is famous for its mud pools and hot springs, but we picked a half-day tour which took us to the Adventure Park nearby. When we arrived, we went to the top of the hill that overlooks Rotorua, by gondola, and we enjoyed views of the town and lake during our climb. The reason for doing this particular trip was for us to go on the luge, which is built along the hill side in the Adventure Park. I have never done anything like this before, and I was nervous of sitting in a basic sledge and hurling myself down a steep race track! But, once I knew how to clamber into our vehicle, and I knew that it had a brake and handlebars, and I had a briefing of how to stop and where to go, I felt a little more confident and less stressed. There were three levels of tracks – easy, medium and fast. We started with the easy one, so that we could get our feel for the trolley, and to make sure that we weren't going to go speeding downhill and not be able to manoeuvre or to stop, without crashing into the sides of the track or another rider.

All I can say was that this first ride was BRILLIANT! I could not wait to get back up the hill, which was done with the aid of a chairlift, and go on my next run. Our package entitled us to three rides on the luge and we increased the difficulty with each trip, leaving the fast route to last. This advanced track had drops and swirling banks, which made it a lot harder to control our sledge, but I squealed with delight as we both raced around. There was a café and a shop on the hilltop where we enjoyed a bite to eat and a bottle of wine, sitting out on the veranda and enjoying the views all around us.

Our final port was the capital of New Zealand, Auckland and, as you always have to disembark very early, we had booked a city tour with a transfer to our hotel, The Langham. Our first stop was the Sky Tower, and we went up this observation and communication monolith, which is three hundred and twenty-eight metres tall and is the tallest freestanding structure in the Southern Hemisphere. The views of the city from this height were truly breathtaking – we had a three hundred and sixty degree view, and this included our ship in the port, which had been joined by the Sun Princess.

Our tour continued around the city, where we saw a number of key sights before heading for the Sea Life Aquarium. They had a lot of aquatic life in there, but the key exhibit was a great collection of penguins. However, it did remind me of the film "Happy Feet", when Mumble is rescued after chasing a ship and placed in an aquarium where he was very sad and lonely! I know that it's a cartoon, but I thought that this film was actually thought provoking and made me think about the damage that we are doing to our world, without considering the impact on wildlife. There was a shark tunnel, an exhibit of sea-horses and tanks with coral and tropical fish – very pretty.

We just had one night in Auckland, as we had booked a three-night tour, through Viator.com to visit the Bay of Islands, an area in the very north of North Island. We had an early start, getting picked up from our hotel at six-thirty a.m., transferring to the main coach and then setting off at seven-thirty a.m. We arrived at Phiaia at eleven fifteen a.m., and checked in at the Maritime Centre as our first night, was going to be spent on a boat. The town of Phiaia is a nice coastal town, and, although it is only small, there are some descent restaurants, nice shops and pleasant walks along the shoreline.

After spending a couple of hours walking around town, we returned to the Marine Centre, and then boarded another coach to take us to Opua, where we boarded the Ipipiri, our home for the next sixteen hours. We were pleasantly surprised with the size of our cabin as, although it was small compared to those on cruise ships or river boats, it was a reasonable size, with en-suite facilities. We were just above sea level and we had large picture windows, to be able to enjoy the view while we were in the cabin.

As we set sail, the skies cleared and we had a lovely sunny afternoon sailing around some of the hundreds of islands, which make up this beautiful area. You had the opportunity to partake in some activities – kayaking, snorkelling or walking on the beach, but we opted to stay on board and enjoy the views and the sunshine from the top deck of the boat. This was so relaxing and peaceful and, I have to say, as close to perfect as we could possibly imagine.

Once the adventurers returned to the boat, we set sail to find another peaceful bay where we would spend the night and, hopefully, get a good sunset. We didn't, but it was still a pleasant area, where we spent the evening at sea. After changing for dinner although it is very informal on board, everyone changed their attire for the evening. We had some pre-dinner drinks and then enjoyed a three-course dinner, which consisted with a choice of a starter, a buffet main course and then a choice from a selection of deserts. We washed it down with a bottle of Pinot Gris and by the end, we were quite stuffed! There was a disco for those inclined, but we had an early night, tired after spending so much time relaxing in the sun!

The following day, we had opted to do a helicopter flight over the Bay of Islands, but we woke to grey skies, low clouds and rain. I thought that the flight would be cancelled as it was expensive at four hundred and sixty dollars, and I was worried that we would see nothing but still have to pay for this excursion. But, it went ahead, and we boarded a tender to be taken out to the floating helipad located in a sheltered bay around the headland from where we were moored.

As we waited for the helicopter to arrive, it started to rain again, and we donned our waterproofs and resigned ourselves to having a dismal flight. There were five of us from Ipipiri taking the flight and the helicopter seated seven, including the pilot, which meant we all had a window seat. To begin with, the windows were steamed up, and with the low clouds and the rain, we could not see anything at all. But, as the windows cleared, so did the clouds and we were greeted with beautiful sunny blue skies, as we soared over the many islands that make up this stunning area. We saw the Hole in the Rock, and the pilot did sharp, exciting turns so people from both sides of the chopper could get a good view. The flight was supposed to be just fifteen minutes, but we were up there for a lot longer, so we certainly got our money's worth and we really enjoyed the trip.

Back on the boat, breakfast was still being served, and we tucked into a big plate of bacon and eggs before we packed, ready to disembark once we were back in port. The sail back was very pleasant as the morning, which had started off so bad, was now glorious, and we had great views on our return journey.

We were transferred to the Copthorne Hotel in Waitangi by minibus, but could not check-in yet as we were too early, so we left our cases and headed back to Paihia on the shuttle bus, where we went around a craft market and enjoyed some lunch in town before returning to the hotel and spending the afternoon sitting out on our patio, enjoying the views and the warmth. The hotel is located within the Waitangi Ceremonial Grounds on the sea front, and we were able to watch passengers on the cruise excursions joining the local Maori's in the long canoes, and taking to the water, for a cruise around the bay. We actually managed to catch a bit of the ceremonial Haka being performed.

Included in the package we had booked with Viator.com was a full day excursion to go to Cape Reinga, the most northerly tip of New Zealand. Another early start – we set off for Northland with a big group but Barry, our driver and our guide for the day, was great as he was funny, philosophical and very knowledgeable – a perfect tour guide. Our first stop was a forest, where there were some of the large Kailua trees that are native to the region. We went for a walk around the forest and we were told to "hug a tree", as this gives you vitality – I made Richard hug it twice! We stopped for a short time in Maninui, which means "Big Shark", a fishing port with a lovely, quaint harbour.

We had a picnic lunch on a hill overlooking a beautiful bay, before heading for the main attraction, the lighthouse at Cape Reinga. This is the point where the Pacific Ocean meets the Tasman Sea, and it can be a treacherous stretch of water. According to Maori legend, this is where spirits leave this world and pass to heaven – it was a lovely, peaceful location, and it did feel very spiritual. Our last stop was the ninety mile beach, which is a highway along the sea edge used by cars and buses. We whizzed along this massive stretch of smooth sands for twenty minutes before turning off and heading for home. The icing on the cake was that we saw a herd of wild horses, who trotted along the side of the bus, before galloping into the long grass – what a perfect ending to a very good trip.

We were due to return to Auckland the next day in the afternoon, which gave us time to explore the Bay of Islands a little more, before our departure. We took the hotel shuttle into town and then took the ferry to cross over to the opposite shore line, to visit Russell, the very first capital of New Zealand back in 1845. Now, a sleepy harbour village, back in the nineteenth century, it had had quite a reputation as a lawless town. We went into the church, which still bore bullet holes from the past, and we walked around the graveyard. Many of the grave stones were very old, and the writing was indecipherable, but some had been cared for and were clearly legible. The earliest birthdate that we found was 1780, which dated back to before the country was colonised.

On our last full day in New Zealand, we took a full day tour from Auckland to visit Waitomo and Hobbiton. Waitomo Glow Worm Caves are listed as one of the key sites to see on North Island, and there are a number of different excursions which include this tourist attraction. We would always prefer to do a half-day excursion on holiday, to give us more downtime, but, on this occasion, as we were travelling quite a distance to the caves, we combined the film set used in both the "Lord of the Rings" and the "Hobbit trilogies".

The drive from Auckland to Waitomo is two and a half hours and when we arrived we had time for a coffee before our tour started. We walked down into a large stalactite cave first, and had an explanation as to how they had been formed, then we climbed aboard a small rowboat to drift through the caves, where the glow worms light up the darkness like tiny little stars in a jet black sky. The glow worms can only be found in New Zealand, and there are thousands of them in the cave. Everyone on the boat was silent as we drifted along, enjoying this natural phenomenon and this made the trip quite special and surreal.

We stopped at a place called the Agrodome for lunch, which had lots of information about sheep rearing in New Zealand, and you were able to watch some sheep shearing, if you so wished, as well as buying local wool and other souvenirs. Our tour group split at this point, with some going to Rotorua and the rest of us boarded an alternative shuttle bus and continued with our hour drive to Hobbiton. Purposely created for the film, this village, built into the hillside, was lovely, with lots of colourful little round doors surrounded by tiny picket fences, and beautiful wild gardens. The set had remained as a tourist attraction; open to the public after "The Hobbit" was completed. The whole village was so picturesque, the grass was green and there were loads of butterflies flitting around the gardens. It was just like an Olde English Village for little people. When J.R.R. Tolkien wrote the books, he used Oxfordshire as inspiration for The Shire, and this location was ideal for Peter Jackson's portrayal of Frodo and Bilbo's home. The doors were just a façade; there were no Hobbit homes behind any of them except for Bag End, which did open up and had a small area behind so that you could pose for photos, peering out of this famous abode.

The tree above Bag End had to be perfect and match the detail of how it is described in the books. Although the location was perfect for Hobbiton, there wasn't a tree on top of the hill overlooking the village, so Peter Jackson created the Oak Tree by cutting down a tree from nearby Matamata, transporting it to this location and then bolting it back together again. Artificial leaves were imported from Taiwan and individually wired to the dead tree. We walked around the village enjoying this fairy-tale landscape, eventually crossing the bridge and going to the Green Dragon, where we had Amber Ale. Even though we spent a lot of the day in coaches being transported between sites, this was a great tour.

The next day we flew to Singapore. The first leg to Sydney was with Jet Star, a member of the One World Alliance, which meant that we were able to use all our Silver Executive benefits for extra luggage and use of the lounge, and then we flew on Qantas to our final destination. We had arranged to be collected at the airport on a private transfer, and we were taken straight to Raffles, where we would be staying for two nights. Previously, we have had a drink in this iconic hotel and lunch during a port call on a cruise, but this was our first time staying in this luxurious five-star hotel. I was not disappointed with the service that we received or our room which was large, very well furnished with colonial furniture and fittings, and we had chairs and a table on the outside balcony-corridor overlooking the courtyard – a perfect setting for our evening Cuba Libra.

We returned to New Zealand in 2017, but on this occasion, we concentrated on travelling around the South Island only, as we had been hampered with bad weather on our first visit. We flew out with Cathay Pacific to Sydney, with a stopover in Hong Kong. We had several hours in Hong Kong, so we left our hand luggage at the airport in left luggage, and took the train to Hong Kong Island. We had hoped to be able to go up to Victoria Peak on the funicular, but the queues were horrendous, so we didn't bother waiting. We had a wonderful lunch at Mott 32, a dim sum restaurant. It was a beautifully decorated restaurant and the food was delicious – expensive, but certainly first class service, ambience and food. We had been to Hong Kong before, so this flying visit did not give us time to plan much. However, our day was cut short, as we were overwhelmed by the number of people "camping" out on the streets, sitting on cardboard boxes in large groups in underpasses, along pavements and in the gardens. It was as if a refugee camp had sprung up in the centre of the city. As a result of this, we decided to head back to the airport, as it was not pleasant walking around because of the heat and the number of people around us.

We found out later the reason for this invasion. In Hong Kong, those who are employed in service in homes of the Hong Kong people are given one day a week off, and that happens to be Sunday. All these service people meet up, but as they do not have their own accommodation, they gather on the streets and create their own little private space to meet and to chat, using cardboard boxes. It was just unfortunate that our stopover fell on a Sunday.

We had two nights in Sydney; mainly to get over the jet lag, before flying on to Queenstown. We flew on Air New Zealand, and we had to change planes in Auckland, which meant that this transfer took up most of the day. We had added an extra night in Queenstown at the start of our road trip around the island, in case there were any problems with flights; so on our first night, we stayed in a motel outside of town and close to the airport. The following day, we were able to walk back to the airport, to pick up our car and then collect our luggage and drive on to our hotel, where we would be staying for the next four nights – the Hotel St Moritz.

We knew that we would be too early to check in, and the manager of the motel suggested that we take a drive along Lake

Wakatipu to Glenorchy, which is located at one end of the lake. The weather was beautiful and the scenery was stunning. The water was so calm it acted as a mirror reflecting the mountains and the cloudless sky above. There was not a lot to see or to do in Glenorchy; it was the journey there that made this a worthwhile morning excursion. In 2017, the BBC aired a drama series called "Top of the Lake", and it was actually filmed on location in Glenorchy and Queenstown.

In the afternoon, after checking in at our hotel, we walked into town, which was very busy with holidaymakers, as this is a very popular tourist location, offering a selection of adrenalin sports and activities. We managed to get a table at the harbour, where we sat out and enjoyed a bottle of Pinot Gris over lunch, watching the boat trips depart and return to the quayside; parasailers soaring into the sky; canoeists silently drifting out onto the lake, and other water activity trips beginning their daily ritual. It was very pleasant; so much so that we returned to the same place for lunch the next day. Queenstown offers lots of restaurants, souvenir shops, cafés, bars and activity centres – an ideal holiday centre.

We had booked a tour the next day with Outback NZ Ltd, to do a 4 x 4 drive to Macetown. This was classed as a small tour with maximum of four people and that was the number of people in the 4WD, including the driver and another guest. We left Queenstown and headed for Arrowtown, an old gold mining town which offers an alternative location for accommodation in the area. The main street is lined with old wooden buildings and there were many classic cars parked there during our stop. It had a feeling of being on a western film set – you expected gunfighters to appear at either end of the street! We stopped to buy some water, as it was very hot and to take a few photos of this pleasant town.

Once back in the car, we headed off-road and the fun began! We travelled along the River Dart, which was very shallow in this area, but we still managed to create quite a splash! We then left the base of the valley and climbed up to the mountain roads which were very narrow. I was terrified that a car might come the other way, as there were no passing points and all we had was a sheer drop on our left that would have taken us crashing down the mountain to the floor below us! Luckily, the only time that we did meet a car coming in the opposite direction was at a place where the road was wider, and we were able to pass one another, albeit very slowly! The views along this route were spectacular, looking forward to the mountain range and below us to the river valley.

Macetown itself was very disappointing as there is nothing left of the original gold town, but they have tried to create something by rebuilding the school and a store, so you can get some idea of what sort of conditions they lived in when this remote town was populated. But the location of the town did offer magnificent views of the strange mountains that appeared to ripple, and were covered in lush green foliage. Our driver told us various stories about the town and previous tours that he had brought here in the past when the jeep had got stuck in mud, which did not fill us with confidence, when we were returning through deep water! It was an interesting tour; not a comfortable one as the roads were very rough, especially along the river bed, and we were shaken to our core – but it was the views that made it worthwhile.

There are loads of excursions and tours that can be taken from Queenstown, ranging from high adrenalin activities like white water rafting, to sedate lake cruises. It is also an ideal location for visiting the Fiordlands National Park either on a day trip or on an extended stay, including spending a night on a boat in one of the beautiful Sounds which create this area of outstanding beauty. We did a day trip to Doubtful Sound as this is the most remote inlet available, and it can only be reached by sea or on an organised excursion. It was a long trip but it was worth it.

We started with a coach journey from Queenstown and then a boat trip over Lake Manapouri, which brought us out at the base of Wilmot Pass. The tour company we used, Real Journeys, had a fleet of coaches waiting here to be able to take us over the pass and on to Doubtful Sound. As there is no direct road access to Wilmot Pass from Queenstown or Te Anau, this is the only way that you can make this journey. We stopped at the summit of the pass to admire the view and to take photos. What a sight! We had beautiful weather to be able to enjoy this majestic, sweeping view of the mountain pass, leading down to Doubtful Sound below us.

Once we reached sea level, we boarded a boat and set sail for our three-hour cruise on the Sound. The scenery is breath taking! The mountains surrounding the inlet soar towards the sky – they are covered with plants and trees, and I cannot say that I have ever seen anywhere that is so naturally wild and remote. Doubtful Sound is made up of a number of islands and inlets, and we meandered around these, approaching the sea entrance

where it did get a little rough as we met the Tasman Sea, and enjoying the views and the wildlife that met us on this trip. We saw dolphins, penguins, seals and loads of other bird life who call this beautiful place home. We were very lucky with the weather as we had clear blue skies and sunshine – especially as we had been here on the cruise in 2013, and then we could not see anything because of the low clouds, the rain and the mist. Our return journey took us back over the Wilmot Pass and across Lake Manapouri, before arriving in Queenstown fourteen hours after we had departed that morning. It was a long day, but worth every minute. My only regret was that we did not overnight in Doubtful Sound aboard one of the boats which offer this facility. I messed up the booking and we just did the Wilderness Cruise, not the overnight cruise, as we had planned. Duh!

As I had expected us to be travelling back from Doubtful Sound the next day, we did not have anything planned. I had meticulously planned every overnight stop, excursion, tour and expedition from the comfort of the settee at home, arranging everything myself over the internet. Only the cruise that was to be taken at the end of the holiday had been arranged through a tour operator. But luckily, I had made our hotel reservation at the St Moritz for four consecutive nights even though I had expected us to be on a boat for one of these – this meant that we did have accommodation for that extra night, when we returned, unexpectedly, to Queenstown. On our surprise free day, we wandered around the shops, the pier and the bars of Queenstown and we had a very pleasant lunch on the pier, before we boarded one of the lake cruise ships to enjoy the views from the water.

In the evening, we went on the gondola to visit the Skyline Restaurant. This Skyline cable car is the steepest in the Southern hemisphere, and takes you to the top of Bob's Peak. The views from the top, looking down on Queenstown, across Lake Wakatipu and over towards The Remarkables were, yet again, magnificent! The restaurant has two sittings in the evening and is very popular so it is wise to book. The meal is a buffet, but offers many different types of food with many international dishes, so that there is something for everyone – even those with a fussy temperament. We went to the late sitting so that we could go up the mountain in daylight and then come down in the dark, giving us the opportunity to see the view by day and by night. With being so high up, at night Queenstown was lit up like a fairyland and it was a very memorable last night in this fabulous town.

The next day, we left Queenstown and started our road trip heading north towards Mount Cook (or Auraki in Maori). Driving was very easy in New Zealand as they drive on the left, as we do in the UK. Although the roads are mainly single lane, passing was fairly easy and most drivers would be courteous and move over slightly to allow you to pass. The journey to Mount Cook was not too long, taking us around four hours including stops, to admire the views and to take photos of the highest mountain in New Zealand. We were blessed with beautiful clear weather again, and we could see Mount Cook when we were miles away with still an hour to drive, as it was so prominent on the horizon.

We stayed at the Hermitage Hotel, which is located in the National Park and offers amazing uninterrupted views of Mount Cook. I cannot think of any hotel which has such a prominent position, with the most remarkable views that I have ever seen! We were too early to check in, so we sat out on the veranda with a bottle of wine and enjoyed the wonderful views. When we were allocated our room, we were very pleased to find that we had a room on the side of the block which had a small balcony and fabulous views of the mountain. We set our alarm early for the next day, so that we could capture the sunrise, and we weren't disappointed, as we drew back the curtains and watched the transformation from dark to light with the golden glows of the rising sun reflected off the snowy glaciers and the mountain peaks.

There are many options for walks and hikes, tours, helicopter flights and other activities arranged through the hotel or alternative tour operators. There is a shop at the hotel, a café and a restaurant with bars, and a museum. This is the location of The Sir Edmund Hillary Alpine Centre, a tribute to this great explorer and features a theatre with choices of presentation.

We only stayed one night at The Hermitage, and we set off the next day to head for the eastern Canterbury region and the main city of the South Island, Christchurch. We had expected the city to have recovered from the earthquake of 2011, but we were so wrong; it was still a building site!

The earthquake struck on the 22nd of February at dinner-time – it caused so much damage because of its proximity to the city, and it was a shallow quake, at around five kilometres below ground level. A hundred and eighty-five people died as a result of the earthquake and the damage to the city was drastic. Many people evacuated the city, as parts of it were totally uninhabitable. The army moved in, and cordoned off the city centre, making it a no go area, as repairs needed to be done to the infrastructure, replacing drainage, water and sewage pipes, communication lines and roads, before they could even start to rebuild the city. This work was still in progress in February 2017, with traffic chaos and limited access to famous sites in the city.

We had decided to stay in Christchurch, in order to go on the famous train journey along Arthur's Pass, which had not been affected by the quake. Unfortunately, there had been a lot of recent fires in the Canterbury area, and some of the bridges along the line had been damaged and as a result of this, our train journey was cancelled and replaced with a road trip instead. We had poor weather on this day, and, despite our guide trying to make up for the fact that we were not travelling through the pass by train, the day was very disappointing. The views were not as spectacular as we had expected, and our stops were not that interesting. Maybe if we had had blue skies and had taken the train, we might have felt differently, but we felt that we had been let down, and we would not recommend this trip to others travelling out to South Island. In fact, I would go as far to say that Christchurch should be missed out until the city is fully functioning again.

We did go on the Christchurch Tramway in the evening, which was enjoyable. Just one of the famous street cars has been converted into a restaurant, and offers a three course meal with a small choice on each course, which is beautifully presented by silver service and very good quality. During the evening, the tram continually loops around the small circuit, which is currently accessible, with a detour for a short comfort break into the Cathedral Junction. It was a nice way to see more of the city and to enjoy a good meal served with wine.

When we left Christchurch, we were hampered once again, by earthquake damage, but this time it was the more recent hit in November 2016. The coastal road along the east coast, which goes through Kaikoura, was badly damaged in the quake – it had been closed to all traffic. We had intended on taking this road to Picton and stopping in Kaikoura to go whale watching, but due to the road closure, we had to take the detour inland over the mountains instead. This was a very laborious route as all transport was diverted along these roads, including large trucks and motorhomes. The mountain roads were not designed to take so much traffic, especially HGV's, and as a result of this, the road was collapsing in some areas, and there were a lot of road repairs being undertaken. This meant a lot of traffic lights, long queues and very slow progress. A drive that should have only taken four hours, plus the break for whale watching, took us almost twice as long – around eight hours!

We were so glad when we eventually arrived at the Harbour View Motel, Picton; especially as we had beautiful sunny weather and fabulous views over the harbour, which we enjoyed over a bottle of wine on the balcony.

We liked Picton so much when we came on the cruise in 2013, that we decided that we wanted to return to the Marlborough area, located in the north of the island, in order to enjoy the beautiful scenery and to taste more of the delicious wine that is produced in this area. There are lots of options for wine tasting trips, but I found a private one on the internet and I booked a tour through Bubbly Grape online before our visit.

We were collected from our hotel and proceeded to visit several of the wine producers in the Marlborough area, where we tasted lots of the different local wines – especially Pinot Gris, which is our favourite. Our guide had the day planned and provided us with a book to record our tastings and showed details of each of the places we visited. They ranged from the very large to the small, and we were not disappointed with any of the wine selections at each location. Because we were on a private tour, we could take as long as we liked and, because we weren't doing the driving, we could really enjoy this pleasurable pastime.

Included on our tour was lunch at the most beautiful elevated restaurant located at one of the wine producers, where we had a three-course meal, served with wine, of course, and some more wine tasting, while we waited for our meal to be served. At our final stop we were invited into the boardroom, where we were allowed to mix our own wine, using a number of different grape varieties, to create our own white wine. This was great fun and we learned a lot about the blending process that each winemaker uses, to be able to create their brand. We found out that last year Prince William and Kate had enjoyed doing the same process in the same room during their stay in New Zealand – it made us feel very special to have been given the same privileges!

Needless to say, that we were quite tipsy by the end of the tour, but this did not stop us from enjoying another bottle of wine, which we bought on our visit, later in the evening, while we enjoyed watching the sun go down from our balcony.

We left Picton the next day and we started our return journey to Queenstown, but this time driving along the east coast, stopping overnight three times, to break up the journey. We also stopped to admire the views on the first day, as we went around Queen Charlotte Sound. The first day was our longest drive, and we arrived at the tiny Birds Ferry Lodge near Charleston late in the afternoon. This four-star accommodation only has two rooms and a separate cottage, and the stay included breakfast and dinner, which was served in the lodge as a set meal, where we were joined by the people staying in the other room. It was very friendly, and we felt as though we had been invited into someone's home to enjoy this pleasurable meal. The lodge is located in a wildlife area on the edge of the wetlands – it is a very remote location with very few properties in the area, so at night, it was wonderful to listen to the bird calls in the dark, and to look up at the clear, night sky which was not affected by any light pollution.

We continued our journey to our next overnight stop, which was Franz Josef. It was here that we encountered our only problem with accommodation that we had arranged prior to our visit over the internet. I had found a hotel to stay called Te Waonui Forest Retreat which offered excellent accommodation in the village, and had a Maori influence, which was very different from the other hotels where we were staying. I shopped around and found the best deal through hoteling.com and made my reservation online through them, paying three hundred and forty-nine pounds and thirty five pence for a deluxe king on a half-board basis. As with a lot of hotel sites on the internet, we made the payment at the time of the booking, which was twelve months before our stay. Unfortunately, when we tried to check-in, we discovered that hoteling.com had ceased trading, and had not paid the hotel for our room. We had no idea that this had happened as the company had not contacted us, and certainly had not refunded the money!

The hotel did have vacancies for the night, but the rate that they wanted to charge us was astronomical, and we refused to pay this; especially after we had already paid out so much already. We knew that it was not the hotel's fault, but we would have expected some compassion from them, knowing our situation. Franz Josef is a very popular tourist village, and we knew that there would be other hotels offering a room at a much lower rate, so we called their bluff, and refused to pay the charges that they were quoting, until it came down to a reasonable price, about one hundred and fifty pounds for bed and breakfast. We accepted this, as we thought that the price was reasonable, and it was easier than getting the car back, loading all our luggage again and trying to find somewhere else to stay.

In Fox Glacier we had reserved a flight over the glaciers, as this location is very close to the Southern Alps and there is a lot of choice for scenic flights. We had booked with Air Safaris to do the Grand Traverse Scenic Flight of Mount Cook and the Glaciers, which would be in a small plane. When we arrived at the little airfield just outside Franz Josef, we found that there was only one other passenger, meaning that, with just three of us in a plane which could seat ten, once in the air, that we would be able to move around to get the best views and photos. We did spread out in the plane, to even out the weight distribution and I sat at the back, so that I did not have to move to be able to see out of both sides of the plane.

The weather was a little grey and dull on the ground, but once we reached the glaciers, we were lucky to have clear blue skies and the views we encountered were wonderful. We flew around Mount Cook, getting so close that you felt like you could touch the mountain. We also flew low over the glaciers to be able to see the grit and the lines within these huge icy carpets. There are many high snowy peaks that make up the Southern Alps and our one hour flight gave us plenty of opportunities to see the spectacle offered by this mountain range. This flight was a real treat and, although it was expensive at three hundred and sixty New Zealand dollars each around two hundred pounds it was money well spent.

The next day we had a long drive, but we stopped several times to enjoy the views of Fox Glacier and the Hawea Conservation Park, which had the most wonderful forests, mountains, lakes and rivers, to accompany us on our long drive to Wanaka for our final night in New Zealand. Originally, I was planning on returning to Queenstown to be close to the airport for our flight back to Sydney the next day, but I had read that Lake Wanaka was exceptional and listed in my book – Five Hundred Places you have to See – so I made the decision to stay there, and leave earlier, to make the short drive to the airport in Queenstown the next day.

There is a lot of choice for lodging around Wanaka, as it is a very popular holiday destination, due to the activities that you can enjoy on the lake, and the walks around the surrounding area. We did not participate in anything other than sitting out in the sunshine, enjoying a bottle of wine, and the views from the Edgewater Resort, located on the banks of Lake Wanaka. This was a very relaxing and pleasurable way to while away the hours before we rearranged our suitcases and spread the weight, ready to fly back to Australia and continue our holiday, which consisted of an overnight in Sydney and then a twelve day cruise around the Pacific, stopping at Noumea, New Caledonia; Lifou, Loyalty Island; Mystery Island, Vanuatu, Suva and Lautoka in Fiji.

Unfortunately, we did not make it to Lautoka, as we left the ship early, disembarking in Suva and flying home from Fiji, instead of returning to Sydney and taking our booked flight with Cathay Pacific back to the UK. This was due to us receiving the devastating news when we were in Vanuatu that Margaret, Richard's sister, had died the night before. She had been in hospital before we departed for the holiday, but we had no idea that her illness was so serious, and news of her passing was a total shock to both of us. Our holiday was over, and all we wanted to do was to return home to offer comfort and support to the rest of the family. The logistics of doing this were a nightmare, as we were on the other side of the world, with a twelve-hour time difference and we were in a remote area.

It was impossible to fly back from Vanuatu, so we booked flights for when we arrived in Fiji, to return to Heathrow via Los Angeles. The concierge on the Celebrity Summit assisted us in arranging for us to leave the ship early, and we managed to find a company who was able to transfer us, and all our luggage, from Suva to the International Airport in Nadi, which was on the opposite side of the island, and a four-hour drive away.

It was not a good way to end a holiday, but we were glad that we took this decision. As a result of this change in direction, it meant that we actually flew around the world, crossing the international dateline between Fiji and the USA, so that we arrived in Los Angeles before we had taken off!

New Zealand is a beautiful country, and there is so much to see and to do. The people are very friendly, helpful and accommodating and, as English is the main language, and they drive on the correct side of the road, it was like being at home. I would love to go back and go to Stewart Island; cruise overnight on Doubtful Sound; see the whales at Kaikoura; visit more of the inland area of North Island and manage to visit everything that we missed out on this trip. But it is a very long way to travel, and it is expensive to get there, before you add–on the costs of accommodation and transport, so I doubt that we will ever return to this wonderful country.

Just a final note – we did not see a kiwi in the wild during our stay, as they are actually very small, timid, shy birds, that are nocturnal and not visible during the day. But we did see one in Franz Josef in a sanctuary or museum – well, I'm saying we saw one – it was so dark in the enclosure, that your eyes struggled to adapt to the light, and we just about made out a tiny little blob rustling around in the undergrowth, so as far as I am concerned, I can tick that box to say we have seen this little, elusive enigma!

CHAPTER 34

Niagara Falls (15), USA and Canada – September 2013

We originally booked to take this cruise and tour in September 2012, but after Richard's heart attack in July 2011, we delayed all our holidays by twelve months, and we went to Alaska in 2012 instead. The cruise company, Princess, were very good, as they allowed us to transfer the deposit we had made on the original booking for 2012 to 2013. Sometimes cruise companies can be very stubborn, and would see that change as a cancellation, rather than a transfer, but; on this occasion, with both the Alaskan cruise and this transatlantic cruise, they agreed to honour our initial reservations without any penalty. In fact, because we were very early booking onto the 2013 cruise, we were able to select the Grand Suite. This is the largest and most luxurious suite on many Princess ships – there is usually only one, and it gets booked very quickly. This cruise was for fifteen nights, sailing from Southampton to New York, and at around ten thousand pounds for the two of us, we thought that this would be the only time that we would be able to take this option as it was a good price and the cruise was long enough for us to make the most of the facilities in the suite.

As normal, we used the cruise as a starting point for our holiday, and then we added to the trip with extensions in New York and booking a five-day tour with Viator.com, which would take us to Niagara Falls, Pennsylvania and Washington DC, with transfers by private jet! All in all, this was going to be a five-star holiday!

This was our first transatlantic cruise and, I suppose you could say, that we were going the wrong way! But most cruise ships will normally do repositioning cruises during the year when they leave one touring area, to head for another, which would offer the right weather conditions in that season. The Caribbean Princess had spent the summer cruising around Britain, the Baltic and Iceland, and was now heading for New York and the short season for New England cruises in the fall, before heading down to the Caribbean and the long winter period, cruising in the warmth from Florida to the islands. We did another transatlantic crossing with Celebrity in April 2016, and came the other way, sailing from Miami to Southampton with many days at sea.

Our Princess cruise was due to call at Bergen, Norway; the Shetland Islands, the UK; the Faroe Islands, Denmark; three stops on Iceland; Greenland, Denmark; Newfoundland, and Canada, before finally arriving in New York. Unfortunately, there were storms in the North Atlantic, and, in order to avoid the really high winds and torrential rain, the captain made the decision not to call at Shetland and the Faroe Islands; instead we had an overnight in Bergen, to spend two days in this pleasant Norwegian town, and have an extra night at sea before arriving in Iceland on time. This is one of the issues with cruising; you are dependent on weather conditions being favourable to ensure that you are able to complete your selected itinerary. We have missed out on quite a few ports due to bad weather – Geraldton, Australia; Kingston, Jamaica; Bermuda; Guernsey, Channel Islands and, in Canakkale, Turkey, due to the lack of tugs in the port, they only had one – the ship was not able to be pushed into position to dock. My brother and his wife were diverted on their South American cruise, due to a medical emergency and they missed out on Puerto Madryn, Argentina. I have heard that some cruise ships have been refused admittance into Argentina after calling at the Falkland Islands, but this did not happen to us when we did our Antarctic cruise in February 2015.

We were actually quite glad that we had the opportunity to visit Bergen over two days, as the first day was wet and miserable and the views of this pretty port was not pleasant, but the next day we had clear, beautiful blue skies and we went into town under our own steam, wandering around the brightly coloured shops at Bryggen, and taking the little train on a tour around the city and into the hills, providing us with some good photo opportunities.

At our first stop in Iceland we docked in Akureyri in the north of the island, just above the Arctic Circle. From there, we did an excursion which took us out to Godafoss Falls. We were lucky, as the sun was shining, and we had some blue sky for the photos, but it was bitterly cold! We also went to see some lava flow remains, which had created some weird shapes, and the Icelandic people had created stories about them, imagining that they were built by trolls and elves. This sounds quite interesting, but it was not really as good as it sounds.

Our next port, on the north-west coast of Iceland was Isafjordur. This was a tender port and, although the town had very little to see and even the shops were for locals, not tourists, the location was stunning, with crystal clear, calm seas and snow-capped mountains, that reflected in the mirror-like bay, where we were moored. Our final stop was Reykjavik, our second time in the capital. We went on a 4x4 adventure and, with only six cars in the convoy; we had a pleasant drive, stopping several times to enjoy the views. These included a stop on a hill outside the capital to get a great elevated view of Reykjavik; a climb onto a small plateau, where they filmed episodes of "Game of Thrones", to view smoking volcanoes in the distance including Grimsvotn, the volcano that caused chaos in 2011, with the ash cloud that caused hundreds of flight cancellations and travel chaos. We went off-road across lava fields and through rivers before stopping for a break in a small town where a crevice had been created after the earthquake in 2010, which measured six point three on the Richter scale. This excursion was only a half-day one, so we had time to go into the city for something to eat and to do some shopping.

As we sailed away from Reykjavik, the weather was perfect – sunny with brilliant blue skies, and it was lovely sitting out on the balcony, which spread across half the back of the ship, watching the city and Iceland get smaller and smaller, until it vanished from the horizon. We were able to see the stunning Imagine Peace Tower, a tribute to John Lennon, conceived by Yoko Ono.

Our next port of call was Nanortalik in Greenland, which is still a territory of Denmark. Up until June 1944, Iceland was also part of Denmark, and it was the Danes who named these two islands. The latter they found to be very green and fertile, with lots of natural resources, and they wanted to deter people from settling there so they called it Iceland, to dissuade settlers simply from the name. But they wanted to encourage people to relocate to the former location, Greenland and to encourage this they called this barren, cold, miserable place Greenland! I think that this is called reverse psychological thinking!

From my description of Greenland, I am sure that you can understand my feelings for this place. We had intended on getting up early to experience sailing into the bay, from where we would get our tenders into town, but we arrived early. However, when we looked out of the window, we could see high, snow-capped mountains; a small, sparsely built town and some floating ice-bergs! But by the time we went ashore, the fog had descended, and you could not see any mountains at all. We could only just see our destination point in the distance. There was so little to see in this town – we did the circuit within an hour, stopping at the village hall to see some school children singing and dancing but not in National costume as promised. The information centre was the only shop in town, and it was filled with two and a half thousand passengers from the Caribbean Princess or that is how it seemed having to queue to get in, quickly grab anything from the shelves and queue again to pay, which took twenty minutes, and a remote, simple church. It started to rain on top of the heavy mist we had encountered on land, and we were glad to be heading back to the ship, although we had to queue yet again to get the tender back. In the afternoon, there was an announcement stating that there would be no further tenders due to the fog. We thought that this was just relating to tenders leaving the ship, so as not to allow any more passengers to depart from the ship and go ashore, but we found out it also related to the tenders leaving the shore, so no-one was being allowed to leave the town and return to the ship!

We were told later that, as the tenders did not have any satellite navigation, one of them had actually got lost returning to the ship, and had ended up heading out to sea towards the floating icebergs! So, it was for safety reasons that no one was allowed to go or to return until the fog had lifted. Luckily, this was not too long, but we did find out that although we knew what was happening, the passengers in Nanortalik were not being updated and some people were queuing in the cold and the rain for hours with nowhere to sit or shelter and with no information. There were a lot of unhappy faces on the ship that night!

Saint John's in Newfoundland was a lovely small, colourful city, set in a natural harbour at the head of an inlet off the North Sea, surrounded by coastal mountains. Over five hundred years old, it is the oldest and the most easterly city in North America, and the capital of the province. We did a photographic tour of the city calling at Signal Hill to see the lighthouse, and view the coastal area around the city; Quidi Vidi, a charming, quaint fishing village and finally a quick photo stop at the city park. It was a really nice place, and I am sure that those people who did the hiking, kayaking or other strenuous activities, managed to see a completely different side of the place than our relaxing coach tour.

After two days at sea, we eventually arrived in New York. I set the alarm early, so that we could witness our arrival into this famous harbour. It was still dark at six a.m. when I opened the curtains, but as we crawled along the Hudson River and the sun began to brighten the night sky – we sailed past the Statue of Liberty, Ellis Island and Lower Manhattan before eventually docking in Brooklyn. This iconic cruise port has to be one of the best in the world, and the views you get from the ship are spellbinding – it certainly competes with Sydney Harbour as my favourite.

On this occasion we stayed at the Sheraton Tribeca – a nice hotel, but the location was not good, as it was in the Soho area of New York and a long way from Times Square, which is where we like to stay. But it was convenient for our tour, as this was the pick-up point and, although we did not have to stay there, we thought that it was better to stay at this location both before and after the tour, so that we could store the bulk of our luggage, while we did an extended tour to Niagara Falls. We arrived at around eleven-thirty a.m. after disembarking from the ship, which can be a lengthy affair in the USA, due to immigration. Once we had unpacked we had some lunch, and then we went around the shops which were very good in this area. In the evening, we took the metro and went to Times Square, where we went to see Jersey Boys – a great musical, and it was certainly the right place to see it.

The next day we went for lunch in Little Italy, as it was just one stop away from our hotel on the metro. When we arrived, we were surprised to find that there was a festival taking place and that the main road was closed to traffic, as it was taken over by food stalls and entertainers celebrating the Feast of San Gerona. The atmosphere was electric, and the aroma of the delicious food being served all around you was intoxicating! We ate at a streetside café and enjoyed watching the bustling crowds go by. Everyone was good humoured, and there was no threat or fear from the huge crowds who were enjoying this annual feast. I felt as though we had stepped back in time, to the years when the original Italian immigrants had first settled in that area.

From there we took the subway to Fulton Street to visit the 911 Memorial. We had booked a time slot online, as we knew that the queues to visit the reasonably new site would be huge. Entrance is free, but they requested that you donate five dollars per person to go to the 911 Foundation. There were thousands of people there when we arrived, so if everyone honoured that request I am sure that the foundation would be raising half a million a day. This site had opened on the tenth anniversary after the disaster on the 11th of September 2011, but there was still a lot of building work taking place around the gardens, which were surrounded by wooden panelling; as the museum was due to open the year after in 2014, but despite this, the memorial was still very moving. Towering above us was the new World Trade Centre, or Freedom Tower, which is the tallest building in the Western Hemisphere standing at one thousand seven hundred and seventy-six feet tall – a deliberate number to recognise the year that America declared its independence. When we were there, the building was almost complete, and it opened the following year.

In the gardens are two large, black marble pools, built on the exact spot of the foundations of the original Trade Centre destroyed in 2001. Water cascades down the sides and vanishes through a central drain. All around the edges of the two pools are memorials to those who had died in the disaster and in the attack in February 1993 – all two thousand nine hundred and eighty-three men, women and children. By the side of each name there is a small crevice in which a red rose is placed on the birthday of each of the victims – where a woman died who was pregnant, there are two roses, one for her and the other for the unborn child. It was very moving. Although we had to queue and be searched on entering the gardens, and there were thousands of visitors, it seemed as though everyone wanted to show their respects and walked around the memorials and gardens in a calm and quiet manner, with no pushing, shoving, shouting or disorder of any kind. I was very impressed with the whole site, as it was done with taste and dignity; not something that the Americans are renowned for!

The next day we needed to be in the foyer early, six a.m. ready to be collected for our tour, which we had booked through Viator.com. There were about twenty-seven in our group from Australia, Poland and the USA – we were the only British people on the tour. We were taken out of New York and we drove for about an hour to a small airport just outside the city. We boarded our jet, which was just large enough for the group and our guide, and we flew for one hour and twenty minutes to an American airport close to Niagara. Because our flights were private and on a small plane, we were able to hop between smaller airports and we did not have to bother with formal check-in, security and baggage checks, which meant that all our city transfers were quick and easy.

A coach collected us and we went over Rainbow Bridge into Canada, from where I got my first sight of Niagara Falls. These falls are very commercialised, with both the US and Canada operating big tourist sites on both banks of the river. Once we were in Canada, we started our visits to all that this natural wonder has to offer, visiting Walk on the Wild Side, a footpath that leads down to the river bank where you are able to walk alongside the torrent of water that flows away from the falls. The rapids here are grade six, and very forceful – there was so much speed and power to the river, as it crashes over rocks and against the cliff sides. We continued into the town centre, where we boarded the Maid of the Mist, the popular boat excursion that gets you up close and personal with the lower level of the falls.

If you don't want to get wet – stay inside! We donned our Maid of the Mist plastic ponchos and went onto the top deck, to be able to take photos, but this was impossible because of the spray that we encountered almost as soon as we cast off, we needed to hide and to protect the cameras, to stop them from being damaged by the wet. We did get a couple of silly shots with us wrapped up to try and stop getting soaked – it didn't work!

The boat approaches the American Falls first. I think I should explain that the falls are split into three. The first, the American Falls, is a wall of thundering water and Bridal Veil Falls is separated by an island from these -they are both in the USA, and the other, more spectacular, is Horseshoe Falls, a curved spectacle which lies in Canada. It felt as though we went right underneath the wall of water crashing over the ridge, but it was just the spray from the falls that was soaking us to the skin. We then approached the Canadian Falls, but these were even more forceful than the first, churning the water below to rock the Maid around, as we got as close as safely possible. It was great fun and you have to do this iconic boat trip when you visit Niagara – unless you don't want to get wet, that is!

Niagara Falls has the highest flow rate of all the great waterfalls. Angel Falls, Venezuela is the tallest at three thousand two hundred and twelve feet. The Victoria Falls in Zimbabwe and Zambia is the largest singular falls at one point seven kilometres in length and three hundred and sixty feet high and Iguazu Falls, Argentina and Brazil is the biggest, consisting of some two hundred and seventy five separate waterfalls and cascades, measuring two kilometres in length and a height of two hundred and ten feet. This high flow rate is because the falls are created by Lake Erie emptying into Lake Ontario, via the Niagara River. The falls were created in the last ice age, at the same time as the Great Lakes. It was as the ice melted that the river was created, and over time, it cut a gorge through the north-facing cliff which is made up of different rocks. The top level is limestone, which is mostly erosion resistant, but underneath was softer, weaker rock, mainly shale, and as this gave way, the gorge collapsed, to create the falls. In the last ten thousand years, they have moved southward by about six point eight miles, due to continued erosion, but this has slowed because of the river being managed and being used for hydro-electricity. The Horseshoe Falls are the largest – a hundred and eighty-eight feet high. It started as a small arch, and changed its shape to a horseshoe; hence its name, but now, it is more of a gigantic "V" shape. The American and the Bridal Veil Falls are not as high, ranging between seventy to one hundred feet because of huge boulders that lie at the base; the remains of the collapsed wall that was created by erosion.[2]

After lunch, we went to visit the attractions at the Horseshoe Falls, doing the Journey Behind the Falls and the Niagara Fury. The first is a walk that has been cut into the rock behind the falls, with windows that peer out at the crashing water of the falls. The path ends in a platform that is behind the main section of the falls. The final sight is good, but most of the time you are just walking through a corridor, with nothing much to see. The latter was a bit corny and aimed at children, using a cartoon to show how the falls were created and explaining what will happen in the future. This was followed by a 4D ride, where we flew over the falls, as though in a boat on the river above, and we were pelted with rain and snow to make it feel real!

We stayed at the Sheraton, and upgraded, to get a room with a Falls view – well worth the extra money just one hundred dollars for two nights, as the view was fabulous and we could see the changing colours reflected off the Falls when it went dark. The whole group returned to the Canadian Falls in the evening, to dine at the restaurant located in the tourist centre there – good food, great company and an ideal location. We could not ask for more!

The next day the weather was beautiful compared with the day before when it was cloudy and cold, and we met early for our day trip into Toronto. The drive was about two hours on a very good highway running along the side of Lake Ontario, which is huge! Our first stop was the CN Tower, and we had time there

to go up to the first viewing platform where we stood on the glass floor, peering down to the pavement below us. We would have liked to have taken the lift to the upper level, which was fourteen floors higher but, unfortunately, we ran out of time.

We went to a museum and then to the Parliament Buildings, where we went inside to see the lower gallery and a picture of the founding fathers. We were very lucky, as we were allowed to go into the actual chambers, which were beautifully decorated with carved wood, leather seating and a huge mace used on formal occasions. We had some free time in Eaton Place, a large shopping centre; to be able to have lunch and/or to shop before we headed back to Niagara Falls.

We left Niagara the next day, crossing back over the Rainbow Bridge, going through passport control, as we were returning to the United States, and then stopping for an hour to be able to view the Falls from the American side. Here, there is a park by the side of the Niagara River, so that you can see the ferocity of the water before it crashes over the falls. As you walk along the path, you come to the top of the falls and a number of platforms and paths take you close the top of the American and Bridal Veil Falls, so you can look down the wall of water. Seeing the ferocious river at this level was amazing, as there is so much water in a swollen river, which gathers into a small channel before it crashes over the precipice into the river below. You continue along the path to the edge of the Horseshoe Falls, but the view is not as good from above as it was head-on from the Canadian Side.

We headed for the small private airfield in Buffalo, to board our jet again and to head for Harrisburg in Pennsylvania, where we drove to the Hershey factory in Lancaster. Hershey is a renowned institution in America, famous for its chocolates, sweets and philanthropy. There is a theme park at the location with many thrill rides, but we did not have time to visit that particular part of the park as we concentrated on the chocolate making and the history of Hershey. In all, we had three hours there, to be able to do the corny ride around the imitation factory, learning about how chocolate is made; we did chocolate tasting, and who would not enjoy that! Finally, we boarded the trolley tour which took us around the grounds, the old factory, the workers' cottages and Hershey's grand house, where we learnt all about the history of the man, and his dream, which included many generous donations to charities and workers' rights. With some time to eat lunch and visit the shop, we left the park and headed for the Amish area in Lancaster County, Pennsylvania.

Here are some facts about the Amish, which, personally, I think are fascinating:

The Amish people in America are an old religious sect, direct descendants of the Anabaptists of sixteenth-century Europe. They moved to the US after breaking away from the European Mennonites led by Jakob Ammann. The first sizable group of Amish arrived in America at around 1730 and settled near Lancaster County, Pennsylvania, as a result of William Penn's 'holy experiment' in religious tolerance.

All aspects of Amish life are dictated by a list of written or oral rules, known as **Ordnung***, which outlines the basics of the Amish faith and helps to define what it means to be Amish. For an Amish person, the Ordnung may dictate almost every aspect of one's lifestyle, from dress and hair length to buggy style and farming techniques.*

The Amish dress in a very simple style, avoiding all but the most basic ornamentation. Clothing is made at home of plain fabrics and is primarily dark in colour. Amish men, in general, wear straight-cut suits and coats without collars, lapels or pockets. The trousers never have creases or cuffs and are worn with suspenders. Belts are forbidden, as are sweaters, neckties, and gloves. Men's shirts fasten with traditional buttons in most orders, while suit coats and vests fasten with hooks and eyes. Young men are clean-shaven prior to marriage, while married men are required to let their beards grow. Moustaches are forbidden.

Amish women typically wear solid-colour dresses with long sleeves and a full skirt, covered with a cape and an apron. They never cut their hair, and wear it in a braid or in a bun on the back of the head concealed with a small white cap or black bonnet. Clothing is fastened with straight pins or snaps, stockings are black cotton and shoes are also black. Amish women are not permitted to wear patterned clothing or jewellery.

The Amish are averse to any technology, which they feel weakens the family structure. The conveniences that the rest of us take for granted such as electricity, television, cars, telephones and tractors are considered to be a temptation that could cause vanity, create inequality, or lead the Amish away from their close-knit community and, as such, are not encouraged or accepted. Most Amish cultivate their fields with horse-drawn machinery, live in houses without electricity, and get around in horse-drawn buggies.

The Amish believe strongly in education, but only provide formal education through the eighth grade and only in their own private schools. The Amish are exempt from state compulsory attendance beyond the eighth grade based on religious principles. One-room Amish schools are private institutions, operated by Amish parents. Schooling concentrates on the basic reading, writing, maths and geography, along with vocational training and socialization in Amish history and values. Education is also a big part of home life, with farming and homemaking skills considered an important part of an Amish child's upbringing.

Amish marry Amish – no intermarriage is allowed. Divorce is not permitted and separation is very rare. Because of their religious beliefs, Amish try to separate themselves from "outsiders," in an effort to avoid temptations and sin. They choose, instead, to rely on themselves and the other members of their local Amish community. Because of this self-reliance, Amish don't draw Social Security or accept other forms of government assistance. Their avoidance of violence in all forms means that they also don't serve in the military. [2]

We did a tour around the Amish community, stopping at a shop where they sell their wares and we visited a replica home/school house where our guide told us all about their beliefs and way of life. It was all alien to us, as we rely so much on technology. I could not imagine life without computers and television! We had dinner with the community, which was meant to be simple home cooked fare, but the meal was plentiful and satisfying with large helpings of fried chicken, beef stew, mashed potatoes, pasta and vegetables.

The following morning, we had a short visit to the Parliament Building in Harrisburg which is the state capital of Pennsylvania and not Philadelphia which is the largest city and then we headed back to the airfield, to take the short flight to Washington DC. Richard and I have been to Washington before, spending Easter weekend there in 2001, and we visited the majority of key sites on this occasion. In 2013, we returned to many of the key attractions – Union Station (great shopping and eateries); the White House; the Capitol Building; Mount Vernon; the Smithsonian Institute and Arlington Cemetery, but we still managed some new experiences on that visit.

We walked to the Capitol Building from Union Station, which wasn't too far, but with all the walking you do around the building afterwards, I was quite exhausted by the end of the day. Our tour started with a very interesting film telling us about the two houses, the Democrats and the Republicans; the development of Washington DC and the construction of the Capitol Building, before visiting the Hall of Statues, where there are images of all the previous presidents. We were very lucky on this occasion that the Hall of Representatives was in session, and we were able to attend, sitting in the public gallery. Although we didn't stay long, it was really interesting, and I would have liked to linger a bit longer, but things to see, places to go!

From there, we took our bus to see the major memorials located in Washington DC – the Lincoln Memorial; the Washington Monument; and the two war memorials for Vietnam and Korea. The Vietnam Veteran Memorial is very simple, but also very striking and moving. It consists of two walls of black granite, engraved with the names of all who had served in the war, whether they are alive, died in the conflict or have passed away since. Each wall consists of seventy-two panels, seventy are engraved, but the smaller two panels on each wall are not engraved. The length of each wall is approximately two hundred and forty-seven feet, and the wall starts at a height of ten feet with each panel decreasing in size until the last one is just eight inches in height. It was completed in 1982, but names have continued to be added, and in May 2017 the total numbers were fifty eight thousand three hundred and seventy two, including twelve hundred who are still missing.

The Korean War Veterans Memorial consists of a wall sandblasted with photographs of the war, a pool of remembrance, and nineteen stainless steel statues in full combat gear, walking through a field of juniper bushes and granite segments, to represent the Korean rugged terrain.[(2)]

Our next stop was the White House, where we walked around the grounds, peering into the gardens, to try and catch a glimpse of the president – I don't even know if he was in residence or not, but the number of guards and security around this iconic building certainly indicated their need to take any threats of terrorism very seriously.

The next day we visited Mount Vernon, the family home of George Washington, the: first president of the USA. We had been there before, but the house had not been open to visitors in 2001. This time it was, and we were able to walk around the slave quarters, the grounds and the house, and we walked down to the river to see George and Martha's grave. It was a beautiful day and this historic location is set in stunning countryside, and makes for a very pleasurable visit. There were several changes from our last visit, including a film on entry, telling the story of George Washington, and his role in the War of Independence and the creation of the new nation. There was also an education centre that was really interesting and very well presented – more of a tourist attraction than a museum.

When we returned to Washington DC, the group were dropped off at the Smithsonian Institute, which is made up of several museums containing various exhibitions. In 2001, we went to the National Air and Space Museum and the Museum of American History – both very good and worth a visit. This time we went to the National Archive Museum, and queued to be able to see the original documents that are exhibited here – the Declaration of Independence; the Constitution of the United States and the Bill of Rights. It was amazing to see these three important documents and to be able to actually read some of the important contents and see the signatures of such famous people as Benjamin Franklin, Thomas Jefferson and Samuel Adams. We had hoped to see one of the original Magna Carta documents, which are held by the museum, but on the day of our visit they were not on display (on loan or being cleaned or something) – I guess I'll have to go to Runnymede at some point! There are a lot more documents held in the archives, but we just went into the rotunda to see the important US original documents, as that was what we were interested in.

That evening we had a real treat as we got a cab to Arlington, to have dinner at the Melting Pot with friends, who live near the capital. Sarah, the daughter of Richard's best friend Malcolm Maw who sadly passed away in 2009, worked in South Korea after she had finished her degree at Exeter University. During her time there, she met Will, a United States marine, and as they say, the rest is history! I mentioned in our New York chapter that we bumped into them on New Year's Eve, just around the corner from Times Square, but this time our meeting was pre-arranged. It felt very cosmopolitan to be meeting up with friends for dinner thousands of miles from home! We had a great meal – a fondue, with cheese, meat, seafood and chocolate (not all at the same time!) with excellent company – a lovely way to spend the last night of our tour around the major eastern cities of America.

After a very late night; the next day, we had an early start to be able to visit Arlington National Cemetery. This is a military cemetery covering over six hundred acres and still expanding. It was established in the grounds of Arlington House during the American civil war, and since then, many members of the military have been interred here. There are also many other famous graves in the cemetery that are non-military, including John F Kennedy and his wife, Jackie; his stone is lit by an eternal flame; his brother Robert F. Kennedy and other members of the same family. There are memorials to the Space Shuttle Challenger, which exploded on launch in 1986, killing all those on board; the two hundred and seventy victims in the Lockerbie disaster when Pan Am. Flight 103 was destroyed by a bomb flying over Lockerbie in Scotland, and a memorial to those who died on the 11th September 2001, when there was a terrorist attack on the

Pentagon in Washington DC. There is the tomb to the Unknown Soldier, which has a permanent guard of honour, and it is possible to see the changing of the guard; which is one of the highlights of a visit here.

There is a trolley bus tour that takes visitors around the cemetery, explaining where memorials and graves are and providing information on the history of the site, as well as prospects for its future. There are several stops including the Tomb of the Unknown Soldier, the Kennedys' grave and Arlington House. I know that this sounds morbid, but it is very tastefully done and is an interesting place to visit.

This was our last visit on the tour and we headed straight to the military airport for our return flight on our private jet to New York. We stayed one night at the Tribeca again, as that was where we were being dropped off and it seemed to be our best option. This time we had a suite which gave us club access, allowing us to be able to use the lounge on the twenty-first floor, where there was an outside terrace offering a great view of the city and the Hudson River. We had the next day to ourselves, to be able to accomplish other activities from our wish list, including a ride around Central Park in a horse and carriage it is very expensive at one hundred dollars plus a tip, but we did get to see a lot of this huge park; visiting Trump Tower and having a drink in the bar; shopping along Fifth Avenue and returning to Little Italy, to enjoy the sights, sounds, smells and tastes of the Feast of San Gennaro, for one last time before we flew home that evening.

CHAPTER 35

Sri Lanka (41) and The Maldives (19) – December 2014

This was it, we were about to complete our list, and visit the last two places that made up the Fifty. Sri Lanka had not been high on our own personal bucket list. In fact, I think that it's fair to say, it was very low down, mainly because of Richard's dislike of spicy food, and after his disappointment with India. Barry, my younger brother, spent his honeymoon with his first wife, on an accompanied tour around the island and he loved it. He went to Japan with Fi, his second wife, and they had a brilliant experience, travelling by themselves, visiting many areas without a guide.

We did not really fancy the cultural side of Sri Lanka – it just did not appeal – but we discovered that there were a lot of game parks and reserves, and we decided to turn our trip into a wildlife visit. I used Responsibletravel.com to search for a company that was able to arrange a private tour that suited our plans. We have used this website on several occasions, initially for our Northern Lights holiday in Lapland, and then our private tour of Myanmar, a wildlife tour of Sri Lanka, and our planned tour of Indochina, which, unfortunately we had to cancel. This website has access to many specialist companies, who offer eco-tours with many different alternative tours for singles, couples and families. You basically select where you want to go, what you want to do, how you want to do it, and then find the ideal match from the list of possibilities. You have the opportunity to join an organised group tour or push the boat out and have a private, personalised tour, that meets your requirements perfectly. Rosy at Responsibletravel.com is very good, and will help and assist you to make the right selection. We have found the options to be very reasonably priced, even for private tours, and the agencies are really co-operative, making several adjustments and changes until you finalise your ideal trip.

I did a lot of research myself, looking at different game reserves, hotels, sights and locations in Sri Lanka, that I thought that this would be of interest to us. I studied tours offered by the big agencies which are not flexible to change, so I could get ideas of the route that we would take, and the best options for stopping and viewing. I have followed this technique for many of our road trips; including Italy, New England and New Zealand, and I will do this again when I finally start to plan our Route 66 trip in the USA, hopefully in the summer of 2020.

We flew out with British Airways, on a very crowded flight which stopped in Male, Maldives before continuing to Colombo, Sri Lanka. The majority of the passengers left the plane in the Maldives, which meant that when we arrived in Colombo, that there were not many on the flight so we got through immigration quickly and our luggage arrived just after we did. As we came out of the airport we easily found our representative, who took us to meet our driver for the trip, Manoj. Quickly loading the car with our luggage, the front seat had to be used, as well as having a packed boot, we set off to our first stop on the tour, The Beach, just outside of Colombo. This short journey was selected so that we could get over the long, overnight flights before starting the main tour the next day. When we arrived, it was a full moon and this results in a day's holiday in Sri Lanka, and they don't serve alcohol on these auspicious dates. Luckily, we had the rum that we had bought at duty free, so we were able to get our usual sundowner in our room, so we did not cause any offence to the locals.

We had an early start the next day; meeting our driver at eight-thirty a.m., after a very good breakfast at The Beach we drove north through the Sri Lankan countryside but, I'm afraid to say, we didn't see much of it, as both Richard and I nodded off. After three hours, we stopped at our first location on the itinerary, where we would be doing white water rafting. Neither of us had ever done anything like that before, and, as Richard cannot swim and I am not confident in the water, we were both rather nervous of exactly what would be involved.

At our stop, there were facilities to change but we already had swimwear on under our regular clothes, so very quickly we got transferred to our truck and drove seven kilometres to our starting point. On arrival, we had to walk down a steep slope to get to the water's edge. I suppose really in order to go rafting, the river needs to be going through a gorge of some kind to create the rapids and the white water. There were several rubber dinghies waiting to be launched, and quite a lot of people milling around, but we had a dinghy to ourselves, with two guides to paddle with us. After some brief instructions, we were off, hitting white water almost straight away. I was sitting on a bench seat in the centre of the dinghy, while Richard was near the front, and we were both given paddles to help. I can honestly say that we got soaked! Our clothes did not matter; we were in costumes, but our trainers were absolutely sodden and Richard did not have another pair packed! When we came to the rapids, which were much fiercer than the regular white water, we were told to crouch down and hold on, while the professionals steered us through it. I kept slipping off my bench and ending up in the bottom of the dingy, and I really struggled to lift myself up to regain my seat – very undignified!

Along our trip we saw the spot which was used for the location of the bridge in the film "Bridge on the River Kwai" – they used this location, as there was more jungle to give better affects than the actual river in Thailand. We also saw some wildlife, including a kingfisher, a kite, some cormorants and something swimming in the river, although we could not make out what it was! When we arrived back at our camp from where we initially departed from, we were able to dry off a bit, change and have some lunch, before we set off on the road again and headed into the mountains.

As we got higher, the weather and temperature changed, going from sunny and warm to misty and dull, but not too humid and sticky. The scenery was very pleasant, and we stopped to view a waterfall in the distance and some of the tea plantations which line the hillsides. We arrived at The Grand, Nuwara Eliya at four-thirty p.m. and had some tea before being shown to our room.

Nuwara Eliya is a town high in the hills, and offers the city residents a respite from the heat of the lower regions. The Grand lives up to its name and is the grandest hotel in the town, offering a colonial style of accommodation. I felt as though we had stepped back in time, to when the British forces occupied the country. The benefit for me was that the hotel was beautifully decorated for Christmas with trees, a grotto, and loads of ornaments, all around the public areas. We even had piped Christmas music in our rooms, but this very soon got switched off, as it was a bit overpowering!

We stayed in Nuwara Eliya for two nights as it is such a lovely location and an excellent hotel. It should have been Manoj's day off, but he arranged to take us to a tea plantation to see the factory, Pedro, and to do some tea tasting. The tour around the factory and the information we were given regarding the production of tea was actually very interesting. This was followed with a drive around the town where the main employment sector was anything related to tea! Pedro employed thirteen hundred people at the factory and plantation, including seven hundred pickers and there were lots of other plantations dotted across the hillside. As I have said, this location is very popular as a holiday destination for Sri Lankans, who want to escape the heat of the cities and with it being so green and the many buildings being mock Tudor, it is known as Little England.

Our hotel offered manicured lawns and topiary, and the town had a golf club, racecourse and cricket club. The town centre was run down and resembled places we had seen in India. Many of the locals are Indian in appearance with dark hair and dark skin and the women wear saris.

We left Nuwara Eliya the next day, and we headed for our first wildlife stop – Udawalawe National Park. This small reserve – thirty-one thousand hectares in area – is famous for its elephant population and is the only park in Sri Lanka that guarantees a sighting. We drove through the mountains to get to our pick up point and the views were lovely, especially a big valley which we viewed from the high road. We stopped at a waterfall which was located by the side of the road. There were lots of cars and buses stopped, with tourists enjoying the falls, which were quite spectacular with the road being so close – the river flowed underneath the road. As a result of this anticipated stop, there were many locals' selling their wares, begging and offering crystalline rocks for free. I will not fall for that again after Cairo, but I feel so ignorant when I appear to refuse a gift, but I know that they will want something in return.

We continued until we arrived at a junction on the road, where we would transfer to another vehicle to take us to our next stop for two nights, Mahoora Luxury Tented Camp. We did not take all the luggage as we needed to travel light, just our cameras and one bag between us; the rest remained in the car, and we went with Manoj to the place where we were staying. We continued for about an hour in the jeep until we turned off the road, and headed into a field where our camp was located. I had researched this place before we had booked the holiday and it looked very good, especially as its location was supposed to be right by the side of the National Park. But when we arrived, my jaw dropped! This luxury camp was actually very basic! I had expected it to be like The Hide in Zimbabwe – now that *IS* a luxury tented camp. But Mahoora consisted of about eight tents for guests plus others further on for the staff, a covered reception area and that was it! There was no main house for meals or a place to relax and to meet other guests, and certainly no bar or restaurant. When we were taken to our tent I could not believe how sparsely furnished it was – a small tent with one chair and a small table where we could put our bag so that it was off the floor; a double bed which did not look very comfortable; a curtain covering the "bathroom" area which had a camp basin and no hot water, a western toilet which did not flush and a shower stand with a shower head to hold over you. There was nowhere to hang your clothes, and we had to live out of the bag during our stay. Outside the tent were two folding chairs and a couple of pairs of flip flops which you needed to use when entering the tent, so that you did not take mud or insects inside with you. There was electricity in the tent, but this was only available between six a.m. and eleven p.m. after that you were in the dark!

We had arrived in time for lunch and as we were the only people at the camp at this time, we ate on our own on an outside table – luckily the weather was fine! At two-thirty p.m. we went on our first safari drive and I got my second disappointment. The camp had been forced to move by the Sri Lankan government, and was now located a thirty minute drive from the park – this was one of the reasons why the camp was so basic, where we thought it was a permanent camp, it wasn't – it was actually semi mobile! There was only Richard and I, on the drive with Dumi, our camp guide, and when we entered the park a spotter was allocated to our jeep, to assist in locating wildlife and making suggestions on where to go. Almost as soon as we entered the park, we saw a small herd of elephant. During our drive we saw lots of these gentle giants – single males and families, including some really young calves. When I call them gentle giants, they are gentle most of the time but you need to give them a lot of respect and caution, as they can be aggressive, destructive and dangerous if provoked or spooked in any way.

Our other sightings on this drive consisted of black hare; buffalo; spotted deer and birdlife. To be honest, birds make up the majority of sightings on safari in Sri Lanka, and some of them are really spectacular with their iridescent colours and calls. I made a list of every bird we did see, but I am not going to recite them here, as they won't mean anything to anyone, but there were certain birds that were really beautiful, and we saw a lot of them including the Blue Tailed Bee Eater, White Throated Kingfisher and Green Bee Eater, and I finally saw a bird I have read about, the Hoopoe. We stopped for tea and biscuits at the lake, where there were lots of water birds including a Spoonbill. As we headed out of the park, the heavens opened! We had to have the sides brought down on our jeep, which meant we could not see a thing – luckily, it was right at the end of our drive that this took place, otherwise we would have had a pretty dismal safari drive!

When we got back to the camp it was totally dry – the rain had been very localised close to the park. Others had now returned to the camp and they were sitting around having herbal tea and biscuits and we joined them for a while, to listen to their tales of sightings in the park. We returned to our tent in the dark, where we had to go through a ritual of having our feet washed in a basin outside our lodgings. I did not like this as it seemed very demeaning, having someone crouch-down and wash my dirty, smelly feet! We did not have time to shower as dinner was due to be served at seven-thirty p.m. and we only had twenty minutes to get ready! By now it was pitch black and the makeshift paths were lit by oil lamps to guide us to the campfire, where we had a drink before dinner. It was very strange as it seemed as though the camp purposely kept the guests apart even though we had all been chatting nicely just moments earlier! I certainly could not complain about the evening meal, which was five courses and served with a very nice wine, although the food could have been a little warmer, but we have that problem in so many places. When we finally retired to bed, we took a bottle of coke with us, and sat out on our chairs listening to the noises of the dark which was mainly dogs barking from the nearby village and chanting of Buddhists from the monastery.

We were up early the next day, five a.m., which is normal for a safari. We retraced our steps from the day before, with a fast drive to the National Park and it was light by the time we had entered it. Because of all the rain the previous day, the roads were very muddy and you could see numerous footprints, including a set of three leopard tracks, which really excited our guide and spotter! We continued our journey, and came to a rocky outcrop and sitting on top, in the early morning sunshine, was a leopard! It had its back to us, but kept turning around to look at us, and all the other jeeps that were parked up on the road, trying to get the best view. It was great to see the leopard but what was not good was the way that the drivers of the jeeps kept pushing-in, to try and get the best view, with no consideration for the occupants of the vehicles who kept being blocked off by new arrivals. As we manoeuvred to try and get a better view, after being obstructed by yet another jeep, we realised that there was another leopard in a tree, and we were able to watch it climb down before disappearing into the undergrowth. We were told that this family consisted of a mother and two cubs, that were almost fully grown. We did get another sighting of a leopard walking away over the outcrop – we weren't sure whether this was the third member of the family or the same one we had seen earlier, sunning itself. We were told by our guide that leopards are actually quite rare in this park, so we were very lucky to see three. He re-emphasised that, as the day before, we had seen a "tusker" and there were only five of these in the park. The Sri Lankan elephant is smaller than its other Asian relations and it does not normally have any tusks, but due to interbreeding with Indian elephants, some have now started to develop tusks, and this is what we saw the previous day.

Most of the sightings that we saw over the rest of our drive were bird life. There were hundreds of peacocks in the park, which we found exciting at first, but after seeing so many of them, we started to ignore them. They were everywhere, even sitting on branches in trees, which was quite bizarre at first, as they are such big birds but even this grew tiresome. We did see a male performing its mating dance with a fully stretched tail and scuffling around the female in a frenzied manner, trying to attract her attention – this was different, and we sat there for a while, watching this performance before heading back to our camp for breakfast, arriving back at ten a.m.

We knew that we would be going out on another drive later in the afternoon and we had hoped to have a rest before setting off again, but Dumi had other ideas. He turned up at our tent with several books on Sri Lankan birds and mammals, expecting us to read them before we set off again. He even provided us with bean bags, to be able to do this whilst sitting outside in the shade of a tree, rather than lying on the bed! I did try, but we were both so tired that we ended up having a sleep instead!

After lunch at one-thirty p.m. we came back to our tent, and the heavens opened! – I have never seen so much rain fall in such a short time, it was a deluge! We had a stream form around our tent, as if it was a castle moat, but when it started to come through the canvas roof of the tent, dripping onto the cameras, was when we sprang into action! The rain was collecting in a huge dip in the roof, which was getting bigger and bigger, and we pushed the bulge out, to get rid of all the water collecting there, but by this time the waterproof canvas was no longer working, and the dripping got worse and worse.

We did not think that we would do the drive in the rain as we would have to have the sides of the jeep down and it would be impossible to see any wildlife at all, but we were wrong. At two-thirty p.m. the jeep was reversed towards our tent so that we only had a very short walk to climb aboard in the pouring rain! However, by the time we got to the park it had stopped raining, and we drove down towards the Walawe River. There was not much going on by the river, or in the park, and our only new sighting was a large monitor lizard.

When we got back to the camp just after five p.m. we were told that we were moving to a new tent, as ours was no longer waterproof, and we needed to transfer everything. But instead of allowing us to go to our tent in our shoes and start packing, we had to go to our new tent, and have the ritual feet washing, before waddling back through the mud in our flip flops! We were then told we had five minutes to get ready for dinner at seven-thirty p.m.. We said that we needed more time and we were given fifteen minutes to wash and change. It had rained on and off since our return to camp, and because of this we ate under canvas that night in a large tent, but we discovered at that point that we were then the only ones staying at the camp for this, our second night; the others had moved on. The meal was good, five courses again with wine, and, as we were the only guests, we got a lot of attention from all the staff. We retired to our new tent with two cokes, to be able to have our sundowners before we finally retired to bed, absolutely exhausted.

We left the camp the following day, but we had one more visit in the area before we would meet up with Manoj again – the Elephant Transit Camp. The lake in the National Park had been created by the building of a dam, and we crossed this to get to the transit camp. There were a couple of elephants on the grassy bank between the waters' edge and the road but one elephant was standing right by the side of the road. As the side was on a slope, his body was below the line of the road but his trunk was outstretched in front of him and rested on the path by the roadside. Dumi told us that this particular elephant had learned that if he is patient and stands like this for a long time, people will come along and feed him so he does not have to work at finding his own food. It was sad to see this magnificent beast begging for food, which is basically what he had learned to do.

We arrived at the camp at eight forty-five a.m., ready for the feeding ritual at nine a.m., the reason for our visit today. We were told where to stand to get the best view and at nine a.m., we saw the young elephants start their parade, walking in single file, like Colonel Hathi's troop in Disney's Jungle Book, before coming into the feeding area. This camp had been created to house, to care for and, eventually, to repatriate these orphans back into the wild. The inhabitants came from all over the island, and were at various stages of development. The first to enter the arena were the very young elephants – they were so little and covered in dark fur, one seemed to have a Mohican haircut! He dashed forward to get his quota of milk from the machine, and when he was fed, he kept going back again and again to get more, but was moved on each time by the helpers – it was comical to watch his efforts, but at the same time very sad that his mother was not there to be able to offer him his breakfast every day.

The older elephants had leaves and branches to munch on which they did with gusto – they were obviously all hungry little animals! There were around forty to fifty elephants in the camp, and they dashed into the feeding ground roaring with delight, and sometimes squabbling between one another, as they headed for the milk station. Those that came in at the end missed out on the vegetation, as the others had eaten it. I hoped that they reversed the order of entry, when they came back for their afternoon feed, so that those that missed out in the morning would manage to get their share later in the day. It was sad to see so many orphan elephants, but it was good to know that they were being cared for and eventually returned to live in the wild and to fend for themselves. We stayed watching them until they all left the arena, retracing their steps out of the gate, along the path and back to their pens.

Manoj was waiting for us, and we transferred our luggage back into the car and headed off to Yala, a journey of around one and a half hours. After we went through a large town called Tissi, we turned off the main road and went over a very rough, bumpy temporary road that shook us to our core, eventually arriving at the much larger permanent camp, the Cinnamon Wild Hotel, just five minutes from the entrance to Yala National Park. We had a round chalet there which was so much more comfortable than the tents at Mahoora. This time we had closet space, air conditioning, a proper shower with hot water, and a flushing toilet.

After lunch, at two-thirty p.m. we went on a game drive and we had a private jeep again, although this time we were accompanied by Manoj, our camp guide and a spotter. We drove around the park for a long time – our only new sightings were Ruddy Mongoose and wild pigs, so, a disappointing afternoon. We did see a couple of elephants in the distance and lots of birds again, but this huge park seemed to be almost devoid of animals! It's certainly no Ulusaba in South Africa which is where we had had our best safari drive. We stopped for a drink of tea at a beach with beautiful sea views. This particular location was hit by the Boxing Day tsunami in 2004, which killed around two hundred and thirty thousand people in fourteen countries. There was a memorial there to those who had lost their life on this beach – nineteen Japanese, twenty locals, and two foreigners.

We were suddenly called back at our jeep as a message had come over the radio, saying that a leopard had been spotted, and once on board, we sped off to the location given. We were not on our own. There were dozens of vehicles all vying to get the best location. While our spotter and driver were concentrating on trying to see the leopard in the bushes, Richard saw it cross the road a little further on, and we quickly leapt into action to get ahead of the crowd and follow our prey. I hated this chase and what I considered to be harassment of this poor creature, but to be honest, he could not have cared less. He just sauntered through the bushes to hide from view again.

We had time to change before we went for dinner. The Cinnamon Wild Hotel was a large camp, and there was a main building where you found reception, a shop, the bar and the restaurant. The meals were all buffet style, but there was plenty of choice between Western cuisine and local food; in particular curries. We had to be escorted back to our little cabin, but we sat outside on our covered veranda having our sundowners until suddenly we were ordered to go inside, as there was an elephant in the camp. Sure enough, within minutes of us taking refuge, a huge bull elephant appeared right by the side of our cabin, taking a liking to our tree, which he practically destroyed within minutes! We turned the lights out and very cautiously opened the door, just a little, to peer out at him, just ten feet away from us. Quite a thrilling end to our day!

To be honest, the next day was very disappointing, as we hardly saw any game at all, despite starting our drive very early at five-thirty a.m. Even the bird life had decided to disappear that morning! In the afternoon we went to Bundela, a small park on the coast, but it was an hour's drive from Yala. We did see crocodile, tortoise, black necked hare and lots of birds, but there was no big game at all, and a bit of a waste of time. I think that we would have preferred to have had the afternoon to ourselves to rest, read and relax.

On our final day, we agreed with our spotter to do an extended game drive, taking a breakfast box with us, and leaving at five-thirty a.m., but returning in the afternoon. This meant that we would be able to drive a lot deeper into the park, and go to areas not normally visited by those on a morning safari. That was the plan, but we had a new spotter, and he basically led us to exactly the same places we had been to on our previous drives. It seemed as though we just drove around and around in circles trying to find leopard, and I didn't think that our new spotter had any idea how to locate a big cat! I became annoyed, as he spoke mainly to the driver and Manoj in the local language, and hardly gave us any information at all. We eventually found a car park, full of jeeps and buses, all parked around a grassy area, surrounded by bush, where leopards had been spotted. We had no idea where to look, until I shouted at our spotter to get him to speak English and to tell us where we needed to look!

There were two leopards, a male and a female, and we watched them cross the grass, disappear into the bush and then go their separate ways; the male climbing into a tree, while the female sauntered through a herd of spotted deer that raised their alarm, and then she also climbed a tree and was hidden from view. We did get the odd sighting of these beautiful animals, despite jeeps jostling around and in front of us, and our driver parking in a manner where he could see them, but those in the back were completely obstructed by others. Not a pleasant experience really – much better at Ulusaba, South Africa. We got fed up with going around in circles, and seeing nothing of any interest so we asked to return to the camp a lot earlier than we had planned, getting back at around noon.

That evening, whilst we were sitting out having our Cuba Libras, a herd of wild pigs wandered past, but did not cause us any problems at all. Then, while we were getting ready for dinner, we got a knock on the door to say we had to stay inside – our elephant was back! and he finished off the tree that had been damaged the previous night.

That evening, we opted have do the Dine in the Dark dinner which cost us sixty dollars each. When we arrived at our meeting point, we were led down to the beach by the lake, where a table was placed, surrounded by candles or lamps. The water's edge and beach were well lit, which was good as this meant that we would be able to see crocodiles or buffalo emerge from the lake before we got attacked! I didn't think that this dinner would have taken place if there was any danger, but we were the only ones anywhere near the lake, sitting in the dark, eating a sumptuous meal! We had our own private waiter and chef, who served us a fabulous four-course meal, cooked in the open air on a barbecue, located just behind our table. It was very good – location, food and service, and it was certainly a memorable evening, our last night in Yala.

We were looking forward to our lie-in the following morning as we were leaving later that day, and did not need to be up early for a game drive but we were rudely awakened at six a.m. by such a commotion which sounded like somebody, or something, was in our roof rafters! When I went into the bathroom and saw a little face appear in the window I realised who our attackers were – a troop of monkeys (Gray Langurs, to be precise) were going crazy all around our cabin. They jumped from tree to roof to fence, making such a racket. At one point they started to wreck our patio furniture, throwing the table on its side, and even rolling it away! We tried to shoo them away, but they sat there just watching us, showing no fear whatsoever! The way that they watched us – it felt like we were in the cage and they were the spectators. It was an amazing experience but, at the same time, a little unnerving, as there were so many of them.

At nine-thirty a.m., we left for our journey to Galle which is located on the coast. We didn't stop and arrived at our hotel, the Galle Fort Hotel, at one p.m. This was a lovely hotel located in the old four-hundred year old fort, which had been converted to a very nice colonial boutique hotel. The design was a little like a Moroccan Riad, with rooms on all four sides, looking onto a central garden where the swimming pool was located. The room had high ceilings and was decorated with teak wooden furnishings. Our room, number LS2, was on two floors, and was beautifully furnished and had shutters instead of curtains.

We had the afternoon to ourselves and we had a stroll around the shops, which were plentiful in the beach town. Some of them had some beautiful clothes, and others offered a big selection of local teas. There are ramparts in the old town which can be climbed, but we found it to be very hot and did not want to get too exhausted. We ate in our hotel that evening and, even though there were others staying at the hotel, we were the only ones in the restaurant, which surprised us as we had not seen many other options in town for dining.

The next day we were back to our early starts, as Manoj picked us up at five-thirty a.m., to drive us further up the coast to Mirissa, where we joined a whale watching excursion. The boat was quite large, with a big group of Indians and a few other

Europeans, but we managed to find seats at the back, which gave us the opportunity to be able to see from either side of the boat. Unfortunately, there wasn't much to see! The problem with whale watching is that when these huge mammals' surface, they don't hang around for long, and if you are looking in the wrong direction at the time, you miss the spectacle. We did see blows of water and the occasional arched back – Richard even saw one dive, including a raised tail. We were told that the whales that we saw were Brides Whale and Blue Whale – the largest living animal on the planet – and that was the reason for visiting this area of Sri Lanka.

When we returned to our hotel we were both exhausted due to the early start, long drive and the heat, so we just relaxed in our air conditioned room, to recharge our batteries. We decided to eat out that night in Galle, and we wandered around inspecting different menus before we settled on a lovely place we found called the Heritage Café, which had tables surrounded by pots of plants, giving you the feeling that you were sitting in a garden. We had wine and drinks back at the hotel, before we retired to bed, exhausted, at nine-thirty p.m.

The next day we left Galle to drive inland again, into the rainforest, to stay at a place called Boulder Garden in Sinharaja. To get to the hotel, we had to leave the main road and travel along a very rough and bumpy track, before we reached the car park, that was located below the raised up reception area. We had to climb many steps to get to our room, and the main lodge area, which is like no other hotel we had ever stayed in. As you can probably guess from the hotel's name, the lounge and the rooms are built into the rocks. To be honest, the lounge area and the dining room were open-air and protected from the elements by a rock overhang. Our lodge, the largest at the hotel, was built into the rock, and had a balcony looking out onto the rainforest, and we also had a rooftop patio. The room was equipped with a fan, TV and fridge so, although it was quite basic, we had all the mod cons to keep us comfortable for our one night stay.

There was an option to take a walk in the rainforest in the afternoon, but we decided against this for five very good reasons:
1. It was likely to rain – well we were in the rainforest!
2. The park was a thirty-minute drive away, and we did not want to put Manoj through that awful hotel road more than he needed to.
3. I am frightened of leeches, and we had been told there was a chance of one attaching itself to us
4. The park only offered bird life and we had seen enough of our feathered friends in the other parks
5. We preferred to sit and drink wine than walk!!!

So, instead of visiting the rainforest and we did not need to visit it as we were already in it, we went to the lounge and enjoyed two bottles of wine, taking in the sights and sounds of this unique place. It did start to rain while we were drinking and it was torrential, with thunder and lightning, but we were protected from this deluge by the rocky overhang, which, as the guidebook states, is like sitting under the prow of the Titanic. We returned to the same location in the evening for our dinner, where we met another couple who were staying overnight. All in all, a very pleasant rest in a really unique setting.

It was our last day in Sri Lanka and we headed for the motorway, which would take us back to the capital, Colombo. As we approached, we hit heavy traffic for the first time on this holiday, and this slowed us down, so as it took us three hours before we finally got out at Independence Square for a short tour of the city. There was a nice mix of old colonial buildings from the time of the British occupation, and new buildings; in particular a theatre and conference centre donated by the Chinese. The traffic was very, very slow in the town centre, and we decided to go the hotel rather than spend time at the shopping centre. I must have been ill – I love shopping! We were staying at Tintagel, the former home of the President and Prime Ministers of Sri Lanka, and even as we approached this beautiful building I knew that it was going to be the best place that we had stayed in, during our sojourn. The conversion of the building to an eighteen-room, five-star hotel had been done by an Australian, and he had utilised the small rooms downstairs to create intimate public areas, including a library, whilst keeping aside the large, high ceilinged rooms upstairs, to create luxurious bedrooms. The décor had a hint of the orient, with big, wooden chests and wall hangings and decorated with dark wood and cream walls. The bathroom was huge, with double sinks, a bath and a shower. Talk about saving the best for last – this hotel was stunning!

We relaxed in our comfortable room all afternoon, before changing to go for dinner at The Gallery, a restaurant owned by the same Australian who had created the hotel. Manoj collected us and took us to this fine dining restaurant, which was a treat arranged by our tour operator, Ampersand, and a total surprise to us. The restaurant was very modern, built partially inside and partially outside. It was dark and brooding and decorated with modern art which was for sale. The meal was lovely, probably the best we had had, during our stay in Sri Lanka.

We had to leave very early the next day, being picked up at four-thirty a.m., for our drive to the airport, our last time with Manoj. He lives in Colombo and had spent the evening at his home with his wife and three children. I'm sure that he was glad to see them. We gave him, what we thought, was a good tip, as he had done a lot for us over the last ten days. Arriving at the airport was a little chaotic, with people going through scanners, but not the luggage and then checking in for our flight with Sri Lankan Airlines to The Maldives. I slept most of the flight, the consequence of getting up so early.

As we were at the front of the plane in Business Class; when we arrived in Male, we were first off, and went through passport control very quickly. We had to wait for our luggage though, and, despite us having "priority" stickers, it still took a long time to arrive.

But, once we came out of the airport, we privately celebrated as we had just completed our quest of visiting the **fifty places to see before you die!**

The Maldives are made up of hundreds of little islands, many of which just have a single hotel resort built on them offering luxurious, five star accommodation. To get to the resorts, you have to either fly or travel by boat. We were staying at Baros and our transfer was by speedboat. The journey was very fast and rather bumpy, as we skimmed over the top of the waves. When we arrived at Baros we were greeted by quite a few members of staff and taken to check-in where we had a glass of champagne. This greeting was really nice, making you feel very welcome and rather special. We were given a tour of the resort, which did not take long, as the island is quite small, but the hotel had several eating options, which is the reason why I selected this particular hotel, and then we were taken to our over-water villa which was beautiful.

It was actually quite modern, with wooden floors and furniture; a large bed situated in the centre of the room looking out onto the veranda and the sea, and a very large bathroom with an open shower, as this was very private and not looked onto by anyone. We also had a fridge and a wine chiller, and the large teak deck outside had a lounging bed for two, sun loungers, chairs, a table and a sun umbrella. Our only disappointment was the weather, as the sky was very grey, and as a result of this, the sea was also grey – not what I had expected.

We went to reception for a drink and booked the restaurants where we wanted to dine during our short stay. Both lunch and dinner that day was in Lime as Cayenne had an Asian buffet that evening which was not really our cup of tea. The food was good with enough choice to satisfy our picky appetite – we were very pleased to see Pinot Grigio on the wine list, at just thirty nine dollars a bottle, which we thought was very reasonable and it meant that we would not break the bank with our drinks bill during our stay. It rained in the afternoon, but we were in our villa, so we did not get wet; it just stopped us from exploring our resort. We managed to get to the restaurant in the evening, without getting wet, but the heavens opened while we were there, and we were very glad that they had umbrellas located at every public building, which we needed to make our return journey.

The next day was mixed again – some rain, mostly dry, but the sky was still grey. It was warm enough and did not stop us from enjoying this restful element of our holiday; it just meant that our photos were not particularly colourful. There is an aquatic centre at the resort where you could book excursions to go diving, fishing, or take boat trips to other islands, but I just went there to get some flippers and a snorkel. I am not a strong swimmer, but I wanted to go into the water at least once during our stay, and hopefully see as much as we had done in Bora Bora. The water was lovely and warm, and was quite shallow around the villa, so I felt safe enough that, if I got into any danger, I was able to put my feet down and stand up. I found a nice piece of coral, that had a multitude of little fish swimming around it, and spent some time watching them, before I climbed our stairs and sat out on our veranda. I made the mistake of not realising that, just because it was grey and cloudy, the sun was still really strong and I burnt my shoulders as I did not put suntan lotion on – when will I ever learn!

In the evening we dined in the grill at Cayenne, and had a very romantic meal sitting on the balcony, close to the sea, looking onto the lighthouse. In the distance you could see the lights from other hotel resorts, which were not visible during the day, as they were so far away from us. We were able to peer over the side of the balcony into the water underneath, as it was lit up to enable you to see into the depths below, and we saw both a sting ray and a shark swim underneath us while we ate our meal.

There was a spa at our hotel – to be honest, I think that every resort in the Maldives will offer a spa and an aquatic centre and Baros was certainly no exception. I had made an appointment to have the Signature Massage, but I was concerned after getting burnt the previous day that a massage might be too painful. I was wrong, the massage was wonderful and relaxing, and the cooling balms that they used actually made me feel a lot better.

The weather was much better that day, with patchy blue skies and we made the most of it by swimming, sunbathing and enjoying a walk around the resort, sitting out with drinks at the Sails Bar and having our sundowners on the veranda; the first opportunity to do this due to the rain on previous nights. In the evening, we went for dinner at the Teppanyaki and enjoyed the meat feast at one hundred and thirty five dollars for the two of us. As is normal with this style of dining, we sat with two other couples, one from Vienna and another couple who were originally from Malaysia but now live in London. The chef was very entertaining, juggling his knives, tossing the eggs, and certainly making the meal quite a spectacle. It was really a very enjoyable evening and, back at our villa, we were able to sit out in darkness, as it was still lovely and warm and have our Cuba Libras before retiring for the night.

Our final day at Baros certainly offered us the best in sunshine with beautiful clear, cloudless skies, which meant that the sea was very blue and clear – beautiful! This was what I had imagined the Maldives would be like and, after the first few days being wet and grey, it was really nice to be able to see this tropical paradise at its best. Whether it was because the sun was out, I'm not sure, but we had some large fish swimming under our villa, rather than the little tiddlers we had been watching on other days.

In the afternoon, we took the excursion to return to the main island of Male, which is the capital of the Maldives and where the airport is located. It cost us seventy dollars each to do this sightseeing and shopping excursion but, compared to the other excursions on offer at the hotel, this tour was probably the best value for money. There were two other couples on the speedboat, but one of them went shopping rather than doing the tour. We each had our own guide, which meant that we could go at our own pace and visit the places that were of interest to us – especially important when it came to be doing the shopping element.

Our guide, Amez, spoke good English and he was interesting to listen to, while he told us about the history of this little country. There was not a lot to see, but what was of interest was located in a small area and we went to two mosques, various government and presidential buildings, a tomb, the fish and fruit market and a memorial to the martyrs who were killed by the Tamil Tigers, when they invaded the island in 1988. We did find out that there are around twelve hundred islands that make up the country but only a hundred or so have hotels on them, and many of the others are actually uninhabited. The shops were not very exciting, mainly local craft shops, and they all sold pretty much the same things – we went into three, but did not bother with any more as, from what we could see, there was nothing new to excite us in any of the others. We returned to the pier and waited for the others to join us, and then we sped back to Baros, giving us time to enjoy the beautiful sunset that evening from our deck.

On our final night; and we had saved the best restaurant for last, we dined at the Lighthouse, where they offered a fine dining experience. We had drinks first in the lounge, and then sat out on the upper deck, looking out over the sea towards Male and the other resort island – it was very romantic, and the food was beautiful! The weather was good enough for us to sit out at the villa, and enjoy our last evening at that beautiful resort. I understand why people keep returning to the Maldives. It is so peaceful, romantic and relaxing, and it was ideal for us to wind down in, after the hectic tour and early mornings in Sri Lanka.

We left Baros the next day, after a relaxing morning as we were due to be transferred to Male and the airport at one-thirty p.m. We paid our bill, which was a big one, for just four nights – two thousand dollars, but this included all of our meals, drinks, massages, purchases and excursions. As we left, many of the staff accompanied us down to the pier, which was a lovely touch. As we boarded our speed boat to jet off to Male, they stood in a row on the jetty and waved us off. They remained there, waving, for as long as we could see them and, I assume, that they could see us. It was a wonderful farewell, making us feel more like family than just residents. I would love for us to be able to return here as it was a wonderful hotel and an amazing experience. I am so glad that the Maldives were the last of the fifty places that we visited, as it was very special, and will remain in my memories for a long, long time.

Epilogue

I hope you have found this personal record an interesting one and that it has given you the urge to travel and experience the world in more detail. I suppose that you could call it our bucket list, but theoretically, it wasn't *our* top fifty places, as it was decided and voted for by the British public for the BBC's television programme. But, while we have been ticking off these selected places, we have been able to do everything, well almost everything, that we wanted to do; so I suppose that we have really done our own bucket list. We are still travelling; finding new places to visit, ticking off more countries and enjoying meeting new people from around the world.

We have travelled around the world on one holiday, when we flew to Sydney via Hong Kong; we spent twelve days in New Zealand before boarding a cruise around New Caledonia and Fiji; then flying home from Fiji via Los Angeles. But our travels over the years have taken us East and West, as we clocked up the miles, ticking off each of the Fifty. This is the reason why I have called this story "Around the World in Fifty Sites". I would like to explain the reason for the subtitle – well this is **my story**, recorded in my travel journals and retold in my words; it is **our journey**, as Richard and I have been to all fifty sites together, since we met in August 2000; and it is **your itinerary** as the British public voted for the fifty and we have stuck to that selection, even when it has been amended slightly in later years.

There are a few places on the BBC's list which we don't necessarily agree with; we think that there are some alternatives that should have appeared in the top fifty. For example, we think that Barbados is there to represent the Caribbean Islands, and in our opinion, there are other islands which are a lot more beautiful and have more to offer than Barbados; for example Saint Lucia. I know when we say to fellow travellers that Barbados is one of the fifty places to see before you die, they are very quick to disagree and come up with their own opinions. I think that this is because of Barbados being very British that it was chosen. The other islands have more of a feel of America, France or the Netherlands.

We agree that Rome, Paris and Venice are the real highlight cities in Europe, taken from the list, but we think that there are a lot more that exceed the benefits and the sights that you find in Barcelona. These include Saint Petersburg, Istanbul, Florence, Budapest, Dubrovnik and Vienna. Don't get me wrong, there is nothing wrong with Barcelona, and we have returned several times. We just think that some of the other cities that I have mentioned offer more. The Matterhorn is a fabulous individual mountain that towers above the surrounding peaks in the Alps and Zermatt is a perfect Swiss town that is free of cars. You can only get there by a special train, and then you are transferred to your hotel by little electric buses or horse drawn carts; so with both of these together, we cannot think of a better natural sight that should be on the list.

We are not beach lovers, so it was difficult to tick off places like Bora Bora and the Maldives, but we added these onto other holidays and this way, we were able to visit these resort or beach locations. Bora Bora really is paradise and is so much more beautiful than Tahiti. It is on the other side of the world from us in the UK, and it takes several flights to get there, but it was worth it just to experience this little piece of heaven on earth for a few nights. With the Maldives, it can be added on to a trip to Sri Lanka, which is how we managed to visit and have this as our final destination of the fifty. But our views have changed in later years; probably an age thing, and we now actually enjoy restful holidays. I certainly would not say no to returning to French Polynesia, the Maldives or the Caribbean Islands, to enjoy a resort break, as we now recognise the benefits of a beautiful location, guaranteed sunshine and relaxing, five-star accommodation.

I am amazed that Japan was not on the list – maybe not many who voted had visited this amazing country that offers so much and is so totally different from British culture. We did a fully escorted tour of Japan in 2011, starting in Tokyo and staying in Kyoto, Hiroshima and Osaka. It was so different from anywhere else that we have visited. In particular, the restaurants! In the UK we have Japanese restaurants that will normally offer every dish that you associate with Japanese cuisine – sushi, teppanyaki, yakitori, tempura etcetera, but in Japan, each restaurant specialises in just one of these dishes and the whole menu is based on that dish. So, you have sushi restaurants, yakitori restaurants etcetera. A lot of them also have plastic replicas of the dish on show in the window of the restaurant and when you look at them, you are totally turned off trying any of the dishes, as they look so unappealing. We are not very adventurous with our food, but my younger brother, Barry, went on his honeymoon to Japan with his new wife, Fi, just before we went in 2011. They are a lot more adventurous, and they enjoyed the food very much, eating all manner of dishes, including eel! Food and wine can be expensive in Japan and, as we were eating teppanyaki a lot, we used up most of our budget on restaurant bills. We didn't starve, but we certainly did not put weight on whilst we toured the country.

One of our best holidays was in March 2014, when we had ten days touring Myanmar (Burma). This country had been closed to tourism for a long time. We first considered it back in 2001, and since then, it very rarely appeared in any of the travel brochures that we picked up. We went through Responsible Travel, an internet company that will put you in touch with travel companies that specialise in exotic holidays that are also environmentally friendly. This is how we found Odysseyworld, who tailor-made our trip to fit in the sites and the cities that we wanted to see, plus a bit more that we had not anticipated. We started in Yangon, the capital, and then travelled, by plane, to Bagan, Mandalay and Inle Lake. The hotels were very good, and offered good restaurants at a reasonable price – the food was more international than local, but at Inle Lake Resort and Spa, I did have a plate of local dishes and they were very good. We went to a restaurant in Yangon, Le Planteur, and had an excellent meal, probably one of the best we have eaten anywhere. It was fine dining offering international food with an Asian touch, and it was absolutely delicious! A word of warning if you go; they do not accept credit cards, it's cash only.

The country was so unspoilt as it is so new to tourism. You won't find a MacDonald's, a Starbuck's or a Pizza Hut, even in the capital. They drive on the right hand side of the road, but all the cars and trucks have the steering wheel on the right – this seemed so foreign to us, and quite hazardous, but they manage fine. In Bagan, there are thousands of temples, stupa's and pagoda's. It is a very rural town, quite different from Yangon, and does not yet have the thousands of tourists that you get in India or China. Inle Lake and the floating village was one of the most amazing sights that we have ever seen. A whole village including workshops, boat building, gardens, homes, restaurants and bars are all built on foundations of mud and hyacinth. It was green, organised and fascinating to watch, as we whizzed around the little channels in our very long, motorized canoe. This is also the home to the legendry one-legged fishermen, who balance on one leg, wrap their other leg around the tiller and move across the lake in this way, keeping both their hands free to cast their nets and catch the fish. Their whole life is spent on the lake, and they have all adapted, and they manage to live in relative comfort as they all had satellite dishes and electricity, and in a manner that would be so foreign to us. If you get the chance, you MUST go to Myanmar, before it becomes too popular and is spoilt by the increase in tourism.

Both North and South Island New Zealand appear on the list and the two islands are both very different. The South Island offers lots of adventurous activities, especially around Queenstown, and is also very rugged with high, snow-capped peaks and mystical, sheer cliffs at the fjords. When we went in 2013, Christchurch was still recovering from the earthquake that caused so much damage and loss of life the year earlier. Also, we did not have good weather, and therefore we did not see the real beauty of the country, that is known to so many of us, as being the backdrop used in the "Lord of the Rings" film trilogy. That was why we returned in 2017, to spend more time in South Island, and we loved it!

I do not agree with the new definition of naming Auckland as one of the fifty; it has to be North Island in general as, in my opinion, there is very little to see in the city itself. You just use it as a base, to visit the sights nearby. If you want to see somewhere beautiful in North Island, go to the Bay of Islands. We did this as an extension to our cruise, and we booked it through Viator.com. It included a night on a catamaran moored at one of the little islands and, after spending the afternoon and the evening enjoying this wonderful spot, you wake to the beautiful views at this unrivalled location. We then had two nights at a hotel giving us the opportunity to see other sites in the area, including the most northerly point of New Zealand.

I could go on for many, many more pages telling you about the sights that we have seen and the adventures that we have had. But here are just a few:

We have been on the Orient Express from Venice to London; the Rocky Mountaineer from Jasper to Vancouver and the Bullet Train from Osaka to Tokyo.

We have walked behind a waterfall in Canaima, Venezuela; we have sailed under waterfalls at Niagara in Canada, and we have flown over waterfalls at Iguazu, Brazil and Victoria Falls, Zimbabwe.

We have seen the sun rise over the Ganges in Varanasi, the sun set over the Irrawaddy in Bagan, and I have seen a total eclipse of the sun in Normandy, France.

We have fed tigers in Thailand, walked with lions in Zimbabwe, and ridden elephants in Thailand, Africa and India.

We have sailed around Cape Horn, and stood at the farthest point on the Cape of Good Hope. We have sailed through the Panama Canal, to cross from the Caribbean to the Pacific and we have floated over the Valley of the Kings in Egypt, in a balloon.

We have gazed at the Olgas at sunset in Australia, seen the Northern Lights perform their magical dance in Norway, and watched the sunset from our water bungalow in Bora Bora.

We have slept under canvas at the Masai Mara; stayed in luxurious five-star hotels all over the world, and lay back in the desert near Hurghada, to witness the Milky Way, and the myriad of stars that decorate a jet black, unpolluted night sky in Egypt.

We have tasted wine in the Languedoc region of France near Carcassonne; taken a private helicopter flight for wine tasting in the Hunter Valley near Sydney, and enjoyed a glass or two in Montevideo, Uruguay before dancing the tango.

We have toured around the back streets of Bangkok on a tuk-tuk; we have been driven to the banks of the Ganges in a rickshaw to witness the sunset ceremonies, and dodged the tourists in Florence, whilst we whizzed around on Segway's.

We have climbed the staircase to visit the City of the Dead on the Yangtze; we have skimmed along the snow in dog sleighs, and on snowmobiles in Finland, and we have released flaming lanterns into the night sky, at the Lantern Festival Pingxi in Taiwan.

We have been to over a hundred countries – and still counting; and many more territories and independencies. We have been to all seven continents; we have seen many of the most famous mountains in the world (Everest, Mount Fuji, Mount McKinley, Mount Kilimanjaro, Mount Annapurna, Mount Uluru, Mount Cook, Mount Etna) and sailed on many of the worlds' greatest rivers (the Amazon, the Yangtze, the Ganges, the Irrawaddy, the Nile, the Zambezi, the Mekong). We have sailed all the Seven Seas, crossing the equator on many occasions, and we have actually circumnavigated around the world.

We have done so much, but there is still so much more that we want to see and to experience – we're still travelling and we hope to continue to do so for many more years – and I will continue to write my diaries, as a memory of our journeys around the world, to be able to look back, to reminisce and to relive our amazing adventures.

Appendix 1

Fifty Places to see Before You Die – in order of preference

Original	Revised
1.	The Grand Canyon, USA
2.	The Great Barrier Reef, Australia
3.	Disney World, USA Florida, USA
4.	South Island, New Zealand
5.	Cape Town, South Africa
6.	The Golden Temple of Amritsar, India
7.	Las Vegas, USA
8.	Sydney, Australia
9.	New York, USA
10.	The Taj Mahal, India
11.	Lake Louise, Canada Canadian Rockies, Canada
12.	Uluru (Ayers Rock), Australia
13.	Chichen Itza, Mexico
14.	Machu Picchu, Peru
15.	Niagara Falls, Canada/USA
16.	Petra, Jordan
17.	The Pyramids, Egypt
18.	Venice, Italy
19.	The Maldives
20.	The Great Wall of China, China
21.	Victoria Falls, Zambia/Zimbabwe
22.	Hong Kong, China
23.	Yosemite National Park, USA
24.	Hawaii, USA

25.	North Island, New Zealand
	Auckland, New Zealand
26.	Iguazu Falls, Argentina/Brazil
27.	Paris, France
28.	Alaska, USA
29.	Angkor Wat, Cambodia
30.	Mount Everest, Nepal/Tibet
	The Himalayas, Nepal/Tibet
31.	Rio de Janeiro, Brazil
32.	Masai Mara, Kenya
33.	Galapagos Islands, Ecuador
34.	Luxor, Egypt
35.	Rome, Italy
36.	San Francisco, USA
37.	Barcelona, Spain
38.	Dubai, United Arab Emirates
39.	Singapore
40.	Seychelles
	La Digue, Seychelles
41.	Sri Lanka
42.	Bangkok, Thailand
43.	Barbados
44.	Reykjavik, Iceland
	Iceland
45.	Terracotta Army, China
46.	Matterhorn, Switzerland
	Zermatt, Switzerland
47.	Angel Falls, Venezuela
48.	Abu Simbel, Egypt
49.	Bali, Indonesia
50.	Bora Bora, French Polynesia
	French Polynesia

This list was taken from Travel Forums website to get the positions of each of the fifty sites, and to find the revised definitions. The original list was the location/site that was listed by the BBC in 2002. You can still search the internet by entering "BBC 50 Places to see before You Die", to obtain your own list.

The BBC also did a programme called "50 Things to do before You Die", but as this included the climbing of Kilimanjaro, I did not even consider this as a bucket list to follow!

APPENDIX 2

A list of countries that we have visited (and stepped foot on!)

1. Andorra
2. Antigua and Barbuda
3. Argentina
4. Australia
5. Austria
6. Bahamas
7. Barbados
8. Belgium
9. Belize
10. Benin
11. Botswana
12. Brazil
13. Bulgaria
14. Cambodia
15. Canada
16. Cape Verde
17. Chile
18. China
19. Colombia
20. Comoros
21. Costa Rica
22. Croatia
23. Cuba
24. Cyprus
25. Czech Republic
26. Denmark
27. Dominican Republic
28. Ecuador
29. Egypt
30. Estonia
31. Fiji
32. Finland
33. France
34. Germany
35. Ghana
36. Greece
37. Grenada
38. Haiti
39. Honduras
40. Hungary
41. Iceland
42. India
43. Indonesia
44. Ireland
45. Israel
46. Italy
47. Japan
48. Jordan
49. Kenya
50. Latvia
51. Lithuania
52. Luxemburg
53. Madagascar
54. Malaysia
55. Maldives
56. Malta

57. Mauritius
58. Mexico
59. Monaco
60. Montenegro
61. Morocco
62. Myanmar (Burma)
63. Namibia
64. Nepal
65. Netherlands
66. New Zealand
67. Nicaragua
68. Norway
69. Oman
70. Palestine
71. Panama
72. Peru
73. Poland
74. Portugal
75. Romania
76. Russia
77. Saint Kitts and Nevis
78. Saint Lucia
79. San Marino
80. Senegal
81. Serbia
82. Seychelles
83. Singapore
84. Slovakia
85. South Africa
86. South Korea
87. Spain
88. Sri Lanka
89. Swaziland
90. Sweden
91. Switzerland
92. Taiwan
93. Tanzania
94. Thailand
95. Togo
96. Trinidad and Tobago
97. Turkey
98. Ukraine
99. United Arab Emirates
100. United Kingdom
101. United States of America
102. Uruguay
103. Vanuatu
104. Vatican City State
105. Venezuela
106. Vietnam
107. Zambia
108. Zimbabwe

It is difficult to get a definitive answer as to how many countries there actually are, as new ones form occasionally and others are disputed. On a recent viewing of Wikipedia, it stated that there are one hundred and ninety three member states of the United Nations, two observer states – the Holy See and the State of Palestine and eleven other states – making two hundred and six. WW Travelog states that there are one hundred and ninety eight countries, which includes two that are disputed – Taiwan and Chechnya.

There are apps that you can download for free for iPad and iPhone that allow you to select the places that you have visited. It is a great way of keeping track of your travels, and it will register the number of countries, states etcetera, that you have visited. Some of them produce a map to show exactly where you have been.

The Travelers Century Club, (travelerscenturyclub.org) is a worldwide organisation that you can join when you have travelled to over a hundred countries, it recognises three hundred and twenty seven countries and territories and they actually have members who have ticked off every single place listed. They claim to have the definitive standard list for naming every country.

In 2017, Cassie De Pecol from Connecticut completed her project to visit all one hundred and ninety six countries in the world in the shortest time, taking just eighteen and a half months, smashing the previous record of three years and three months.

Another interesting app for the iPad is Countries, which gives you lots of facts and information without being logged on, as well as a quiz that can expand your knowledge of the world.

There is so much information on the internet relating to this, and there are many quizzes and apps available to help track your travels and to keep-up your interest in geography – take a look and make your own mind up as to which are the best.

APPENDIX 3

Territories, Islands and Dependencies that we have visited

1. Alaska, USA
2. Antarctic Territory, Chile
3. Aruba, Netherlands
4. Bermuda, UK
5. Canary Islands, Spain (Tenerife and Gran Canaria)
6. Cayman Islands, UK
7. Ceuta, Spain
8. Channel Islands, UK (Jersey and Guernsey)
9. Dodecanese Islands, Greece
10. Falkland Islands, UK
11. French Guiana, France
12. French Polynesia, France
13. Galapagos Islands, Ecuador
14. Gibraltar, UK
15. Greenland, Denmark
16. Hawaiian Islands, USA
17. Hong Kong, China
18. Newfoundland, Canada
19. New Caledonia, France
20. Prince Edward Island, Canada
21. Puerto Rico, USA
22. Saint Barthelemy, France
23. Saint Croix, US Virgin Islands
24. Saint Maarten, France
25. Saint Thomas, US Virgin Islands
26. Tasmania, Australia
27. Turks and Caicos Islands, UK
28. Vancouver Island, Canada
29. Victoria Island, Canada
30. Virgin Islands, USA
31. Zanzibar, Tanzania

APPENDIX 4

Glossary, references and useful e-mail and website addresses

(1) Information taken from the reference box on memo's app on iPad
(2) Wikipedia extracts
(3) Various Lonely Planet tour books covering several countries
(4) AA Explorer Guides – India
(5) http://www.sacred-destinations.com/
(6) www.victoriafallshotel.com
(7) eyewitnesstohistory.com
(8) www.chichenitza.com
(9) Zermatt.ch
(10) imaginepeacetower.com

I. www.viator.com: ours, excursions and extensions
II. www.vjv.com: tour operator based in the UK
III. www.kuoni.com: tour operator specialising in long haul
IV. www.ba.com: British Airways website
V. www.seatguru.com: seating advice for flights, all airlines
VI. www.thailandtourscenter.com: tours of the tiger temple near Bangkok
VII. www.travelcenturiesclub.org: definitive list of countries and territories
VIII. www.responsibletravel.com: eco-friendly holidays

APPENDIX 5

Some personal travel tips; money, airline benefits, security and cruising

Over these last seventeen years, we have made our own discoveries, whilst we have been travelling around the world, some of which I wish we had known beforehand to avoid the problems that we encountered whilst abroad. Some of these may be common sense and I apologise if it appears as though I am preaching to the professional, but I thought that it might be useful to add these few insights at the end of the book.

Money: There are basically four ways you can pay for goods, services and souvenirs when you travel; in cash, by credit or debit card, by traveller's cheque or by using the new "cash card", but we have come unstuck on a couple of occasions and I want to tell you about these, and how we now handle our money.

With the cash card, you purchase a special travel card, from a bank or from the travel agent's bureau de change, where you pre-load it with money, before you travel. Do NOT pre-load it by using a credit card, as you will be charged interest on your credit card account, as though you have actually withdrawn cash, which is higher than the interest charged on normal transactions. Supposedly, you can then use these cards to purchase items anywhere where they accept credit cards and to withdraw money from an ATM machine. As long as you have used a debit card or cash to load the card, it is interest free, you have no exchange charges, and it is a safe way to carry money. But, if I give you three tales of caution regarding these cards, then you will understand why we do not use them at all.

The first time we used this card was in Seattle, and we wanted to withdraw money from the card at an ATM. We could not find an ATM that accepted the card – we wandered around the city for several hours, trying to find one. Eventually we did find a bank that was open (it was a Saturday) and we were able to get some cash from the bank. However, this was not possible when we were in Marrakesh. Yet again our card was not accepted at the ATM machines around the main square, nor would they accept it at the bank or the post office which is where the bank sent us. We even tried at a bureau de change, and they would not accept the card. On this occasion, we had to use a credit card to withdraw cash from an ATM, which proved to be an expensive lesson learnt!

Our second issue was when we used a card as the charge card on a cruise. For anyone who has not cruised before, every cruise ship operates a cashless system, where you register a credit or a debit card when you board, and any purchases that you make, including excursions, go-off against that card. With a money card, you have a limit set for the amount that you pre-loaded onto your card, and if you exceed that limit, as we did, you start getting messages, letters, and phone calls from reception telling you that there is a problem with your account – very embarrassing! It is easy enough to make a payment against your account with another card, but there are times that the ship cannot get a satellite signal for their card link, and it can take several days for that payment to be processed, during which time you still get more messages, letters and phone calls!

Finally, you can only withdraw money from an ATM in certain denominations; probably the lowest is ten dollars in the USA. But because you use your card for other payments (hotels, shops etcetera) you may find that there is a residual balance on your card that is less than the minimum amount you can withdraw from an ATM – well you lose it! You cannot get that money refunded! So because of these issues, we stopped using these cards a long time ago.

Credit cards are probably the safest method of payment overseas, but you have to be careful that your card is not "cloned". The recommendation is that you always make sure that your card is kept in your sight, whenever you pay for anything. Have you ever shopped in Turkey? The transaction never takes place in front of you; your card is always whisked off and processed behind closed doors! Maybe we are too trusting to let this happen, but so far, we have not had a problem with our card details being stolen. You also need to take into consideration the fees that you will incur when you pay by credit card. The exchange rate may not be as favourable as the salesman indicates, and you will incur a transaction fee, which will vary depending on the card provider. I have been told that the Post Offices issue a credit card where you do not incur a transaction fee for overseas purchases, but I have never used one, so I cannot give you reliable information on this. But you need to be aware that some countries may not accept credit cards, like Myanmar, so check before you go. When we did our tour of Myanmar in March 2014, we contacted all the hotels before we went, to check on whether they took cards or not. Out of four hotels, the Inle Lake Resort Hotel and Spa only accepted cash, and the Hotel @ Tharabar Gate in Bagan had real difficulties with their connections, so you have to get to reception early when checking out to pay your bill and hope that the card will go through.

 With a debit card, the same issues with cloning can occur, but there is a single fee for using your card to make payments, as opposed to a percentage transaction fee. This is around one pound and fifty pence per transaction, so if you are buying a one dollar and sixty cents cup of coffee with your debit card, it could cost you almost three pounds! But a debit card is by far the best way to withdraw cash from an ATM whilst on holiday. Just remember to tell your bank where you are travelling to before you go on holiday. They are very security conscious, and if they do not know that you are travelling it is impossible to withdraw cash, and that can cause some real problems late at night if you need to pay for a taxi to get you back to your hotel and you have no cash!

 With contactless cards, things have changed recently, but many countries do not have this facility and in a lot of cases we have found that you have to sign as well as provide your pin.

Forget traveller's cheques – they are outdated, and I think that most places do not accept them anymore as a method of payment. You could probably use them to exchange for cash in a bank or a bureau de change (not in Marrakesh by the way!) but we would not take the chance. We always use a debit card to get cash, and don't bother at all with travellers' cheques whether they are dollars or pounds.

After all our issues with money cards and travellers' cheques, we now take cash with us to cover our expenses on holiday. Wherever we can, we pay by credit card (for security) but we do not rely on machines, bureau de change or hotel concierges. We take our cash with us, purchased in the UK at a rate that we have researched on the internet to make sure that we are getting the best deal. A word of warning, do not use the banks or bureau de change at airports, as their rate of exchange is the worst you can get, and their fees are normally quite high too.

It is true that you can use US dollars in most countries for making payments, but if you want to buy a small item (say a bottle of water) on the city streets, then you will struggle to pay with any foreign currency. It is also more difficult to haggle over an item that you want to buy, when you ask them to convert their price into dollars or euros – they will certainly make sure that they win on the exchange rate. But cash is by far the safest way of making a payment. You just have to be careful with how much you carry, where you keep it and keeping it secure in your hotel room. When we are travelling with cash, we split the money between us, and then put it in different locations too, always in hand luggage of course. In some countries, you can only get local currency at the airport or in the hotels. If you travel to Myanmar, you can exchange dollars at the airport for the local currency but make sure that you have got large notes – the bigger the note, the better exchange rate you get, and I am talking fifty and one hundred dollar notes!

There is always a possibility of losing your wallet or your purse. Two Americans we recently met on a cruise both lost theirs in Johannesburg. Everywhere in the world has problems with pickpockets, thieves and muggers; the latter probably being the most dangerous, as there is a possibility that you may be hurt in the process. Richard takes the precaution of carrying a second wallet with him, which contains a couple of out of date credit cards, and a small amount of cash. If he were to be accosted and had to hand over his wallet, he would give them this one, in the hope that once they see it has money in it, that they would run off and leave us alone. Thank goodness, he has never had to put his theory to the test.

Airline benefits: I am sure that everyone has their own favourite airline, ours is British Airways, but I have some advice for those who book with the cheapest one that goes to their destination, or take the one offered with a package holiday. Very early on when you start to increase your travelling plans, check the airline that you like, to see if they are part of an alliance, and see what other airlines are members of that alliance. By doing this, you can see what benefits you can get from that alliance when you build up your loyalty points as you travel. The two main airline alliances are One World and the Star Alliance. Once you make a booking with any of the airlines, make sure that you register with them as a member, and allocate your booking to your membership, and do this with every flight you take with that particular group.

We are Executive Members of British Airways, and every flight that we take with a member of the One World Alliance is recorded on this membership, earning us Avios points and Tier points. The Avios points are air miles, and we can exchange these for flights all over the world. The Tier points give you your membership level and the more you fly; the higher up the membership ladder you go. We are currently Silver members, and have been able to retain this level for several years. We think that the benefits at this level are really good – we are able to take two pieces of check-in luggage each, regardless of the seat limitations; we can check in at business class; we have priority boarding; we can use the allotted lounge at any airport (as long as the airport has a lounge and we are on a One World flight); we receive higher Avios points and Tier points every time we fly; and we have a better chance of receiving a complimentary upgrade if one is available. Check out their website on www.ba.com for the full details, and what you can get for each Tier level – Gold is the highest, but I think that you need to be flying business class many times a year on business to achieve this level.

We had not known about the benefits of membership when we started to travel a lot, and we lost out on the air miles that we could have earned a lot earlier. Even so, with the Avios points (air miles) we have earned on our flights and through the British Airways American Express card we have travelled to Cape Town (twice), Houston, Johannesburg (twice), New York (twice), Mauritius, Miami, Kuala Lumpur and Singapore/Hong Kong. Most of these were premium economy, some of them business class, and one was in first class. Not a bad exchange for simply registering with the airline!

The reason we like British Airways is because they offer Premium Economy on their long distance flights. We would love to travel Business Class on all our long haul trips, but this would be too expensive, and we would have to cut down on the number of holidays that we take! But with Premium Economy we get that bit of extra comfort at a price that is right for us. It also increases the number of Avios points and Tier points that we receive, by upgrading to this next level above economy. Many of the other One World members do not offer this seating class, that is why we prefer to fly with British Airways and request this option for any holiday we book at our Travel Agents. Qantas and Cathay Pacific now have these seats on their A380 planes, which are used for travel between the UK, Asia and Australia.

One other benefit of being a Silver member is that we can reserve our seats, free of charge, on any British Airways flight that we book. If you want to check which are the best seats on your plane go to www.seatguru.com as they show the layout of all the planes operated by every airline, and suggest where you should sit (or not sit) on your flight.

Security: Before I met Richard, I used to travel on my own, and I was very careful of where I went, who I spoke to and how I travelled. Most of the holidays I booked were touring holidays, so I was with a group of people during the day, and I knew that my transfers, hotels and tour guides were all "safe". Even so, I was still in Hong Kong, Bodrum and Delhi on my own, when the tour ended and I extended my holiday to enjoy it just a little bit longer. With being a single female traveller, members of the tour would always take me under their wing and make sure that I was not on my own at night. Richard, however, did not have the same experience when he travelled alone. He was fine during the day, but in the evening, everyone did their own thing, and he would dine alone every night. We both discovered Solo's, a company that specialises in holidays all over the world, aimed at the single traveller. On most of the holidays there is not a single supplement charge which can be incurred on the normal touring holidays, but they can be a lot more expensive too. When we went to Venezuela, we booked through Sovereign Small World, which is another company specialising in holidays for singles. I have mentioned Voyages Jules Verne in the past – they also have some holidays where you do not have to pay a single supplement, but places are normally limited.

Once we started to travel together, we would book holidays on the internet, and create our own package combining flights, hotels, transfers, car hire, tours and experiences. This is where you need to be careful and take some extra security precautions. We always make sure that tour operators are ATOL registered and that tour companies and airlines are registered with ABTA – this gives you some confidence that if something goes wrong then you are covered, and will get your money back, or, if you are on holiday and something happens to the company, that you will be able to get back home. We have had several holidays cancelled on us in the past, but we have never had a problem with either getting a transfer to another one or getting our deposit back.

I don't mean for this to be a case of telling your Grandma how to suck eggs, but always make sure that you have got adequate insurance to cover you for your trip, especially if you are planning on any adventurous activities while you are away. Inform them of any medical issues that you have before you travel, as they will not cover you if something happens and they were not made aware of existing problems. The price may go up, but it's better to be safe than sorry.

There are a lot of scams that can happen to you while on holiday, I am glad to say that we have never been a victim of them, but I think that it may be worth mentioning them. We have heard about bogus taxis at airports where they will pick up unsuspecting holiday makers; especially if you are travelling on your own, and take them to an unknown location in the city, where they will rob you of everything you possess and then ditch you. I understand that this is especially an issue in Rio de Janeiro. If we are travelling to a dubious country, we pre-book a transfer with a reputable company on the internet, pay for it up-front, and arrange to be met at the airport by their representative. Viator.com have transfers, both shared and private, at many airports around the world.

Another is at hotels where someone will pose as a hotel doorman and open the door of your taxi or your limousine when you arrive and welcome you to the hotel. You then proceed to hand over your luggage to a complete stranger, and you'll never see it again! Always wait and check that all your luggage is transferred onto a trolley, and brought inside the hotel, preferably being handled by someone in uniform, or at least who looks as though they belong to the hotel.

We had an issue when we went to Marrakesh. It sounds like we had an awful holiday there, but we enjoyed it, honestly! I had booked a Riad online for a weekend stay and included transfers, booking flights separately. I spent a long time trying to find the perfect place with the gardens in the centre, the rooms looking down into the oasis, a large comfortable room with a hammam, and I had found it at Riad Eden, which was within the walls of the old town. Our transfer from the airport took us to the edge of the walls where our luggage was loaded into a cart, and we walked the rest of the way down the little paths to our hotel (where we had a suite by the way!) As we arrived and we went inside it looked perfect, just like the photos. But suddenly we were confronted by waving arms and a Moroccan woman shouting, "No! No!" and we were turned around and taken to a different Riad. This one was NOT what I had booked, as there was no garden, it was small and dingy, the room we were taken to it had no hammam and was certainly not a suite. I was dumbfounded and I complained – we were taken to a different room, but this was no better and I refused to unpack. We saw another couple staying at this Riad who should have been at Eden, and they said that Eden had overbooked and were sending people to stay there instead – they were happy because they had a better room.

Luckily, when I had booked the hotel and the transfer it was through a company site, not direct with the Riad, and they had given us their number to contact them if anything went wrong. So they got a phone call! Within a couple of hours they had us booked into Riad Clementine, a beautiful place, offering us everything that we wanted and more. The location was not quite as good as it was on the edge of the walled old town, but a longer walk did us no harm at all. So it does show that booking through an agent does have its benefits.

Finally, and I know that this is probably an obvious comment but, always have your medication, valuables, keys, travel documents and money in your carry-on luggage, do not take the risk of putting it into your check-in luggage. I have learnt from experience that airport officials cannot be trusted, and as your check-in luggage can now be inspected anywhere it is not safe to leave anything of value in your check-in luggage.

We were once travelling in China before we were to go on a cruise from Beijing to Bangkok. We were flying from Beijing to Xian and then on to another city, where we would board our boat for a three-day cruise on the Yangtze, before returning to Beijing. Most of our cases were left at our hotel in the capital, and we travelled light for our extension. We were told that we were only allowed one small bag as a carry-on, and our check-in luggage was fifteen kilograms each. Richard had his camera bag for a carry-on, and as the bag that I used was a tote bag that was tied with a string, I did not think that this was a safe place to be walking around China with my jewellery box in a partially open bag. So I put a small amount of jewellery in a box in my check-in luggage, thinking that it would be safe as it was locked with a TSA approved lock. In Xian we arrived so late at the hotel that all we did was get out our overnight bag and clothes for the next day, I never touched my jewellery, but we did notice that things had been moved around in the suitcase. When we got onto the Yangtze boat we unpacked quickly and my jewellery went into the safe, it was only the next day when I went to change my necklace that I discovered that two diamond rings and a gold pendant were missing.

We reported it to our guide, who told his head office, but I don't think that it was reported to the police at all, as there was no way of telling when the items were stolen, but we are certain that it was at airport security, when they searched the suitcase after check-in. They did not take everything in the box but obviously took small items that could be easily put into a pocket and would not be missed immediately. But they were valuable and, the pendant, had sentimental value, as I had bought it on our Galapagos cruise – it was a gold turtle and I always received nice comments whenever I wore it.

Anyone hearing this story has always said that you should not have put it in your check-in luggage! but I thought that it was safer there than carrying it around Xian. One of the men on the tour did have his wallet stolen when we were visiting the Terracotta Warriors at Xian, so be very careful when you go there. But as they say, you learn from your mistakes. I was able to claim for the stolen items from our insurance, despite not having a crime report, but I was not able to get the same rings, I had new ones made to replace the two that were stolen.

Just a final note on this story, the following year in October 2013 Richard presented me with a wrapped gift and when I opened the box, there was a gold turtle pendant! My first thought was that he had found it or that the police had been able to retrieve it, but the solution to this mystery was even better. He knew how much I loved this turtle and he had contacted Celebrity to get the name of the jeweller who had come onto the Xpedition during our Galapagos cruise. He then contacted her by email, sending a photo of me wearing the pendant. She sent him a replacement turtle, all the way from Quito, Ecuador – it had to go through customs on arrival in the UK, and Richard had to pay duty on it, but it was worth it, as this has to be the greatest gift he has ever bought me.

Cruising: A great way of seeing the world is by going on a cruise. You very quickly tick off countries and cities while you tour around; taking your hotel with you. Touring holidays in general can be very tiring and you can spend a lot of time at airports, but if you want to see a country in detail, this is the only way to do it. But a cruise offers a lot more relaxing method of travelling, as you unpack once. You don't normally get a lot of time in a port to be able to see everything there is to see, but you can certainly get a feel for the place, and can return to do more at another time.

The benefits of taking an excursion with a cruise line is that you are accompanied by a reputable agent, and the ship will wait for the tour to return, should there be a delay or an emergency, the tour company or cruise line will pay to get you to the next port, if this is the only option, in extreme cases. But ship excursions can be expensive and, in most instances, they can be crowded and very restrictive. Viator.com have started doing some shore excursions, and they provide the guarantee of getting you back to the ship on time, or paying for you to get to the next port. We have recently used a company called Cruising Excursions, introduced to us through our agent, Thomas Cook, but we have used them twice and had an issue on the first occasion, so the jury is still out on this company.

If you are booked on a ship tour, in the event that the ship does not dock in a port, you will get an immediate refund. We had this problem when we were unable to dock in Jamaica, but we had booked a Viator.com tour. We contacted them and explained what had happened and, once we made our claim in writing; we received a full refund. My brother had arranged car hire in Guernsey, during a mini-cruise in the English Channel, but he was not able to get a refund, when we were unable to dock, as the car hire had lost the possibility of hiring the car elsewhere.

Normally, at a port, the cruise line or the local government will provide a shuttle bus that will take you from the port into the town centre, or to the port gates where you can get a taxi. If a taxi does not have a metre, always agree a price before you take the trip.

In some instances the cruise line will offer overnight excursions, which enables you to see a lot more of a place, rather than a short visit on a single day in port. We did this on our Holy Land cruise where we had an overnight in Jerusalem, while we were in Israel. The ship stopped at two different ports; we got off at the first and re-joined it at the second. It did the same in Egypt to do a trip to Cairo, but as we had been on the Nile cruise and stayed in Cairo previously, we did not bother with this excursion.

But these overnight options can be expensive, especially if they include a flight. When we were cruising in Asia and due to stop in Cambodia, we looked at the extended excursion to do Angkor Wat, and we were shocked at the price that they were charging – from memory it was around one thousand two hundred dollars each! In this instance, we added our own trip to Siem Reap, when we stayed in Bangkok before we boarded this Australia/Asia cruise. We flew from Bangkok to Siem Reap, had two nights in a lovely hotel with breakfast and transfers included; arranged for a private tour through Viator.com and had a wonderful full day in Angor Wat, visiting the main temple, Ta Prohm and Bayon. As we were on our own, we could stay as long or as short a time as we wanted. We were not restricted with time or location. We returned to Bangkok and stayed there for a couple more nights before flying to Sydney to board our cruise ship. Our extended stay in Cambodia, including a private guide, cost less than the cruise line were charging for one night and a group tour, so do your research before travelling, as there may be better options available to you.

We will quite often extend our stay in a country, either at the start or at the end of a cruise. Cruising is a great way to get a taste of a place, but to really "see" a country, you have to tour the interior, and more often than not, the excursions offered do not go too far from the port.

Most cruise companies have loyalty schemes that improve every time you cruise with that particular line. Most of them are not transferrable but the points you earn on P&O can also be used on Princess, but not the other way round. The more you cruise with a particular cruise line, the more benefits you receive. We are now Elite members with Princess and Celebrity/Royal Caribbean and get priority boarding and disembarkation, a free mini-bar set up at the start of the cruise, and with Princess, free laundry services and a ten percent discount off boutique purchases.

We have cruised with Silversea, Celebrity, Cunard, African Safari Club, Oceania and Royal Caribbean. With Cunard, they have different restaurants depending on the level of cabin you book – we have had suites on both occasions, and ate in the Queens Grill which was wonderful – the food and the service were excellent. If you are in a mini-suite you dine in the Princess Grill and all other cabins dine in the Britannia, which is by far the largest dining room and, my brother and my sister-in-law have told me, was fabulous.

My friend's mother, who was an experienced cruiser, told me once that when you book a cruise, select the best cabin that you can afford, and then go up one level! In other words, go for the best! However, on one of our cruises, the Future Cruise Specialist said that a cruise takes you from A to B, it does not matter which cabin you are in, and everyone goes to the same place, but at a different price. Do not rely on getting an upgraded cabin on a ship when you board. Upgrades only occur if your cabin is required by another passenger and you will only go up one level if you are fortunate enough to receive one. If you take time selecting your cabin for example – mid-ship, higher level, unobstructed balcony etcetera, then there is every chance that if you receive an upgrade, that you will not be in the same position and could end up with a slightly larger cabin, but in totally the wrong location. My brother and his wife have received many upgrades, and a lot of these have been into a suite. They have invested in buying shares in the cruise companies, and it may be as a result of this that they get the upgrades, as we have only had this happen to us once.

I know that a lot of cruisers will say that you don't spend a lot of time in your cabin, as you are busy doing things from the ships daily itinerary, but we disagree with this. We spend a lot of time in our cabin and on the balcony, as we don't like to challenge people over the deck chairs that they are saving for their friend, or have reserved from four a.m. that morning. This is not supposed to be done, but I'm afraid it happens the world over. We enjoy the peace and the tranquillity in our own space – boring, you might say, but we like it.

There are now more and more River Cruise specialists too. We have done cruises on the Neva in Russia (Saint Petersburg to Moscow), on the Danube through several East European countries (Bucharest to Budapest and Budapest to Nuremburg), as well as on the Nile and the Yangtze. They can be more expensive than ocean cruise liners, but this is because the ships are a lot smaller. We have cruised with Scenic Tours on the Danube, and they offer a fully inclusive programme with flights, transfers, excursions and drinks, all part of the package. .

We enjoy cruising – as I have said, it is a great way to tour, as you take your hotel with you. We have been to all seven continents and enjoyed every single cruise that we have done. It's not for everybody, we were reluctant before we did our first cruise to Alaska in 2006, and, since then, we have never looked back! We normally have several cruises planned in advance, trying to go somewhere different each time. We are repeating a lot of the locations on each cruise that we take, but there's always something new to see, and different people to meet, so I think that we will be cruising for quite a few years to come.

The cruise lines are continuing to build new ships year on year – some are monsters with a capacity of over five thousand passengers. But Scenic Cruises are launching their first cruise liner in August 2018 and it looks spectacular. Unlike the new ships being built by Celebrity, Royal Caribbean and Princess, they are starting with a very small ship. The Scenic Eclipse will only take two hundred and twenty-eight passengers and is classed as a discovery yacht! It is all suite; all-inclusive, and has submarines and helicopters on board, for the purpose of hiring for excursions. It sounds amazing but it has a price tag to match!

We are returning to South America in March 2019, when we will cruise from Santiago, Chile to Los Angeles, USA. This has given us the opportunity to add a short excursion before our cruise, and I have booked a short break of four nights on Easter Island, flying from Santiago. Having now completed the bucket list set by the British public on the BBC's programme, I am now able to organise holidays where we tick off our own list, and the giant heads on this remote Pacific island are top of my list.

Who knows where we will travel to next – as they say, the world is our oyster and there is so much to see, to do and to experience. I hope that we will be able to travel further in the years to come, and that I'll continue to write my travel books to be able to look back and to remember.

Rate this book on our website!

www.novum-publishing.co.uk

The author

Susan Battersby was born on the 10th of October 1957 in Manchester, England. She achieved her A-Levels at Senior School. She is a professional Finance/Management Accountant. Susan is married to Richard who she met while on holiday in Venezuela in August 2000 and hence her relocation to Sheffield. She and her husband both have a passion for travel and they have travelled around the world together. Since they met in 2000 Susan and Richard have travelled to 108 countries and many other territories, islands and dependencies. They do not have children. Susan loves cooking and reading when she and Richard are not busy travelling or taking cruises to exotic places. "Around the World in Fifty Sites" is Susan's first book.

novum 🞄 PUBLISHER FOR NEW AUTHORS

The publisher

„ *He who stops getting better stops being good.*

This is the motto of novum publishing, and our focus is on finding new manuscripts, publishing them and offering long-term support to the authors.
Our publishing house was founded in 1997, and since then it has become THE expert for new authors and has won numerous awards.

Our editorial team will peruse each manuscript within a few weeks free of charge and without obligation.

You will find more information about
novum publishing and our books on the internet:

www.novum-publishing.co.uk